The Business of a Woman

The Business of a Woman

The Political Writings of Delarivier Manley

RUTH HERMAN

Newark: University of Delaware Press
London: Associated University Presses

© 2003 by Rosemont Publishing & Printing Corp.

All rights reserved. Authorization to photocopy items for internal or personal use, or the internal or personal use of specific clients, is granted by the copyright owner, provided that a base fee of $10.00, plus eight cents per page, per copy is paid directly to the Copyright Clearance Center, 222 Rosewood Drive, Danvers, Massachusetts 01923. [0-87413–792–6/03 $10.00 + 8¢ pp, pc.]

Other than as indicated in the foregoing, this book may not be reproduced, in whole or in part, in any form (except as permitted by Sections 107 and 108 of the U.S. Copyright Law, and except for brief quotes appearing in reviews in the public press).

Associated University Presses
2010 Eastpark Boulevard
Cranbury, NJ 08512

Associated University Presses
Unit 304 The Chandlery
50 Westminster Bridge Road
London SEI 7QY, England

Associated University Presses
P.O. Box 338, Port Credit
Mississauga, Ontario
Canada L5G 4L8

The paper used in this publication meets the requirements of the American National Standard for Permanence of Paper for Printed Library Materials Z39.48–1984.

Cataloging-in-Publication Data is on file with the Library of Congress

PRINTED IN THE UNITED STATES OF AMERICA

Contents

Acknowledgments 7

1. "Particulars relating to her Life and Behaviour": Introduction 11

2. A Liberty to Abuse Their Betters: *The Secret History of Queen Zarah* 35

3. "Some Artificial Poisons": *The New Atalantis* 66

4. "Some faint Representations": *Memoirs of Europe* 95

5. Mistress *Examiner* 126

6. "Several little pamphlets and papers": Manley's Pamphleteering 152

7. "Pride of our Sex, and Glory of the Stage": Manley's Plays 179

8. "Ascribed to other Pens": Possible Additions to the Canon 206

9. "A Thousand Years Hence": Manley's Posthumous Reputation 225

Appendix I. *An Heroick Essay Upon the Unequall'd Victory Obtain'd by Major General Webb over the Count de la Motte at Wynendale* 247

Appendix II. Manley's Unpublished Correspondence: 1710–1719/20 252

Notes 263

Bibliography 301

Index 319

Acknowledgments

Trying to remember and thank all the people who have helped me over the past few years through my Ph.D. and the resulting book is extremely difficult. I must therefore beg all those I have not thanked to forgive me and put it down to my defective memory rather than my ingratitude. I can genuinely assure them that all help offered during this period was gratefully received.

With this in mind, I would like to thank W. R. (Bob) Owens for his patient, meticulous and scholarly supervision of my original thesis and all the advice offered since. Chris Mounsey's suggestions and genuine friendship are also much appreciated as was the ocean of cups of tea and coffee shared in various British Library refreshment areas. Others without whom this book would have been difficult, if not impossible, are Sarah Hutton for introducing me to Manley in the first place, Rachel Carnell and Anita Pacheco for reading and commenting on the last chapter to be written and Stephen Colclough for being a good listener and also making innumerable useful suggestions. Donald Mell of Delaware University Press needs special thanks for showing interest in the project from a very early stage and for his subsequent support, as does Hermann Real for his unfailing kindness. All the libraries I have used have been of incalculable help, but I must particularly thank Reader Services in the rare Books Room at the British Library and also the ever-cheerful staff at the Open University Library at Milton Keynes. Indeed, without the Open University's generosity in funding my doctoral studies, this book may never have seen the light of day. Of the scholars who have made useful suggestions and tactfully corrected my mistakes I really ought to mention Paula McDowell, Brean Hammond, and Nicola Watson and, right at the end of the project, W. R. Speck. There are lots of others who have read, listened to, and commented on my ideas including Ros Ballaster. I must thank them all. The remaining errors are, of course, my own. Thanks must also go to the unnamed editorial staff at Associated University Presses who have helped in getting my words into better order.

There are others, of course, who have simply been good friends and listened to me while I progressed through the research and writing periods. Among all these, I think I should single out Catherine Lennon as one of the most empathetic people I could have had "on my team." Peter Fraser and my friends at the University of Hertfordshire all also played their part in showing a genuine interest in my work and offering encouragement.

Most of all, however, my husband, my daughter, and my son-in-law have been patient and helpful, each in their own way. They welcomed Mrs Manley into their lives as well as mine, and provided me with vital support throughout the project.

The Business of a Woman

1

"Particulars relating to her Life and Behaviour": Introduction

In 1714 Delarivier Manley declared that "Politicks is not the Business of a Woman."[1] It is hard to take this statement at face value. If there was any woman who had made politics her business during the previous decade, it was surely Manley herself, England's first professional woman political journalist. Manley was undoubtedly being ingenuous. She had been reminiscing on her literary output, and, as if to give the lie to her own words, she continued by saying that she was ashamed of her work, "saving that Part by which she pretended to serve her Country, and the ancient Constitution."[2] Perhaps her comments were meant to show a bitter edge to her memory of the efforts she had expended in support of her beloved Tories. For she also asked herself, "*Who bid her write? What good did she do? Could not she sit quiet as well as her Neighbours, and not meddle her self about what did not concern her?*"[3]

It is my intention to suggest answers to these questions by examining Manley's writing in the context of contemporary parliamentary politics. Through a consideration of the techniques she uses, I will discuss how innovative they are; by looking at her methods and comparing them to the contemporary conventions she followed, I will show how she developed them to achieve specific polemical goals. This process of contextualization is not only fascinating if one considers Manley's development as a writer; it is essential if we are to measure her achievement as a leading figure among the propagandists of the reign of Queen Anne. And since I will be arguing the case for an increased recognition of her importance within that community, and also as a political writer, I will be placing the majority of her work in its natural milieu, the propaganda wars of Queen Anne's reign.

How do we most often think of Manley today? She is best known for her Tory scandal fictions: *The Secret History of Queen Zarah* (1705), *The New Atalantis* (1709), and *Memoirs of Europe* (1710). These were the *romans à clef* which detailed salacious scandals of the rich and famous of the royal courts from Charles II to Queen Anne. It is true that before these pieces, during her first active writing period from 1696 to 1705, Manley's literary output does not, at first glance, appear to be explicitly political. Her first two plays, *Royal Mischief* and *The Lost Lover* (both 1696), make no direct comment on current affairs, although as we shall see they are easily decipherable as posing serious questions about the position of William and Mary *vis-à-vis* the "abdicated" James II. Less problematic, however, is her light little epistolary diary, *Letters Writen* [sic] *by Mrs. Manley*, an entertaining account of a journey from London to Exeter, supposedly published "without [her] Leave" by an admiring friend.[4]

After these three pieces, Manley appears to have published nothing more until 1700, when she contributed two poems, under the pseudonyms "Melpomene" and "Thalia," to a small (women only) anthology entitled *The Nine Muses* in memory of the poet Dryden.[5] Here we can detect the political journalist trying to surface from the depths of the eulogizing poet. It was an indication of the direction of her future career that Manley was the only one of the Muses who chose to highlight Dryden's political commitment, reminding readers that "The Monarch CHARLES he has Divinely sung."[6]

The suppressed political commentator could not remain hidden for long, and Manley's burgeoning interest in politics clearly became more intense. In 1705 she published the explicitly Tory *Secret History of Queen Zarah*,[7] her first known excursion into overt political satire. The book allegorizes the domination of Queen Anne in the early part of her reign by the Marlboroughs (Sarah and John Churchill) and their associates, the small set of powerful Whig Lords known familiarly as the Junto. Sarah Churchill is clearly the eponymous central figure.

In 1707, two years after the publication of *Queen Zarah*, Manley published an unsuccessful play, *Almyna*.[8] This work, while appearing to be an apolitical, protofeminist demand for a recognition of women's intellectual and marital equality, was quickly recognized as a piece of sedition. It appears to have been so blatantly dangerous that the clearly nervous dedicatee, the countess of Sandwich, demanded that one particularly offensive scene be removed entirely. Given this reaction, it was probably lucky for Manley that the play was not well-attended: its "ill-fated" performance clashed with a fashionable eunuch's debut and went unnoticed in the week before Christmas.[9] Less contentiously, the same year also saw the publication of a second epistolary text, *The Lady's Pacquet of Letters*,[10] which included copies of her correspondence with the Whig, Sir Richard Steele.

The next piece that we can ascribe to Manley with absolute certainty is *The New Atalantis* of 1709,[11] her best-known work, which again allegorized the contemporary political scene. Written as a series of anecdotes and novellas told by the Lady Intelligence to two visiting deities, Virtue and Astrea, it was the most notorious exposé of alleged Whig misdemeanors of its day. As before, it featured the Churchills and the Whig Junto as its main targets, but this time predicted that their rule would end in disaster and the queen would eventually be free of them. It was considered sufficiently subversive to prompt the Whig secretary of state, Charles Spencer, earl of Sunderland, to issue a warrant for the arrest of Manley and her printers.

During 1710, the Whig government against which Manley had written so effectively collapsed, to be replaced by a Tory ministry. In the meantime, she produced *Memoirs of Europe*, a third scandal fiction.[12] As well as providing the familiar mix of romance and titillating gossip that had characterized *The New Atalantis*, the new *roman à clef* continued the story of the Churchills' domination of Queen Anne. In line with the changing political scene, Tory success is celebrated and Anne is finally freed from Whig control with the help of her faithful Tory followers, principally her new favorite, Abigail Masham, and the leader of the new Tory ministry, Robert Harley.

Harley's Tory ministry retained power until the queen's death in 1714, and during this period Manley wrote no more scandal fiction. Harley was perhaps the first political leader in England to realize the power of the printed word and the importance of influencing and controlling public opinion through a regular and well-organized political press.[13] Manley played a significant part in this first age of "spin," contributing several important pamphlets to the powerful Tory propaganda machine. She reached the zenith of her career in 1711, when she took over writing the subsidized Tory ministry periodical, *The Examiner*, from Jonathan Swift. In 1714 she published her fictionalized autobiography, *The Adventures of Rivella*, principally to preempt the publication of an unflattering biography rumored to have been written by Charles Gildon under the auspices of the unscrupulous Edmund Curll.[14] After Queen Anne's death, she appears to have shied away from writing overtly political propaganda, although the highly successful play *Lucius The First King of Britain* (1717) has detectable proto-Jacobite undercurrents.[15] The only other work we can be certain of is a set of novellas entitled *The Power of Love* (1720).[16]

Scholarly interest in Manley over the past few decades has focused almost entirely on her major scandal fictions. Critics such as J. Paul Hunter, Michael McKeon, John Richetti, and Robert Adams Day have drawn attention to Manley's contribution to the development of narrative fiction in its various forms.[17] Lennard Davis has pointed to the part her work played in bridging the gap between nonfictional texts and the new occupation of "novelist."[18] Manley's position as one of the earliest female professional writers in English has also excited the interest of feminist scholars.[19] Ros Ballaster has demonstrated that the roots of much of Manley's fiction can be traced back to sixteenth-century French texts such as the *roman à clef,* and in particular the writings of Madame d'Aulnoy.[20] Janet Todd has looked at Manley's treatment of the corrupt society within which she lived. While acknowledging Manley does not always put feminist issues to the fore, Todd has dealt with Manley's seeming preoccupation with the vulnerability of women and her depiction of "virtue in distress and . . . love betrayed."[21] More specifically, Caroline Gonda has used the passage concerning the Duke and his ward Charlot in *The New Atalantis* to examine eighteenth-century attitudes to incest.[22] In *The Whore's Story,* Bradford K. Mudge looks at the overtly lascivious aspects of *The New Atalantis*.[23] Other critics examining gender issues in early modern England have also found Manley's work a rich source of study.[24]

Here, of course, I must set out my own stall in respect of Manley's place in the evolution of the novel and feminist thought. My study is specifically on her position as a political propagandist. The detailed and scholarly discussions of the place of her scandal fictions in the development of prose fiction are outside the scope of this book, as are the continuing debates on Manley's position with regard to the feminization of late Stuart political discourse.[25] As noted above, many writers have interrogated the gyno-centric elements of Manley's work. One of the most recent is Rachel Weil. While I might dispute Weil's claim that Manley's "genre of choice was the scandal novel," I can agree wholeheartedly with her conclusion that Manley "breaks down the barrier between sex and politics, not by making sex a metaphor for political power, but by making behaviour in sexual liaisons a test of character and political trustworthiness."[26]

This is clearly an important distinction, and illuminates Manley's position with regard to the development of scandal fiction. Nonetheless, its validity rests on a clear understanding of Manley's reaction to affairs of state not only in their sexual sense, but also from a *parliamentary* perspective. Any conclusions about Manley's political writing that are based on a less-than-detailed critique of her view of the political world cannot provide a complete picture. As historians such as Geoffrey Holmes have shown, the Whig-Tory struggles in the reign of Queen Anne are complex and we simplify them at our peril. While I make no claims to be a historian, I am convinced that the minutiae of parliamentary activity is significant in the consideration of any politically oriented literature. We should devote the same detailed attention to a woman's writing as we do to Swift's or Defoe's. Crucially, therefore, I will be discussing Manley's work in terms of political strategies and factional conflict.

It is my intention that my contribution to the burgeoning scholarly activity on Manley will be the factual groundwork upon which subsequent discussions of gender and genre can be profitably built. This detailed archival exploration of the context of the writing has hitherto been missing in the field of Manley studies. While I am fully cognizant of the importance of Manley as a writing woman, we should not ignore that she was a fully functioning member of a highly politicized section of society. As Kathryn King so astutely comments, "Too intent a focus on gender excludes from consideration elements at least as important as those it makes visible."[27] With this in mind, it is clear that once the foundation provided by a thorough examination of contemporary events is in place, the arguments on Manley's position in a broader literary and cultural context can be made ever more fruitful.

However, to return to Manley's undoubted importance in the development of narrative fiction, I am persuaded that the novellas embedded in her texts offer opportunities for further productive discussion. Manley clearly seeks to entertain and titillate her readers with stories such as that of Charlot in *The New Atalantis*. In this they are obviously close relatives of the novels Manley borrowed from her elderly aunt during her formative years, and equally they can be seen as stepping-stones to the longer, more homogeneous narratives of her successors. While these embedded tales are perhaps too short and too incidental to be regarded as full-blown novels in their own right, they undoubtedly belong to the great eighteenth-century tradition of the "digression." Indeed, these interludes might be regarded as embryonic novels, with plot and some character development. In addition to these novellas I would suggest that the essentially linear narrative style of *Queen Zarah* points to a future novelistic tradition.

For the purposes of this book, therefore, I would rather look beyond the confines of gender and genre and continue in the footsteps of scholars such as Catherine Gallagher and Paula McDowell, who have examined Manley's efforts to make her way in the predominantly masculine world of early modern print.[28] Equally importantly, scholars such as Melinda Alliker Rabb and Carole Fabricant have discussed a more comprehensive selection of Manley's texts and have begun to examine her propaganda as the work of a political journalist, rather than as an adjunct to her novelistic discourse. Their exploratory work has indicated that there is still much to be done to enable us to judge more exactly Manley's standing as a participant in the pamphlet wars of Queen Anne's reign.[29]

Apart from these specifically literary approaches, scholars have also included Manley in more general surveys of early-eighteenth-century propaganda. Important works here include J. A. Downie's seminal *Robert Harley and the Press,* and doctoral theses by Paul Baker Patterson and Frances Harris.[30] More recently, Heinz-Joachim Müllenbrock has written about Manley in his discussion of the rhetoric of Tory pamphleteers during Robert Harley's ministry.[31] However, despite this wide acknowledgment of Manley's contribution to the propaganda industry, no full-length study has been devoted to the political implications of Manley's unashamedly partisan texts.

This is the reason I have undertaken the task of reexamining Manley's writing and its place in Augustan literature. My first step therefore must be to locate the contributory factors to the formation of her political perspective. The concise narrative of her life that follows focuses primarily on these political influences.[32]

The fullest contemporary account of Manley's youth is contained in her autobiographical *Adventures of Rivella*. However, as a biographical source *Rivella* is unreliable, since its objective was clearly literary effect rather than absolute truth. Moreover, it finishes its narrative just after the publication of *The New Atalantis* and Manley's subsequent arrest. But despite its drawbacks, *Rivella* does provide us with a number of verifiable facts. Manley was certainly the daughter of a Cavalier scholar and soldier, Sir Roger Manley, and if we are to believe her own testimony she was born "in one of those Islands, which formerly belong'd to *France,* where her Father was Governour."[33] Her year of birth remains uncertain, but following her own evidence, it must have been during her father's term of duty as lieutenant governor of Guernsey, between 1667 and 1672.[34] She was proud of her pedigree as the daughter of "the Second Son of an Ancient Family."[35] In political terms the most important fact about her lineage is that she was born into a long-established gentry family, the Manleys of Chester. More particularly, she was extremely proud of her father's Royalist loyalties and his exile during the Interregnum. As she said herself, her upbringing had made her a "perfect *Bigot* from a long untainted Descent of Loyal Ancestors, and consequently immoveable" in her Toryism.[36]

Her support of the Tory party was no doubt further facilitated by her irregular marriage to her bigamous cousin, John Manley, who was well known as a "Parliament man."[37] John Manley was a career politician. Trained as a lawyer, he stood as Tory M.P. for Bridport in 1688/89 and finally gained the seat for Bossiney in 1695, remaining in Parliament more or less until his death in 1714.[38] Delarivier's liaison with her cousin must have begun no later than 1690, since she gave birth to a son in June 1691, and she and John Manley christened the child in St. Martin-in-the-Fields, Westminster, in July of that year.[39]

According to *Rivella*, she spent the next three years abandoned in London, her "husband" returning to Cornwall during the winter of 1693 at the latest, his legal wife having given birth to a son who was christened in August 1694.[40] At the same time, Manley made her entry into the London world of the aristocratic gambling salon, when she went to live as the companion of the aging countess of Castlemaine in early 1694.[41] Yet after six months she fell out of favor with the fickle Castlemaine, and, on the pretext that she had begun a liaison with the old lady's eldest son, she was turned out.[42]

According to her epistolary work, *Letters Written by Mrs. Manley*, she had seen enough of the bright lights of London by 24 June 1694, and began a journey to the West Country to "retire to starve alone in Solitude."[43] Exactly what she did and where she stayed during the eighteen months she was away from the capital is uncertain, but by March 1695 Manley was bored with her rural retreat and complained that "there's no real satisfaction without Conversation."[44] She was desperate to return to London even though, as she wrote, "when that will be I have not the pleasure so much as to imagine."[45] However, she was back in London a few months later, and possibly wrote a poem in support of Catharine Trotter's play *Agnes de Castro* when it was performed at Drury Lane in December 1695.[46]

In the first letter Manley sent back from her journey into the West Country she quoted the gentleman poet, George Granville, whom she may well have known through her husband's political connections.[47] Indeed, since Granville was later to become one of her most important sponsors, John Manley's association with the family of the young nobleman could have done no harm to his "wife's" future career prospects. The Granvilles controlled a significant electoral interest in Cornwall, and as a prospective Tory Cornish M.P., John Manley was part of that interest.[48] He worked closely with the Granvilles, initially as legal advisor to John Granville, first earl of Bath. Later on, he acted as electoral right-hand man to the poetically inclined George Granville in the 1705 and 1708 electoral campaigns. Granville subsequently rose to become secretary-at-war and treasurer of the royal household.[49] However, in 1695 this was still some way off. It is most likely that at this time, Mrs. Manley and George Granville first heard of each other through the world of the theater rather than the Houses of Parliament.

In the closing years of the seventeenth century Delarivier Manley and George Granville both had their sights set on writing for the stage. Granville's play *The She Gallants* and Manley's *Lost Lover* were both produced during the 1696 season at the Theatre Royal. Given the confined nature of the theatrical world during this period it is unlikely that they did not meet. Just how small the world of the theater was at this time may be illustrated by the way the same names appear time and again. Fidelis Morgan, Manley's most recent biographer, identifies the *"J. H."* who signed the preface for Manley's first play as James Hargreaves, about whom little is known.[50] It is equally possible (and I would suggest more likely) that the initials represented John Hughes, who along with the ubiquitous Bevil Higgons sent Catharine Trotter a set of verses in 1698.[51] Higgons, a Jacobite Tory, is also reported to have written commendatory verses "on a Blank Leaf of Mrs. *Manley*'s Tragedy, call'd *The Royal Mischief*," which is particularly interesting given the ambiguous content of the play.[52] In addition he provided an epilogue for Granville's play, *Heroick Love*,[53] and a prologue for his *The Jew of Venice*.[54] Another possible association between Manley and Granville is noted in Giles Jacob's *Lives and Characters of the English Dramatick Poets*. Jacobs claims that commendatory verses to "Delia" (one of Manley's diminutives for Delarivier) prefixed to Manley's second, more successful play, *The Royal Mischief* (also produced in 1696) was written by a "Nobleman now living." The most likely contender for this honor is Granville, to whom Jacob's book was dedicated.[55] Manley herself claimed that the verses were written by a "great Hand," although she is coy about revealing the author's name.[56]

It is equally intriguing that in *Rivella* she refers to a "certain Gentleman, who was a very great Scholar and Master of abundance of Sense and Judgment," from whom she requested an introduction to Sir Thomas Skipwith.[57] Skipwith owned a controlling interest in the Drury Lane Theatre, where her first play, *The Lost Lover* was performed.[58] It is possible that this "gentleman" was Granville, who had not yet been elevated to the peerage. The flattering description of him is echoed in *The New Atalantis*, where Granville is said to have a "wonderful deal of good sense" and is credited with having "touched the drama with a truer art than any of his contemporaries."[59] Granville may well be intended as the target for Mr. Awdwell, "a gentleman of sense and education" in *The Female Wits*, produced at Drury Lane in 1696.[60] This play cruelly satirized Manley, and included Awdwell as one of her followers. Curiously, a later play of Granville's, *The British Enchanters*, included a cameo part for a "Delia," handmaiden to a sorceress.[61] It does not take too much speculation to see this as a joke between old friends. And perhaps it was for old time's sake that in 1720 Manley dedicated her final work, *The Power of Love,* to Lady Lansdowne, Granville's wife. Once again in her dedication she is at pains to praise him for "His exalted Notions of Honour, join'd to the Graces of his Mind and Person."[62]

There were other people on the fringes of the theatrical world of the late seventeenth century whom Mrs. Manley would find even more useful in later years. Granville's play *Heroick Love* boasted a prologue by Henry St. John, the future Lord Bolingbroke and member of Harley's Tory ministry of 1710–1714.[63] We can only guess at the level of intimacy Manley enjoyed with these exciting young men, but she herself admits to being an eager participant in the hedonistic atmosphere surrounding the stage. She enjoyed "the Incense that was daily offer'd her upon [the success of her play] from the Men of Vogue and Wit: Her Appartment was daily crouded with them."[64]

Manley's coyness about naming her influential connections during this period of her life is particularly frustrating. Whoever these connections were, they were certainly powerful. *The Female*

Wits, the play that personated "Mrs. Manley, a Gentlewoman sufficiently known for a Correspondence with the Muses," did not find its way into print until 1704. The preface to the published version comments on the play's truncated run in 1696, claiming that the run was not cut short for failure to "oblige the Taste of the Town in general." On the contrary, the preface asserts, it was "acted six Days running without intermission" and "with great Applause," but its run was shortened because "some particular Persons" placed pressure on the management.[65] The identity of these "particular persons" remains obscure, but it may be significant that *The Female Wits* was written for the theater in Drury Lane, which was increasingly Whig in its affiliations.[66] Manley, with her strong Royalist sympathies, may already have become fair game for the Whig wits—who were, however, forced to bow to pressure from Manley's wealthy and powerful, perhaps Tory, friends. Whether or not this was the case, there were other reasons for her unpopularity at Drury Lane, not the least of which was the fact that she had allowed *Royal Mischief* to be transferred to the rival Lincoln's Inn Theatre. Whatever the precise motivation for the anti-Manley satire, the preface to *The Female Wits* confirms that she was already popular enough to be satirized and that she was certainly not without some influence.

At this time, or shortly after, Manley made the acquaintance of Sir Richard Steele, the Whig playwright and essayist who was never long absent from any of her political writings, usually as the victim of a vituperative attack. The origins of their friendship are obscure, but it seems likely that they had met before 1696. This is the most likely date for Steele's letter congratulating Manley on her "success," probably a reference to the favorable reception of her play, Royal Mischief.[67] The letters which passed between Manley and Steele were printed in *The Lady's Pacquet of Letters*, and they provide evidence of an affectionate relationship.[68] The level of Steele's fondness (or more) for Manley can be assessed from the following quotation:

> You imprint your self too deeply in all the Hearts you conquer, to exact an Admiration without either Complaint or Praise of the lov'd Cause of their Affliction. . . . Pray let me hear from you . . . ; for tho' your Anger will be a very quick Sorrow to me, I think I can bear it much easier than your Indifference.[69]

Dolores Duff conjectures that the liaison may have developed into a sexual one, but there is no direct evidence of an affair,[70] though one letter written in 1701 suggests that Steele was at least flirting with Manley. Significantly, the letter hints that Steele was pretending a greater passion for her than he actually felt: "I shall I [hope] pay my debts with my play [*The Funeral*], and then in spite of [D]elia, be very easy, for whatever I may tell her, nothing can really make my heart ache but a dun."[71] As noted earlier, Delia was one of names by which Manley was familiarly known in print. At around this time Steele also wrote two poems to "Delia." Blanchard suggests that "Delia" is someone called "Black Moll," who also figures in Steele's letter to Revett. However, the implication in the letter is that "Moll" and "Delia" are two different people, in which case Delia is probably Manley. The Delia poems are certainly written as testaments to love: "Yet let her so much Sorrow know, / As to conceive her Lover's Woe."[72] This is only strengthened by further instances of Steele's amorous inclination toward the desirable Delia:

> When the Three Charming Beauties of the Skies,
> Contended Naked for the Golden Prize;
> The Apple had not fall'n to Venus share,
> Had I been *Paris*, and my *Delia* there.[73]

Blanchard dates the poems at about 1701.[74] If Steele was toying with Manley's affections during this period, it may explain why some of the vitriol in her later descriptions of him went beyond pure political antipathy.

In the meantime, Manley did not lose touch with her "husband." Indeed, according to *Rivella*, it was through John Manley that she met John Tilly, the unscrupulous warden of the fleet, whom she describes in *Rivella* as the person who "indeed fix'd her Heart."[75] Tilly was a married man, and Manley became his mistress. Both John Manley and Tilly were by profession lawyers, and both of them were involved in the closing stages of an inheritance dispute involving the Whig Montagu family and the Tory Granvilles.[76]

Manley's politics may at this time have been more fluid than she later admitted, since Tilly was one of the lawyers acting for the Montagu interest. At the same time, John Manley was part of the legal contingent working for John Granville, the earl of Bath, and he was chairing a parliamentary committee looking into Tilly's corrupt management of the Fleet Prison.

According to her own account of the affair, Delarivier Manley was first introduced to Tilly when Catharine Trotter begged her to mediate between John Manley and Tilly.[77] Manley claimed in *Rivella* that her "Kinsman and Husband" was very likely to use his position on the parliamentary committee to "joyn Revenge and Retaliation" on his opponent in the lawsuit, "by which Means [Tilly] was to expect very severe usage, if not a worse Misfortune."[78] In fact, Manley did more than simply mediate, and the three of them tried to effect a settlement of the lawsuit whereby they, as the facilitators of a speedy conclusion to the case, would be rewarded with some kind of financial benefit.[79] The attempt failed, and the three were all left out of pocket. Manley later claimed that even if she had earned some pecuniary acknowledgment for her efforts from the Bath interest, it had found its way into John Manley's pocket rather than hers.[80] Though this episode took place long before Manley's entry into the political world proper, it adds further evidence for the hypothesis that she was known to the Tory Granvilles long before she took up pamphleteering.

All through her relationship with Tilly, Manley maintained her friendship with Richard Steele. In an equally futile pursuit of wealth, Manley, Tilly, and Steele were all concerned to some degree in sponsoring an alchemical projector, an activity that drained Steele's limited resources until Manley (as she claimed in *The New Atalantis*) warned him of the hazardous nature of his investment.[81] While Steele never denied his debt to Manley, writing to her several years later that "I had the greatest Sense imaginable of the Kind Notice you gave me when I was going on to my Ruin,"[82] Manley, for her own reasons, chose to ignore the acknowledgment.

In 1702 Tilly's wife died, and Manley and Tilly decided between them that the most effective way of curing his financial problems was to marry a rich widow, which he duly did.[83] The heartbroken Manley made her way to the country. It was at this time that she also broke with Richard Steele. The catalyst was his refusal of a loan for the fare out of London, and although

Steele later claimed that he "had not the money," it took Manley fifteen years to forgive him.[84] The reconciliation, when it came, was a public one. In her dedication to *Lucius*, which Steele produced at Drury Lane, she at last admitted that "I have not known a greater Mortification than when I have reflected upon the Severities which have flow'd from a Pen which is now, You see, disposed as much to celebrate and commend You."[85]

Between 1702 and 1705, Manley seems to have led a peripatetic existence, first returning to the West Country and then visiting her friend Sarah Fyge Egerton in Buckinghamshire.[86] Thereafter, Manley became involved in a scam in which she hoped to help a lady whose lover had died to gain some benefit from the deceased man's estate (and obtain a £100 annuity for herself). Unfortunately, they appear to have falsified evidence that the woman and her lover were married. Egerton testified against them, and the case failed.[87]

After this disaster, Manley found her true *forte* in the production of propaganda material, producing her first scandal fiction, *The Secret History of Queen Zarah*, in 1705. It was also at this time that she first came into contact with John Barber, who became the Tory's chief printer and Manley's lover.[88] According to a biography of Barber published at the time of his death, he was already, when Manley met him,

> up among the Booksellers and Authors in general; . . . [and] was become the Idol of a Set of Persons of Distinction. . . . His Fame among others, drew the Beaux and the Belles. . . . Among the Number of those, who paid Regard to Mr BARBER, we shall at least find two, to whom he was under greater Obligations, as a Printer, than to any other Persons upon the Face of the Earth.[89]

The two to whom he owed such a great obligation were Henry St. John and Delarivier Manley. Barber's meetings with them "proved very fortunate and happy to [him]; from hence a Friendship and Intimacy commenced, which raised him in time, to be above wanting the Friendships of any other Persons but themselves, and of those they led him to an Acquaintance with."[90] According to the biography all this took place in 1705. Manley's network of influential friends was, at least according to this report, already wide enough to prove as useful to the ambitious young printer as that of Henry St. John, secretary of state for war. Another biography of Barber, also published on his death, confirms Manley's contribution to his success, describing her as "his best Friend, . . . through whose Interest all those Persons who contributed to make his Fortune were owing."[91]

Barber was responsible for printing a significant percentage of the Tory propaganda output during the last years of Anne's reign. That he owed a large measure of his success to a woman known to be his mistress was remarkable, and it was not only her circle of friends and associates who were of benefit to Barber. Her own writing was sufficiently influential to make her physical presence at Barber's place of business beneficial:

> For the Sake, *only*, of being near the Press and more at hand, to see her own Work done *correctly*, and better attended to than it had been; she had an Apartment fitted up for her, at the House of Mr *Barber*, with whom she resided, to the Day of her Death.[92]

It may well be that Barber's biographer was trying to hide the more intimate details of the printer's relationship with Manley. However, there is no doubt that their association was to a large extent founded on a firm business basis.

After *Queen Zarah*, it was several years before Manley is known to have embarked on more explicitly political ventures, although her dramatic work was suspect. As we have already noted, in 1707 she published *Almyna: or the Arabian Vow*, which had been performed the previous year without conspicuous success. In the same year her second epistolary work, *The Lady's Pacquet of Letters*, was published in the same volume as Madame d'Aulnoy's *Memoirs of the Court of England*. Manley's portion of the book contained a selection of her own correspondence with both Richard Steele and Sarah Fyge Egerton. It also included a version of a scandal that had rocked London in 1694—the mysterious death of a young man named Beau Wilson—and a romantic story of a mysterious beauty in a country house.[93]

We must now return to John Barber, for in 1709 he was the printer of Manley's second and most notorious scandal fiction,

Memoirs of the New Atalantis, and its sequel the following year, *Memoirs of Europe*. From this point Manley's and Barber's names are inextricably linked, and they both enjoyed the benefits of their ever-widening circle of influential acquaintances. Barber (and therefore Manley) were by this time mixing with many of the prominent Tory politicians and writers of the day, including those who were to play the most significant part in Manley's career, Robert Harley and Jonathan Swift.[94]

Swift is so often linked with Manley's pamphleteering and journalism that it is crucial to establish the nature of their association. They both worked for the Tory ministry during the years 1710 to 1714, and while they did so they became good friends. Swift was undoubtedly the ministry's most important writer, acting as the Tory party's *chef de propagande*,[95] while Manley also wielded her pen on the Tories' behalf. However, this does not imply that Manley owed her pamphleteering career to Swift's influence. Her association with the Tory propaganda machine predates her known acquaintance with Swift, and in fact in the summer of 1710 she was already claiming in a letter to Harley that her requests for recognition by the Tories were upheld by "many Great and Good."[96] At this date Swift had only just come to London from Ireland; he was still consorting with Whigs, and in September 1710 he was still having his post directed to Richard Steele.[97] He knew of Manley's work, but did not think much of it at this point. He wrote to Addison on 22 August that he had read the poet's character in "Mrs. Manley's noble Memoirs of Atalantis."[98] He proceeded, rather unflatteringly, to comment on her style, judging that she had "about two thousand Epithets, and fine words putt up in a bag," and that she "pull'd them out by the handfull, and strewed them on her Paper, where about once in five hundred times they happen to be right."

Manley had already published the first volume of her final scandal fiction, *Memoirs of Europe*, when on 14 September 1710, probably at the behest of St. John, she made her initial contribution to the official Tory mouthpiece, *The Examiner*. Swift, however, was not far behind, and the company he kept changed rapidly after he made the acquaintance of senior Tories such as Harley and St. John in October 1710.[99] Shortly after this date he took over the sole editorship of *The Examiner*,[100] and began abusing Steele, describing him as "the worst company in the world, till he has a bottle of wine in his head."[101]

No doubt Manley approved of this reversal in Swift's opinion of her enemy, and three months later, Barber and Manley hosted the impecunious Irishman for the first time. He described them to Stella, his friend in Dublin, as people she "had never heard of, nor is it worth your while to know."[102] While this is rather deprecating, it is entirely understandable given the circumstances. One of Swift's friends in Ireland was Isaac Manley, the Whig postmaster general in Dublin—John Manley's brother, and therefore Delarivier's "brother-in-law" and first cousin. There was a strong suspicion that he was opening letters, and it appeared that his tenure on the job was none too secure. Despite being on the other side of the political divide, John Manley was strongly supportive of his brother, which Swift makes a point of mentioning,[103] as he does the handsome nature of John Manley's hospitality.[104] Given the possibility of Isaac reading Swift's letters and the delicate nature of the relationship between John and Delarivier, it is hardly surprising that Swift was reticent about mentioning the printer or the authoress by name, or with any hint of approval. It is equally probable that it was not in his professional interest at this point to be associated too intimately with hot Tory propagandists such as Manley and Barber, who had both been arrested in 1709 for the publication of the second volume of Manley's scandal fiction *The New Atalantis*.

However, as time went on Swift's attachment to Manley appears to have become one of genuine friendship. The evidence for this is convincing. Charles Ford, one of Swift's intimate circle, wrote to him in 1714 that Manley's state of health had "alarmed" her friends in London.[105] Barber's most recent biographer nominates Manley as one of the "grateful" names on an undated list of the "characters of some of [Swift's] friends."[106] Swift's accounts also refer to losing money to "M——y" at hazard, which the editors of the account books read as most likely a reference to Manley, since Swift often gambled in a modest way at Barber's residence.[107] The account books further reveal that Swift made frequent trips on the river, presumably to Barber's house, and one trip was made on the day of Swift's probable loss of 6d. to Mrs. Manley.[108]

The friendship may even have been close enough for her to read with equanimity *Corinna*, Swift's satiric poem to her, in which Swift teases Manley with an excessive reticence over her age, claiming that he "dare not tell" the year of her birth. The same poem also satirizes her unfortunate marital experience and the publication of her autobiography:

> At twelve, a poet, and coquette;
> Marries for love, half whore, half wife;
> Cuckolds, elopes, and runs in debt;
> Turns authoress, and is Curll's for life.[109]

Swift's friendship extended to Manley's widowed sister, Cornelia Markendale, who also lived in Barber's house and inspired Swift to compose a Rebus to her: "What few Men can hit [that is the Mark], tho' most can spy / At the Foot of a Hill or from Mountain on High, / Is that fair Lady's Name, with a Black rolling Eye."[110]

As Manley acted as hostess in Barber's house when Swift dined there,[111] she also cultivated her acquaintance with men of more tangible political power. Some of the young aspiring poets she had met in the theatrical world of the 1690s had by now gained high ministerial rank. Granville, for instance, was secretary-at-war in the new Tory ministry. St. John was secretary of state. Manley also made other important friends and she knew the value of name-dropping when asking for recognition for her services. In a letter to Harley in 1711 she wrote, "my Lord Peterborow as well as Mr Granvile have promised to recomend me to your Lordship's Protection."[112] Only two weeks after this letter had been sent to Harley, she paid a visit to the earl of Peterborough at his home in the west of London. Swift bears witness to this. He reported to his friend Stella, "I met Mrs. Manley there, who was soliciting him to get some pension or reward for her service in the cause, by writing her Atalantis, and prosecution, &c, upon it. I seconded her, and hope they will do something for the poor woman."[113] Clearly, with their Tory friends in power, Swift was no longer reticent about his friendship with Manley. More significantly, the wording of this passage shows that Manley was there acting on her own behalf, with Swift merely "seconding" her solicitations. She was more than capable of pleading her own case, and it would not have been at all strange had Manley gone to the earl of Peterborough without Swift or other intermediary. As we shall see later, there had been Whig suspicions that Peterborough was already one of her patrons when she wrote *The New Atalantis*, and she had also featured him as the hero of *Memoirs of Europe*.[114]

At the same time that she was soliciting the earl of Peterborough, London literary society also provided a means by which she could make use of her political associates: the Society of Brothers, whose inauguration took place in June 1711.[115] An informal dining circle, the club was initiated by St. John and thereafter organized by Swift. It consisted of Tory wits and gentlemen and one of its declared ambitions was to reward "deserving persons with our interest and recommendation," in imitation of the help given by the Kit Kat club to Whig men of letters. St. John wrote to Lord Orrery,

> I must before I send this letter, give your lordship an account of a club which I am forming and which, as light as the design may seem to be, I believe will prove to be of real service. . . . The improvement of friendship and the encouragement of letters are to be two great ends of our society.[116]

Granville joined St. John and Swift as a founding member, as did the duke of Beaufort, dedicatee of *The New Atalantis*. While the dedicatee of *Memoirs of Europe*, Abigail Masham, could not join because of her sex, she was represented by her husband, Lord Masham, and her brother, Jack Hill. Robert Harley's son was also a member, as was John Arbuthnot, the royal physician and author of *John Bull*. The Society was therefore clearly one of influence and power, and Manley's friend John Barber "constantly" attended its dinners.[117] She was therefore likely to have been familiar with their proceedings and projects, just as they must have been well aware of her pamphleteering. She refers to their promises to help her in a letter to Robert Harley in June 1714:

> Mr Barber was orderd to bring me from a number of Great men who were call'd The Society of Rewarding of merit. I had hopes

> yt. my poor endeavours to do service might have given me some mark of your Lordships favour; particularly I was assured that my Lord Masham and Sr. William Windham, two of the Society were commissioned by the rest to desire in their names, that your Lordships would send me an hundred pound, with assureances att the same time of their farther Favour. I have been likewise informed, that your Lordship agreed to their request, and that my Lord Harley ingaged to put you in mind of it.[118]

In this letter, Manley cites the backing of some of the most powerful men in the country. William Wyndham was secretary-at-war. Lord Harley was the lord treasurer's son and heir. It was an impressive array of notables to claim as supporters.

There was, however, another person who was excluded from membership, and he was the most important man in the country. Swift and St. John had decided not to admit Robert Harley to the club, even though they had welcomed his son.[119] Nevertheless Harley, lord treasurer during the last four years of Queen Anne's reign, was probably the most significant of Manley's patrons, and it becomes evident from the scraps of Manley's correspondence that remain that they were in personal communication.

We can be certain this was the case during the four years of Harley's ministry, while Manley was actively pamphleteering for him, although Sarah Churchill, duchess of Marlborough, thought that Manley had "kept correspondence" with Harley even before the publication of *The New Atalantis*.[120] While such early contact is unlikely, after the publication of *Memoirs of Europe* Manley was assiduous in bringing herself to his personal attention. She sent him a copy of the book, and (probably also in 1710) requested his help in obtaining a naval commission for a young man of her acquaintance.[121] The letters she addressed to Harley over the next four years are invariably requests for money, but they also contain confirmation that she visited him in person. The fact that her correspondence with Harley is as a petitioner, continually reminding him of what she has contributed to the "Cause," reveals little of their relationship, but this was probably inevitable given the erratic methods of recompense in place for eighteenth-century political journalists. The only payment for which there is any evidence is fifty pounds from Harley, only two months before Anne's death, so it may be argued that she had good reason to complain.¹²² However inadequate this may appear to us, we should of course remember that this was precisely the sum Swift rejected from Harley in 1711, while Swift was engaged in editing *The Examiner*.¹²³ Despite the plaintive nature of much of her correspondence with Harley, her usefulness to his ministry is indubitable. Her last extant letter to him makes it clear that the two Tories enjoyed a reasonably easy relationship. Right up until Anne's death and the return of the Whigs, she was full of ideas in her role as Tory propagandist, suggesting, at the very end of the period, an official version of recent events: "I take Leave, most humbly, to ask your Lordship's Opinion, whether a true account of the Changes made just before the Death of the Queen, would not be very acceptable to the Publick?" It is also apparent that she was used to presenting her proposals to him in person: "I should have presumed to have waited upon you myself, but want of Mourning keeps me in the country."¹²⁴

Manley's association with Harley did not end with Anne's death. Manley stayed in contact with his family even after the Tories' fall from power and continued to enjoy some form of patronage from them. In one surviving letter written six years after the fall of the Tory ministry, she thanked Harley's son and daughter-in-law for their kindness to her. While it appears that the patronage had been administered through the offices of her fellow Tory propagandist Matthew Prior, it is clear that they had not forgotten her: "I have deferred till your Comeing to Town to return my most humble thanks for the honour of your letter; and for Lord Harley and Lady Harrietts Bounty."¹²⁵

But Manley cannot have relied solely on handouts after the fall of the Tory ministry, and she also seems to have involved herself in Barber's printing business. There is convincing evidence that in 1719 Manley played a part with her landlord and another notable printer, Benjamin Tooke, in negotiations over the granting of the reversion of the patent to print the *Gazette*. The *Gazette* carried official notices and obligatory advertisements for insolvent debtors. It was a lucrative contract worth around two hundred pounds profit per year, and was at bottom a political appointment.¹²⁶ The exact nature of Manley's financial interest in this is uncertain, but we know that it existed from one of Swift's letters.¹²⁷ In a letter to Charles Ford, Swift refers to an "Inmate" of Barber's—probably Manley—who had written to him asking for arbitration when Tooke attempted to renege on the agreement.[128] Although at the time of writing Swift was evidently unable to render much service, he must have made some attempts to help. Manley's will confirms Swift's involvement in her pursuit of payment. She acknowledges the "Deans Letters" and begs

> my much honoured friend the Dean of St Patrick Dr Swift as he was Privy to the promise that was made me of the said ffifty [sic] pound a year to be received from the said patent that he will aid and assist my Executors in getting the same or having it secured to them.[129]

While she struggled to establish her business claims, in other respects Manley's life appears to have become less strenuous during her last ten years. Although dogged by ill health, she apparently enjoyed a period of some prosperity. Perhaps it was the huge sum of six hundred guineas that Richard Steele gave her for her play, *Lucius The First Christian King of Britain*,[130] that enabled her to purchase a house in Beckley, a pretty village near Oxford. She seems to have enjoyed spending her summers there, spreading "the bright contagion of Romance," as James Moore, the son of one of St. John's closest associates, put it.[131] Manley's pen was not entirely idle during these latter years, and in addition to her set of novellas, *The Power of Love*, she wrote a number of poems, one of which, written to Moore, was published in a miscellany printed in 1720.[132]

These late works testify to a newfound political tolerance. There were connections between the Manleys and the family of John Hervey, earl of Bristol. Manley fostered a friendship with the earl despite his strong Whig affiliations, and he, in turn, showed himself extremely grateful to Manley for taking a young Oxford undergraduate (possibly his son) under her maternal wing:

> May that part of [the Hervey family] which you have thought worthy of interesting yourself so zealously for (& who for that reason I shall take more particularly into my protection,) live to deserve but half the trouble you have given your self for him, &

then I shall think all the cares of his education thoroughly repaid.[133]

She did well out of the friendship, being paid a handsome twenty guineas for a poem to the countess of Bristol.[134]

None of Manley's final publications show any indication of political interest. However, if Edmund Curll is to be believed, she had not abandoned the Tory cause. Curll wrote to Walpole claiming that he had seen

> A letter, under Mrs. Manley's own hand, intimating that a fifth volume of the Atalantis had been for some time printed off and lies ready for publication; the design of which, in her own words is, "To give an account of a sovereign and his Ministers who are endeavouring to overturn that Constitution which their presence is to protect; to examine the defects and vices of some men who take a delight to impose upon the world by the pretence of the public good; whilst their true design is only to gratify and advance themselves."[135]

If the text ever existed, it has not yet been recovered. However, the very fact that Curll reported (or fabricated) a story that Manley was up to her old tricks is a testament to the potency of her name. In fact, Charles Townshend, the Secretary of State, took the warning seriously enough to issue a warrant for a search of Barber's house and his next-door neighbor's:

> Whereas I have received Information that a Seditious and Traiterous Libel entituled the New Atalantis Vol. the Fifth or with some like Title is now ready to be publisht and that part thereof lyes in the House of John Barber and other Part in the House of Groves Widdow also on Lambeth Hill.[136]

If Manley had written such a book, it was the last thing she wrote. She died on 11 July 1724 at John Barber's London house.

It is clear from this brief outline of her career that Manley was a significant figure in the world of Tory propaganda from 1705 to 1714. Her political colleagues clearly recognized her strength in this field, and her political opponents were equally cognizant of her abilities, placing her in the same "Honourable Society" alongside Swift, "the Author of . . . *The Conduct of the Al-*

lies," and John Arbuthnot, the author of the famous *John Bull*.[137] The remainder of this book will set her among this illustrious Tory company, and we will see how her carefully targeted scandal fictions, pamphlets, and periodicals made her a writer to be admired by her friends and feared by her opponents.

2

A Liberty to Abuse their Betters: *The Secret History of Queen Zarah*

The publication of *The Secret History of Queen Zarah and the Zarazians* in 1705 marks the beginning of Manley's career as a Tory propagandist.[1] This text is the one that comes closest to a coherent fictional narrative in the Manley canon, and the story line is relatively simple. Unfortunately, despite its deceptively straightforward plot, the veiled political allusions make this secret history opaque and confusing to the modern reader. For Manley's more knowing contemporaries, however, the immediacy of the events she focuses on and the sheer volume of propagandist literature available for reference made the political allusions readily comprehensible: the principal characters would have been obvious to most well-informed readers. However, discretion is an admirable quality, and the libel laws were such that it was not advisable to be too explicit. Consequently, to avoid trouble with the authorities Manley, like her fellow propagandists, employed pseudonyms when referring to real people.[2] Yet, often the references were almost as blatant as using real names, as some of the epithets she used were not original. For instance, in *Queen Zarah* Manley refers to Sidney Godolphin, the Lord Treasurer as "Volpone," a name he had already been given in "Faction Display'd" in 1704.[3] No doubt these names would have been so obvious to her contemporaries that she and her colleagues did not consider that *Queen Zarah*, unlike her later scandal fictions, would have benefited from a published key.[4] Handily enough, however, it was later published in French, and the translator took the trouble to construct a guide to the principal characters. In fact, he or she took even greater pains for the French audience, providing an additional section of detailed political background, explaining about *"Tories & . . . Wigs, qui sont deux partis toujours opposez,"* and referring to the characters by their real names.⁵

Bearing all this in mind, the problems inherent in such an opaque text for the modern reader are obvious. It is clear from the careful explanations contained in the French version that one had to be familiar with contemporary English politics to recognize all the characters. However current the aliases, there was a clearly felt need to make the pseudonyms more immediately obvious, and there were apparently still some contemporary readers who found they needed recourse to keys and explanations. For us, distant from the heat of the action and contemporary gossip, the satire may be lost in the welter of aliases. To avoid confusion, Manley's fictional names will be followed, in this and subsequent chapters, by the characters' real names in parentheses on their first appearance, and thereafter if there is likely to be any uncertainty.⁶

The Secret History of Queen Zarah is a political allegory that centers around Zarah and, to a lesser extent, her husband Hippolito (Sarah and John Churchill, duke and duchess of Marlborough). The book charts their progress from relatively humble origins to quasi-monarchy, showing in detail the unscrupulous means by which they manipulated themselves to the highest rank. Beginning with the advantage Hippolito (John Churchill) makes of his affair with Clelia (Charles II's mistress, the duchess of Cleveland), Manley illustrates the trickery used by Zarah's mother (Frances Jennings) to trap him into marriage with her daughter. Zarah (Sarah Churchill) becomes the close companion and confidante of Albania (Princess, later Queen, Anne), whose secret love for Mulgarvius (Buckingham) she betrays to the King (Charles II) and Albanio (James, duke of York, later James II). After Albanio's accession, and when it becomes obvious that he can no longer retain control of the country, Hippolito (John Churchill) deserts him, his original patron, and joins the forces of the invading Aurantio (William III). From this point the text becomes a catalogue of Zarah's vices, particularly her avarice and lust for power. Zarah, having wrested details of Aurantio's war plans from Hippolito, tries to retain influence with all parties and is suspected to be sending sensitive information to the exiled

Albanio's supporters in France. As a result she and Hippolito are in temporary disgrace.

Meanwhile Zarah (Sarah Churchill) has encouraged Princess Albania (Anne) to hold herself remote from the new king, and has become indispensable to the princess. On Aurantio's death, and once Albania has ascended the throne, Zarah's aggressive domination of the new queen becomes the main theme of the narrative. Manley also ensures that Zarah's private and public life are inextricably linked with details of her rumored affair with her kinsman, Volpone (Godolphin), the country's most senior statesman. With his assistance Zarah is seen steadily to gain control over all official positions, while draining the country's resources into her own coffers. Despite setbacks from opposition groups, such as the universities, Zarah's grip on power becomes complete, and at this point the text ends abruptly.

Politics is at the heart of *Queen Zarah*. Manley was keen to ensure that the text was as topical as any of the pamphlets circulating at the time, and in form it most resembles an extended piece of allegorized political propaganda. Lennard Davis astutely describes the text as "a commentary on most of the major political and aristocratic figures of the age . . . a work that is at once true and false—as any allegory would be."[7]

However true or false the representation, the fact that *Queen Zarah* is a political commentary inevitably implies that it had a political purpose, and even a politic deviation from verifiable fact. Manley saw that her role at this point in the Tory propaganda campaign was to present not a history, but a secret history, an intriguing interpretation of rumor and hearsay. Therefore, while she provided her eighteenth-century reader with an easily recognizable account of contemporary politics, it was one that deliberately pandered to a set of prejudices already defined by other propagandists. Intended for a Tory audience, her frankly biased version of the means by which the Marlboroughs and their Whig allies rose to power was deliberately exaggerated. Her disclaimer in the preface to the second volume, in which she denies that there is *"any such Country in the World as* Albigion, *nor any such Person now Living, or ever was, as* Zarah, *or the other Names Characteriz'd, either in This or the First Part,"* tacitly indicates that while the tale is not true, the reader should detect the irony in the claim and recognize that it is based on reality. The disclaimer is made to sound ridiculously solemn sited next to its ludicrous provenance of being written by Cain in the "*Land of Nod*" (II, sig. A2–A3). Tory readers, all too aware of the real Sarah Churchill's behavior, would have noted the mockery in Manley's assurance that *"I almost believe it impossible any Nation under the Moon ever cou'd produce a Creature of so little Use to the rest of Creation besides her self, as this Wonder of her Sex, Queen Zarah is feign'd to be"* (II, sig. A4).

Manley's monstrous allegorical world was therefore clearly based on the real political one, and it was an exciting model.[8] 1705 was a general election year, and while the Commons that had sat since 1702 was predominantly Tory, the party was now dangerously divided, principally by divergent attitudes on the issue of occasional conformity.[9] This was the practice of non-Anglican Protestants (Dissenters) taking Anglican communion on an occasional basis while continuing to worship regularly in their own meeting houses. By this means the Dissenters succeeded in circumventing the Test and Corporation Act, which had been designed to keep them out of employment by the state. More than thirty years earlier, zealous Tories had failed to prevent Dissenters, who were popularly perceived as Whig in their party loyalty, from becoming members of Parliament.[10] Not surprisingly, the Tories believed that the Whigs relied on Dissenting votes for their parliament men, and that their party funds were kept supplied with Dissenting money. Consequently, Tories felt that the Whigs could not be trusted with maintaining Anglican hegemony, since their loyalty to the established Church was equivocal. As one contemporary pamphleteer put it, the Whigs were "for the Church of England as long as the Dissenters share in the Places of Trust that belong to it."[11] Repeated attempts by the High Tories to pass legislation outlawing occasional conformity had failed in their passage through the Lords. In frustration, Tories even planned to force the legislation through the Upper House by "tacking" it to a money bill, a strategy that ended in controversy and failure and came to be called the "Tack," earning its proposers the name "Tackers."[12] The result of this failure to reinstate absolute control of state office by members of the established Church was a scaremongering campaign encapsulated in the slogan, "The Church in Danger." The Tack and the perceived threat to the Church of England were key political issues in 1705. Tories particularly feared that the rise of the Whigs, with their traditional association with the Cromwellian Republic, would in some way diminish the authority of the Crown. They believed that, as one exasperated pamphleteer was forced to declare to Queen Anne, "Madam, you're *ravish'd*, your Queenship's invaded."[13]

The other significant worry for the Tories was the progress of Sarah Churchill's husband, John Churchill, duke of Marlborough, in the War of the Spanish Succession. The Tories had long mistrusted Churchill. He had been James II's favorite, but had supported William III in the Glorious Revolution. Under William his career had originally flourished, as he became lieutenant-general and Gentleman of the Bedchamber. However, William came to feel that Churchill's outspoken criticism of William's Dutch favorites and Sarah Churchill's close friendship with Princess Anne, the heir to throne, was a threat to his sovereignty. Charges were leveled against Churchill for treasonous communication with the exiled Stuart court and for betraying state secrets to the French, and he was dismissed from all his offices.[14] Other rumors circulated that he had been dismissed for "the excessive taking of bribes, covetousness and extortion on all occasions," accusations repeated throughout the rest of his career.[15]

For the Tories, Churchill had shown himself duplicitous in his early career, exhibiting disloyalty to both James II and William III. Furthermore, they thought that his family connections were taking him too close to the seat of power. His wife, Sarah Churchill, was the intimate companion and confidante of Queen Anne. His eldest daughter, Henrietta, was married to the son and heir of the Lord Treasurer, Sidney Godolphin, controller of the nation's finances. In addition, by the time *Zarah* was published Marlborough had been appointed captain-general, with considerable ministerial power and responsibility for the management of what the Tories considered an overly expensive land war against France. Not surprisingly, the Tories were deeply concerned with the extraordinary power and influence which was concentrated in the hands of the Marlboroughs and their Godolphin in-law.

Although the Duumvirs, as Marlborough and Godolphin were called, had always been thought of as supporting moderate Tory rather than Whig ideology, by 1705 their "Toryism had ceased . . . to be much more than nominal."[16] Indeed, up until this time they had enjoyed relative independence from the factional antagonism between the parliamentary Whigs and Tories, and their ministry had managed to govern the country and fund the war without resort to heavy reliance on one party. They were supported in their occupation of the middle ground between party extremes by Speaker Robert Harley's unparalleled management of the Commons. This interfactional accommodation was generally referred to in the literature of the day as "Moderation." The word, which figures so heavily in *Queen Zarah*, became a term of abuse directed by High-Flying Tories at anyone who offered to negotiate between the extremes of party. High-Flyers particularly despised what Defoe urged as "General Peace, abstracted from the Prejudice of Parties," even though, as he pointed out, this kind of accommodation would be in the overall interests of the Church.[17]

By 1705, the situation had become critical for the High-Flying Tories. Harley, mistrusted because of his Dissenting Country Whig origins, had been persuaded to accept the post of Secretary of State, elevating him to the ministry. Concerns for the Church and the expense of Marlborough's campaign made Tory members increasingly restive. It was becoming clear that if the ministry wished to ensure vital army supplies they would have to work with the Whigs, and in particular with the Junto, the small group of powerful Whig Lords who had formed the ruling oligarchy under William III. The General Election of 1705 brought in a finely balanced Commons. The Whigs wholeheartedly supported the continuation of the war. In order to vote funds for future campaigns, they needed to be helped into a position of power. The situation prompted John Churchill to write to Godolphin, informing him that he had begged the Queen "to advise early with you, what encouragement might be proper to give the Whigs."[18] The problematic election result also meant that party control of the vacant Speakership was now of prime importance, since it fell to Parliament to vote or deny funds for the continuation of the war.

Given the volatility of the political situation at the time and the vigor of the electioneering, it is unfortunate that there are no newspaper advertisements or any other external evidence to determine the exact publication date of the first volume of Manley's *Queen Zarah*. Paul Bunyan Anderson suggested that the text appeared either before, or as part of, the electioneering conducted between April and June 1705.[19] However, this dating is undermined by the lack of any reference within the text to the Tack, a key issue that inspired lampoons, pamphlets, and poems galore.[20] It is therefore doubtful that any of *Queen Zarah* was written before July, when the final results and the full implications of the election were known, and all hopes of the Tack buried in the Tories' disappointment.[21] It is more likely that the first part of Manley's allegory was published with the intention of influencing voting in the crucial Speakership elections of October 1705. However, until more conclusive evidence is found the precise dating of the first volume of *Queen Zarah* must remain questionable. Fortunately, we can be considerably more certain about the dating of the second volume. It is recorded in the *Term Catalogues* as being published in Michaelmas Term (i.e., before November), 1705. More precisely, Harley's press spy, Robert Clare, reports it as appearing between 22 and 26 September 1705, just in time for the deciding vote for the Speakership.[22]

While the dating of parts of *Queen Zarah* may be problematic, we can be absolutely certain that Sarah Churchill was the principal target. Manley was not original in her choice of victim; Sarah Churchill was a popular subject for Tory pamphlets and lampoons.[23] The accusations against her were legion, but one of the principal complaints was that she was prepared to sacrifice anything to serve her own and the Whigs' interest. Tory antagonism to Sarah Churchill had begun in the previous century. One early anonymous author claimed that she was a facilitator in the rumored homosexual junketing at William III's court.[24] Perhaps the most scurrilous proposition of this period was the accusation that she had committed adultery with Shrewsbury "not for joy / But only to obtain a boy."[25] The truth of either of these ideas is very doubtful, but the implication is that the Churchills' political dishonesty was compounded by their amoral attitude to sex, a theme running through all of Manley's anti-Churchillian satire.

The roots of Manley's jibes at Sarah Churchill's sexual behavior were well established, starting in the 1690s and continuing well into the eighteenth century. Only the year before the publication of *Queen Zarah* Sarah Churchill had been compared with Sempronia, a former prostitute of ancient Rome who had taken up politics, a suggestion that clearly provided inspiration for Manley.²⁶ Manley therefore plays upon settled Tory prejudices, declaring that she is providing

> *A kind of Prophesie against some Wicked F*[emale] *F*[a?]*te that shou'd in Future Days come into the World with this Mark of the B*[eas]*t upon her, that she should be a Second P*[ope] *Joan, and R*[uin?] *the Ch*[urch]*, by Reigning Absolute over her Sovereign, who ought be Supream Head, both in Matters Civil and Ecclesiastical.* (II, sig. A3)

Besmirching Sarah Churchill's name had become a central tactic in the Tory propaganda campaign against the Whig Junto. Her political significance was in her close relationship with Anne, which was seen by all parties as an efficient means of influencing the queen.²⁷ While the perceived threat to the monarch's neutrality provided a fertile topic for scurrilous journalism, the Tories also considered it an issue of sufficient weight to prompt parliamentary debate. Gilbert Burnet recorded that in the Commons, "some reflected very indecently upon [Sarah Churchill and] many . . . virulent things [were said] against her; for indeed she was looked upon by the whole party, as the person who had reconciled the Whigs to the Queen, from whom [the queen] was naturally very averse."²⁸

The Tories' dislike of Sarah Churchill sprang not only from her proximity to the Queen, but was also partially prompted by her family contacts with the Junto. Manley's reader could not fail to be aware that, in addition to her connection with Godolphin (as the mother-in-law to his son), she had married all her daughters into prominent Whig families. Charles, earl of Sunderland, himself a Junto Lord and Secretary of State from 1706 to 1710, married Anne, her second daughter. Her third daughter, Elizabeth, married the heir to the earl of Bridgwater (Master of the Horse to George of Denmark), and Mary married the son of another Junto Lord, Ralph, earl of Montagu.²⁹ Such politically advantageous matches prompted pamphleteers to refer to Sarah's progeny rather unkindly as "the Spawn of her Grace," who held "Nanny [Anne] fast in their clutches."[30] Above all, the Tories feared the grip Sarah was supposed to maintain over the appointment of the royal attendants, making it impossible for Tory wives and daughters to gain influential access to the royal person.[31] Sarah's value as a Whig power behind the throne was not only recognized by the Tories; her own party also estimated Sarah's power at the same high level. Her son-in-law, the earl of Sunderland, assured her that "if England is saved it is entirely owing to your good intentions, zeal, and pains you have taken for it."[32]

This, then, is the political context for *Queen Zarah*. Using it as a backdrop, we can now better understand how Manley gives expression to the Tories' misgivings over the Junto's encroachment on royal power and how the Whigs had undermined the previously secure Tory position. From this standpoint we can judge how Manley's allegorical treatment of Zarah and the Zarazians (Sarah Churchill and the Whigs) is used to personify the perceived nepotism and moral bankruptcy of the Tories' parliamentary opponents.

Manley was by no means an innovator in tackling political topics in an allegorical or fictional fashion. She was following on from an earlier French tradition, and taking a lead in part from Aphra Behn's *Love Letters between a Noble-Man and his Sister*.[33] John L. Sutton and Ros Ballaster have both shown how much of a debt Manley owed to texts such as Bussy-Rabutin's *L'Histoire amoureuse des Gaulles* and to Madame d'Aulnoy.[34] William Warner sums up how Manley's predecessor Aphra Behn developed her earlier brand of political intrigue:

> Behn [braided] together several distinct elements: the stingingly abusive satiric discourse of early English party politics; the secret histories of Lafayette and Gabriel de Bremond with their disguised reference to public figures; and the Spanish dramas and novellas of court intrigue.... The love plot [is transformed] into a kind of political discourse.[35]

Manley's *Queen Zarah* certainly follows in this tradition, but uses the ingredients identified by Warner in strikingly different proportions. While the French *chronique scandaleuse* may have served as an initial inspiration for her first political secret history, the amatory escapades of the lovers are deliberately replaced by the overtly political ambitions of a set of scurrilous *ad hominem* caricatures of leading Whigs, in the style of contemporary English lampoons.[36] Manley's characters do not find in sex "politics pursued by other means,"[37] and her aims are, as Rachel Weil points out, often to attack the ways in which "people maintain their own reputations by ruining those of others."[38] In what was perhaps a disappointment for more prurient readers, Manley characters very quickly eschew sex, preferring the really exciting intrigues of factional jostling. What begins as a conventional novel of court amours quickly becomes a biting political satire, dealing with specific issues made familiar to contemporary readers by the increasingly political periodicals.[39] And while the themes of political stratagem are universal, Manley makes the circumstances absolutely relevant to the moment of publication.[40] She is adapting a native tradition in doing this, while clearly drawing on French examples. Paula Backscheider points out the different techniques adopted on either side of the Channel:

> The English political memoir differed from the longer French ones by being limited to the "history" of a remarkable event rather than embedding the event in an extended, rather fabulous adventure narrative. . . . The French expectation that amorous intrigues would be included had carried over into English memoirs to some extent.[41]

It is the extent to which Manley subsumes the amatory element within the political that is innovative. *Queen Zarah* manages to tantalize us with the promise of a love story and then removes it almost entirely, replacing it with a cynical pleasure-seeking that exhibits all the self-centered interest of factional activity.

Zarah (Sarah Churchill) begins her courtship of Hippolito (John Churchill) by fooling us with a traditional (if manipulative) feminine submissiveness. It is not long, however, before we realize we have been duped by the sexually aggressive Zarah's role play, and she quickly loses all vestiges of romantic passivity. Instead, we are presented with a calculating, predatory female. While the political advantages of betraying Albania's (Anne's) secret passion for Mulgarvius (Buckingham) to her uncle, the king, are uppermost in her mind, Zarah is also attracted—but obviously less so—by the possibility of "gratifying her Pleasure with *Mulgarvius*, who was one she greatly admired"(I, p. 40).

Manley's strategy of including, but playing down, the romantic element of a French-style Romance involves more than a regrettable facility for mimicry. It has recently become evident that she plagiarized other writers in her first secret history,[42] incorporating substantial portions of *chroniques scandaleuses* into the main body of her work. She includes large chunks from an English translation of one French novella, *Hattigé*, which had first appeared in 1680. The original text had related the amorous entanglement and abandonment of Charles II's mistress, Barbara Villiers, by John Churchill, a story that of course forms part of the narrative of *Queen Zarah*.[43] While we may deplore Manley's plagiarisms, she did in fact do more than simply transfer the passages across; in many instances she deliberately politicized them. An excellent example of her technique appears in the first pages of *Queen Zarah*. In *Hattigé* she found, "The young people incourag'd by their Fathers Examples, get themselves Mistresses before they get rid of the Rod of their School-master."[44] In *Queen Zarah*, the sentence becomes, "The Youth of that Country, encourag'd their Parents Examples, Aspire to be Privy Counsellors before they get rid of the Rod of their School-masters" (I, p. 2).

The borrowings from *Hattigé* in *Queen Zarah* have been discussed elsewhere, and are considerable.[45] On the political level, though, Manley's small changes in emphasis reveal that she was less concerned with the voyeuristic gossip of her French original than with matters of more national significance. It is unquestionably the suitability of the people who appeared to be in charge of the country in the wake of the 1705 election that worried her. In a long digression in the second volume, Manley reveals a Tory concern for continuity and order:

> we ought of Necessity to Worship aright before we can know how to govern so....
> But this was a Doctrine *Zarah* and her *Zarazians* was [sic] so far from practising, that they were rather for abolishing natural Laws of Government, and instituting new ones of their own, ac-

cording to their Modern Scheme of Policy, and far-fetched Notions of Government, quite different from any yet Instituted by Divine or Humane Right before. (II, p. 103)

For a Tory the natural law of government was the right of those who were traditionally the ruling class to remain in this position. As Holmes describes it, the Tory squires' "deepest animosities" were aroused by those people who, despite not belonging to the governing class, had "waxed fat on the profits of war, and were using their new wealth to wrest political power from those whose birthright it was."[46] With this in mind, Manley precedes Zarah's family history with the following complaint:

> Mechanicks of the Meanest Rank plead for a *Liberty* to abuse their Betters, and turn out Ministers of State with the same Freedom that they smoak *Tobacco*. *Carmen* and *Coblers* over coffee draw up Articles of Peace and War, and make Partition Treaties at their Will and Pleasure. (I, p. 2)

A description of Zarah's "Obscure Parents" and her mother's "low Sphere" follow immediately (I, p. 3). The intention is clearly to cast doubt on the suitability of the scion of such a lowly family for her eventual high office. Even worse, her rise had not been through the recognized channels of lineage and hierarchy, but through "little Arts" of an apparently sexual nature (I, p. 4), learned from her mother. Such slurs on Sarah's lineage were not new. She was not an aristocrat from birth, but hailed from a relatively poor branch of the Hertfordshire gentry.[47] Accusations of her mother's acquaintance with the arts of prostitution were also not new. An earlier lampoon had described Sarah Churchill as the "Spawn of a bawd."[48] Even the power the Tories believed she wielded over her heroic mate was common gossip. The author of "Moderation Display'd" had earlier claimed that "not all [John Churchill's] Valour" could withstand "The Witchcraft of Sempronia's [Sarah Churchill's] Golden Hand."[49]

Manley's new idea in *Queen Zarah* was to consolidate these disparate rumors and incorporate them into her text. She also ridiculed the threat of the Churchills' power by reducing it to a domestic level—transforming, for instance, Zarah's "Witchcraft" into uxorial nagging. For Tories overawed by Churchill's apparent invincibility on the battlefield, Hippolito provided a comforting alternative. In *Queen Zarah* he is nothing more than a henpecked husband, bowing to his wife's treacherous designs to avoid "the Risque of a Perpetual Noise in his Ears" (I, p. 77)

Self-interest in a political sense is another major theme in this text. As has already been noted, the Tories suspected the Churchills of an ungovernable ambition and insatiable avarice, which had left them bereft of integrity and willing to stoop to any level for advancement or money. Manley illustrates their reputation for lack of principle by reducing the marriage of Hippolito and Zarah to a union inspired by lust but achieved through mutual deceit. Hippolito enters the story as little more than a gigolo, advancing himself through the bed of his king's mistress, Clelia (duchess of Cleveland). Zarah, having advanced rapidly from Maid of Honor to the favorite of Clelia, has fallen desperately in love with Hippolito, knowing full well how her lowly position disadvantages her with a man of Hippolito's ambitions. She also understands why Clelia is so attractive to him: *"The Title of Chief Mistress to the King gives her both Power and Favour to oblige him, and affords him the greater Pleasure and Ambition to be obliged"* (I, p. 7).[50]

Inspired by her "Love-Sick" daughter's excessive desire for Hippolito (I, p. 6) Zarah's mother arranges for Clelia to be called away to spend the night with the king. Consequently, when Hippolito arrives for his scheduled visit to his mistress, he finds the lovely Zarah awaiting his embraces. After a brief flirtation they settle into a compromising situation. Her mother, who has conveniently posted herself outside the door to catch the lovers, storms in and demands that Hippolito marry her daughter. His future wife's superior cunning is revealed when, despite her passion for Hippolito, Zarah refuses to give up her most valuable asset, her virginity, before receiving some concrete benefit: *"Since he had profess'd such a Passion for her, and her Mother was now become a Witness of it, she did not know how he cou'd part from her without giving her such Satisfaction as Parents in those Cases expected"* (I, pp. 21–22). Hippolito has been trapped by the two women. As his prospective mother-in-law points out to him, one option is that "*Clelia* be made Privy to this Affair" (I, p. 22), which would result in a loss of all the benefit he had gained from being her lover. Alternatively, he can marry Zarah, which would have the advantage that the "King wou'd be better satisfied to have his Rival Married, and then *Clelia* . . . cou'd not Reproach you with a dishonourable Action" (I, pp. 22–23). Before the dismayed, trapped, but nevertheless besotted future son-in-law has time to argue, a parson is produced, whereupon they are promptly wed.

Manley reveals each participant in this episode as involved in some illicit activity, all of which reflect on their political history. The fictional Hippolito's amatory treachery and inconstancy are easily translatable into an indictment of the real Churchill's political opportunism, foreshadowing his later apparent vacillation between James II and William III.[51] With the initial focus on Hippolito's trespass into the king's domain, in the person of Clelia, his possession of the royal mistress's body becomes an act of treason, a trespass on his sovereign's (adulterous and therefore equally illicit) prerogative. Hippolito takes for his own lust and profit that which is intended for his monarch's private pleasure. At the same time he deceives the instrument of that pleasure, his mistress, in an act of self-gratification, by the attempted seduction of her female favorite. The effect is to make Hippolito appear doubly dishonorable, his sexual opportunism with Zarah equalling his professional opportunism with Clelia. Manley is recycling the story of Churchill's shoddy treatment of Barbara Villiers (as depicted in *Hattigé*) as an explicitly political, rather than amatory, exercise. Manley reminds her readers how Hippolito, "Well Born, Young and Vigorous, who had pleas'd other Women, and was reputed to make his Fortune that Way" (I, pp. 4–5), had prostituted himself sexually, corroborating the distrust already engendered in Tory consciousness by Churchill's deception of both James and William.[52] He was indeed an "Ungratefull Toadstool."[53]

No doubt it gave Tories in 1705 some consolation to be reminded of Churchill as an impecunious young soldier gaining advancement through such unsavory means. They would have remembered his problems with William III as they read how Manley's Hippolito laments his sexual double-dealing and "made a Thousand Reflections on his Ill Fortune that had drawn him into such a Fatal Snare" (I, p. 24). They would have relished how Hippolito is torn between satisfaction with his new bride and the likely loss of favor following his treatment of the King's powerful mistress. Again, Manley was following a well-trodden path. Hippolito's dilemma echoes an earlier poem in which Churchill, dismissed from court after being accused of betraying his new king, William III, to the exiled James II, is found bewailing his fate: "My Master dethroned / The true Prince disowned / I fall by the Man I unjustly have crowned."[54] Manley's metaphor of the marriage plot is simple. Churchill had experienced the same difficulties when he tried to keep his influence with both William and James. His self-serving activities and his essential disloyalty have again backfired, and his lack of sexual integrity has left him easy prey to the ambitions of Zarah and her mother. At the same time, the complex double deception sets the tone for Zarah's future intrigues. In Manley's scenario Hippolito functions both as deceiver (in his role as lover of the king's mistress) and deceived (by Zarah in Clelia's bed). Hippolito initiates the deception, but he is outwitted by Zarah, who has been launched in her career by her mother. The Tory reader would also not be surprised to see that Zarah soon outgrows her need of maternal assistance; from an early point in the text, her ambitious, devious, and treacherous activities are her own.

Again the progress of Manley's satire parallels reality. At the beginning of her married life, propagandists saw Sarah Churchill as a woman who participated in, rather than initiated, the nefarious projects of others, particularly her husband. For instance, in the 1690s it was said that "They do agree so, in the main / To sacrifice their souls for gain."[55] In the first years of Anne's reign this changed. Churchill's desertion of James and his alleged treachery toward William, although emotive memories, were in the past. By 1705 Sarah Churchill had developed a persona independent from her husband. She had become a hated symbol of the Junto and Whiggery in general, and Manley's goal in *Queen Zarah* was to show Zarah's self-serving political activity as symbolic of the Whigs' undermining of royal authority. The motivating force throughout *Queen Zarah* is therefore the thrall in which the Tories believed the Whigs held the Queen. In order to make this explicit, Manley makes Zarah a conflated symbol of

Sarah Churchill's perceived influence over Anne and her husband's treachery toward James II and William III. Zarah is shown to be the driving force behind the couple's success.

A foretaste of the overpowering Junto's unsavory political tactics is neatly provided when Albania hears of Zarah's intention to persuade Hippolito and Volpone to abandon Albanio. Albania is horrified. Hippolito, she points out, is as a soldier bound by certain rules of conduct: "Would you perswade your Husband to be a treacherous Villain to his Master, and A Traytor to his King? ... *Hippolito* ... is a Soldier, and should have more Honour than to betray his Prince." (I, p. 65). Zarah's answer sums up the ethos of the book, and of the Tories' perception of the Junto: "Well Madam, ... if you depend upon Honour, I hope you never expect to succeed to the Crown of *Albigion* [England]" (I, p. 65).

The themes of treachery and desertion run through *Queen Zarah*, as they do through other pamphlets circulating at the time. The treachery, the Tories claimed, was not only to the monarch; it was also to the Church of England, the symbol of national unity. If we look at the most controversial of the Tory productions of 1705, *The Memorial of the Church of England*, the metaphor becomes clear. Whig toleration of Dissenters and the concomitant diminution of Anglican authority meant that the Duumvirs' accommodation of Whig principles made them equally guilty of treachery to the Church. The dismissal of several High Tories from their ministerial positions was tantamount to a "desertion" by Godolphin and the Marlboroughs of the Church of England. *The Memorial* groups "the L[ord] T[reasurer], and D[uke] and D[uchess] of M[arlborough]" together, ironically suggesting that it would

> be more Honourable to suppose 'em *Abus'd* than to think they left the Cause [of the Church of England] by which they have been rais'd out of *Levity* of *Temper*, or *Premeditated Treachery*: But however that was, being possest of the Q[uee]n's Favour, they were resolv'd to admit no *Sharers* with 'em in it.[56]

The implication is that their actions were, indeed, "premeditated Treachery." The passage demonstrates that through her association with her husband and Godolphin, Sarah Churchill had become invested with a political authority that had no institutional foundation. Manley seems to have acknowledged this reality in her portrait of Zarah at the beginning of Albania's reign:

> *Albania* had not been long set upon the Throne of her Ancestors, and as yet indeed it was not to be expected she shou'd understand how to hold the Reins of Government steadily, but *Zarah* pluck'd the slack Ones out of her Hands and tho' she left those of *Power* behind her, she made sure of all that were of *Profit*, knowing like a skilful Politician, they wou'd at last produce whatever her Ambition cou'd desire. (II, pp. 9–10)

Manley acknowledges that Zarah has had to take a backdoor route to power. She is, nonetheless, the power behind the throne, as well as the driving force in the Zarazian party. It is she who dictates the distribution of power: "By this time the C[ourt] and M[inistry] were almost all modell'd to her Mind; *Volpone* [Godolphin] redoubled his Care and Diligence, to see that none were admitted unto *Albania*'s [Anne's] Service that wou'd fly in the Face of their Benefactors" (II, pp. 66–67). Translated into contemporary political terms, it is now Sarah Churchill who dictates the Duumvirs' actions. As one modern historian has put it, "Godolphin . . . was thought too timorous and too easily browbeaten by Sarah and the Junto."[57] In effect Sarah Churchill becomes the symbol of the Whig Junto, with whom the Duumvirs were forced to negotiate to get the necessary funds to continue their war.

To achieve this transformation from Zarah as representation of Sarah Churchill, the woman, to Zarah as symbol of corrupt Junto authority, Manley also had to transform her from the wife of a public/political figure into a public/political figure in her own right. Manley took an obvious route by giving Zarah's notional Lord, Hippolito, a diminishing role in the text, effectively subsuming his political persona into the body of his partner in the Duumvirate, Volpone (Godolphin). In fact Hippolito makes only sixteen appearances in the second volume, while enjoying seventy-eight in the first. Manley's Zarah by this means is able to stand independent. Her primacy in creating political discord means that she also takes on the role of the eighteenth-century concept of Faction, or destructive party strife, for which, as a female and a political activist, she was well suited.

The figure of Faction was a relatively new one identified by contemporaries as female at least as early as 1704, in "Faction Display'd"—and perhaps earlier, in "The Dispensary" of 1699.[58] Both predated Swift's 1711 portrait of "Miss Faction" in *The Examiner*.[59] Physically, Sarah Churchill was an ideal candidate for the Tories' vision of the disruptive deity. William Shippen had already portrayed the goddess sporting "a Crown of Eating Flame," reminiscent of Sarah's own magnificently abundant, reddish-gold hair.[60]

Making Sarah Churchill the embodiment of "faction" becomes yet more serious in light of her connection with Anne, a topic requiring especially sensitive treatment. The Tories naturally disapproved of the queen's favorite. The difficulty for the propagandist lay in illustrating the unworthiness of Sarah to be Anne's companion without indicting Anne's intelligence or capacity to recognize Sarah's unsuitability as a counsellor. Some lampoonists throughout Anne's reign solved the problem by allegorizing the relationship as that between a lady and her domestic pets or farmyard animals.[61] Manley, faced with producing a much longer text, could not resort to this somewhat simplistic device. Instead she chose to concentrate on Albania's (Anne's) loyalty to Zarah, emphasizing both Albania's integrity and Zarah's lack of it. Manley was undoubtedly aware of the risk she took by implying Albania's weakness in accepting Zarah's influence, and she took pains to give an explanation, acknowledging that there were those who

> Reproach'd *Albania*, the best Woman in the World, for giving such Liberties to a Subject as Sovereigns themselves have been check'd for. But all the World agreed she was impos'd on by the subtle Insinuations and Devices of *Zarah*, who got such an Ascendant over her in her Youth, she cou'd never shake off all her Life after. (II, pp. 14–15)

The wider applications of Zarah's dangerous sway over the queen are made explicit. Having used "*Hippolito*'s Fame" as the means to power (I, p. 110), Zarah becomes increasingly sinister. Her manipulation shifts from bedroom to throne room, and, borrowing heavily from *Hattigé*, Manley describes Zarah's intervention in the proper running of the state.

> The Government of the Kingdom was in a manner in her Hands, and whoever expected Favours or Rewards must apply themselves to *Zarah*, by whom all was granted, as the Pipe that convey'd the Royal Bounty to the Subject; . . . *Albania* took the Crown from her own Head to put it on *Zarah*'s. (I, p. 100)

Manley's scenario once again recalls the spirit of passages in the *The Memorial of the Church of England*, in which the writer recalls how Catherine de Medici had dominated the young French king Henry III, "by reason of his bas Age [youth], and afterwards thro' his Weakness," tolerating the Protestant Huguenots and encouraging party strife within the administration: "[the] *King* was made to Act on all *Occasions* contrary to his *Interests*, *Inclinations*, and *Promises*, in Compliance to the *Desires* of the *Factions*, and became thro' their *Means* very *Unhappy* and *Contemptible* to all his *People*."[62]

In the *Memorial*, as in *Queen Zarah*, at issue is a power struggle, with the Junto and the forces of faction on one side, and the monarch and the High Church on the other. Manley adds a further element to the fairly straightforward allegory of the domination of Albania by Zarah: the Junto's ever-increasing demands for power are depicted in the growing difficulty of relations between Volpone and Zarah. The relationship between Zarah, as the symbol of the Junto, and Volpone, the representative of the Duumvirate in Parliament, is central to the later sections of the text; the assertion that Zarah could "no more be Govern'd by *Volpone* than *Albania* could Govern her" serves as a stark warning that the Duumvirs had already succumbed to the Junto's insatiable desire for domination of ministerial policy (II, p. 60). It is made equally clear that the Whigs' advocacy of "Moderation" was simply a demand for power.

For the Tory reader, the close association between Godolphin and Sarah Churchill was unnerving, particularly with Godolphin's increasing tendency to Whiggish "moderation," which for the Tories connoted a shocking willingness to abandon Anglican principles in the interests of political expediency and the unconstrained accommodation of potential political allies. Manley shows the dubious nature of Volpone's Moderation and the way the word, as well as the sentiment, had become corrupted. Discovered in his liaison with Zarah, "his L[or]ds[hi]p's Pretensions to *Moderation* [were almost ruined,] for he was forced to summon all his Conduct and his Reason to support himself" (II, p. 38).

Volpone's "Moderation" is shown to be nothing more than a cover for his unprincipled accommodation of Zarah and her Zarazian Junto. Volpone's consciousness of his own political corruption is made manifest in "the impetuous Stream of Blood that boyl'd into his Face" (II, p. 38). Despite his embarrassment, Volpone, like Jonson's antihero, is an accomplished confidence trickster, "who knew perfectly how to wear Two F[ace]s under One H[oo]d, that was F[ud]ge, Flatter and Dissemble, and never to speak as he thought" (II, pp. 23–24). As a result, he soon recovers his equilibrium with truly Whiggish duplicity.

Contemporary pamphleteers echoed Manley in warning that the Duumvirs' Moderation was a sham. They too were suspicious of the Duumvirs' passing "for *moderate* Men," when inevitably they would be "discover'd by every Body to be factious Incendiaries that make the Cry of Moderation a Vehicle for Slander."[63] Rather than pursuing a conventionally "moderate" course, the Duumvirs, once they had joined forces with the Junto, would simply abandon their temperate façade. Once England had been won to their moderate scheme, the pampleteers claimed, "the Ravish'd *Goddess* [Faction]" would "bless the Isle."[64] Manley's degenerate Zarazian Queen would be the head of a debased state religion. Thus, for Tories Moderation amounted to little more than a "lukewarmness in Religion, and Indifference in every thing that relates to the Service of God, and the Interest of his Church."[65] The shiftiness of the men who subscribed to such an ideology was apparent: how could "Men of Common Understanding," one pamphleteer asked, "pretend to look two Ways at once, to blow Hot and Cold, and fancy that every Body does not see thro' the pitiful Disguise and Artifice?"[66]

Volpone's proposed policy of Moderation is therefore central to an accurate political reading of *Queen Zarah*. He claims his policy would "[banish] Hatred and Quarrels" (I, p. 114), but his definition of Moderation comes immediately after his promise to banish Zarah's enemy, the Tory Mulgarvius (Buckingham), from court. The Duumvirs' Moderation, and Volpone's strategy for achieving "Peace and Union" (I, p. 114), can clearly be interpreted as the elimination of opposition—or more specifically, for Manley's purposes, loyal Tory opposition.

The account of the liaison between Volpone and Zarah vividly represents how the voraciously ambitious Junto had seduced the erstwhile "moderate" Duumvirs, and subsequently emasculated them. The Duumvirs' representative, Volpone, is seen to have capitulated, and ignoring his duty to his queen he pays "more Court to *Zarah's Couchee* than *Albania's Levee*" (II, p. 22). A little later in the text, the Junto, in the shape of Zarah, demonstrates that they are anything but moderate when loyal Tories defy them, and Zarah lashes out at Volpone after Urania's eldest daughter (Oxford University) destroys Zarah's "Mask of M[oderatio]n" (II, p. 56), revealing her "Fashionable" face, a term also used to describe Moderation in the *Memorial of the Church of England*.[67] Volpone's (Godolphin's) subjugation to Zarah is complete. He begs her, *"Pray tell me coolly what I have done that is not for your Interest and your Glory . . . Weak as I am, I wou'd willingly serve you, tho' at the Expence of my own Life"* (II, pp. 61–62). Volpone's craven submission to Zarah evokes the disgust Tories felt at the Marlborough-Godolphin ministry's surrender to the Junto, and how in their view its policies had become indistinguishable from those of the powerful Whig peers.[68]

The Tories also considered that the coming together of these two previously oppositional institutions, the mildly Tory Duumvirs and the Whig Junto, was likely to produce some terrible outcome, in the same way that an incestuous relationship inevitably runs the risk of engendering deformed offspring. Indeed, for some writers any kind of factional activity was likely to produce unnatural results.[69] The connotations of incestuous coupling relate directly to the fears of the most committed Tories. The union between Zarah and Volpone was not only adulterous, and therefore treacherous, it would also have been considered legally incestuous because of the marriage of their children. The conjunction of the Duumvirs and the Junto would inevitably bring forth a monstrous republicanism. Once again, Manley uses her text to echo real Tory fears. Two senior Junto members were already tarred with the brush of antimonarchy, "Chief of all the Rebel-Race" Wharton and "Republican" Somers.[70] Beside them stood Sunderland, the Churchills' son-in-law, who "hoped to see the Day, when there should not be a Peer in *England*."⁷¹ How could the High Tories, the believers in passive obedience to a divinely appointed monarch, bear to be "Lorded over by our Fellow-Subjects"?⁷²

Frightening as these ideas were, an even more unpalatable and more immediate source of distress was the thought that a union between the Duumvirs and the Junto would result in a further easing of the laws restricting Dissenters. Manley's stress on the incestuous nature of the liaison between Volpone and Zarah, and its potentially terrifying outcome, illustrates the fear with which the Tories viewed such a close association between the Junto and the Duumvirate.

Manley continued to use already familiar concepts to illustrate her allegory for the contemporary reader. She was not original in suggesting an intimacy between Sarah Churchill and Godolphin. Writings contemporaneous with *Queen Zarah* made similar claims of sexual impropriety and many contemporary pamphleteers delighted in portraying Godolphin as besotted with her. Joseph Browne wrote in 1705 that the Fox (Godolphin) was "much taken" with the "golden locks" of a neighboring Lioness (Sarah Churchill). The Lioness asks,

> Sir Ren . . . I hop'st no Sin
> Since you and I're so near a Kin
> To talk in Private now and then,
> And settle Matters where and when.⁷³

The poem was published in November 1705, two months after the second volume of *Queen Zarah*.⁷⁴ Browne is less explicitly sexual than Manley, being largely concerned with Godolphin's wily management of the different factions and Sarah Churchill's position as the sovereign's manager: "You rule the Country, I the Court," she tells him.⁷⁵ Browne reinforces Manley's hints at Godolphin's unhealthily close friendship with Sarah Churchill, but stops short of further attacks on her personal conduct. Manley makes it clear that Zarah's attachment to Volpone is both sexual and political. She refers to Volpone being "in [bed?] with Zarah [and] tax'd with In[ces]t and A[dulter]y" (II, p. 38). Clearly these rumors of a possible liaison were commonplace at around this time; in fact they persisted. Swift, several years later, suggested that Godolphin's "Alliance with the *Marlborough* Family, and his Passion for the Dutchess, were the Cords which dragged him into a Party, whose Principles he naturally disliked; and whose Leaders he personally hated."[76]

Not surprisingly, Manley's account of the affair is more highly colored than Swift's. Sexual misdemeanor is, of course, more exciting to read about than political intrigue, but Manley restrains her voyeuristic interest in the amatory aspect of the relationship, and the sexual nature of Zarah's and Volpone's liaison is for the most part subsumed into the overall danger of the political partnership. Melinda Rabb suggests that the sexual promiscuity that Manley pictures so vividly "indicates a lack of coherence that endangers political stability."[77] However, while Zarah is relatively sexually promiscuous, her activity is marked by a chilling political coherence. Although Zarah is described as "fill'd with *Love* and *Ambition*," leaving "no Stone unturn'd to secure to her self the *First*," we are led to suspect that it is in fact Ambition that is her motivating force, and that this is the reason her "Life [is] one continued Scene of political Intrigue" (I, p. 41). The three men Zarah is associated with in this text are Hippolito, Volpone, and Salopius (Shrewsbury). The first two are Duumvirs whom the Junto was anxious to dominate after 1705. The peculiar liaison she enjoys with Salopius not only echoes the earlier rumors of her affair with him, it also allegorizes the Duke's long-standing association with Marlborough and Godolphin. In 1696 all three men had faced charges of Jacobitism. In addition to this, in 1702 and 1705, as Zarah's pursuit of him suggests, the Junto was trying tempt Shrewsbury back into office.[78] Although they failed, Manley's portrayal of Shrewsbury as Zarah's lover indicates continuing Tory distrust of him.

The trepidation with which the Tories beheld such relationships, particularly those between Godolphin, Marlborough, and the Junto, was not simply a matter for discussion in the coffee houses. In 1705, with the speakership elections in view, the specter of Whig domination of the Houses of Parliament promised "ruthless exploitation of place, high taxes, [and a] vigorous war." For those Tories who were closer to the seat of influence, it also meant real disadvantage and little opportunity to gain "jobs, influence, profit, [or] the control of spoils."[79]

In tandem with Zarah's growing importance in the text is an increasing emphasis upon the sphere of public affairs. Zarah can be seen coming out of her role in the bedroom and wardrobe, and encroaching on the proper role of the monarch, who takes "the Crown from her own Head to put it on *Zarah's*" (I, p. 100). The inappropriateness of Zarah's activities is evident in Manley's treatment of elections and electioneering. She articulates a Tory disapproval of Whig electoral manipulation while simultaneously entertaining readers with a reminder of the real Sarah Churchill's failure to influence the electoral result in her home constituency. An examination of this central topic enables us to see clearly how Manley exploits Sarah Churchill's unpopularity to make her alter ego, Zarah, the personification of Whiggish malpractice.

The first reference to electoral misdemeanor recalls an attempt by the Whigs to dominate the Commons in a dispute between the two parliamentary houses. Manley allegorizes Sarah Churchill's Whig Junto allegiances through Zarah's inability to control a "Milk-white *Steed*" (I, p. 112). This obscure symbol, not explained in any of the keys, most likely refers to the long-running Ashby-versus-White controversy. This issue, which had caught the public imagination, centered on efforts by the Lords to dominate the Commons over a case of alleged electoral corruption in Aylesbury in 1701.[80] White was the Tory mayor of Aylesbury; Ashby was an enfranchised Whig "who care[d] not a T[ur]d, for a Whig or a L[or]d,"[81] and who claimed that he had been denied his right to vote by the Tory constables. The dispute had been revived in early 1705 under the auspices of Lord Wharton—Manley's Artonio, "the vilest *Zarazian* in *Albigion*" (II, p. 96). The argument generated considerable anger, as the Tory Commons expressed their resentment at the attempted incursion into "the Privileges of their House," and it subsequently turned into an acrimonious parliamentary wrangle between the two Houses.[82] The Lords went so far as to appeal to the public in print, using the case to argue their point in other electoral disputes.[83] In Manley's version Zarah's function is symbolic. The real case had little direct connection with Sarah Churchill's actual political activities. Therefore, at this point Zarah should be seen purely as a representative of the Junto, with its difficulties in controlling the resentful Commons.

The trope of the female Zarah attempting to bestride the white horse, while a powerful image with all sorts of sexual resonances,[84] is likely to have been intended originally as a factional conceit, conjuring up the striking picture of the Junto Lords attempting to tame and break the independent spirit of the Tory Commons represented by Mayor (Mare?) White. The Lords were indeed "kick'd off at the Court-Gate" with the Commons' aggressive defense of its privileges (I, p. 112). Manley gives Zarah the task of forcing the Commons to bow to her will because she represents the Junto. Equally, it is Zarah as representative of the Junto, not of Sarah Churchill, who cannot endure "*Lawn Sleeves*" (I, p. 112), a metonym for the High Tory priesthood; it was the Junto's latitudinarian bishops, not Sarah, who were wrestling with the rebellious clergy in Convocation.[85]

Notwithstanding my arguments about the purely symbolic significance of Zarah, the real Sarah and her monstrous counterpart do occasionally come together in the text. Zarah is given a central role in the campaigning for the 1705 general election, where the real Sarah Churchill did have some personal, although limited, involvement. Thus it becomes the duty of Zarah, the leader of the Zarazians, to take upon herself the management of "Affairs against the next great Sitting of the States of *Albigion*" (II, p. 49–50). In effect, she becomes responsible for the Whig electoral campaign:

> She sent Circular Letters with Secret Instructions to all those Petty States and Provinces, who sent R[epresentatives] to *Lodunum*, to debate about the Grand Affairs of *Albigion*, that they shou'd Elect no D[eputies], but such and such as were by her H[ighness, i.e., Queen Zarah] nominated and appointed, as fit to answer the great Ends for which they were design'd, under the Penalties of her Displeasure, and Forfeiture of her future Favours. (II, p. 51)

Obviously, with the General Election just over, electioneering strategy was particularly topical at the time of the publication of *Queen Zarah*. It was also a sensitive issue in a period of increasing suffrage, which occurred not only through the natural expansion of the electorate but also through the deliberate manipulation of the qualifications for voting. In some instances unscrupulous managers found it was possible to extend the franchise temporarily to achieve electoral victory in a particular constituency.[86] High-Flying Tories regarded the prospect of a growing electorate with horror, considering it an attack on the prerogative of the Crown. Charles Leslie, the High Tory propagandist, claimed that parliamentary determination of voting rights robbed the monarchy of an important part of its jurisdiction: "The Power of Voting for Parliament-Men; and the Limitation of the Free-holds, who shall Vote, and who not; and which Towns shall send Representatives, and which was never from the People or ever cou'd be; but all this was wholly from the Crown."[87] Manley's suggestion that Albania (Anne) has placed the crown on the head of Zarah, the Whig leader, echoes this fear of a diminution of royal involvement in government (I, p. 100). Clearly, this was a particularly galling prospect for the Tories, since they had just lost their strong majority in the Commons.[88] Conveniently for Manley's desire to implicate the Marlboroughs in as much malpractice as possible, they were also reckoned to be guilty of employing underhand tactics to make the electoral system work in their favor. In order to secure the election of his own candidate in New Woodstock, a constituency situated near the recently started Blenheim Palace, the duke enfranchised several of his dependents by making them freemen of the town in an honorary capacity.[89]

The timeliness of Manley's text becomes even more obvious when we look at the manner in which she celebrated the elections in Oxford and Cambridge. She allegorizes the situation, imaginatively weaving into the results of the recent General Election a transformation of the University of Oxford into Urania's eldest daughter and the University of Cambridge into her younger sister. The University of Oxford was staunchly Tory. The county was even more so, with all its nine members voting for the Tack, as had one of the Cambridge University M.P.'s.[90] At the prompting of Zarah, Albania visits the intelligent elder sister, Oxford, showing her "the Virtues she wou'd have her imitate" (II, pp. 54–55).

In fact Anne did not visit Oxford in 1705, but she did go to Cambridge in April, just before the General Election. In real life, as in *Queen Zarah*, the university lavishly entertained her and her

Whig Junto companions: "Nothing was too costly, nothing too good, that they could treat her with" (II, p. 72). Cambridge even bestowed honorary doctorates on twenty-one of the queen's companions (of whom twenty were Whigs, including three Junto Lords—Somers, Wharton, and Orford). The visit was a huge success, and made the Whigs optimistic of a win in the forthcoming Election. As Manley accurately reports, one of the candidates was "no less than a *Zarazian*, one who had Married *Zarah's* Daughter, and was *Volpone's* son [Francis Godolphin]" (II, p. 74).[91] But the universities are not deceived by the Whigs' attempts at winning them over. Oxford sees through Zarah's efforts, and a little later in the text Cambridge also "prov'd as Errant a B[awd?] to 'em as the Eldest, and instead of choosing a *Zarazian* of any kind, sent them a Red Hot [High?] C[hurchma?]n, an *Albigensis* [Tory] worse, if possible, than a *Bruscus* [Bromley]" (II, pp. 81–82).

The Red Hot Churchman is probably Annesley, who defeated the young Godolphin. His counterpart at Oxford University was indeed the "promising young zealot," Bruscus (William Bromley),[92] who is described as one of Urania's daughter's (Oxford's) "lovers," alongside the fanatically High Church Danterius (Nottingham) (II, p. 58). It is worthwhile noting that Manley chooses Oxford to warn Albania of the implications of allowing the unscrupulous Zarah to dominate her. Bromley was also the Tory candidate for the eagerly contested vacant speakership, which I have argued was the motivating force for the entire text. It is therefore not only Oxford's M.P. Bruscus (Bromley), but the party he represents, who accuses Albania "of Fickleness, who had been applauded for unalterable Constancy." It was the whole Tory party that "began to Lampoon her, by comparing her to the *Wind*, which is always Subject to Change; in short [Oxford] talk'd strangely even of *Albania* herself" (II, p. 57). The warning to Albania is clear: if she allows Zarah to continue to exercise undue influence, her erstwhile loyal Tories will begin to regard her as unreliable, and she will ultimately lose the respect of her subjects.

The whole episode uses Zarah symbolically, for Sarah Churchill had little personal involvement with the electioneering at Oxford and Cambridge. Manley does, however, find an opportunity to subsume the political activities of the real Sarah Churchill into the practices of the mythical Zarah. Despite her efforts, Zarah's own home constituency of *Sancta Albania* (St. Albans, Sarah Churchill's birthplace and family seat) had "despis'd her Overture of Greatness, and laugh'd at her Threats" (II, p. 80). St. Albans also refused to return the Churchills' chosen candidate. Manley's text directly echoes and allegorizes Tory periodical writing of the time; a contemporary newsletter reported that on 10 May "Mr Gape has carried it at St Albans, notwithstanding a great Lady [Sarah Churchill] went down thither to oppose him."[93] These personal disappointments aside, in Manley's version of the election campaign Zarah takes on a role far beyond her scope in real life. The idea was to rally party spirits by representing the few Tory victories as triumphs over Sarah Churchill's allegorical persona. It was a brave but ultimately futile attempt to demonstrate that even the apparently invincible Zarah-Junto could not achieve domination of the kingdom entirely on her/its own.

Despite the best efforts of the Tories, the Whigs did seem to have the advantage. They also had some initially surprising supporters. Included with the Whig villains is Robert Harley, the same Harley who became Manley's employer during the great Tory ministry of 1710–1714. It may be unexpected to see Harley vilified in a Manley text, but at the time that *Queen Zarah* was published Harley was suspected of being "In Show a *Tory*, but a *Whig* in Heart."[94] He had been persuaded to accept the office of Secretary of State in the previous year, as a symbol of the association between the moderate Duumvirs and the moderate Tories, and as such presented another example of the dubious nature of moderation. High-flying misgivings about Harley are well illustrated by the Whig Arthur Mainwaring's reference to the unlikelihood of his being made a "Smithfield Martyr" for the established Church.[95] If nothing else, Manley writes, Harley's telltale Dissenting ass's ears (I, p. 109) would show him for what he really was. Manley's use of this image is reminiscent of *The Memorial of the Church of England*, in which Whigs are describ'd as "Prick-ear'd," a term that "came to be applied to any dissenter or even ... low churchmen."[96] The anonymous "On the New Promotion" likewise laments Anne's "new Friends and Prick-ear'd Court."[97]

At this point, then, Manley had little respect for Harley as "the symbol of coalition."[98] She sneeringly describes him as a politician who can "fawn like a true C[our]t D[o]g, and lick the Feet of his M[aster]s" (II, p. 49). However, her attitude to Harley indicates that she had a thorough understanding of the politics about which she wrote. For if she displayed contempt for Harley, she realized, as he did, that there were other, more dangerous politicians on the scene. She knew that if the Tories' archenemy, Sunderland, succeeded in his strenuous efforts to be appointed to the Privy Council the Whigs would dominate the queen, and the *"Make-Shift"* Harley would be stripped of his power (I, p. 109). It is worth nothing that Harley also realized as much, writing himself a note at this time, just before seeing the queen: "Can you stop the Whigs that they will not possess themselves of your authority if you stand not here?" (i.e., by blocking the appointment of the Junto Lord, the earl of Sunderland, to a senior ministerial position).[99]

Examples of Manley's understanding of the dynamics of political life are evident throughout her propaganda work, and their presence marks *Queen Zarah* as a typical Manleyan text. However, circumstantial evidence of this kind is not cast-iron proof, and the authorship of *Queen Zarah* is still regarded in some quarters as problematic, despite Edmund Curll's unequivocal statement in 1741 that she was indeed the author.[100] Curll may well have taken his information from the title page of the 1711 edition, which announced that *Queen Zarah* was now available "by way of appendix to that of *The New Atalantis*."[101] However, the fact that Manley did not dispute this association of the text with her work is significant. At least twice in her career she responded vigorously to the unauthorized use of her name. She certainly showed no fear in 1714, when she took the notorious Curll to task for publishing a spurious *New Atalantis for the Year 1713*, directing the readership of *The Examiner* "to take notice, that this Book was not writ by the Author of . . . the Atalantis . . . the Author of those Volumes having never seen this Book, nor knowing any thing of the Contents, will not be answerable for whatever may be display'd therein."[102] She was clearly not intimidated by Curll, despite having just delivered the manuscript of *The Adventures of Rivella* to him, simultaneously urging him to "keep the Secret" of her forthcoming autobiography.[103] The risk of offending the underhanded bookseller was clearly less important than preventing the use of her name for other people's profit.

Not only was Manley apparently content to allow *Queen Zarah* to be associated with her, she had no objection to its re-issue in 1711. Such complaisance contrasts sharply with her response to the appearance of another text, the pirated edition of *The Lady's Pacquet of Letters*, which was published in the same year under John Morphew's imprint.[104] Her long-standing working relationship with Morphew (and his association with her lover, John Barber) did not prevent her from using the *The Examiner*, also published by Morphew, to complain about the unauthorized edition. Indeed, she described the new edition as "ridiculously mangled, and very uncorrectly Reprinted by the Management of a Grubstreet Pen, without the Consent or Knowledge of the Author of the Atalantis."[105]

This all points to the likelihood of Manley's authorship of *Queen Zarah*. There is, however, some contradictory evidence. It is contained in a collection of pieces published in 1715 called *State Tracts: Containing Many Necessary Observations and Reflections on the State of our Affairs at Home and Abroad; with some Secret Memoirs*.[106] The two volumes are attributed to Joseph Browne in the *English Short Title Catalogue*. Despite this claim to single authorship, the contents display such a dazzling variety of conflicting political views (including a scurrilous attack on the queen's Tory favorite, Abigail Masham) that it is difficult to believe that any one person could have been responsible for the whole collection. More specifically, the "Secret Memoirs" cited in the title are merely a reset edition of *Queen Zarah*. They are attributed to "the Author of the Examiner," an accurate description of Manley, and this would seem to add to the evidence that *Queen Zarah* was her work, but for the fact that Browne, too, had edited a publication called *The Examiner*—one that he had the "assurance to continue" when the original was "discontinued by Swift, Prior, Atterbury, Oldisworth and Mrs Manley."[107]

Robert Allen suggests that the new *Examiner* may have been produced in collaboration with Mrs. Manley and William Oldisworth. Patricia Köster, however, dismisses Manley's association with this later *Examiner*. The whole question is made in even more confused by the fact that Joseph Browne is also said to have contributed to the original *Examiner*.[108] This is extremely doubtful, but even if it were true it makes his authorship of *Queen Zarah* no more likely than, say, that of Atterbury or St. John.

Where are we left in this welter of evidence? The best explanation, as Allen credibly argues, is that *Queen Zarah* was included in *State Tracts* as one of a number of poems and pieces that Browne had "collected . . . to help buy off his latest crop of creditors," using the new *Examiner*'s "name and space to advertise" the volumes.[109] Since the only contributor to *The Examiner* ever known to have produced texts in the same vein as *Queen Zarah* is Manley, she is the most likely author. Finally, and perhaps most pertinently, the fact that Browne declined to use the text's original title suggests that the many publishers (ten in all) were attempting to smuggle Manley's text into the volume incognito.[110]

I think we can therefore safely ascribe *Queen Zarah* to Manley. And no doubt, she was pleased with her first foray into straightforward propaganda, since *Queen Zarah* became an influential text, continuing to play its part in the Tory arsenal of print warfare throughout Anne's reign. The two editions in 1705, its reissue in 1711, and the French versions of 1708 and 1711 are testimony to its popularity. Even more remarkably, it also enjoyed the rare distinction of creating a new term of abuse for the Whigs, with Tories eagerly attacking their "Zarazian" political enemies in such pamphlets as *The Devil of a Whigg: or Zarazian Subtilty Detected*.[111] For Manley, as the likely author, *Queen Zarah*'s success was even more important. It must surely have helped to inspire her to create her next, and best known, secret history, *Secret Memoirs from The New Atalantis*.

3

"Some Artificial Poisons": *The New Atalantis*

Four years after the anonymous publication of *The Secret History of Queen Zarah* Manley wrote her most famous text, *The New Atalantis*—or perhaps I should say most notorious, because it made such a remarkable impact that not only did Richard Steele accuse her of bringing "many persons of both Sexes to an unrimely fate" with her "artificial poisons," but she was arrested on publication of the second volume.[1] It is fair to say, however, that it was not only its notoriety that made *The New Atalantis* different from its predecessor, it was also significantly distinct structurally. In fact its organization makes a startling contrast to the relatively uncomplicated linear plot of *Queen Zarah*. Instead of an easy-to-follow story line, we are confronted in *New Atalantis* with a collection of anecdotes and lengthy self-contained stories. However, before we claim that the book is a complete departure for Manley, we should note that there are also striking similarities between the two texts. For instance, once again we have an elaborate and obviously fictional provenance. Manley claims that the "secret memoirs" have made their way to England from an Italian-speaking island via France and Brussels. Then, as if to cover her tracks more efficiently, she alleges in the dedication that it has been translated out of primitive Italian into French and subsequently into English (I, p. iii). Nevertheless, the body of the text is very different. She changes the format, eschewing the services of an omniscient narrator and opting instead to structure the narrative as a dialogue between three deities and an occasional informative mortal.

The basic framework of the memoirs is provided by the descent of Astrea, the goddess of Justice, who, having once abandoned Earth in disgust at human behavior, returns to investigate the progress, or otherwise, of humanity. She does this as preparation for the task of educating a future king, wishing to acquaint herself with the sins and vices of humanity in order to "fit him for all that Grandeur which the Destinies have allotted him" (I, p. 8). Once on earth, Astrea is blown off course and finds herself in Atalantis (England). She is almost immediately surprised to meet her mother, Virtue, who is depressed at being abandoned by the vast majority of mortals. The mother and daughter take a coastal voyage to gain a swifter passage to the capital city, Angela (London). This device conveniently allows Manley to enlarge upon mismanagement of the navy by the Whigs, who defraud "the Seaman, that labours incessantly for a sorry Subsistance" (I, p. 16). Upon arrival at Angela, they are met by Lady Intelligence, groom of the stole to Princess Fame, "of whom all the Monarchs on the Earth stand in awe" (I, p. 18). Fortuitously, mother and daughter have arrived on the day that Henriquez (William III) has died and Princess Olympia (Queen Anne) has succeeded to the throne. Intelligence is immediately concerned to tell her mistress of their visit, but instead the visiting goddesses insist that she give them a guided tour of the country and its leading figures.

With the framework established, from this point the text consists of Intelligence's retailing of a number of largely unrelated stories, separated by brief pen portraits of well-known contemporary individuals; these sometimes consist of little more than a few comments. *New Atalantis*'s loose structure and divergent theme has been the focus of much of the scholarship devoted to it. In the main, the text seems to fit John Richetti's description of the genre of the scandal novel as "a series of anecdotes, some swollen to novella length and complexity, unified only by a narrative occasion similar to that which unifies such well known framework collections of stories as the *Decameron* and the *Canterbury Tales*."[2]

Yet this is something of a simplification, for *New Atalantis*'s contents are so diverse as to defy any categorization. While there are plenty of self-contained episodes featuring variations on a romantic theme, such as the account of Charlot and the Duke (Stuarta Howard and the earl of Portland, I, pp. 50–83), there are other elements that seem to owe more to lampoon and farce than straightforward romantic fiction. We are not even on safe ground if we describe it as homogeneously anti-Whig. Tories too come under fire.

A typical anti-Tory episode concerns John Manley, Delarivier's cousin and "husband." He is ironically dubbed the "Stallion of the Senate House," and described as "one of those that intend ever to be Young tho' in despight of time, let his Looks contradict his Tongue never so much" (I, p. 194). John Manley's exploits are hilarious. Trapped in an upstairs room of his mistress's house when her husband returns early, he dozes off, but in his sleep wakes the entire household by banging with his cane on the floor, causing uproar throughout the establishment. It is a situation closer to Fielding than to a *roman à clef*. And while we can understand Manley's personal motivation for presenting this unflattering portrayal of her "husband," he was nevertheless a senior Tory M.P. In stark contrast to this mischievous satire on her Tory "spouse," some sections are pure propaganda—particularly in the second volume, where Don Haro (Harley) emerges as a Tory hero and is depicted rescuing Olympia (Queen Anne) from the clutches of the Whig Junto (II, pp. 148–153).

Close examination of the details of the stories reveals that Manley took advantage of the opportunities offered by the loose framework of *New Atalantis* to develop a format too diverse to fit comfortably onto any single literary template. This is partly because they span such a wide thematic range. Some contain elements already familiar to contemporary readers, as with the descriptions of Hilaria (Abigail Masham) and Don Haro. These do not differ greatly from other contemporary allegories, such as *Arlus and Odolphus*, a pamphlet concerned exclusively with Godolphin and Marlborough's fall and Harley's subsequent assumption of power.[3] Equally, the story of Madam St. l'Amant's (Cary Coke's) unacknowledged love for Baron de Mezeray (Sir William Baron or Sir Edmund Bacon)[4] is most likely to have been adapted from the popular seventeenth-century French novel, *The Princess of Cleves*, and subsequently assigned to contemporary figures (I, pp. 106–30).[5]

In complete contrast to these examples, Elonora, whose lengthy story is contained in Book II, seems to be a newly created fiction (or at least one which Manley found in a source not yet recognized). The protagonists remain unidentified in the keys, leading us to surmise that Elonora's romantic interlude was included without even the pretense of a basis in reality, political or otherwise, and with no recognizable individual hidden behind the central character. The episode can therefore be described neither as scandal fiction nor political allegory. Certainly, Thomas Hearne, the eighteenth-century antiquary who meticulously copied out the key for the first volume on 24 October 1709 and did the same for the key of the second volume in May 1710, made no effort to identify who lay behind Elonora.[6] Manley introduces a further element that owes nothing to romantic fiction and less to political expediency. Some of her malicious satire is inspired by sheer animosity, no doubt affording her personal satisfaction and providing the reader with a voyeuristic insight into the author's *bêtes noires*.

Sometimes, of course, Manley could satisfy more than one authorial aim, and could claim an ideological excuse. Her uncomplimentary portrait of her avowed enemy, the Whig essayist and M.P. Richard Steele, as Monsieur Le Ingrate (I, pp. 187–93) can be partly explained by Steele's Whig loyalties. However, there was little political capital to be gained by attacking the poet Sarah Fyge Egerton or describing her as a "She-Devil incarnate" (I, p. 159). It can only be assumed that Manley took the opportunity to settle the long-standing score with her former friend by turning her into the ridiculous figure of a Poetical Wife who throws a scalding pie at her husband.

Overall, then, *New Atalantis* may seem anarchic. Yet it is important to remember that despite its bewildering diversity, Manley herself regarded it above all as a political text. Two years later she described it as a "publick attempt made against those designs & that [Whig] ministry which have been since so happily changed."[7] The conclusion to be drawn from this statement is that she did not consider herself primarily a writer of popular fiction. Her avowed mission was to provide her fellow Tories with ammunition in their increasingly successful attacks on Godolphin's ministry. It was the Whig Junto's domination of the parliamentary process that drew her fire. Scandal fiction, romance, and *ad hominem* satire were included because they helped to sweeten the pill of pure political comment. With an eye to the wider audience she also realized that a more diverse approach than that employed by other propagandists would be advantageous, attracting those who might normally shun politically oriented texts. A further, and important, consideration is that such an approach was likely to prove commercially more lucrative. We can only speculate on her motivation, but there is no doubt that Manley's narrative strategy was effective. The historian G. M. Trevelyan has suggested that of all the Tory propaganda, *New Atalantis* did the "most harm to the [Whig] Ministry,"[8] and Gwendolyn Needham observes that "Its help in undermining public confidence in the Whigs came at the psychologically right time for the Tories, who were striving to overthrow the Ministry."[9]

The volatile nature of parliamentary politics between the publication of *Queen Zarah* and *New Atalantis* explains why *New Atalantis* was so timely. In the four years between the two books, Tory fortunes had at first slumped disastrously. The Junto had gained an ascendancy over Anne, who admitted that the Whigs had had from her hands "so many favors . . . of late that I fear a very few more will put me insensibly into their power."[10] In the General Election of 1708 the Whigs gained their only Commons majority during Anne's reign.[11] Tory fortunes reached their nadir during this period, but even while the situation seemed hopeless, the tide was turning. As Manley had predicted in *Queen Zarah*, Godolphin and Marlborough, in their increasing need for funds to continue the war, were forced to capitulate to the Whig Junto and give up the myth of coalition government. This at least helped to polarize the parties more effectively, persuading those politicians still occupying the politically neutral center, such as Harley, that there was no longer any hope of cooperating with even the most accommodating of the Whigs. It was a period in which the Tory party temporarily settled its internal differences to present a united front against the Whigs, making the most zealous and the most moderate Tories temporary, if uneasy, bedfellows.

Along with this internal peacemaking, the Tories were also encouraged by the sight of Sarah Churchill losing all remaining vestiges of the influence she had once had with the queen. It was now Abigail Masham, Anne's new favorite, who talked politics with Her Majesty.[12] Abigail was a kinswoman of both Harley and the duchess of Marlborough,[13] and Harley had begun using her as a means of communicating his intentions to the queen during his period out of office.[14] He had been forced to resign his position as Secretary of State in 1708 after his efforts to separate the two members of the Duumvirate had failed. His aim had been to discredit Godolphin, allowing Anne to retain her favorite general while he took over the job of Lord Treasurer. However, Godolphin threatened to resign if Harley did not. Marlborough, on whom the war effort relied, refused to remain in post without Godolphin. Once he had resigned, Harley went into open opposition against his former colleagues, Godolphin and Marlborough and his only means of access to Anne was via the back stairs and Masham.

At the time Manley was writing the first volume of *New Atalantis*, Harley was actively collaborating with the Tories (although it took some time for party members to place their full faith in him), while Tory antagonism to Marlborough and the Junto had increased. In May 1709 Britain's allies and the French signed a peace treaty in which Louis XIV agreed to thirty-nine of forty articles. Marlborough and the Junto ultimately rejected the treaty because it did not meet their requirements on the Spanish Succession. To Tory eyes, it seemed that they were determined to continue the war for their own financial benefit. The strain the war was placing on the economy became ever clearer and the Tory farming interest increasingly felt it was suffering unduly from land and malt taxes.[15] The perceived need for peace and the Whigs' reluctance to pursue policies that would bring it about undoubtedly gave the Tories the cachet of being the peace party, an advantage in the eyes of all but committed followers of the ministry.

Whig moves to naturalize foreign Protestants also angered voters at all levels, and there was widespread disapproval of the passing of the Naturalization Bill in March 1709.[16] Swift, in his role as spokesman for the Tory party put it succinctly, if xenophobically, in 1711, describing how the Whigs had invited over "a great Number of foreigners . . . who understood no Trade or Handicraft; yet rather chose to beg than labour; who besides infesting our Streets, bred contagious Diseases, by which we lost in *Natives*, thrice the Number of what we gained in *Foreigners*.[17] A combination of factors thus made Tory protectionist attitudes begin to appear far more attractive to many hard-pressed English voters.[18] And adding to secular concerns, the Whigs' increasingly latitudinarian outlook in religion was also suspect. Swift dryly suggested that Protestantism "was still too much limited by *Priestcraft*, notwithstanding all the good Intentions of the Legislature."[19] Fears of Whig disloyalty to the Anglican Church were further fueled by rumors of plans to repeal the Test Act in Ireland. The addition of all these fearful moves together strengthened Tory resolve to oust the Whigs from the ministry.[20]

It is clear from this scenario that at the time of publication of *New Atalantis* the Whigs found themselves in an increasingly vulnerable position. The extent of their sensitivity quickly became apparent to Manley when she was arrested after the publication of the second volume of *The New Atalantis*. Narcissus Luttrell recorded that on 29 October 1709 Manley and her publishers and printers were "taken up,"[21] and she immediately became a *cause célèbre* even outside the small world of politics and publishing. For instance, the young Mary Wortley Montagu, living far away from court in the country, was concerned about the implications of the ministry's reaction to Manley's text. It was not the text itself that she felt needed defending—she was of the opinion that others would "succeed better than the Authoresse of the Memoirs of the New Atalantis." She blamed Manley's arrest on overreaction by the authorities, and complained to her friend, "I lament the loss of the other parts which we should have had; and have five hundred arguments at my fingers' ends to prove the ridiculousness of these creatures that think it worth while to take notice of what is designed only for diversion."[22] Her real concern was that such actions on the part of the government might deter independent writers in the future. Judging by Lady Mary's reaction (even though she appears to have been fooled by Manley's deceptively light touch), outside government circles readers were not particularly shocked by the book. The reason for her arrest and subsequent brief detention is therefore something of a mystery.

It is unfortunate that we have to rely for the details of Manley's arrest and interrogation on the account to be found in her own fictionalized autobiography, published five years later.

She claims to have given herself up to the authorities on finding that "Lord S[underlan]d had granted a Warrant against the *Printer* and *Publisher*" of *New Atalantis* because she could not bear knowing that "three innocent Persons were taken up."[23] She seems to be putting herself in a rather better light than such facts as are available would suggest. A practically illegible note in the Public Records Office throws some doubt on the veracity of Manley's claim (or the accuracy of Luttrell's commentary). The note records the warrant for the arrest of John Morphew and John Woodstock, the publisher and a printer. It reads: "Nov. 11 1709. Secret Memoirs and Manners of Several Persons of Quality of both Sexes from the New Atalantis, an Island in the Mediterranean. John Morphew, John Woodward. War[rant] for apprehending these[?] for printing[?] and selling[?] Scandalous Book, particularly [?] Jo. Charw [?] Thos. Smith & Fla Shock[?]."[24] The note is dated nearly two weeks after Manley was taken into custody, and four days after she was admitted to bail.[25] This suggests that Manley did not heroically present herself to the authorities to save her colleagues, as she claims in her autobiography,[26] but that they pursued the unfortunate printer and bookseller after she was released. Whatever the truth of the matter, Luttrell continued to chart the progress of the criminal proceedings against Manley, which eventually ended in all charges being dropped on 13 February 1710.[27] It is ironic that her well-known former friend (now adversary), Richard Steele, seems to have had something to do with her release. She grudgingly thanked him in her later work, *Memoirs of Europe*, for his "reconcil'd Friendship (promis'd after my Application to him when under State-Confinement),"[28] and there is also a letter from Manley to Sir John Hopkins, the undersecretary of state, stating her application to Richard Steele's interest.[29]

It is interesting that part of Manley's defense against her accusers was that *New Atalantis* was full of "old Stories that all the World had long since reported" and that she had no "farther Design than writing for her own Amusement and Diversion in the Country; without intending particular Reflections or Characters."[30] It was certainly a popular publication, and despite the high percentage of recycled gossip, *New Atalantis* was eagerly read. The scholar Thomas Hearne records two impressions in

1709, presumably for the first volume.³¹ The keys, which appeared at the same time, were equally popular. Lady Mary Wortley Montagu was keen to swap her key to the first half of *New Atalantis* for her friend's second volume.³²

Perhaps it was its popularity that worried Sunderland. The lengths to which he went to stop Manley's activities indicate that there was certainly something about *New Atalantis* that he perceived as dangerous. It may have been his suspicion that Manley enjoyed Tory patronage that worried him. He wrote to Sarah Churchill, his mother-in-law:

> I believe Mr Manwaring [sic] has given you an account of the Lady, I have in Custody for the New Atlantis [sic] & of the noble worthy Persons, she corresponds with, I shall spoil their writing, at least for some time for I promise them, I will push it, as far as I can by law.³³

The Duchess of Marlborough suspected that the "noble persons" were the Earl of Peterborough, Robert Harley, and Abigail Masham, Anne's new favorite, and Harley's assiduous supporter with the queen.³⁴ It is unlikely that Manley had any personal contact with Harley at this point, but if the Whig ministry believed that Manley was indeed patronized by such important people (even by proxy), it could explain the anxiety that *New Atalantis* aroused.³⁵ Sarah Churchill herself had been alarmed by what she had heard of the contents of Manley's book, and she requested Arthur Mainwaring, her secretary, to give her a written account of it.³⁶ He dismissed *New Atalantis* as "all old and incredible stuff of extortion and affairs with [Godolphin] and [the duke of Shrewsbury], which not a soul living believes a word of." However, like Sunderland, he appears to have been alarmed at the possibility that the hand of unnamed "nobles" may be behind it.³⁷ Sarah, perturbed at what she heard of the contents of *New Atalantis*, passed on her anxieties to the queen, warning her about a

> new book that is come out; the subject is ridiculous, and the book not well written, but that looks so much the worse, for it shews that the notion is extensively spread among all sorts of people.³⁸

It is clear that Sarah Churchill did not read the book herself, and that, ironically, she had confused it with a piece of Whig propaganda. She describes it as "dialogue between Madame Maintenon and Madam Masham" that dealt with "passions between women."[39] What Sarah was actually describing was *The Rival Dutchess*, a scurrilous attack on Abigail Masham accusing her of lesbianism, which had appeared in 1708.[40] It is not surprising she was confused: she would have had a good choice of lampoons and broadsheets, from both parties, which were at least as insolent as anything contained in Manley's text.[41]

Sunderland certainly overreacted, despite Mainwaring's astute warning against having the "the rise taken from this trifling book, which . . . would only make it spread more."[42] One suggestion is that Sunderland might have felt himself to be a principal target in *New Atalantis*, even though he appeared only once in its pages (II, p. 17). The very absence of such an important figure as Sunderland in *New Atalantis*, where so many other leading Whigs are featured, must prompt the reader to question why he had been omitted. One suggestion is that his own sexuality was open to question, making him hypersensitive to real or veiled criticism. Twelve years later Sunderland's enemies openly accused him of homosexuality, and he was no doubt already vulnerable to such accusations.[43] Manley had already included the scandalous Beau Wilson affair, which was rumored to involve Sunderland and a murdered male lover, in her *Lady's Pacquet of Letters*. In a gender-bending technique at which she later became adept, she had cautiously transformed the rich and powerful aristocrat into an unnamed woman.[44]

In 1709, with Sunderland as Secretary of State and at the height of his power, a direct exposé of his sexual peccadilloes would have been disastrous. Sunderland's panic may well have been prompted by the curious and complex manipulation of gender and sexuality in *New Atalantis*.[45] The text is remarkable for the boldness with which Manley transforms the actively heterosexual James II into the female Princess Ormia, and describes an aristocratic lesbian cabal (II, pp. 43–52). Male homosexuality is also hinted at as Manley describes how The Duke (William Bentinck, William III's favorite) saved his king's life having thrown off his Cloaths got into Bed to the *Prince* [William III], embracing closely his Feverish Body, from whence he never stirr'd, 'till the happy Effects of his kind Endeavours, were visible" (I, p. 45).

Although she ingenuously explains the Duke's action as intended as a cure for a "malignant Distemper," readers would remember the rumors of open homosexuality that had surrounded William III's court a decade earlier.[46]

Scurrilous hints of this nature were one way in which Manley ensured that her readers would immediately recognize that satirical allegory was at the basis of her second "secret history." Even the title was ironic, a direct reference to Francis Bacon's *New Atlantis*, published in 1626. Tory discontent with the Whig Britain of 1709 makes the allusion to Bacon's famous work unmistakably quizzical. Manley matches Bacon's utopian island of Atlantis with a far less satisfactory location. In Bacon's text strangers sail to a foreign land and are confronted by, among other things, "Salomon's House," named after King Solomon.[47] As the great judge of the Hebrews, Solomon provides a forerunner for Manley's Astrea, the goddess of justice. Manley deliberately provided the negative alternative to Bacon's great allegory, bringing her judge in by boat to a corrupt nation. Where Bacon's inhabitants are truly Christian, praying that God would bless their labors "turning . . . them into good and holy uses,"[48] Manley's Atalantis is filled with people "void of *Religion*" (I, p. 6). Bacon's New Atlanteans are noted for their reverence for the family and their chastity, celebrating large and thriving family groups with state-sponsored feasts.[49] In Manley's New Atalantis "*Hymen* no more officiates at their Marriages," (I, p. 4) and the text is filled with seduction scenes and betrayals of innocent women. The parallels run deeper. In borrowing her title, Manley was no doubt also mindful that Bacon had himself been a statesman. It is clear that the island of New Atalantis, as depicted by Manley, reflects not Bacon's idealistic society where men holding state office disdain extra payment, but the realities of the corrupt public life that existed less than a hundred years after Bacon's death.

For Tories in 1709, corrupt public life was epitomized by the Whigs, and Manley could hardly have found herself a more disaffected Tory than the duke of Beaufort, an "ill-disguised" Jacobite, to whom to dedicate the work.⁵⁰ However, Manley was also acutely aware of the dangers of identifying herself too closely with Beaufort's political ideology. She was therefore careful to emphasize her Hanoverian Tory loyalties by making the whole text revolve around the education of an unspecified Hanoverian king. Ballaster suggests that the young prince in the care of Astrea is George II, aged nineteen in 1702 (the year in which the text is supposedly set) and twenty-six in 1709 (the year it was published). This is unlikely. As a child George had been brought up by his grandmother, Sophia, Electress of Hanover,⁵¹ and in *Memoirs of Europe* Manley is extravagant in her praise of the Electress. She is someone from

> whom we learn by her prodigious Knowledge of all things, that so much Experience cannot be obtain'd without a long Application; . . . she takes in with her prodigious Views, Nature, Philosophy, and History, which are her Intimates.⁵²

It is extremely unlikely that Manley would have risked describing the much-respected Sophia as inflicting "the greatest of Misfortunes, the want of Royal Education" (I, p. 8) on her grandson. It is far more likely that she was in agreement with other Hanoverian Tory pamphlets, such as *The Devil of A Whigg*, which talk in respectful terms of the old lady. For Hanoverian Tories, Sophia

> and her *Family* had purposed to live among them [the British], and free them from the fear and danger they had such just reason to apprehend from the secret Contrivances of the *Zarazians*.⁵³

If Manley is referring to a specific prince at all, she is describing the future George II's son, Frederick. However, Frederick had not been born in 1702, the date of the opening of *New Atalantis*, and he was only two years old in 1709. Again, it would be unwise to suggest that any scion of the future ruling house was being deprived of a good education. It is therefore more likely that Manley has given Astrea responsibility for the future Hanoverian dynasty, unschooled in the ways of the British monarchy, who will, with Astrea's help, "be fond of [their] People's Good, both in War and Peace" (I, p. 8).

The figure of Astrea is also open to interpretation. Critics have suggested variously that she represents Aphra Behn, or even Manley herself.[54] Another view which should also be considered is that Manley chose Astrea for her links with Elizabeth I. Gloriana was the monarch most commonly associated with Anne (principally for her gender and vigorous defense of the established Church against the threat of Papacy and Dissent). All ranks linked the two great Protestant queens and Elizabeth's birthday was celebrated with considerable enthusiasm during Anne's reign.[55] Clearly, Astrea is not Anne herself. But Astrea's function in Elizabethan imagery was the "One Virgin whose sword of Justice smote down the Whore of Babylon and ushered in a golden age of pure religion, peace and plenty."[56] Religion, peace, and plenty were concepts as powerful and popular in 1709 as they had been for the Elizabethans. It is therefore deeply significant that Manley makes the goddess of justice choose the moment of Anne's succession, the moment she is divinely appointed to the throne, to visit the earth she has avoided so long.

However, while we are invited to admire Astrea's noble mission among the mortals, there is an element of subversive satire which also runs through the text. Astrea has a naiveté that undercuts her high-minded character, betraying what Paula McDowell calls Manley's "lack of interest in the didactic."[57] We should contrast her to Intelligence who is in, and of, the real world. Astrea, for instance, is likely to launch into convoluted speeches declaiming "Better! O Better! for the unhappy *Race*, that *Creation* had never been, this Glorious World in its first *Chaos*, the Seeds of Things buried in their Pristine *Obscurity*" (II, p. 2). Meanwhile, Intelligence speaks for both author and reader when she comments, "Your *Eminences* are declaiming a Length beyond my Understanding" (II, p. 7).

It is this touch of humor that distinguishes Manley's text from other writers' tediously pompous propaganda. It is paralleled on the political front by incidents that distinguish the text from the formulaic nature of other pamphleteers' secret histories. For instance, while the author of *The Devil of A Whigg* might recoil at the thought of a Tory receiving the same satirical treatment as the Whigs, we have already seen that Manley does not hesitate to poke fun at her own Tory husband. And she goes outside her own family to give her text the illusion of balance by including figures such as Humphry Mackworth, a high Tory who was notorious for his fraudulent sale of worthless mining shares. Even his impeccable Tory record as a loyal M.P. and an active pamphleteer does not save him from being described by Manley as an "old *successful projecting-Chevalier*" who enjoys "the *present Benefit*" while feeding the "*Multitude*" with "distant *pretended Hopes*" (II, pp. 256–57). We could excuse her, saying she was on safe ground with Mackworth, since his suspicious financial dealings were infamous. There were, however, other Tory figures named in the keys are less likely targets.[58]

A good example of this is the identification of the High Tory Lord Haversham. He is named as the dead father of the incestuous Polydore and Urania (II, pp. 19–38), but this appears to be unlikely and not surprisingly, Ballaster and Köster query the assumption.[59] The story itself does not match Haversham's biographical details. The two children in the story were orphaned young and, as they became adolescents, they initiated an incestuous affair. When their guilty secret was discovered, the brother went to sea and died in heroic circumstances, while the sister perished giving birth to the product of their illegal union. In reality, the young Havershams comprised a large family of one son and seven daughters, only one of whom remained unmarried, with no hint of impropriety.[60] The story itself is a good one, containing lust, incest, betrayal, and tragic death, and it is obvious why Manley included it. However, why someone implicated the Havershams in this story appears at first to be a mystery. While that may seem to be a simple (or malicious) identification, it is not the only time that Haversham appears. In addition to this rather outlandish depiction of the lord's family, there is another much more down-to-earth representation of Haversham as "an old out-of-Fashion Lord (in everything but Politicks)." This time the story is ludicrous rather than shocking. The lord cuts a ridiculous figure pleading with his mistress not to move on to a new lover. The mistress dismisses the sacrifices he is willing to make: "My Lord, you offer me nothing, your *Estate* is *entail'd*, your *Wife* you don't *love*, and your *Children* are none of your *own*" (II, p. 217).

In both cases it seems strange that Manley should seek to denigrate a Tory such as Haversham. However, before we dismiss his identification in the keys as completely worthless, the political atmosphere of 1709 suggests that there would have been some political point in besmirching Haversham's good name. In good Tory eyes his background did indeed make him suspect. He was a Whig-turned-High Tory "blood brother of Bromley, Nottingham and Rochester," and like many converts had become overzealous.[61] In 1709 many Tories did not trust him, a fact that is borne out by his failure to achieve office in Oxford's new ministry of 1710. The slights on Haversham and his family also go some way to explain Manley's sneering attack on Haversham's political mentor Nottingham. She describes the senior peer as "a grave Seignior" who had "too much neglected" his responsibilities in the government and as the head of the Tories in favor of the delights of an opera singer (I, p. 172). Such an unflattering picture of the distinguished statesman also shows how political opinion had changed in the years between the publication of *Queen Zarah* and the *New Atalantis*. In the earlier text Nottingham is the man who "was much valued by all Men for his Wise Counsels" and who had given up public business because he "found he was going to be made a Tool" to the Whigs.[62] In *New Atalantis* he has become nothing more than a foolish old man.

Manley's attitude towards the Tory Coke family also requires some explanation. The romantic interlude of Madame St. Amant is associated in the keys with the late Cary Coke, but there seems no particular political reason why Manley should have wanted to attack her or her dead husband. The text and the keys suggest that Manley had written their elegies as a subcontractor for Mary Pix, who "defrauded the poor Labourer of h[er] Hire" (I, p. 90). However, Manley's resentment over Pix's failure to pass on her fee would hardly justify criticism, however mild, on the unfortunate deceased couple. Their identification in the keys, either by Manley, or another Tory supporter, suggests that it was their family that was under fire. If the attack on the Cokes is politically motivated, it was because of the family association with the M.P. Thomas Coke who, like Lord Haversham, is ridiculed for his pretensions as a lover. Coke, a "Dapper, squat Gentleman," has been "bubbl'd" by "a young *Courtezan* . . . and 'tis thought he may be such a Fool as to marry her, which is more than ever her Mother could persuade her Father to do for her" (I, pp. 183–84). Again, it seems strange that the Tories might want to mock Coke, who was known as a rake, but was also one of their own.[63] A discernible strategy emerges, however, if we link comments on Coke to another Tory M.P., Charles Caesar, whom Manley first points out as a "gallant" who has effectively bought someone else's "handsome wife" for a "Settlement . . . a Jewel for her Neck, and a Chariot for the *Prado*" (I, p. 164). A few pages further on, the tables are turned on Caesar and he is ousted in the lady's favors by the notorious gambler, Sir James Ashburne, becoming categorized by association as one of the "Fools [Ashburne] has cheated out of their real Estates" (I, pp. 179–80).[64] Caesar, again by virtue of his enthusiastic Toryism, should have been exempt from her satire. Indeed, Caesar should have earned her praise, since he had once been briefly thrown into the Tower for an "impetuous" attack on Marlborough in the Commons.[65] The link that emerges in these surprising jibes at Tory M.P.s lies with another of Manley's unlikely victims, the High Tory Henry St. John. The reason for Manley turning her sights on Coke and Caesar lay with their associations with St. John, the rising young star of the Tory party.[66] Manley's distrust of St. John may have stemmed, at least partially, from his unlikely devotion to Marlborough, whose "support was commonly thought to be behind him."[67] While it was probably Harley who suggested St. John as Secretary of War in 1704, once he had met Marlborough, the young M.P. was dazzled by the general, and never lost his esteem for him.[68] Manley, who had expended such energy in undermining Marlborough's reputation must have found it difficult to support one of his most ardent admirers, allowing her suspicions of him to taint Coke and Caesar, who rallied to St. John's banner.

This hypothesis is validated by Manley's comments on St. John. Her antipathy is such that she is willing even to follow a Whig lead in her references to St. John's literary aspirations. William Walsh's description of him in *The Golden Age Restored* as "*Thracian St. John,*" echoes the phrase "Thracian Orpheus" in an earlier mock-Jacobite panegyric *The Golden Age*.[69] Remembering St. John's verses from her early days in the theater, Manley continues in this theme of classical versifying:

> He has but to fall in labour of some little Trifle, a *Prologue, Epilogue, Song* . . . and be generous to the next Poet he can (get his Friend) to dedicate to him, and presently he's *Virgil* and *Mecenas* too. (I, p. 176)

Manley clearly did not trust the young politician. St. John had resigned his post when Harley had been forced to resign in 1708, but Manley raises doubts about the motives for this act of selfless solidarity. She claims that his political integrity was pretence and in reality he had given up his "troublesome Place in the Government" to devote himself to his mistress. She also slyly suggests that he would have had to resign soon anyway because of Harley's "ill Management," a surprising comment to make about the future Tory leader (I, p. 177).

In trying to understand Manley's motives, we should note that she was not the only Tory satirist who commented on St. John's resignation. In *St James' Park*, which had appeared in the previous year to *New Atalantis*, Joseph Browne (who had had his own run-ins with Harley)[70] also suggested that the young rake was acting a part:

> Now view young *St. John's* stepping it with State,
> Affecting to be thought still very Great:
> He forces on himself an easy Air,
> And studies unconcern'dly to appear.[71]

It does seem as though Manley and Browne were on the same wavelength here at least. They also both make a point of praising St. John's friend, George Granville, Harley's chief supporter in the southwest. [72] Manley refers to Granville as having "Wit, without the pride and affectation that generally accompanies and always corrupts it" (I, pp. 177–78). For Browne, Granville was "a hopeful beauteous Youth . . . / Blooming in Vertue, as he grows in Years."[73] Why these two very different writers should make such a deliberate point of praising Granville is unclear, but it indicates that the comparisons were being made around the Tory coffee-houses and political salons. In Manley's case, the answer is straightforward. Her personal regard for Granville may well have been strong enough to make allowances for his support of Harley.

Harley, of course, was the leading figure in Tory circles, and Manley's changing attitude to him is crucial to our understanding of her politics and her career. If nothing more (and of course there is far more) her treatment of the future Lord Treasurer gives clear indications of her sensitivity to the dynamics of the political scene. Her first accounts in *New Atalantis* of the man who later became her employer contrast forcibly with the panegyric to him in the second book. In the first volume Manley declares that Harley was "discharg'd from [his] Office" and as we have noted, even his own henchman, St. John had made "such Discoveries against the ill Management of the Minister that it was but vain for him to hope to keep it after" (I, p. 177).

Just how far her position moved is evident in this short passage, for she is making two extremely grave, and possibly libelous, statements. Firstly, she must have known that Harley was not officially discharged from office, although Whig scandal suggested that he was.[74] Harley had no choice but to step down. Godolphin certainly wanted him removed, but Manley's claim that he was sacked is simply untrue.[75] Manley's second charge, concerning Harley's mismanagement, is more difficult to interpret, but she is presumably referring to the case of William Greg, a clerk in the Secretary's office who had been arrested for treasonous correspondence with the Jacobite court in France. The Whigs made a serious attempt to implicate Harley in the affair, but Greg stubbornly denied Harley's involvement. His final confession in Newgate, suppressed until after his death, made it clear that he had acted entirely independently of his employer, much to the chagrin of the Whigs.[76] Manley's veiled accusation is therefore hard to substantiate, although we may interpret it as a slight on his inability to control and supervise his office staff. Whatever its original implications, it undoubtedly contrasts sharply with her extravagant praise of Harley at his second appearance in the text as Don Haro. If we are looking for a reason for Manley's curious attitude to Harley we might find it in the politician's own relationship with the party prior to May 1709. We saw in *Queen Zarah* how much the Tories distrusted the former Whig, with his Dissenting background. As late as October 1708 the Tories were unsure of Harley's true intentions, and his overtures were treated with reserve.[77]

However, this changed in the intervening months, and Manley executes a complete *volte-face* in the second volume, describing Harley as a statesman who "had not only Capacity for the Affairs of the *Cabinet*, but eminently possess'd a Virtue that often vanishes, as it approaches *there*. He was *Honest*! He was *Brave*!" (II, p. 148). The key to the change in Manley's attitude in the second volume of *New Atalantis* may of course be that Masham, his kinswoman, offered her patronage after she saw the first volume of *New Atalantis*. It is notable, for instance, that Manley is careful to paint Harley as an appreciative and biddable politician, with the two women, Abigail and Anne, as the dominant figures in the trio. In the pages where Manley describes Hilaria's (Masham's) dealings with Don Geronimo de Haro (Harley) he is portrayed as passive. Instead of directly approaching Olympia (Anne) he "made his Applications" to Hilaria, and indeed, as Manley indicates, and as we have seen, Harley's opportunity of access to Anne was limited at this time.[78] Manley emphasizes Masham's influence with the queen, placing the stress on Hilaria's qualities, and Don Haro's response to them. It was the "awful Esteem he had of her Thousand Virtues" (II, p. 148) which encouraged him and it was "her fine *Sense*, and *Judgment*" which appreciated Don Haro's qualities. Equally, once admitted to the Royal Olympia's (Anne's) presence, Don Haro becomes aware of the "*Depth* of Judgment, ... *Capacity* of Government, [and] *true* and *surprizing* Taste of *Politicks* in the Princess" (II, p. 149). It is Don Haro's willingness to listen to Olympia that endears him to her, in contrast to Biron (Godolphin), the "*Arbitrary*, self-sufficient Minister" (II, p. 149).

Masham's nonappearance in the first book of *New Atalantis* reinforces the idea that she stepped in as Manley's backer after its publication, thereby requiring Manley to revise her approach to Harley. In contemporary opinion Masham's fate is inextricably linked with Harley's and with St. John's. Whig propagandists confirm the popular association of these three key Tory figures.[79] Everybody, indeed, knew that Harley and Masham were closely connected and that St. John followed wherever they led. A contemporary commented on the closeness of St. John, Harley and Abigail Masham and their secretive communications network.

> On his [Harley's] being dismissed, these gentlemen [St. John and Sir Simon Harcourt] . . . passed the evenings together . . . where they had messages from the Queen, generally by Mr Harley . . . and sometimes by Mrs Hill [Abigail Masham] [80]

While we may put Manley's changing attitude to Harley down to personal patronage, her depiction of James II is less easy to explain. In the second volume of *New Atalantis*, the abandoned Princess Ormia [James II], is no longer the "bigotted Christian" of the first book. In Manley's retelling of William of Orange's invasion, James's crime was merely to try to change the succession in favor of her (his) young son (the Old Pretender). There is no hint that the real problem between the monarch and his political opponents is his adherence to Roman Catholicism. Surprisingly, for a loyal Hanoverian Tory, Manley claims that the people opposed James because "they lov'd Opposition" and through their "natural Perverseness" (II, p. 119). To explain this change of emphasis is difficult without speculating on the possibility of Manley experiencing moments of Jacobite sympathy. When we come to discuss the plays, this is a topic which will again become problematic. But, as far as her prose work is concerned, or even in the personal correspondence that remains, there is no suggestion, without unsubstantiated speculation, that she was ever diverted from her support of the Hanoverian succession. In *Rivella*, indeed, she claims that even to save herself from imprisonment she would not flee to the Jacobite Court, and as regards

> the Queen [Mary of Modena] that was once to have been her Mistress . . . [S]he said the Project was a vain one, that Lady being the greatest Bigot in Nature to the *Roman* Church, and she [Manley] was, and ever would be, a *Protestant*, a Name sufficient to destroy the greatest Merit in that Court.[81]

For the moment, I will discount the idea that she entertained, or was willing to exhibit, any Jacobite leanings. We should instead look at this from the perspective of a professional (or at least a would-be professional) propagandist. I would suggest therefore that the most likely explanation for the different emphasis is that Manley was in the same difficult position in which her political leaders found themselves. The increasing need was to bind the varying factions of the Tory party into allegiance with each other in order to defeat the Whigs. Inevitably, this meant that some accommodation had to be made to the conspicuously Jacobite element.[82] Manley's equivocal portrait of Princess Ormia (James II) was flexible enough to allow the contemporary reader's own prejudices to prevail. Ormia (James II) can therefore be interpreted either as a pathetic, misguided figure obviously unfit to reign or, alternatively, as a monarch betrayed by her own self-interested followers.

Manley's attitudes to some members of her own party and even to her former monarch may appear fluid. In one thing at least she was consistent: she never let up in her attack on the most obvious of her targets, the Marlboroughs. We have seen that the Tories were slowly building up for a ministerial victory over the Whigs. By 1709 it was Marlborough's and Godolphin's political influence that was declining. Public pressure to end the war was increasing. Despite Marlborough's continuing success there seemed to be no prospect of peace in sight, and even his victories were perceived as increasingly pointless and expensive. The appalling carnage of Malplaquet[83] had taken place between the publication of the first and second volumes of *New Atalantis*. The slaughter gave an extra edge to Manley's comment on "the Expense of the People's Blood" and "Successes which could not be obtained but with the *Purchase* of the bravest Lives" (II, pp. 152–53). It is also clear that by the time she came to write the second volume, Manley was in tune with Harley's propaganda requirements and knew what ammunition he needed in his campaign against the Marlborough-Godolphin duumvirate. Harley's own description of them gives invaluable insight into Manley's strategy in dealing with the general, his wife, and their mutual friend, the Lord Treasurer:

> As long as these rule victorys obtained are employ'd for their private advantage & profit . . . None of [the characters of former Tyrants] will entirely fit them . . . From the one they have borrowed ingratitude, from another restless ambition, from another falsehood, & to make the mixture more strong they have added the impotent rage & illbred haughtiness of a wild woman.[84]

This is exactly the picture of the Marlboroughs and Godolphin that Manley presents in the *New Atalantis*. She changed her 1705 portrayal of the captain-general as a disloyal, uxorious, but still brave, hero in *Queen Zarah* to a coldly calculating, avaricious, and self-interested commander in 1709. The transformation is well-illustrated by comparing Manley's competing fictional versions of his affair with Barbara, duchess of Cleveland. In 1705, it was Zarah (Sarah Churchill) and her mother who were in control of the situation, with Hippolito (Marlborough) as their dupe.

In *New Atalantis*, however, the Sarah Churchill character, Jeanitin, plays little more than a secondary role. She is merely

> a young Girl then without Interest, or the appearance of any, a Maid of Fortune, that was sent to Court, and plac'd among the Rank of those who generally owe their Establishment to their Beauty, from whence the young unthinking Men of *Quality* and *Estates*, choose themselves Wives of Fancy. (I, p. 27)

It is the Count Fortunatus (Marlborough) who calculates how to abandon the Duchess de l'Inconstant (Cleveland) without damaging his future career. It is he who realizes that

> his only way to come off with honour, was to make her [the Duchess of Cleveland] the Aggressor; cou'd he but fit her with a new Lover, and catch her in the Embrace, he shou'd have a good pretence for his Marriage with *Jeanitin*. (I, p. 32)

Of course, some of the damaging elements in Manley's earlier portrayal of Marlborough are retained. In both texts, the betrayal of Barbara Cleveland, the lover who has lavished affection and considerable material benefits on the perfidious young soldier can be read as a rehearsal for Marlborough's abandonment of his king, James II.

In *Queen Zarah*, however, the implication was that Hippolito (Marlborough) abandoned Albanio (James II) through his wife's influence, and he was in despair at his wife's continued plotting.[85] The motivation for his betrayal of the Prince of Tamaran/ Princess Ormia (James II) in *New Atalantis*, in contrast, has nothing to do with his wife, it is simply a matter of cold calculating politics. Marlborough is aware that he is "more beloved and more trusted" (I, p. 25) than any of Tamaran's other courtiers. He is equally cognizant of the "honours that the *Count* [Marlborough] . . . might . . . expect in this new Reign" (I, 41). Despite these potential advantages, Manley's wily Marquis de Caria (Marlborough) is too experienced in politics to ignore the danger of being the favorite of a king who "had not the Hearts of his Subjects," especially when that king was of "a different Religion from that Establish'd in *Atalantis*" (I, p. 41).

Therefore, when Caesario (the Duke of Monmouth) rebels, the slippery De Caria (Marlborough) decides not to support him directly. Manley makes it clear that this is not through loyalty to his monarch, but because "if [Monmouth] once prevail'd, himself must either fall, as a Favorite of the foregoing Monarchs, or waste the remainder of his Life in inglorious Obscurity" (I, p. 41). De Caria is far too clever to endanger his own future career with Ormia by overtly supporting Caesario's unpromising uprising. He is also too cunning to let slip an opportunity of encouraging a more likely successor to the ill-fated James II.

> He therefore cast about, and, with the Cabal of the principal Lords of *Atalantis* in concert, sent to Prince *Henriquez* [William of Orange], to invite him over to their Relief, from Oppression, and *holy Fears* of Slavery. 'Tis true, he betray'd in this a Master who tenderly lov'd him, but a Master *Indiscreet* and *Bigotted*, that cou'd not in all probability long support himself, and therefore he held it wise to evade a falling Ruin. . . . The *Count* [Marlborough] advis'd that he [William of Orange] shou'd lend Aid to *Cæsario* [Monmouth], who implor'd it, to Invade *Atalantis*, where the Hearts and Hands of the People were ready to assist him: Aid not sufficient to serve, but to betray him [Monmouth]. 'Twas done as projected; *Cæsario's* Enterprize miscarry'd . . . After which *Henriquez* was consider'd as the Successor: He came over with a much more powerful Army. The *Count* had a tender Conscience, and cou'd not act to the prejudice of his Interest; he left an indulgent Master, and went to *Henriquez*. (I, pp. 41–42)

This is a fabrication. Manley has altered the chronology of the period in order to present Marlborough as a scheming Machiavel. She also makes it appear that he was simultaneously manipulating the two princes, James II and William of Orange to his own advantage. William of Orange was not invited to invade England until three years after Monmouth's defeat on 5 July 1685. Moreover, Churchill fought for James in the Battle of Sedgemoor, making it highly improbable that Churchill sought William's aid for Monmouth.[86] Moreover, Churchill was not a signatory to the invitation to William III. In fact during the Glorious Revolution, it took him nearly two weeks to change sides.[87] Manley's intention in falsifying the facts is obviously to make Marlborough seem all the more calculating. Historically, William did not send assistance to Monmouth, but actually sent James's troops in his own service back home to assist their original employer.[88] However, Manley's insight into the ultimate ambitions of both William and Marlborough may have been accurate. According to one historian William was hedging his bets:

> If Monmouth were . . . successful, William would have a Protestant England for ally in his lifelong struggle against Louis; if Monmouth were defeated, a rival candidate for the throne would have been removed from his path. William would be all right in either case.[89]

Not willing to let up for a moment, Manley suffers Marlborough's character to go through even further decline in the second volume of *New Atalantis*. She also expands on the atmosphere of devious double-dealing by bringing in Godolphin, using his close relationship with Sarah Churchill to illustrate the point. Count Biron (Godolphin) has recognized that a liaison with the Marchioness de Caria (Sarah Churchill) is likely to prove both sexually and politically advantageous:

> Count *Biron* foresaw that this Passion which he so ragingly felt for Madam de *Caria*, by her ascendant in the Lady *Olympia*'s [Anne's] Favour, might be brought to introduce and fix *him* there; and Advantage he had then but little prospect of . . . because he was in the *Interests* and *Designs* of the Princess *Ormia* [James II] . . . However, he was sure that thus far he could not be mistaken, openly to appear for the *Princess* [James II], and secretly to assure her Daughters [Anne and Mary] . . . that at Heart he was so far devoted to their Interests, that whenever an Opportunity presented, they should find the good Effects of it.

> So was his Retreat secured, and which way soever the *Dye* cast, himself in *election* to draw a Prize. (II, pp. 123–24)

But if Biron (Godolphin) is devious, Caria (Marlborough) is downright deceitful. Having assured Ormia (James II) that he is "full of Gratitude and Emulation" he will

> do something *Conspicuous*, something deserving of that *Eclat* of Favour, which with uninterrupted Glory has shone upon me. Wou'd to the Gods, that Duke and People cou'd be appeas'd with my worthless Life. (II, p. 136)

From this stirring assurance of his absolute loyalty to Princess Ormia, and his determination to "secure my Divine Princess in her Rights of *Birth* and *Sovereignty*" (II, p. 137), he goes straight to Count Biron and Madame de Caria, who are idling away the time at cards. He takes a very different stance:

> Does not the *Princess* [James II] totter in the Throne? . . . I so plainly perceive her fall, that for my part I have determin'd with my self this very hour to abandon her *Mistakes* and *Her*, and to go over to the Duke.[William of Orange]. No Interest, no Gratitude, should make us act against those Principles of *Honour* and *Conscience*, that are inseparable from the Character of an honest Man. She is *ruin'd!* she is *sinking!* will not she crush us in her fall? If we stay longer, till the Duke have no occasion for us, of what Merit will be our Attempt? She . . . would have me go to the *Army* and fight a *Battle*, with not a *Heart* or *Hand* at her Devotion. Forsaken as she is, by Friends! Subjects! Favourites! and her Better Fortune! What have we to do but to give into the *Tide*, and suffer our selves to be born along the *Current*! (II, p. 137)

It is impossible to miss the irony in this passage. De Caria's emphasis on honor and conscience, the virtues he most obviously lacks, is matched by his admission that all Ormia's (James's) "Friends! Subjects! Favourites!" have deserted. These are all epithets which most closely apply to de Caria (Marlborough) himself, making himself the prime culprit in the abandonment of the princess.

We should recall that in *Queen Zarah*, it was Zarah (Sarah Churchill) who had taken the initiative in Marlborough's desertion of James II.[90] In *New Atalantis* it is Marlborough's idea to desert the last Stuart king. Sarah Churchill is demoted from party leader to a mere agent. She is now simply the means by which Count Biron (Godolphin) and Marquis de Caria (Marlborough) manipulate Olympia (Anne) through "good management" and "arguments." In *Queen Zarah* arguments and management were unnecessary. Zarah's sway over her sovereign was complete, as was Volpone's (Godolphin's) inability to control Zarah. As in the case of his affair with the Duchess de l'Inconstant (Cleveland) in *New Atalantis*, it is Marlborough who takes the lead in the desertion of James II. In fact Marlborough's moral fiber has disintegrated so disastrously that instead of bewailing his wife's influence in making him seek his "Ruin by [*her*] Base Designs," [91] he is found complaining with such force of Biron's and Madam de Caria's "*Apathy* . . . Insipidity, or rather Fearfulness," (II, p. 138) that Biron has to calm him down.

This greater emphasis on Marlborough's culpability is partly explained by the fact that the Tories blamed him squarely for the costly continuation of the war, citing his lack of support for the recent peace negotiations. Moreover, it was also no longer necessary to acknowledge his skill in the continuing military success. One poem circulating at the same time as the second volume of *New Atalantis* makes it clear it was "*Marlborough's* Zeal that scorn'd the proffer'd Treaty; / But thank *Eugene* that *Frenchmen* did not beat ye."[92] Thus, with the Tories sensing that their recovery was imminent Manley could confidently begin to predict the Marlboroughs' downfall. The precise moment for this downfall in *New Atalantis* takes place, not surprisingly, when the rising favorite Hilaria (Abigail Masham) makes her appearance "with a Soul fitted for *Grandeur*; a capacious Repository for the Confidence of *Royal Favour*" (II, p. 147). Manley cruelly presents their political death in discrete ironic narratives, individually tailored for maximum Tory glee. Marlborough, who never lost a battle in his life, suffers fatal defeat on the battlefield with the warning that it is a

> Fate which generally at the long run attends all *Heroes* who still believe they shall *escape*, because they so often *escaped*; and are therefore unwilling to embrace those Opportunities they may find favorable, towards making an *Honourable* Peace. (II, p. 153)

The Marchioness de Caria's (Sarah Churchill's) end is equally figurative. The mob loot her "*Superbous* Palace" (Blenheim) (II, p. 155) of all her valuables and she is rescued by the virtuous Hilaria (Abigail Masham) as the baying mob threaten to "[tear] her to pieces" (II, p. 156). Hilaria then persuades her to enter a religious institution, a satirical reversal of Sarah Churchill's known "[laxness] in religious matters" and open contempt for "ostentatious Anglicans."[93]

But these glorious visions of Tory superiority were in the future. While Manley was actually writing *New Atalantis*, the Whig Junto was still clinging on to power, and Manley could only predict their downfall in allegorical terms. But she could predict that once released from their control, a "new" Queen Anne will be able to rule Britain with the help of a re-formed, reliable Tory ministry. To allow for this rebirth, Princess Olympia (Anne) is made to die in childbirth. She leaves an infant queen, innocent of contact with the Carias (the Marlboroughs) or the Junto, to be brought up by Don Haro (Harley) and her father (ostensibly George of Denmark, though he had died in October 1708). Her new advisors, the Tories, and particularly Don Haro, will show all the good care and guidance required of trustworthy and responsible guardians.

I have shown that Godolphin and the Marlboroughs are the main Whig targets of *New Atalantis*, even though Manley provides very little new or particularly damaging scandal about them. This is equally true of the other senior Whigs, which is curious, given that the text is usually defined as a scurrilous exposé of Whig misbehavior. The identification of these leading Whigs, or at least their precise misdemeanors, is sometimes deliberately obfuscated. This is not to say that the text does not include some extremely easily identifiable targets even in the upper echelons of the Whigs. However, it is noticeable that when the focus of the slur is crystal clear and high ranking, Manley seems to lose some of her bite. The stories she retells about the really important figures are for the most part already well known. It is obvious that Manley was determined not to store up too much trouble for herself, and perhaps she realized that this would be a useful alibi, as she later claimed in *Rivella*.[94] It certainly seems to have been a good strategy, since she escaped actual prosecution.

How far she used these old stories as an insurance policy against future prosecution we cannot be sure, but her cautious treatment of these senior Whigs can be illustrated using the reference to the supposed bigamy of William Cowper, the Whig Lord Chancellor from 1707. This was hardly sensational new gossip. It had already prompted at least one contemporary to make a note in their diary about "Mr Cowper persuadeing his M[ist]r[es]s to think herself his other wife."[95] In fact Manley is so careful about using contentious material that she is even rather evasive about the suspicious circumstances surrounding the drowning of the mistress of Mosco (William Cowper's brother, Spencer Cowper) (I, pp. 242–43). The case had come to trial at the end of the seventeenth century and Spencer Cowper, a Whig M.P., had been acquitted of her murder. The published version of the trial prompted at least one answering pamphlet, which claimed that the participants in the postmortem found that Sarah Stout's lungs had contained no water. The conclusion to be drawn from this was that she had not drowned, and had therefore presumably been murdered before her body was thrown into the water.[96] And yet Manley refuses to be pinned down. Her suggestion that Zarah (Sarah Stout) had drowned herself by holding her breath underwater (I, p. 243) is intended, at best, to be read ironically. Otherwise it is nothing less than a mealy-mouthed prevarication.[97] Indeed, Manley appears to have been circumspect enough about the story that even the brothers' mother, Lady Cowper, was not overly concerned by Manley's revelations. She remarked in her diary, "The main matter is but old Dirt grown so dry it may not stick if it be not mixt with new stuff."[98]

And other Whig grandees got off equally lightly. The most notoriously dissolute member of the Junto, Lord Wharton, is described as "one of the most artificial Men of the Age." (I, p. 156) This a remarkably mild castigation, as is calling him *"An old Antimonarchical Pretended Patriot"* who ridicules "the Failings of others; yet in himself suffering 'em to ripen into Sins, of which there is scarce any but *Bloodshed* of which he has not had a Taste" (II, pp. 151–52). This kind of description was obviously not going to endear Wharton to her, but he would hardly lose any sleep over it, as it was no worse than he had come to expect from other Tory pamphleteers. Wharton's Junto colleagues, Somers and Halifax, are given an even easier time: they are dismissed briefly as "two renow'd [*sic*] *Politicians*" who "have had the lucky Circumstance of finding it to be for their Interest still to remain of the *Party* they first fix'd in" (II, pp. 261–62). Orford, another Junto member does not even merit a mention in *New Atalantis*. Sunderland's absence from the text has already been discussed.

Taking into consideration that Manley avoided antagonizing these easy targets, it is impossible to continue to state baldly that *New Atalantis* was written simply to abuse the Whigs. I would suggest that we begin to recognize that its propagandist elements are far more complex than has previously been acknowledged. Rather, they must be interpreted contextually, both in the light of circulating gossip and rumor, and with regard to the factions within the Tory party from 1708 to 1709. It is equally important to realize that in *New Atalantis* Manley is careful to distinguish between stories which are, or which can be interpreted as, political allegories and those which appear to be intended as pure fiction. In using this strategy we can see how she began to develop her technique as a political pamphleteer.

It is equally important, in viewing her subsequent career, that in contextualizing *New Atalantis*, we pay careful attention to her choice of Tory heroes. One of these is the earl of Peterborough, with whose exploits *New Atalantis* ends, and her next work, *Memoirs of Europe*, begins.

4

"Some faint Representations"
Memoirs of Europe

I ended the last chapter by suggesting that Manley was careful to provide a link to her next book. In fact she finished *The New Atalantis* with a reference to the earl of Peterborough, the central figure of her next *roman à clef*, *Memoirs of Europe*, which appeared in May 1710.[1] The latest addition to her scandal repertoire was published only four months after charges against her had been dropped. No doubt as a result of her brush with the authorities there was an eager audience waiting for it, and for the second volume, published in November that year.[2] Clearly, the fame Manley had achieved through her arrest and subsequent discharge were of considerable value commercially. Equally, the subject and format of the work itself helped boost sales. It was only to be expected that when Manley decided to produce another work in the same genre neither she nor her printer, John Barber, were shy of capitalizing on this fame. Not surprisingly, therefore, *Memoirs of Europe* was advertised as "done into English by the Author of *New Atalantis*."[3] She was determined to be open about her authorship and, with a flourish, she attached her initials to the preface. In addition, on 11 May 1710, in accordance with the newly passed Copyright Act, she signed her name "Delarivier Manley," in the records of Stationers Hall as the author of *Memoirs of Europe*.[4] She was one of the first writers to do so, and certainly the earliest woman. It is a mark of her independence that whereas other authors were content to let their printers and booksellers make the entry for a new publication, it was she rather than Morphew who made the trip to claim the text as her own. Perhaps she made the effort because she had ambitions beyond that of simple scandalmonger. She was now a successful Tory writer, and she had set her sights on becoming a member of the Tory writing team. Her letter to Harley accompanying a complimentary copy of the book is evidence of this. And this was not simply a passive offering to the head of her party. She wanted a reaction: she particularly urged him to get in touch with her so that "If any thing sir moves your curiosity I will explain what you desire."[5]

It was not only Harley from whom she demanded some attention. The success of *New Atalantis* and her arrest had given her some public standing, and she took advantage of her celebrity status to continue her public argument with Richard Steele under his *Tatler nom de plume* of Isaac Bickerstaffe. Steele had retaliated for Manley's unflattering portrayal of him in *New Atalantis* by ironically referring to her as *Epicene*, after Jonson's silent hero(ine), a Professor at an imaginary "College for young Damsels."[6] He had also obliquely attacked her condemnation of Marlborough in a later *Tatler*, written when Manley was under arrest. Steele had taken exception to the "Libels" written against Alexander (i.e., Marlborough) "as he was a profess'd Enemy of their State." Steele also put forward the notion that "all who spread or publish such detestable Pieces should be us'd like Incendiaries."[7] Manley took this as a direct reference to herself, despite Steele's apparent "reconcil'd Friendship (promised . . . after my Application to him when under State-Confinement)." She countered by accusing him of being a hypocrite: he had accepted patronage while calling a Patron *"the Filthiest Creature in the Street"* (I, sig. A2.r.). And just in case any reader (or Steele) did not appreciate the extent of her loathing of him, she included in her Dedication the letter in which Steele protested he was not an *"Ingrate."* With little regard for the rules of evidence, Manley, who was so used to subtly altering texts for her own purposes, tampered with the original letter (despite claiming that she is transcribing the letter *"Verbatim"*). To make her point, and in case Steele might not seem to be the villain she portrayed him, she conveniently omitted a key sentence. It seems that it was a lack of money rather than will which prevented Steele from obliging her in her request for funds: "I had not money when you did me the favour to ask a loan of a trifling sum of me."[8] She had also, as the eighteenth-century editor of Steele's letters points out, changed Steele's word "kindnesses" to "Services."[9]

Once Manley had settled her personal scores, she created a highly complex history for her text, giving her fictional manuscript a long journey across countries, languages, and centuries before setting it down before her reader. Tacked onto this convoluted provenance is Manley's political prophecy:

> *The Legions and Empire rose against her* [Sarah Churchill], *humbly advising, and petitioning* Caesar, [Queen Anne] *That he wou'd dismiss her, and her Adherents, take the Administration of Affairs upon himself, and be pleas'd to Reign alone.* (I, preface)

In confirmation of this glorious prophecy, the political sections in the first volume are concerned with the triumphant revival of Tory fortunes, and the dismissal of the Empress Irene (Sarah Churchill), leaving the Emperor (Queen Anne) to rule independently.

The text forming the support structure for these projections of Tory revival is constructed as a series of travellers' tales told to Horatio (the earl of Peterborough). The earl encounters the travellers by chance on the road somewhere outside Narva in Estonia as he travels to visit Theodorick (Charles XII of Sweden). The opening pages are principally a panegyric on Horatio. But an indication of the triumph Manley no doubt felt at her escape from Whig persecution is shown in the veiled attack on Sunderland, the Secretary of State, and his "perpetual burning Desire of vindicating his Conduct to the Destruction of all Opposers, even to the Imprisonment and Persecution of those who dare so much as glance upon his Errors." (I, p. 16) Whig pamphleteers are also included in the complaints by the two goddesses, Solitude and Sincerity, who become Horatio's first wayside companions. Once Horatio meets with human travellers, he is regaled with romantic tales which act as interludes between the sections of political commentary. The political episodes are narrated to Horatio as a means of familiarizing him with political activity at home in Constantinople (London/Britain) while he has been away fighting in Iberia (Spain). He has been "made to resign" (I, p. 4) despite his dazzling military success. Horatio's travelling companions give an allegorical account of a land where the Empress Irene (Sarah Churchill, Duchess of Marlborough) holds tyrannous sway over her son Caesar Constantine (Queen Anne). In this text Emperor Leo IV (William III) is depicted as Irene's first husband, with Constantine as their son and heir. The empress is expelled from court for espionage and, persuading Constantine to go with her, sets about perverting his natural goodness. Stauracius (John Churchill, duke of Marlborough) is Irene's favorite. Manley briefly introduces a wife for Stauracius who becomes Constantine's chief counsellor and close companion, taking the legitimate place of Constantine's first wife, the sickly Mary the Armenian (George of Denmark). Constantine Caesar, now watched closely by Irene and Stauracius, is enclosed in a ring of surveillance. On the death of Leo IV (William III) Stauracius secretly marries Irene, his own wife having "opportunely" died. Part of Irene's nefarious plans for Constantinople (London/Britain) is to change the state religion from Orthodox (the Tory High Church) and reconcile "the Empire to *Rome*" (I, p. 200), which is Manley's paradoxical term for various forms of Dissenting Christianity. Irene is aided in her schemes by a villainous set of accomplices clearly intended to represent the Whig Junto.

Irene's downfall is her arrogance. Satisfied that Constantine (Anne) is completely her own creature, she loses interest in day-to-day contact with him, and introduces Theodecta (Abigail Masham) into her service. Theodecta is a virtuous young woman, who is subsequently forced by Irene to marry the Emperor bigamously, causing a revolt by the Orthodox (High Church) clergy led by Plato the Patriarch (Henry Sacheverell). By this time, Theodecta (Masham) has already introduced Constantine to Herminius (Harley). Eventually, the people's anger at the proposed religious changes forces Irene and Stauracius (John Churchill) to retreat to their "Superbe and Costly" palace at *Elutherium* (Blenheim) (I, p. 245). By the end of the first volume, Theodecta has taken her place beside Constantine as Empress, and the "sacred Purity" of the Church has been "preserv'd from the Pollution of Hereticks and Idolaters" (I, p. 247).

The second volume of *Memoirs of Europe* was published after the Tory victory in the polls and after Harley had taken over the ministry. Appropriately, by the time the second volume begins Constantine, under Herminius's (Harley's) "auspicious Conduct" (II, p. 30), has overcome his natural laziness and is free from the malignant influence of Irene, Aemilius (Godolphin), and Cethegus (Sunderland), although Stauracius is still in charge of the army. Later on, however, Manley contradicts herself and passes the control of Constantine over to Stauracius following the gift of an enchanted ring, given to Constantine by his general. The ring has "the Power to make the Wearer do all Things in favour of the Giver, to be blind upon his Errors, and persisting in their own" (II, p. 48). Herminius (Harley) bravely ignoring the prophecy that *"whoever shou'd attempt to unpossess Caesar of that fatal Ring . . . should be lost in the Undertaking"* (II, pp. 49–50) restores Constantine to his proper vigor.

At the end of the second volume, Masham reappears as the brave youth, Leonidas, introduced to Constantine by Irene. Leonidas (Masham) becomes so popular with Constantine and Herminius that Irene becomes jealous, tries to oust him from the palace, but is trounced by Constantine's newly developed good sense. Eventually, despite the Junto's worst efforts, the "Time came for the new Elections of Magistrates" (the 1710 General Election) and to the Junto's "Confusion, the *Tribunes* of the People [M.P.s] were all chose from among *Orthodox* [High Church Tories]" (II, p. 297). The main political commentary ends here, leaving Stauracius (Marlborough) in place at the head of the army, with the hope that "Time and Reason wou'd awaken him from the Golden Dream of Lawless Power" (II, p. 299).

Whereas even the key to *New Atalantis* required a certain amount of political knowledge to decipher, Manley takes very little trouble to disguise the main protagonists in *Memoirs of Europe*. Her familiarity with the state of the parties is indicated by the transparency of her political commentary, no doubt facilitated by the further profound change in the political atmosphere between the publication of the second volume of *New Atalantis* and the first volume of *Memoirs of Europe*. On the domestic front, the mood of the country had become increasingly Tory. The trial and subsequent sentencing of the High Tory Henry Sacheverell had proved a catalyst to a revivification of Tory support in the country. By April 1710 Anne was already showing signs of independence from the Junto, replacing the Whiggish Duke of Kent with her own choice of Lord Chamberlain, Lord Shrewsbury. Sunderland's dismissal as Secretary of State in June 1710 paved the way for a Tory takeover. August saw Godolphin removed from office as Lord Treasurer. Thereafter Harley was appointed as Chancellor of the Exchequer with a retinue of his followers on the treasury board.[10] Even Marlborough was no longer secure in the queen's favor, and from this point onward, a considerable proportion of Tory propaganda, including *Memoirs of Europe*, concerned itself with discrediting him, making way for his dismissal and thereby smoothing the path to peace. It was symptomatic of his deliberate marginalization that two appointments which would normally have been channelled through him went ahead without his knowledge. The most serious was the award of the Essex regiment to Abigail Masham's brother, despite the fact that Marlborough had already offered it to someone else.[11] The Whig power base was on the verge of collapse. Meanwhile, the mood of the country was one of even deeper dissatisfaction with the war. If we are to believe Swift, "the absolute necessity for peace" was the underlying reason for all the ministerial changes, an assertion which while not necessarily wholly accurate, reflected public opinion.[12]

The first volume of *Memoirs of Europe* can therefore be read as an expression of the Tory confidence which would flower in the appointment of Harley in August. Foreseeing Harley's return, Manley predicted that "Things took a new Turn at Court; the Idolaters [Whigs] were suppress'd, and the Emperor [Anne] call'd about him his own Friends [Tories]" (I, p. 257). The second volume is likewise a celebration of the new Tory ministry and the overwhelming majority they saw returned to the Commons in October 1710. The passages located in Constantinople in *Memoirs of Europe* are a chronological, if disjointed, account of the fall of the Whig ministry and the Churchills.

Manley is careful to keep some semblance of temporal order within her British history. For instance, the battle of Blenheim in 1704 is accurately placed in the "third Year of the Emperor *Constantine's* [Anne's] Reign" (I, p. 196), and the Whig dominated Convocation of 1708 occurs in the seventh year (I, p. 225). Anne duly succeeds William III, and Manley records the "Joy" of the Tories at the time, and the way that "they Triumph'd before the Conquest was ascertained" (I, p. 190). The political commentary is equally accurate. The benefit of hindsight had shown that over the first few years of Anne's reign, as Manley suggests, the Tories did not seek "wisely to secure" their triumph but "gave their Enemies (who were Masters of cunning, and a lurking Fore-sight) an Opportunity to turn the Tables upon them" (I, pp. 190–91).

Therefore in May 1710, confident that the Junto and Sunderland were no longer a threat, Manley felt able to progress from the encoded and deliberately convoluted *New Atalantis* to a work with a much more streamlined structure. While she retains the customary precaution of aliases for her principal protagonists, there has been a severe pruning of the irrelevant and deliberately confusing material so plentiful in her previous work. As in *New Atalantis*, however, mindful of the commercial advantage of including romantic digressions, Manley provides relief from high politics in sections devoted to the *"Queen* of *Love,* her *bitter Sweets,* her *Hours* of *Pain* and *Joy"* (I, p. 3). Some of the episodes have a dual role, diverting and informing the reader by detailing the sexual activities of the Junto and their followers, although others appear to be for sensational rather than political purposes. There is for instance, the entertaining vision of Gratian (Charles Mohun) "kissing [the] Toes" and "playing with [the] Ears" of Florella (Mrs Edward Griffin) (I, p. 271). Mohun is described by Holmes as one of the Junto's "loyallest but least reputable henchman."[13] He carried no great political weight himself, so the story does not rise above the level of titillating gossip even though it does serve as an illustration of a lack of moral propriety within the Whigs.

As a political opponent whom Manley disliked more than anyone else, Richard Steele merits several pages of abuse, ranging from an accusation of having fathered two bastards (II, p. 309) to his "impudence in abusing the Emperor's [Anne's] best friends [the Tories]" (II, p. 310). Other episodes are more likely to have been included for commercial rather than political reasons, such as the story of Polignac, the French ambassador to Poland and his supposed affair with Agnes (Catharine Gage) the "idiot" daughter of an English gentry family (I, pp. 43–63).

In addition to these nonpropagandist comments, Manley is also unable to resist some attacks on her personal *bêtes noires,* such as Catherine Trotter:

This Thing without a Name [Trotter], is only known by the permission *Julius Sergius* [Lord Somers] gave her to invoke him as a Patron; if she had any other Art of pleasing him, he had best conceal it, lest he make himself the Laugh of those numerous Coxcombs, by whom her Address and Adulations have been so often rejected: Much good may it do you, *Sergius* [Somers], with *Lais's* [Trotter's] Charms, the Leavings of the Multitude. (I, p. 289)

Despite these similarities in content and style to *New Atalantis*, the textual framework of *Memoirs of Europe* is radically different from its predecessor, and consists of conversations between humans, rather than symbolic deities. *New Atalantis* relies on mythological figures to frame an allegorical discussion of personal depravity and political wrongheadedness. The opening pages of the later work indicate that Manley had originally intended that *Memoirs of Europe* would feature the same kind of fanciful element.

However, a different narrative strategy appears to have developed organically as the book was written. *Memoirs of Europe* begins by introducing Peterborough to the goddesses Sincerity and Solitude, and while it appears at first that they will supply the same narratological props as Astrea and Virtue in *New Atalantis*, she quickly finds she can dispense with them. The prospect of a Tory renaissance gave her the confidence to eschew the help of these extraterrestrial figures. In this text it is human beings who relate their experiences of the Whig regime to each other.

We may therefore pass over the divine figures and turn to Manley's principal human protagonist, Charles Mordaunt, earl of Peterborough. Peterborough was an appropriate patron for a Tory propagandist. Originally a staunch Whig, he had been given the command of the Allied Troops in Spain, and charged with placing the Emperor's candidate, Charles, on the Spanish throne in place of the French candidate.[14] He had become a hero to the Tories principally because he perceived himself to have been very poorly treated by the Junto. Rather than give him his due for his spectacular success in taking Barcelona against great odds in 1705, they had found him an embarrassment. They were forced to respond to complaints about his conduct that they received from their German and Spanish allies, and he was consequently accused of mismanagement of the war in Spain.[15] By 1707, as a result of these perceived insults from the Junto, Peterborough was extremely loud in his resentment against the Whigs. In his biographer's words, "Godolphin and his friends must have been cursing the day Peterborough was born."[16] They recalled him to London in the same year where, as one contemporary commentator claimed, Brigadier General Stanhope "misrepresent[ed] all his gallant actions as vain."[17] Peterborough responded publicly through Dr John Freind, Manley's "Immortal" Celsus, (II, p. 247) who had acted as the British forces' medical officer in Spain. Peterborough's "important Services," according to Freind had "in a most Barbarous manner been misrepresented."[18] Freind's *Account of the Earl of Peterborough's Conduct in Spain,* was the result of Peterborough's handing over to him "several attested copies of Instructions, Orders, and Letters & c."[19] His unfailing belief that he had been used abominably by Godolphin and Sunderland over his campaign in Spain meant that even three years later, by means of "flattery, a common hatred of Godolphin [and] prospects of revenge," he was still ripe for the Tories to make use of his resentment.[20] Not suprisingly, Peterborough soon became part of the group involved in overturning the Godolphin ministry.[21] Tory enthusiasm for Peterborough is illustrated by Manley's comment that now the Junto "is dissolved . . . many Pens have broke loose from that silence, their fears seem to have impos'd upon 'em, pressing forward with Emulation, striving who shou'd loudest speak your Praise!" (II, p. 248) We should not take this statement at face value. In her eagerness to present herself as standing out from a crowd of lily-livered sycophantic pamphleteers, Manley was being slightly unfair. Many Tories had vociferously cheered in print for the noble earl in 1707, even before she had included him in her *New Atalantis*.[22]

Peterborough's favor with the Tories meant that his presence in a text may well have been considered a likely way of ensuring good sales. It was no doubt this same consideration which prompted George Farquar's widow to reissue *Barcellona*, a poem extolling Peterborough, in the expressed hope of raising some income for herself and her children.[23] His revived political importance also explains why Manley may have looked to Peterborough for support when she wrote *New Atalantis*. As we saw in the last chapter, Sarah Churchill certainly believed that Manley had "kept correspondence with . . . my Lord Peterborough."[24]

However, Manley featured the earl of Peterborough in *Memoirs of Europe* for more reasons than simple patronage. During the years between 1707 when the Whigs had first attacked Peterborough in parliamentary debate and Harley's invitation to him to join the Tory ministry in October 1710, he had been sidelined.[25] On a symbolic level his exclusion from military command represented the Tories' wilderness years during which the Whig Junto reigned supreme. His personal antipathy toward Sunderland also matched Manley's. It had, after all, been Sunderland who had recalled Peterborough "in a peculiarly offensive dispatch."[26]

Against this background of abuse and ill-treatment, it is no wonder that the Tories could count on Peterborough's support. Peterborough's conversion also no doubt owed something to his own resentment against Marlborough, who was popularly suspected of playing some part in Whig animosity toward him. Contemporaries noted that "the English thought [Peterborough's] praises an obscuration of the duke of Marlborough's glory."[27] And while Margaret Farquhar is understandably more cautious in naming the guilty parties in her preface to her late husband's poem, she too suggests that "had not Envy it self blasted the sure laid Design, my Lord *Mordaunt* [Peterborough] had rival'd the Glory of the Black Prince himself."[28] Manley more directly claimed that Churchill's "Glory . . . tremble[d] from the Pinacle upon which his Flatterers had hoisted" it (I, p. 311) when Peterborough was mentioned.

Manley was clearly following a Tory lead in pointing out how badly Peterborough had been dealt with by the Junto. A notable sign that Peterborough's rehabilitation was an intrinsic part of the Tory's press campaign is indicated by his appearance in an important pamphlet, Simon Clement's *Faults on Both Sides*. Clement's pamphlet is, according to J. A. Downie, the "nearest thing we have, in print, to a full scale exposition of Harleian ideology" and was published in October 1710, one month before Manley's second volume of *Memoirs of Europe*.[29] Clement significantly chose to include the earl's case as part of a not "unprofitable Digression" to illustrate how the Junto had forced their will upon the hitherto more moderate ministry.[30] Both Manley and Clement are effusive in their praise of Peterborough. Clement describes the earl as "Rarely . . . equal'd, never . . . exceeded by any General of the present or former Times; his Enemies had no better Foundation for their proceedings against him than false Reports, Aspersion and Calumny."[31] Manley, in turn, describes her Horatio (Peterborough) in the following terms:

> [Fortune] caus'd the Spirit of *Emulation*, or rather *Envy* to seize upon those who had dismiss'd him to *Iberia*, there to gather *unnumber'd* Laurels . . . *Horatio's* Valour and *inimitable* Conduct, [causing] Things to succeed beyond Humane Expectation, the Empire was highly advantag'd by him. (I, p. 4)

Clearly for both writers the Whigs' appalling handling of Peterborough was a symbol of their self-interest, and their lack of patriotism. Manley gives a political rationale to the Tory encomiums to Peterborough by indicating that the Junto felt threatened by Peterborough's alliance with the Tories:

> *Irene* [Sarah Churchill] her self said he must be remov'd, to prevent the People returning to their old Heathen Worship [the High Church Tories]; you wou'd again incite Idolatry, and force 'em to believe there was more in it than Fiction, since neither *Mars* nor *Hercules* had perform'd things so astonishing as had *Horatio*! (I, p. 311)

Whether the Whigs were quite as frightened of Peterborough's popular following as Manley's Irene suggests is arguable. However, it was true that he had become a symbol of the tide turning against the Whigs, the repercussions of which were even reaching Barcelona, where "Peterborough's creatures were beginning to raise their heads."[32]

Peterborough's consistent popularity among the Tories contrasted with another famous military commander, Charles XII of Sweden, who appears throughout the text. Manley's Theodorick (Charles XII) was, however, an altogether more equivocal hero, and Manley's use of Charles in this text is somewhat problematic. Despite Sincerity's description of him as "a young Triumpher, all

Piety, all Justice . . . so very *sincere*," in real life "Tories and Jacobites had long regarded Sweden in general and Charles XII in particular as dangerous nuisances."[33] The Whigs had, at one time, thought of him as a savior, because he had restored Protestantism in Silesia. In 1706, the Whig Catharine Trotter had proclaimed that "[Sweden's] *Hero will not fail your Ears to move.*"[34] Even more to his credit, Charles had expelled a Catholic king from the Polish throne in 1707, and for the Whigs this had made him a parallel figure to the Protestant William of Orange who had replaced the Catholic James II. He also featured in poems such as Joseph Browne's surprisingly Whiggish *Gothick Hero*, as a European counterpart to Marlborough.[35] However, Charles's popularity with the Whigs was short-lived, particularly in the face of his disastrous defeat by Russia and his subsequent flight to Turkey in 1709. His decline was also partly due to the increasing feeling that he regarded warmongering as an end in itself. Puffendorf had already declared in his *History of Sweden* (which had been in translation since 1702) that Charles was keener on "his own Glory [than] the Publick Good."[36]

Given this and Charles's early popularity with the Whigs, it seems curious that Manley presents a version of Charles in the shape of Theodorick whose "Glory has given . . . Desire" to the truly heroic Horatio to "come so far to behold" (I, p. 315). The only way of understanding Manley's view of Theodorick (Charles) is that we are intended to view it as an ironic example of the deliberate misrepresentation of the real-life Swedish king which had been perpetrated by the Whigs. Horatio wisely wishes to judge Theodorick's *"Renown"* himself, because "Fame" has "spoke[n] so loudly in Favour of his *Person*, *Conduct*, *Temperance*, *Courage* and *Piety*" (I, p. 9). Horatio is well-advised not to take Fame's opinion as fact. In *New Atalantis* Fame's information had come via Lady Intelligence, who was "rarely concerned" with Truth.[37] Further doubt is cast on Theodorick's merit by the fulsome praise of him from Merovius (Polignac, the French envoy to the court of Augustus II of Poland). Even more suspicious is the fact that when Charles XII briefly had control of Poland, he had placed a French protégé on the Polish throne.[38] How could a British reader trust the word of a Frenchman, the representative of a nation with whom they had been at war for eight years? His version must be especially suspect when he was showering praise on someone who had apparently been in league with the French.

Manley encourages us to doubt Merovius's word by showing us that his view of Theodorick is not universal. Ethelinda (Countess of Königsmark, mistress of Augustus, and former fiancée of Charles XII) gives us the opinion we are intended to take as most reliable. She, after all, refuses to discuss the Swedish king with the Frenchman because "I find we shall but little agree about him" (II, p. 22). Her opinion had already been made apparent when she described the king as an uncivilized boor, "a dirty rude insensible Wretch" (II, p. 11).

Ethelinda's provenance as a trustworthy witness is impeccable. She is described to us as a "Lady extream devout, and so tenacious of her [Protestant] Religion" that she would not change it even to become Beraldus's (Augustus's) queen in Poland. She is a woman of integrity, but she also has great intelligence and beauty (II, p. 9). In short, she is a "universal charmer" displaying "intoxicating" beauty and "inchanting" wit (II, p. 11). Her opinion must be taken seriously, and subsequently set against Merovius's (Polignac's) when he later describes Theodorick as "the Prince in the World that is best obey'd, the most belov'd . . . the most ador'd by his Subjects" (II, p. 203). Behind Manley's elaborate conflicting narratives of Theodorick's "Renown" is the assertion that Whig pens "neither *condemn* nor *applaud* but as they are directed" (I, p. 17). Praise for Charles from Whig pamphleteers such as Trotter had not been based on the Swedish king's intrinsic merit but on political expediency (as events later proved) dictated by their Junto paymasters. Whigs are therefore inherently untrustworthy, and their efforts to praise Charles XII are transparently false.

The two main locations of the text, Narva and Constantinople are also significant. Narva was the site of Charles's great victory over Tsar Peter the Great in 1700.[39] Peterborough visited Charles in Leipzig in 1707. Unusually for this text, Manley has taken liberties with the detail of this meeting to show the two great military men on the same road. She has done this to allow the reader to compare Charles's decisive siege of Narva to Peterborough's siege of Barcelona in 1705. The reasoning behind this perhaps is to highlight the military prowess of Peterborough as a Tory military hero every inch as great as Marlborough.

There were other, more general, reasons for using Charles in her narrative. The Swedish king's more recent history also provided the rationale for locating the commentary on British politics in Constantinople. By 1709, the Swedish king was trapped in Bender. He had fled a defeat by the Russians at Poltava and was now under Turkish dominion. His confinement provided Manley with a useful symbol of a monarch in the thrall of a repressive regime, just as Anne was supposedly in the thrall of the Whigs.

The Turkish capital had an even deeper contemporary significance. As one modern historian has put it, "The very word Constantinople evoked shudders of disgust as a byword for tyranny and arbitrary power."[40] It made an ideal location for a story largely concerned with the violation of the British monarch's freedom. Manley was not the only writer who used the Turkish political system as a metaphor for a despotic government. A contemporary Whig allegory comments that the aptly named Obstinato Bigottus (James II) had an "Inclination to the Constitution of Turcomania" in his open contempt for parliamentary rule.[41] Simon Clement also informed his readers that the "Emperor of the Turks" was one of those absolute rulers who "governs alone by his own Will and Pleasure, the Lives, Liberties and Estates of all his Subjects (or rather Slaves)."[42]

While the British reader was pondering upon the repressive Turkish regime, and its resonances with James, their former sovereign, they would also be reminded that Charles of Sweden had been linked to another problematic system of government, that of the Poles. Poland and the Northern Wars furnish the background to *Memoirs of Europe*, and harness useful contemporary prejudices to compare it to Britain under the Whigs. Simon Clement suggested that the Polish system of government, a "Commonwealth [with] a King at the Head on't" was "the only Republick we love."[43] It appears that this was one opinion with which Manley could not agree. For her Poland seems to serve as an exemplar of what could go amiss when the king and administration were too much in thrall to one powerful group of subjects. Bernard Connor's *History of Poland*, first published in 1698, describes the way the elected Polish kings are hedged about with restrictions in a way reminiscent of Anne's subservient position to the Junto. He says:

> The small Authority ... of their Kings, and the Impossibility of them Acting by themselves has at all times exposed *Poland* to the Insults of their Neighbours, and the Rage of their own People, as may be seen in the Civil Wars of the *Cossacks* and the Treachery and Sedition of the Confederates which could never have arriv'd at so great height, if the King had had but sufficient power to have suppress'd them.[44]

In the same way, Manley pointed out "[The Gentry] easily keep the *King* and *Senators* in their *Duty*, and threaten both very often" (I, p. 36). The obvious comparison was the Junto who controlled Godolphin and through him, Queen Anne. Poland reminded many Britons of their own country in other ways too, since it was equally notorious for factious politics. Connor's *History of Poland* had made the country a symbol for faction and internecine struggle, a reputation which Defoe capitalized on in *The Dyet of Poland* in 1705.[45] Likewise, Manley used Connor extensively while writing *Memoirs of Europe*, transposing whole phrases and sentences directly from the earlier book when describing Polish customs. For instance, Connor describes the Poles thus: "I may affirm that they exceed all the Nations of *Europe* in vivacity of Spirit, Strength of Body and living long."[46] Manley uses almost the same words: "They exceed all Nations of *Europe* in *Vivacity* of Spirit, *Strength* of Body, and living *hardily*" (I, p. 35).

We can see from this that Manley narrates her allegorical account of British politics contextualized against the two worst possible regimes available to her as models. She yokes the despotism of a Turkish ruler with the Polish disregard for monarchy. The result is the ideal ambience for a further attack on the controlling Marlboroughs and the supposedly republican Junto with their "Principles repugnant to Monarchy" (II, p. 60), "who kept as little Respect to the Imperial Throne as did her Majesty [Sarah Churchill]" (II, p. 258).

It is through these attacks that *Memoirs of Europe* is most clearly a descendant of her two previous scandal fictions. It is, however, a marked move away from the fanciful allegory of *New Atalantis*, and Manley's writing begins to have more in common with what may be termed partisan chronicling. Here once again it has resonances with Harley's "manifesto," Simon Clement's *Faults on Both Sides*. The similarities in the message of the texts, even apart from the support of Peterborough, demonstrate how close Manley's fiction writing had also come to an affirmation of Harleyite policy. Clement's long pamphlet speaks of

> A certain Lady [Abigail Masham] related to, and introduc'd into her Majesty's Service some Years since by a very great Lady [Sarah Churchill] who had long engross'd the Bounty and Beneficence of her Sovereign; but when the young Lady had by her vertuous Quality and prudent Behaviour gain'd also some share in her Royal Mistress's Favour and Esteem, the Patroness began to look upon her as a Competitor, but by how much more did the former labour to extinguish them by a submissive demeanour and avoiding all possible occasions of Offence.[47]

Manley's allegory also emphasizes Theodecta's (Abigail Masham's) "Greatness of Soul, Humanity, Ingenuity, Religion, and other conceal'd Vertues, that she made no Noise of, for fear of allaruming *Irene* [Sarah Churchill]" (I, p. 211). While Manley's depiction of Masham's expulsion from Kensington Palace and Whig attempts to traduce her is more dramatic, it adheres to the same story as Clement. Manley's Irene "sent a Gentleman to *Leonidas* [Masham], to bid him instantly begone! his Lodgings were given to another, there was no sleeping for him any longer there!" (II, p. 255). Constantine (Anne) is told that "he is thought dangerous, and . . . a Spy to that Party who seeks to dethrone you!" (II, p. 256). Clement's version is similar:

> The great Lady presum'd to turn her out of her lodgings at Kensington, with less decency than became the regard due to her Royal Mistress, and the Mouths of the Party were open'd to traduce and render her odious among the *Whigs*.[48]

Along with the streamlining of her narrative technique, Manley also abandons the confusing strategy she employed in *New Atalantis* of reintroducing characters bearing different aliases. In the previous text Sarah Churchill had been through several incarnations, such as Young Jeanatin, the Marchioness of Caria, a she-favorite and a great lady, all of whom figure in discrete stories and are textually unconnected. In *Memoirs of Europe* Masham is the only major character who is loaded with more than one persona. Even then, she is only given two identities, Theodecta and Leonidas. While Manley declares in *Memoirs of Europe* that she will draw "*the same Persons, in different Manners, sometimes at* length, *sometimes a* Head, *at* Large, *or in* Miniature" (II, preface), it is significant that they are always, unquestionably, the same "Persons," using the same names and occupying the same positions. In *Memoirs of Europe* (outside of the dedication to volume 2, where she is termed the Duchess of Beaujou) Sarah's only representation is as the Empress Irene.

With its markedly more unified characterization, *Memoirs of Europe* represents a development of the harsh, but basically consistent allegorical treatment of the cast list of *Queen Zarah*. It is also more reminiscent of other secret histories published in 1710 and later. The political story line of *Memoirs of Europe* can, for instance, be usefully compared with the Harleyite *Arlus and Odolphus*. In both texts the story lines follow the actual sequence of events with reasonable fidelity, something which, as was noted earlier, happens in neither *Queen Zarah* or *New Atalantis*.[49] It is surely no coincidence that Manley's first known *Examiner*, number 7, which picks up on the story of Charles XII, and is a mixture of journalism and fictionalized comment, made its appearance on 7 September 1710, between the first and second volumes of *Memoirs of Europe*.

Memoirs of Europe and *Examiner* number 7 share more than the appearance of the Swedish Charles. They also feature other current issues, accurately described and only thinly disguised by the most transparent of allegories. Despite this move towards a more factual approach, Manley's writing does not lose its characteristic verve. Her action and dialogue remain entertaining, a benefit which was often lacking in other allegorists' efforts.

Manley's streamlined narrative strategy in *Memoirs of Europe* with its concentration on a few main players is much easier to follow than that of *New Atalantis*. In addition, the travellers' tales structure she adopts gives her the opportunity to include detailed pen portraits of the Junto, from the differing perspectives of the several narrators. Again, Manley's concentration on the party function of Junto members emphasizes again that politics itself is her real theme. Here she can even afford to abandon the frivolous addition of the sexual mores of minor Whigs. With the Tories sweeping into power, Whig depravity was far less important than their political infirmity, demonstrated both by the Tories' healthy majority in the general election of October of 1710, and Sarah Churchill's dismissal from her court appointments.[50]

The whole of the political world in 1710 hung upon Anne's removal of Sarah Churchill from both her affections and her staff. Abigail Masham now occupied this key position. Anne's new confidante had originally gained a foothold in the royal service as a lowly laundrymaid through the offices of Sarah Churchill, her cousin. Sarah had rescued the Masham family from poverty, even taking Abigail into her home, although as probably no more than a poor relation.[51] It is therefore hardly surprising that Sarah Churchill was bitter at finding herself replaced by someone who had been the object of her charity. Whig writers made the most of the reversal of fortune, claiming

> A Dutchess [Sarah Churchill] bountiful has made
> Of me [Masham] a Lady Great.
> . . . .
> Oh! let me then some means find out,
> This Teazing Debt to pay.
> I think, quoth he [Harley] to get her Place
> Would be the only Way.[52]

Manley's dedication to volume 2 is clearly an ironic answer to the Whigs' frequent accusations of ingratitude.[53] Sarah Churchill becomes a foil to the "Brightness of [Masham's] Virtue" (II, sig. A2.r), an "Instrument of Heaven" whose "Only *Meritorious* Action of her Life" (II, sig. A3) was to introduce Masham to court. The dedication of volume 2 to Masham under the name of Louisa of Savoy emphasizes her *"undeserv'd Sufferings! Innocence persecuted!,"* the *"Favourite* of the King, become the *Darling* of the People" (Sig. [A5?]). The theme of Sarah Churchill's resentment of Masham is continued throughout volume 2, so that even in her male guise as Leonidas, Masham is accused by Irene of "Ingratitude to her [Sarah Churchill], his *Maker!*" (II, p. 261).

It may be that Manley was encouraged in her encomiums by the patronage of Anne's new favorite. While we cannot confirm this, she is always careful to avoid any hint of adverse comment about Masham and the royal servant acts as a benchmark of propriety and loyalty. In contrast, the queen's character throughout the text is often equivocal. The prime function therefore of Masham's dual personae, either as Theodecta or Leonidas, is to support the monarch, whatever her actions, in a wholeheartedly positive manner. Theodecta, Masham's representation in volume 1, is female, yet her political advice does not exhibit any feminine timidity. She recommends a government reshuffle, a change of command in the army, and a wholesale sacking of the "Schismatick Bishops" (I, p. 212). Clearly her marriage to Constantine is intended to provide him with a moral and religious antidote to Irene's bullying. She also, crucially, introduces Herminius (Harley) to Constantine's attention. In the second volume Masham is introduced now as Leonidas, a brave youth who is banished, only to be recalled when her return to court is made possible by Constantine's sudden ability to resist the blandishments of the Junto and Irene (II, p. 260). Throughout the text, as in reality, Leonidas (Masham) is inextricably linked to Herminius (Harley) in the Junto's mind. Manley therefore makes a great deal out of their vituperative attacks on the innocent and loyal Leonidas and his attempts to "drive her [Irene] and her Friends from *Augustus's* [Anne's] good Opinion and Confidence!" (II, p. 261).

It is also notable how Leonidas's sensible deference is contrasted with the extremely insulting fashion in which Irene berates Constantine over the way Leonidas and Herminius have prompted the emperor's unprecedented interest in politics in:

> What have you, Sir, to do to hag yourself with Politicks? Since *Leonidas* has turn'd Cabinet-Counsellor and *Herminius* had your Ear, you no longer confess your former Serenity! . . . Cannot you pray and play, and do any thing but puzzle yourself with State-Affairs? which credit me, your Genius was never born for. (II, pp. 257–58)

Perhaps the most symbolic act Leonidas (Masham) takes in this volume is refusing Aemilius (Godolphin) access to Constantine with a "becoming Boldness" (II, p. 292). From that moment there is no doubt that the domination of Constantine by Irene and her Junto henchmen is over. All that remains is their defeat in the parliamentary elections when "the *Tribunes* [M.P.s] of the People were all chose from amongst the *Orthodox* [High Church Tories]" (II, p. 297).

Sarah Churchill's loss of influence and the Whigs' imminent defeat meant that Manley had to create a different role for her in *Memoirs of Europe*, since it was no longer possible to argue that she was the evil genius pulling the strings of a puppet queen. As we noted in the previous chapter, Sarah Churchill's role in *New Atalantis* had been secondary. In *Memoirs of Europe*, in her guise as the Empress Irene, Sarah Churchill regains the symbolic function that she performed in *Queen Zarah*—that of guiding the Whig Junto, this time into eventual defeat. One of Manley's principal concerns is to illustrate the ways the Whigs had lied to the nation, particularly through the activities of Whig writers, the "*Prostitutes* to a *Party*" who are "scorn'd for their *servile* Compliance and Readiness in abusing, and in private ridicul'd for Apostacy!" (I, p. 20). It is no coincidence that it is to Irene that Cataline (Wharton) suggests the employment of Stelico (Richard Steele), "a commodious useful Hireling" who can "metamorphose in a Twinkling the brightest Hero into a dirty Scavenger" (I, pp. 236–37).

However, political reality cannot always be relied on to follow fictional predictions. Events were perhaps not quite as Harley had hoped. After the elections the Tory majority was too large to be manipulated and he was prevented from forming the moderate Whig/Tory coalition he wanted. Instead, he was forced to include the more immoderate High Flyers, such as Henry St. John and his followers. When St. John was securely settled as Secretary of State, Manley was forced to change her tune about him. As a result, in the second volume of the *Memoirs of Europe* in a departure from her previous slighting comments, she sings his praises for several pages, describing him as "A *Star* which is risen in our dusky Horizon, to light the warring Factions into the immortal Day of Concord, and Agreement. If this Task be ever to be accomplish'd *Julius* must be the Man; he only is fit to work the Miracle" (II, p. 300).

This, of course, is an ironic portrait of a man who was soon to split the Tory party in two. Manley noticeably keeps up her subversive edge in her compliments. Most readers would have raised their eyebrows at her next comment. Knowing St. John's reputation as a womanizer, she must have had her tongue in her cheek when she claimed that St. John was "a Martyr to the Empire; to *That* he resigns, in his invaluable Bloom, those Hours so fit for another Monarch [presumably Venus] and which can never return again" (II, p. 300). In direct contradiction to this, stories about St. John's profligacy remained current. Peter Wentworth, a couple of years later, tells how St. John bragged that

> he was the happiest man alive, got drunk, harrangu'd the Queen, and at night was put to bed to a beautyfull young lady, and was tuck't up by two of the prettiest young peers in England, Lord Jersey and Bathurst. [His Lordship] is happy in nothing but armes of common [whores?].[54]

Even Swift, St. John's great friend, was forced to comment to Stella that while walking in the Park with Lord Radnor, St. John met them, "took a turn or two, and then stole away, and we both believed it was to pick up some wench."[55]

She may well have intended to raise a few Tory chuckles, but Manley demonstrated that she was not only familiar with salacious court gossip. *Memoirs of Europe* is also careful to follow the direction of populist political feeling. Few issues roused such public outcry as the trial of the High Church Dr. Henry Sacheverell. In the early part of 1710, Tory hopes had been galvanized by this preacher, whom Manley had elevated in her allegory from a plain clergyman to Patriarch of Constantinople [London] (I, preface). Manley taps into the furor caused by this extraordinary man by featuring his story as one that illustrates the political incompetence of the Whig Junto.

Sacheverell had preached a politically inflammatory sermon entitled *The Perils of False Brethren* in front of the Tory Lord Mayor of London on 5 November 1709. This was the day upon which good Anglicans every year celebrated the foiling of the Catholic Gunpowder Plot, conveniently allied to England's deliverance from the Papist James II. Sacheverell's sermon defended the doctrine of passive obedience, and hysterically condemned "Jews, Quakers, Mahometans and anything, as well as Christians" in order to demonstrate how the hegemony of the Established Church was threatened on all sides.[56] Most significantly, Sacheverell also turned his attention to Godolphin under his popular nickname of Volpone: "In what moving and *Lively Colours* does the Holy Psalmist Paint out *the Crafty Insidiousness* of such wily *Volpones*? *Wickedness*, (says he) *is therein, Deceit and Guile go not out of the Streets*."[57]

The Lord Treasurer was naturally upset at the implications of his inclusion in such an inflammatory sermon. Despite the misgivings of wise grandees such as Somers, the Whigs grossly misjudged the situation and impeached the ultra-Anglican divine. He was put on trial at Westminster and the proceedings in January 1710 became one of the high points of the social calendar.[58] The female population in particular, from peeresses to street girls, were so obsessed with the charismatic Sacheverell and his trial that one amused pamphleteer claimed "the Doctor's Name is a Ticket which admits you into the best Favours of all the *Phillises* in *Drury-Lane*. Strange how the Women love a *High-Flyer*."[59]

More importantly, the trial became a rallying cry for the parties, with Tory support consolidating behind the doctor. The doctor was found guilty, immediately making him a High Church martyr. During the trial, mobs burned Dissenting chapels and roamed the streets.[60] When Sacheverell's punishment amounted to nothing more than a ban from preaching for three years, celebrations were held all over the country.[61] The Whigs, by prosecuting him, had elevated a London cleric to a national hero. They had, even more importantly, given the customarily fractious and factional Tories a single cause behind which to unite.

According to Madan's painstaking bibliography, there were over nine hundred separate publications in 1710 that concerned the Sacheverell episode.[62] Sacheverell's sensational trial and subsequent conviction raised Tory consciousness at all levels of society, uniting the party in a tide of anti-Whiggism that eventually helped sweep the Tories into power. Little else was talked of. Even Richard Steele ironically commented that his own *Tatler* was of no interest as "the Attention of the Town is drawn aside from the reading us Writers of News."[63]

The sheer weight of publications shows how important it was for Manley to make some comment on the issue. Conforming to the more straightforward narrative style that she had espoused, Manley's account of Sacheverell's trial and its effects actually appear far less apocryphal than some of her contemporaries' efforts. *Memoirs of Europe* is certainly easier to understand than say, *Aminadab or the Quaker's Vision*, where Godolphin appears as "A powerful Man, with a Craving Countenance . . . having a huge Purse hanging by his Side."[64] She may even have had some useful inside information, because her description of the deliberations in council over the impeachment of Sacheverell tallies closely with the contemporary relation given by one of her contemporaries, George Cunningham.[65]

Manley puts words of restraint into Somers's mouth, having him suggest that "whatever cou'd happen of Hardship to the Patriarch wou'd but the more indear the People" (I, p. 231). Cunningham too reports that Somers cautioned them to "take care not to consult your passions or affections, more than your own dignity and usage."[66] It would be no surprise to learn that Manley had wangled one of the prized Westminster tickets for herself. (She certainly had the contacts by then.) But whether she did or not, her description of Sacheverell himself and the reaction he drew from the crowd gathered in Westminster Hall to hear the trial ties in with that of witnesses. She describes Sacheverell as acquitting "himself to the Applause of all his impartial Hearers: His Defence was so holy, so moving, so humble, so unaffectedly natural, so free from Ostentation or Vanity, that drew Tears from the Eyes of the Spectators" (I, p. 240). Another contemporary description of the effect the Doctor had on his audience corresponds almost exactly: "It is to be observ'd that the Doctor's Speech made so great an Impression on the Generality of the Ladies there present, that many of them could not forbear shedding Tears."[67]

Manley was also cognizant that while following public opinion was essential, there were other equally important jobs for a Tory propagandist in 1710. The new ministry's most urgent task was to bring the war with Spain to an end and this added a further dimension to contemporary polemical writing. Therefore, *Memoirs of Europe*, along with other propaganda, not only celebrates and supports the new leader's political ambitions, it also participates in laying the groundwork for the program of the new ministry, particularly in the direction of peace. Manley started this task in *New Atalantis*, in which she had concentrated on branding Marlborough, as a political representative of the war party, with the traits of disloyalty and self-interest. In that text it had been his association with Godolphin that she particularly castigated. Manley now turned her attention to specifically discrediting Marlborough as a military hero, as we shall now see.

It is clear from the brief resumé of the political story line provided earlier that the political plot of *Memoirs of Europe* is chiefly concerned with the downfall of the Marlboroughs and the Junto. Irene (Sarah Churchill) represents the Whig Junto's dominance of the monarchy, and Manley's description of Irene as "Haughty! Corrupt! Lascivious! Ambitious! Cruel and Avaritious!" (II, p. 229) ought to be taken as a description of the Junto as a whole rather than Sarah Churchill as an individual. Tory pamphleteers continued to hurl insults at Sarah, because she was an iconic enemy of their cause. They acknowledged as well that "When with Reproaches they the Wife defame / 'Tis at the Husband's Honour that they aim."[68] The reason for this, as has already been indicated, was that Sarah Churchill, now divested of her Court employments, was becoming increasingly irrelevant politically. With the Tories in power, it was therefore the captain-general himself who caught the direct line of satiric fire. He was the living embodiment of a war the Tories wanted to end.[69] His apparently boundless ambition and avarice made him an easy target, made even easier by his wife's long-standing unpopularity.[70] Throughout this period he was accused of avarice, peculation, and ingratitude. Hundreds of contemporary pamphlets testify to this, ranging in quality from Swift"s comparison of Marlborough to Crassus in *Examiner* number 28 to other less well-known efforts.[71] Even his unassailable record as a military genius is undermined, as Ethelinda is made to ask ingenuously, "Then it is not . . . *Stauracius* that has taught his Legions to Conquer, but his Legions that have made a Conqueror of him?" (II, p. 34).

Such slurs were clearly products of popular opinion, but so was the far more sinister notion that he had already shown himself to have an appetite for royal status. Years before he had accepted the small Bavarian principality of Mindleheim from the Emperor.[72] His apparent ambition for "unconstitutional power" no doubt gave Masham the inspiration to nickname him "King John."[73] Conveniently for Tory propagandists his personal ambitions also upset Queen Anne in 1709 when he had requested to be made captain-general for life.[74] It suited the pamphleteers to suggest that this request was more ominous than it appeared on the surface, and that Marlborough sought to follow in the footsteps of Roman generals who had ambitions far exceeding their military role. They began to claim "it was no longer doubted, but [Marlborough] aspired at Royalty."[75] In the same spirit Manley claims that the "Proposition . . . to create him PERPETUAL *Father of the Empire*" would inevitably lead to a presidential system, presumably with Marlborough as the president, although "they had not yet entered upon so detestable a Proposition, as laying the Emperor aside" (II, p. 279). Tory grandees must have been proud of her efforts. Manley was well-known for her experience in the game of denigrating Marlborough, and *Memoirs of Europe* was well up to expectations, bristling as it did with all the aspersions which were regularly cast at him.

With regard to the other villains of the piece, the list of characters is again very different from *New Atalantis*, with the main activities severely restricted to key figures, mainly Junto members, such as "Furious *Cethegus*! [Sunderland], and Precipitate *Catiline*! [Wharton]" (I, p. 219). These politicians are consistently defined by their relationships to each other, their function within the Whig party, and their roles as members of a splintering oligarchy under the leadership of the evil Irene (Sarah Churchill). I have already noted that *Memoirs of Europe,* with its sharp focus on their lack of political integrity, contains rather less emphasis on Whig immorality than does *The New Atalantis*. Nevertheless, Manley could not resist some titillating gossip, and she relates with relish the story of Lord Somers's relationship with Mrs. Elizabeth Blount. The affair was such common knowledge that it cannot be argued to have served much purpose as scandal, and its true significance, other than salacious voyeurism, lay more likely in Manley's insistence on Somers's impotence.[76] Significantly, both Wharton and Somers are deliberately depicted as lacking in virility. Wharton, captilizing on his inability to father a child, tries to tempt to young lady into bed by assuring her that "thou need'st not be afraid of me" (I, p. 302), while Somers is described as "venerable *Cicero*," who "Apes the glowing Lover! . . . personates the fierce Adulterer . . . by help of supernatural Temptations and high-bought Restoratives" (II, p. 93). When we take into account *Memoirs of Europe*'s essential function as a political text, Somers's and Wharton's masculine shortcomings can be read as emblematic of their rapidly diminishing political strength. Here Manley is being innovative. While she and Swift, for instance, agree on most of Wharton's attributes, particularly lewdness and impiety, neither Swift nor apparently any other pamphleteers suggest that Wharton was impotent, merely that he could not be bothered to beget his own heirs.[77] The 1710 *Acrostick on Wharton*, for instance, calls him "O'ergrown in Sin,"[78] while in the *Examiner* Swift thundered that "To recount his abominable Debaucheries, would offend any modest Ear, since so many could not preserve their Daughters and Wives from his Lust."[79]

However, lust in *Memoirs of Europe* most usefully serves a political purpose, as at Julius Sergius's [Halifax's] orgy (I, pp. 280–309). At the most superficial level the orgy provides an opportunity to ridicule Whig grandees through their female relatives in an imaginative variety of situations. The reader is entertained to everything from the scandalously bisexual *ménage à trois* of Ariadne (Lucy Wharton), the singer Philomela (Lindsey), and Bacchus ("the Whig stalwart" Sir Richard Temple)[80] (I, pp. 299–301) to the buffoonery of Sarah Churchill's daughter, Mary, practicing kick-boxing on her husband, John, Duke of Montagu (I, pp. 298–99). The episode carries more serious political undertones, however. Firstly, the opulence of the orgy attests to Sergius's (Halifax's) rapid acquisition of wealth and the way in which, while working in his official financial capacity, he also swelled his own finances prodigiously (I, p. 279). Secondly, he is revealed as unscrupulous and manipulative. He is deliberately funded out of the royal privy purse to "invite, and entertain, the Young, the Fair, the Idle, the Busie, the Wanderer, and even the Sedate; not any cou'd defend themselves against the Charms of his Banquets, and the Luxury of his Rewards" (I, p. 280). The immediate intention is to corrupt: "This religious Introduction to the most notorious Freedoms, banishes all Constraint" (I, p. 281). The result is the elimination of all the rougher Passions . . . you are allow'd to remember nothing but Pleasure and Interest, which is the true Foundation, the invisible Spring on *Julius Sergius*'s Side, that moves the Machine even in this soft, this delectable Retreat. (I, p. 282)

While it is bad enough that the orgies are unwittingly funded by the monarch, their true purpose is worse. The orgies are held not simply to gratify a voyeuristic whim, or for Sergius (Halifax) to gain personal gratification in any way. It is for specifically political ends. There is an explicit accusation that he misuses his power at the treasury, using national reserves to fund bribery. The guests are given

> Inchanted Pieces of Sticks so artificially carv'd, that 'tis but delivering 'em to the Imperial Treasurer, and they shall be converted into Silver, so many Notches so many Talents; there are also Scrips of Paper, upon which are drawn Hieroglyphicks, intelligible to the Surintendants, who upon sight exchange 'em for good Money: What is requir'd here from the Ladies in return to *Sergius's* Generosity, is only, to follow their own Inclinations in pleasing the Men, from the Men to obey and please *Irene* and *Aemilius*. (I, pp. 91–92)

While such accusations, whether founded on truth or not, are to be expected from a Tory propagandist, it is Manley's insightful reading of the Junto's fragmentation which reveals how well she understood the underlying tensions in Sergius's (Halifax's) relationship with his Junto colleagues. Sergius is made to unburden himself to his visitor, the fictional St. Gironne, revealing the resentment he feels that "power did not bring him the rewards he hoped for and expected as his due":[81] "Few Governments, my Lord, are as grateful as they shou'd be! If I had my Deserts, where wou'd *Aemilius* [Godolphin] be? and yet he's the fortunate Man; and tho' I say it, crouds into that Station which is my due" (I, 296). Manley could be as bold as she liked about the failing Junto. However, she had to be more careful when describing the shortcomings of the monarch. Having said this, the most surprising feature of the work is the extraordinary licence Manley takes with Constantine's (Anne's) personality. The peculiarly negative depiction of Anne is demonstrated in the following passage, which is only one of many such to be found in the text:

> working upon her Son *Constantine Augustus's* Youth and native Temper, which inclin'd him rather to be led by others than to go of himself, she [Irene/Sarah Churchill] inveighled him so far, as to make him withdraw from Court, and accompany her in her Disgrace.... Here the Empress laid the sure Foundation of her future Greatness: Here she apply'd her self, not to instruct, but to pervert the young Prince: He was . . . good-natur'd, but no Conjuror, His Inclinations unactive, soft and supine.... 'Tis well he was not Cruel, Voluptuous, or positively Evil, since the Empire has suffer'd so much only by his not being positively Good. (I, pp. 180–82)

It would be hard to find another portrait of Anne as quite so weak and self-indulgent. Clearly it was necessary to be circumspect when attacking the monarch, particularly in the light of the libel laws. As we saw earlier many propagandists felt more comfortable criticizing Anne's favorites through the medium of allegorical references to domestic animals and indulgent owners. Even a fairly mild criticism of Anne for simply acting as spokesperson for the Junto in her prorogation speech was considered too dangerous to publish in 1710.[82] Less confident writers around the time of *Memoirs of Europe* tread very gently in the direction of Anne herself. *The Devil of a Whigg* shows her as having her "Conscience" guarded by a notorious Zarazian, while *Arlus and Odolphus* depicts her as having a "Natural Clemency of Temper" in contrast to the aptly named Lady Hautisara (Sarah Churchill).[83] It was more common to speak of the Churchills or the Whig Junto as taking advantage of her innate goodness.[84] It was far safer to describe Anne as a generous and mild queen, "whose natural Humanity inclines her (where there is the least room for it) to be favourable in her Opinion."[85] At worst, pamphleteers would say,

> So impossible is it to brand her Government with any Instance of Severity, that perhaps it may be more justly Censur'd for Excess of Clemency. A Clemency, the continuance whereof had once brought Her into the utmost Distress, till that tender Re-

gard, which She had always shown for the Liberties of Her Subjects, taught them in Return to struggle as hard for the Liberty of their Sovereign; even for that Common Right of all Mankind, The Liberty of chusing Her own Servants.[86]

Manley is far bolder. Her Constantine (Anne) is not simply indulgent and kind-hearted. He is actually rendered incapable of ruling by Irene's refusal to awaken "his Mind by the Conversation of Persons of Prudence, Fortitude, Capacity and Probity! who might lead him to an Enlargement of his Understanding" (I, p. 188). On occasion, Manley attempts to excuse Caesar's shortcomings by ascribing them to external causes, such as the "powerful lethargick Dormitives" (I, p. 199) administered by his mother's hand, or at the very least "enfeebled by Neglect and Indolence" (I, p. 200). The overwhelming impression in *Memoirs of Europe*, however, is that Constantine is actually mentally incapable of resisting the blandishments of the evil Irene.

Even Anne's religious integrity comes under attack. While pamphleteers are generally careful to emphasize Anne's "Piety, the uprightness of Her Life, Her unwearied Prayers and Endeavours for the Prosperity of her People,"[87] the representation of Anne in *Memoirs of Europe* is anything but pious:

> *Irene* was contented to have her Son preserve Appearances; but because their manner of living was little acquainted with Vigils and Fasting Days, the Empress took care always to have an early private Dinner, secretly provided for him in her Cabinet, from whence he issu'd out with as mortify'd an Air as he cou'd assume; which very well satisfy'd and pleas'd the People, who look no further than they can see, and beheld, that according to the Text, he *appeared unto Men to fast*. (I, p. 189)

While this appears to be an exceptionally risky suggestion to make, there are indications that Manley actually intended her Caesar to be viewed not so much as Anne herself, but more as an indicator of her own fears for the state of the constitution, even for the monarchy itself. The Emperor Constantine does not represent Anne Stuart, per se, but what happens when strong self-interested groups, such as the Junto, are allowed to dominate the British throne.

To make this clear distinction between Anne as Queen and Anne as representative of a well-balanced system of government, it was necessary for Manley to remove her central character from any direct comparison with the queen. She did this by very deliberately changing Anne from male to female. After all, as we noted earlier, as a queen, Anne was frequently compared to Elizabeth I, the epitome of a great, strong, and protective female monarch.[88] The males in Anne's own Stuart dynasty did not enjoy such an untarnished reputation. From James I and Buckingham to James II and his councillors, they had the reputation of allowing themselves to be ruled either by their mistresses or their favorites. This is precisely what Constantine (Anne) does in allowing himself to be dominated by his mother. Making Anne a male ruler allows her to serve as an example of poor royal practice, while casting no aspersions on the living sovereign. By conveniently changing Anne's sex, and her relationship with Sarah Churchill, Manley could remind readers of the damage done to the monarchy by her immediate predecessors, while effectively sidestepping Anne's own heavy reliance on favorites. Having effected this regendering, Manley is also able to make it clear that Constantine is a parallel figure to Anne, with his delicate constitution, without making any direct reflection on the living queen's own insecure health. The enervated Caesar also acts as a symbol of a constitutional monarchy undermined and threatened with overthrow by an overmighty oligarchy, who "thought this little World their own; they found the Reins of Government in their Hands, and by their furious Driving left us to guess, how far they had it in their Thoughts to overthrow the Power of their Sovereign."[89] Changing Anne's sex also allowed Manley to sidestep the unsavory rumors circulated about Anne's preference for her own sex, and Masham's "dark Deeds at night."[90] Manley's strategy for distancing Masham from these aspersions is to change her sex too, creating both male and female personae for her, as appropriate, emphasizing at every opportunity the spiritual and psychological help which Masham (as either a female or a male) offers to Constantine (Anne).

Memoirs of Europe is at bottom a celebration of Tory success. Whether or not Manley was writing specifically for Harley's approval is, of course, unknown, although her presentation of volume 1 to him suggests that she had confidence in the impression it would make. It would be wrong, however, not to point out that there is at least one criticism of Harley in this text. She seems to disapprove strongly of Harley's policy of "temporizing to gain ground," when he had power, which "small Indulgence" Manley points out, "so heartened their unweary'd Industry . . . that the Court and Offices, in a short time, became almost entirely fill'd with Whigs" (I, p. 213). Perhaps she intended to imply that her praise of Harley was sincere, because she was capable of judging his activities objectively.

Memoirs of Europe marks a recognizable development in Manley's writing as she moved away from scandal fiction to political pamphleteering. Within six months of the publication of the first volume she was recruited as an editor of the *Examiner*, and later on the next year she would become a prominent Tory pamphleteer.

5

Mistress *Examiner*

Perhaps the most remarkable career move Manley achieved was her participation in the *Examiner*. If there was a point which marked her arrival as a full member of the Tory writing team it was her appearance as editor of this periodical. It was subsidized by Harley and published throughout the last four years of Anne's reign. Its pages provided the ministry with their most effective regular mouthpiece. Occupation of the editorial chair indicated that her talents as a propagandist were finally appreciated.

The Whig decline that had provided the backdrop to the first volume of *Memoirs of Europe* had accelerated them into a political black hole by the time the *Examiner* first appeared. As a moderate Tory Harley, now installed as Chancellor of the Exchequer, intended to build a ministry which would steer a temperate course through the extreme right and left of political opinion.[1] Moreover, "Tory fever in the country" was making it increasingly difficult to resist calling a general election.[2] The Tories confidently expected a strong majority but there was anxiety that the mere action of "going to the country" would undermine financial confidence.[3] It was in this exciting atmosphere that the *Examiner* was born on 3 August 1710.

Apart from the date of the first issue, nothing about the *Examiner*'s early origins can be taken for granted. If we are to believe Joseph Addison it was "ushered into the world by . . . the Secretary of State [St. John]."[4] If we are to believe John Nichols, it was set up by Harley.[5] Even its original aims are disputed. One scholar has claimed that it was a periodical "specifically designed both to justify past actions and indicate future ministerial policy."[6] Another recent critic suggests that its original function was to act as an organ for St. John's supporters, the ultraright wing of the Tory party, not for Harley's projected moderate administration.[7] The one thing we are sure of is that its most celebrated editor was Jonathan Swift, who wrote numbers 14 to 45 (2 November 1710 to 7 June 1711).[8] He was followed in the editorial chair by Delarivier Manley who took over at some point in issue number 46 (14 June 1711) and continued as solo editor from number 47 until number 52 (26 July 1711). In contrast to the difficulties normally associated with ascriptions at this period, we need not question Manley's involvement. It is indicated by Swift's comment in November 1711 that "the last six [*Examiners*] were written by a woman."[9] Confirmation that the woman was Manley is to be found in her own letter to Harley a few months after her editorship had ended: "I beg your lordship to know that I wrote . . . that Examiner of Antony and Fulvia where by Agrippa's character your Lordship's was designed."[10]

As well as these six *Examiners*, we can probably assign another one to Manley. Internal evidence suggests she is the most likely author of number 7, of 14 September 1711. Suspect as internal evidence usually is, a comparison of this early *Examiner* to number 49 (unquestionably Manley's) makes her the most likely editor. The later paper is written explicitly as a sequel to number 7. Both of these issues closely follow the fortunes of Charles XII of Sweden, the monarch who features so largely in *Memoirs of Europe*. The reader was clearly intended to identify the authors of the two *Examiners* as one and the same. They both take the form of a "letter" and number 49 is directly ascribed to the "same Hand" as the earlier epistle. The opening sentence of the "letter" in number 49 states "I Hope you received mine of the first of *July* last"—the date placed at the top of the "letter" contained within number 7. There are other similarities between the two *Examiners*. The alias used for Marlborough, *Commanding Basha*, is common to both allegories. Both texts set the "*Trusty Swedes* (number 7)" and the "Honest and Faithful *Swedes*" (number 49) against a variety of infidels. Moreover, the themes of the two numbers are identical, that of a beleaguered monarch and a few loyal followers set against the encroaching power of infidels. Of course, the actual content is different because much had happened in the ten months between the two issues, but the allegorical setting is duplicated.

Conveniently, there is some external evidence of Manley's involvement in the *Examiner* at this early stage. It is provided in a comment by Arthur Mainwaring, the editor of the Whig *Medley* (a periodical deliberately intended to "scribble down" the new ministry).[11] He commented in *Medley*, number 21 (19 February 1711) that the writers of the *Examiner* comprised "a Poet [Matthew Prior], . . . a Priest [Francis Atterbury], . . . a Physician [Dr John Freind], . . . a silly academick [William King], and sometimes even an old Woman [Manley]."[12] As indicated by Mainwaring's comment, the periodical was written by a loose consortium of writers in its early stage. The accuracy of the Whig editor's guesswork can be judged from a statement by Swift himself that the team comprised Henry St. John, Francis Atterbury, Matthew Prior, John Freind, "&c."[13] The two lists essentially agree, although we might wish that Swift had been a little more specific about his anonymous "&c." However, given the collateral evidence I think we can safely include Manley.[14]

How did she get onto the editorial team? The uncertain origins of the *Examiner* make it difficult to identify who recruited Manley in the first instance. J. A. Downie has provided evidence that indicates that it was possibly Harley who recognized Manley's early potential as a pamphleteer. Harley is shown to have paid Barber for one hundred copies each of the *Examiner* from number 5 to number 50. Manley's first *Examiner* was therefore one of the run of *Examiners* subsidized by Harley, as were five of her final ones.[15] Perhaps she had made the original overtures to him. Her desire to be recruited is evident in her letter to Harley of 12 May 1710: "I willingly devote my ease and interest where my principles are ingaged and if I have the fortune to do some small service my Design is answered."[16]

Her route to the periodical's editorial chair may be unclear, but even outside the inner circle of Tory propagandists, the identity of the *Examiner*'s supremo provoked keen interest, particularly by the opposition. By 18 June 1711, in *Medley* number 38, Mainwaring had worked out that Swift, "the ingenious Divine," had been the principal editor for some time.[17] Mainwaring's speculations are particularly interesting because he expresses his opinion in the *Medley* which answers *Examiner* number 46, the issue in which Manley took over. In these circumstances Mainwaring's final pronouncement in this *Medley* is suspiciously apt. Mainwaring appears to be suggesting that Swift, since he cannot convert the Whigs to his ideology, should give up the effort and bow out:

> I wou'd advise him to subjoin to the next Invective he makes against the *Whigs*, this short Anathema of *Peter's* in that religious Tale [of a Tub],—if you will not comply in all and singular the Premises, G——d damn you, and all your Posterity; and so we bid you heartily farewel.[18]

The timing of Mainwaring's comment suggests that he was aware that a change of editor was at least in the offing. In fact it is clear that by 16 July he was confident that Swift had gone. His remark in *Medley* number 42 of the same date demonstrates this: "it was not he [the new author of the *Examiner*] who wrote the *scandalous Libel* to Crassus, but one of his Acquaintance."[19] Mainwaring was right, of course. The letter to Crassus had featured in Swift's *Examiner* number 27 in February over four months earlier. Whether or not Mainwaring suspected it was Manley who had taken over *Examiners* numbers 46 to 52, Sarah Churchill seems to be in no doubt that it is her chief persecutor. She wrote to Dr. Hamilton, Queen Anne's physician, that

> I have very good reason to believe that Mr St John's is the chief instruction of the person that writes it, who has not one single qualification of any merit and is notorious for being of a scandalous & profligate life & conversation.[20]

Since the first editors of the *Examiners* include men of exemplary personal character like the cleric Atterbury and the physician John Freind, it is hard to identify Sarah Churchill's remark with anyone other than Manley herself. The real puzzle is determining how many of the *Examiners* Manley actually wrote either in its early days or later on. She may well have been responsible for more numbers than those of which we can be certain. A contemporary biographer of John Barber, the journal's printer, claims that her editorship of the *Examiner* was extensive:

> She often shined in the EXAMINER, without the World's knowing that she had any Hand in it. 'Twas indeed by that Canal that she chiefly conveyed her Thoughts on State Affairs to the Town;

and for several Months together she wrote the *Examiner*, without any other Person's being concerned in it, but herself.²¹

This is entirely feasible. In a supplement to the *Flying Post* in 1712 the *Examiner* was greeted as follows: "All my Services to . . . the admir'd *Delia* [Manley], not forgetting her *Landlord* [John Barber]."²² A later edition of *The Flying Post* itself also talks of "a Woman, a Divine, and two or three gentlemen" as the authors of the *Examiner*.²³ In 1713 Abel Boyer was still convinced that Manley was occasionally responsible for the periodical, complaining that the author of the *Examiner* is "never so scurrilous and impudent" as when he is dressed as a "poor Whore in Petticoats and tawdry Ribbons."²⁴

We can only regret that we have so little evidence to identify more from her pen. However, since we are forced to consider only those which we can prove are hers, we will start with *Examiner* number 7. Manley's first identifiable issue as the editor of the journal, appeared on 14 September 1710. It takes the form of a letter from an officer who has been with the Swedish king, Charles XII, at Bender. The Swedish king's predicament provided an excellent basis for an allegory of the story of Anne's enslavement to the Whigs. He had been detained in Bender since 1709 after fleeing from the Russians, whose territory he had invaded.²⁵ Bender was Turkish ruled, and according to *The Courant*, "The Swedes know not well what to think of the long Stay of their Monarch at Bender; whether it be voluntary or forc'd."²⁶ British interest in Charles's activities in this remote part of the world was intense, with short reports regularly appearing in the London press.²⁷ Indeed, Addison's "upholsterer" was still keen for news four years later.²⁸ Perhaps Manley was inspired to construct her allegory at this particular time by a report in September 1710. The bulletin confirmed that while King Charles's stay, rather than being voluntary, was closer to imprisonment, the Turks had now apparently agreed to escort him back home. The *Daily Courant* quoted the *Leiden Gazette* that, "'Tis confirm'd on all hands that the Porte [the Turkish leader] has resolv'd to guard the King of Sweden through Poland to his own Country by a numerous Army of Turks and Tartars."²⁹ *Examiner* number 7 is based on these reports that the Swedish king "is on his March from Bender to Poland."³⁰ As we saw in the chapter on *Memoirs of Europe*, Manley had already used Turkish rule to signify despotism. Since the High Church Tories felt that the Whigs associated far too much with dangerously anti-Establishment figures for Anglican comfort, the Turks' traditionally anti-Christian Muslim faith now also made them very useful symbols for the Whig Junto's Low Church and Dissenting travelling companions.

The central theme of the allegory is the thraldom of the King of Sweden (and thereby the Queen of England) at the hands of the Turks. It also offers a defense of the king for appearing to have distanced himself from his loyal Swedish subjects (the Tories), remaining with the Turks (the Junto) for an inexplicably long time, particularly since it is made clear that the Turks' religious practices have made him uneasy. The suggestion is that it is merely "hard Circumstances" which had "thrown" him into such company. In truth, the King was "heartily weary of His *new Friends* and *Allies* [intending] to set Himself free, as soon as He can." Equally, it enforces Manley's oft-repeated point that despite the monarch's proximity to these "new *Friends and Allies*" (the Junto) and contrary to the appearances of "State and Grandeur," he is "no better than a Prisoner." Reminding readers of Irene's treatment of Constantine in *Memoirs of Europe*, the king's "Dispatches must be Counter-sign'd by *Turks*; and He is not allow'd to have any Money, but what the *Turks* furnish him with."

This issue was written in the run up to the election in which the Tories gained their massive Commons majority. We can therefore understand Manley's representation of the Whig Parliament as the "*Senators*." For they are acting in conjunction with the Allies (the Dutch) and "*Merchants*" (the money interest). They have no wish to see the king back in his kingdom because "all his Affairs [are managed] so well for him, that neither his Presence nor Interposition at home are necessary." Indeed, they judge that it would be "*hazardous* for him at this Juncture to get back to his *own People*." This could only serve to remind the Tory reader of the extraordinary action of the directors of the Bank of England who had warned Anne that if she dismissed Godolphin and her Whig ministers, the "nation's credit could never recover from such a shock."³¹ Leading on from these dire warnings and mirroring recent political developments, Manley endows Charles (and therefore Anne) with new resolve, so that he will soon be seen at the "Head of his Veteran Troops" (the new loyal Tory ministry).

In this way, Manley celebrates allegorically the queen's successful shedding of the Junto's shackles. She could represent the Tories by Charles's "few *Trusty Swedes,*" who are not "suffer'd to be of His Council." In doing so she mirrored the situation in which Harley and his colleagues had been until August 1710, only a few weeks before this issue. The parallel with Anne was unmistakable and few readers could have missed the echo of Queen Anne's first speech in the fictional Swedish officer's claim that the king's *"Heart is entirely Swedish."* The queen in her first address to the lords in 1702 had claimed her "own heart to be entirely English."[32] In this way the whole of *Examiner* number 7 acts as an extended metaphor, with the Commanding Basha, perfectly representing Marlborough, "always requiring new Presents and Gratifications; whose known Character it is, never to be *Oblig'd or Satisfied with Royal Bounty."*

This early Manley *Examiner* is more complex and significant than this initial reading shows. For Manley does not stop at this simple metaphor. She also makes use of this issue of the journal to counter Whig attempts to tar the Tories with the brush of Jacobitism. It was crucial to confirm to Tories who, like Manley herself, were strongly against a Catholic monarchy, that the new administration upheld the Act of Succession. It was absolutely essential that the *Examiner*, the party journal, demonstrate complete faith in the continuation of the Protestant line. Central to refuting the allegations of Jacobitism is Manley's emphatic declaration in this early *Examiner* that the king (Anne)

> never was, nor ever will be in the Interests of *France*. [S]he is too sincere a *Protestant*, too much a Friend to the King of *Prussia*, and Elector of *Hanover*; and too grateful a regard for the *English Nation* . . . to harbour any thoughts of taking part with the Enemy of all these.

Equally unwilling to miss an opportunity for insulting the Whigs, she declares that the same cannot be said for the "*Ministers* [the Junto], who for some time past have had the chief Direction of his Affairs." When Manley writes "Protestant" it is specifically

Anglican Protestantism that she means, not the Whiggish acceptance of all sorts of deviant Christianity (and perhaps even worse).

However, the Whigs were happy to cast slurs of Jacobitism on the *Examiner* and its writers. The suspicion among Whigs that the Tory organ was guilty of leanings towards the kings over the water was widespread. John Oldmixon repeated the rumor thirty years later:

> The Execution of the Designs of the Friends and tools of *France* came forward daily, and their Secret Conferences at Court began to be avowed, insomuch that a weekly Libel, called the *Examiner*, was publish'd with the Countenance of the new Court.[33]

After *Examiner* number 7 Manley had no part in the journal for some time. Harley, now the Lord Treasurer, provided the periodical's subsidy and he assumed direct responsibility for its management, appointing Swift as the editor. It was nearly a year later when Manley stepped back into the job. The precise details of her installation in June 1711 are not clear, since the motives for Swift's "laying down" the periodical are somewhat mysterious. The first question we ought to ask is whether Swift willingly gave up the task. Other, even more fascinating questions spring to mind. For instance, if he did not step down voluntarily, was it passed on to Manley without reference to him? And why was she chosen in preference to one of the other willing Tory writers of the day?

I think we should now address some of these questions and begin to move Manley out of Swift's shadow. It is certainly a tribute to the awe in which Swift scholars hold him that few are inclined to challenge his claim to Stella that he had "laid [the *Examiner*] down on purpose to confound guessers."[34]

In fairness, however, I should say that there has been some discussion as to the mechanics of the new appointment. Ellis and Downie both question the extent to which Swift willingly resigned the position.[35] This, of course, is important in relation to Manley's appointment. Downie's opinion is that "Swift had been told that if he intended to write without consulting the general policies of the government, then his services were no longer required."[36] And Swift had no illusions that the journal could not exist without him. He knew that it would continue after he left. He wrote to Stella:

> As for the *Examiner*, I have heard a whisper, that after that of this day . . . you will find them hardly so good. I prophesy they will be trash in the future; and methinks in this day's *Examiner* the author talks doubtfully, as if he would write no more.[37]

This was written on 7 June, the day that he wrote in *Examiner* number 45, "I conceive the main Design I had in writing these Papers is fully executed."

In the light of Swift's own comments and his prediction as to the quality of the journal henceforth, we must query the often-expressed opinion that Manley's return to the *Examiner's* editorial chair was at Swift's invitation.[38] Not once in the *Journal* does he imply that he named his own successor. Despite this, even Manley scholars seem unwilling to downgrade Swift's control over the periodical. Melinda Rabb, for instance, has argued that "Swift depended on Manley to carry on the *Examiner*,"[39] as though Manley gains prestige from being Swift's deputy. If this were the case and he had expressly nominated her as the heir to the *Examiner's* throne he would surely have been more generous in his critique of Manley's likely contributions and not referred to them as "trash."

We could wish for more evidence either way, but so far none has surfaced, so we can only say that with or without Swift's blessing, Manley took over *The Examiner* in June 1711. She was not to have an easy task on her hands. Nearly a year after the Tory party had regained political ascendancy it was in a delicate state of health. Harley, as we saw in the previous chapter, now found himself in a very difficult situation with regard to his own lieutenant, St. John. A significant number of unruly backbench Tory M.P.s had formed themselves into the rebellious October Club. They were difficult to control; they were opposed to Harley's moderate policies and worst of all they looked toward St. John, "in whom [Harley] had already begun to find a determined rival for leadership."[40]

All this made the precise timing of Manley's new editorship critical. Two days before Manley's first post-Swift *Examiner* was published, Parliament was prorogued.⁴¹ The country gentry, an influential section of the nonmetropolitan members, the very M.P.s at whom Swift's *Examiner* was mainly targeted, were making their way to their country homes.⁴² It seems that Swift did not know these M.P.s as well as he thought he did. He was certainly wildly out of touch with them if he really thought that "the whole Kingdom finds the present Persons in Power [Harley's ministry], directly and openly pursuing the true Service of their QUEEN and Country."⁴³

Swift did not realize, or refused to acknowledge, that an important section of the political population (at least the High Tory one) was not at all content with the ministry. Apart from any other considerations, they were dissatisfied that there had not been the expected clean sweep of Whigs or moderates from positions of authority within the administration.⁴⁴

Harley was under no illusions as to their discontent.⁴⁵ They had made him painfully aware of it. As Holmes comments, the Tories' Commons Address presented to the queen on 1 June 1711 "lashed with impartiality both the preceding and present administration; the former for its alleged abuses and mismanagements, the latter for its equivocation and its favour towards the Whig enemies of the Church and country interest."⁴⁶ W. A. Speck explains the ministry's problems succinctly:

> By the spring of 1711 the ministry's position . . . was becoming desperate. Harley's moderation was failing to sustain a viable Parliamentary majority, being under serious attack from the October Club.⁴⁷

Brian Hill describes Harley's problem thus:

> As if the task of conciliating the City and the moderate Whigs was not enough, he had also to control the turbulent discontent of the Tories. At times he came near to failure . . . opposition developed rapidly to his policy of retaining all the armed forces at full strength for a further campaign in order to negotiate peace from a position of strength.⁴⁸

Hill suggests that the prorogation of Parliament eased Harley's predicament.⁴⁹ If this was the case, Harley was determined that this advantage should be exploited while these M.P.s were away from the hothouse atmosphere of Westminster. Continuing the *Examiner*, the "official" Tory journal, throughout these early summer months, would be an excellent way of inculcating a more conciliatory frame of mind amongst Tory backbenchers and, specifically, the October Club. They were strong and vociferous, and they had the potential to do more than simply threaten party unity; they could determine policy. Control of the volatile Tory backbenchers was crucial to Harley. Given that the situation was so explosive, we must surely call into question Speck's comment that Swift left the *Examiner* "because the end of the parliamentary session made the paper less important to the ministry."[50] In fact it is clear that Manley was not taking over a journal which had been downgraded. The fact that Harley thought it worthwhile to continue to subsidize it up to, and including, number 50 is powerful proof of this.[51]

The set of *Examiners* Manley produced to tackle this situation are diverse in their format but consistent in their themes. If we examine them individually we can see how the same motifs recur in various guises throughout the series. We will begin with *Examiner* number 46, 14 June 1711. Ellis has maintained that number 46 was a joint effort between Swift and Manley.[52] Therefore, when we come to examine Manley's editorship, the first point of contention must be to establish exactly where her contribution began.

Since Swift had already said his farewells in number 45, it is reasonable to assume that Manley had the principal, if not sole, hand in number 46, with only "some little scraps from the old spirit, as if he [Swift] had given some hints."[53] In fact, the personal control Swift could exercise over this *Examiner* was limited, since he had left town to go to High Wycombe on 9 June, several days before it appeared.[54] Manley was therefore at liberty to incorporate or ignore the hints without Swift's physical presence to inhibit her. How far she used her predecessor's suggestions is difficult to tell. Given the lack of evidence there will inevitably be a difference of scholarly opinion. For instance, Ellis suggests that the phrase "small Bodies" in the opening lines of *Examiner* number 46, are a Swiftian reference to Mrs. Manley's corpulence.[55] I have to answer, in Swift's defense, that this would be a very ungallant, even insulting, comment to make about a gentlewoman friend, even for the fearless author of *Gulliver's Travels*. It seems more likely to be an example of Manleyan self-deprecation. She may even have intended it for the *cognoscenti* as a signing-in device, for Manley made no secret of her size. In *Rivella*, she says of herself, "till she grew fat, there was not I believe any Defect to be found in her Body."[56]

Leaving aside such fascinating, but perhaps peripheral, concerns there is plenty in number 46 of much more consequence. It begins by using military terminology to attack "those Wretches that will still be keeping the War on Foot." These are the Whig writers whose petty attempts to foster "*Faction* and *Mischief*" are satirized in a farcical petition from "fourscore" hacks who wish to be allowed to change sides in order to pursue the only trade they know. Ellis suggests that this mock petition had originally been written for an earlier *Examiner*, but not used.[57] If the writing of the *Examiner* was handed to Manley before she had time to prepare new material, such a prewritten piece would have proved useful, particularly as it emphasized the distance between the two "scribbling" camps. It also led neatly into one of Manley's favorite themes, that of the pretensions to wit of the two Whig grandees, Halifax and Somers, always easy targets in her secret histories. In *New Atalantis*, for instance, where as we have seen, the major Whigs hardly feature, she still found room to refer to Halifax as "A certain Minister, renown'd for Wit, and call'd a Poet by all the Poets, (for fathering one Copy of Verses, by whom ever wrote) the *Mecenas* of the Age."[58]

Manley soon homes in on her main target, and the ironic attack on Whig writers in general becomes an individualized attack on the *Medley*, as a "Dunce out of his Element," with particular emphasis on his poor attempts at irony. Manley clearly recognized that such editorial mudslinging was below her predecessor's high standards—perhaps she had been told that he considered it "trash." She makes amends by apologizing for having "descended so much below the Dignity of this Paper." She offers as her excuse the Whigs' continuing attempts to "corrupt the Minds of weak People, who are at [a] distance from the Metropolis" by "circulating . . . weekly Poisons *gratis*" in order to "prepossess the Reader against the *Examiner*."

It is here that we begin to see Manley's strategy to deal with the October Men develop and why, with his pressing need to pacify them, Harley turned away from Swift, Ellis's "disembodied voice," to Manley with her natural and professional empathy with the High Tories. She addressed the political situation from a different perspective. In *Examiner* number 46 she can be seen to be actively courting the club's approval, specifically with her brazen praise of the M.P.s who had two weeks earlier "lashed" the administration. She refers to them as the

> best House of Commons that ever sate; who come the nearest our happy Constitution, both in the Freedom of their elections, and that True *English* Spirit, which unanimously carried the Majority of them *through*, to the end of this memorable Sessions.

In these conciliatory, even flattering terms Manley, in her Harley-sponsored journal, attempts to persuade the volatile Tory Commons that they and the Ministry are of one mind, that there is no schism.

Behind this facade of approval lies Manley's brief to persuade them to "exercise a little patience over the question of peace."59 The theme is continued in the next *Examiner*. And by ingeniously approaching the issue from another angle the contentious subject of public credit can also be addressed. She begins by reminding M.P.s in the most emotive terms of their ultimate loyalty to the monarch: "Cou'd there amidst that awful Assembly, be any Heart untouch'd at the Voice of such a Q[uee]n?" Then laying praise on even more lavishly, Manley reminds the Commons that they are to be applauded for "disappointing the Enemies of the Nation, *in all respects*." By emphasizing the poor, if not fraudulent, financial management of the previous ministry, Manley particularly plays on the false hopes of the "willing people" that by "chearfully" paying their taxes to a Whig ministry they would achieve an "honourable Peace." Thankfully, she suggests, the economy is again in safe hands. Not averse to throwing the enemy's ammunition back on themselves, she also borrows Addison's vision of "Publick Credit" from *The Spectator* of six months earlier. With delightful irony she claims that under the Whig regime this sensitive maiden was kept alive in "utter Ignorance of her approaching Dissolution."⁶⁰ The Whigs' "remedy" for this sickly young woman's ailments, Manley suggests would be the continuance of their domination of the Queen, under a *"lawless Junto"* and an *"Arbitrary Cap*[tai]*n Gen*[eral]*."*

Examiner number 47 now moves into its second dominant topic, the Church and particularly the *Representation of the State of Religion*. The lower house of Convocation had produced the *Representation* in early summer 1711. The predominantly High Church lower house had ostensibly designed the document for presentation to the queen. It was, however, a frankly confrontational "country" document. It was not surprising that when it was passed up to the Whiggish upper house, the bishops toned down the *Representation*'s High Tory sentiments, so that it became little more than a "platitude."⁶¹ There could be no compromise between these poles of religious dogma. But Manley's task was, as it had been with the Commons, to try to tread a middle path. She had been put in the difficult position of trying to mollify the lower house while not offending the upper house and she decided on the tactic of effecting a compromise by flattering both parties and minimizing their differences. She therefore praises the lower house's *Representation* as "writ with such force of Eloquence and Argument." In an effort to mediate between the two ideological extremes, she points out that

> As to the difference in Style and Spirit, I conceive that does not relate to the Service of Religion in general, any more than when I am excessive Cold, whether I would choose to be warm'd by a quicker or more languid Fire.

The challenge is then made explicit: "Dare any Person imagine that their Doctrine and their Intentions can differ?" Once again the warning is against faction. In this instance the unseemly wrangling would weaken the Anglican Church as a whole. The danger lay in providing the Dissenters, those "Enemies of our Holy Religion (too numerous and politick a Party to be armed by our selves against our selves) [with] a seeming occasion to deride our Divisions."

Having left her readers of *Examiner* number 47 pondering upon the parlous state of the Church, *Examiner* number 48 returns to the theme very quickly. In the guise of opening an overflowing postbag, Manley silently reminds the reader of the "Enemies of the Nation" she described in the previous *Examiner*. She now claims that the Whigs are summoning up

> Reinforcements from the Circumcis'd, as not contented with *Arrians*, *Socinians*, *Free-Thinkers*, all sorts of *Christian Sectaries*; besides a considerable number of *Apostates*, or if you please *Deserters*, from our own Body.

Religion and politics were, of course, never far apart, and the religious commentary becomes politicized immediately with a direct reference to Sir Solomon Medina's "magnificent Ball and Collation" at which a "young Dutchess" gives her hand to dance with a "frowzy *Jew*." Her readership would have known immediately what she meant. Sir Solomon was Jewish, and therefore exemplified a source of dangerously non-Anglican support for the Whigs. Moreover, his payment to Marlborough for the army bread contract was also about to become a contentious issue. It was this contract which later helped pave the way to the captain general's censure in Parliament the next year because "the taking several Summs from the Contractors for Bread . . . was Unwarrantable and Illegal."[62]

Further "correspondents" featured in number 48 complain about the queen's (Whig) physicians and the tardiness of Tories to reward their own. A comment on the *Medley*'s recent attack on Abel Roper's *Post Boy*'s "*unbecoming Familiarity*" in printing the queen's speech also serves as an attack on the Whig ministry, the "insignificant *Pages* and forward *Attornies Clerks*" who presumed "to give Laws even unto their Sovereign!" After these snippets, the final part of number 48 is taken up with a mock invitation for the editor to join the Whigs. Number 49, as we have already seen, follows on from number 7 as a continuation of the letter from an officer at Bender. Number 50, the last which had the benefit of Harley's subsidy, is little more than a literary dogfight with Mainwaring's *Medley*.

But Mainwaring was the secretary of the Duchess of Marlborough and a leading Whig pamphleteer. It was incumbent upon the *Examiner* to answer his attacks. Mainwaring had claimed the week before that "The *Examiner* is grown so insipid and contemptible that my Acquaintance are offended at my troubling myself about him."[63] Manley's irritation can be clearly seen in her comment:

> Methinks this Person . . . puts himself and me to much more trouble than he needs: If he would fairly cavil with me, Paper by Paper, and then have done, there might be some hopes; but without end I am to be perpetually worried and punished this Month for the Sins of the last.

Examiner number 50 continues in this vein, answering points raised by the *Medley*, such as the fitness of the Tories to act as physicians to the "Body Politick" and the provenance of readers' letters, "not all of them," she wittily claims, "wrote by myself."

Taken as a whole, Manley's *Examiners* were significantly different from her fellow journalists' efforts, which ranged from Charles Leslie's hysterically Jacobite *Rehearsal* to Roper's relatively down-to-earth Tory *Post Boy*. It is a worthwhile exercise therefore to analyze three of her issues in more detail. *Examiner* number 49 of 5 July, as has already been noted, was a sequel to *Examiner* number 7. Manley may have been drawn back to the theme of the Swedish king by a virulent attack on Charles XII that had recently appeared in the *Post Man*.[64] But the Tories were not great fans of Charles, as we have already established, and whatever its inspiration, it is true to say that Manley's *Examiner* number 49 has very little to do with the Swedes or their king. Instead she used the same device as she employed in *Memoirs of Europe*, that of using an arbitrary set of aliases to represent a set of well-known English politicians.

When we look at this issue closely it seems, on the surface at least, that *Examiner* number 49 is not a complex allegory. Its purpose was to take readers' minds back to the dark days of 1708 when Harley was forced to resign in the face of the united front of the Marlborough/Godolphin duumvirate:[65]

> The *Commanding Basha* [Marlborough], and the *Basha* who was Superintendent of the *Coffers* [Lord Treasurer Godolphin], came to his Majesty [Anne] and told him, That unless he would remove an eminent Person, (who was then *employed* in his *Dis-*

patches [Harley, Secretary of State]) from his *Presence*, it was *impossible* for them to *serve* him.

While the incident to which Manley refers is obvious she makes it even more pertinent by reverting to her former practice of distorting the chronology of her fables. In order to strengthen the memory of the Junto's erstwhile control she suggests that "a near Relation of the *Great Basha's* was brought into the Office of the *Dispatches*" immediately after Harley's dismissal. Manley presumably means Sunderland, Churchill's son-in-law, who had been a Secretary of State since 1706, and therefore had not replaced Harley. As well as emphasizing the rapacious nature of the Sunderlands' lust for power, Manley may also have wanted to remind the Whig statesman of his recent dismissal in 1710. She must have enjoyed reminding the man who had her arrested of his former elevated position, in comparison to his current political impotence. It was also a convenient fiction with which to enhance the description of the former Whig ministry's tyranny. Better still, it allowed her to resort to another of her favorite topics, her own brave attempts to tell truth about the Whigs. Unwilling to miss the opportunity to enhance her own reputation, she reminds her readers that under the Whig administration it was a "Matter highly Criminal, to *think* or *surmise*" that the nation was in danger. This conveniently allows her to point out that there were a "few Generous Persons" who challenged the law to describe how the national "*Fabrick* [was] *tumbling*" and the "*Foundations Sapped*." I have no doubt she included herself with the "Generous Persons." It may even have been intended as a clue to her authorship. It was after all a theme which she had used in *Memoirs of Europe*. Indeed, it was one to which she would return in *Rivella*, where she asserted her pride in having "more Courage than [the male sex]" and of "throwing the first Stone" against the Whigs.[66]

In *Examiner* 49 she was not the only martyr. She included another figure who had suffered from Whig oppression and who could symbolize the renaissance of true-blue Toryism: Henry Sacheverell, the cleric whose trial had become a *cause célèbre* in 1710.[67] As we saw in the chapter on *Memoirs of Europe*, printed ephemera in support of Sacheverell poured from the presses.

One of the loyalist Tory pamphlets pamphlets told of the

> Wonderful Cures that Dr Sacheverell has perform'd since the 5th November last, on several thousands of People in all Parts of England, in rendering them to their perfect Sight after they had been Blind several Years, to the Wonder and Amazement of all Christendom.[68]

Manley introduces a divine in number 49 who, echoing this metaphor, is said to open "the eyes of the Honest and Faithful *Swedes*." His efforts enable them once more to be confirmed in the

> Precepts of Obedience to Princes, and the true Doctrine of Non-Resistance to the Lawful Sovereign . . . and enforced it so by the Authority of Scripture, and the Practice of the Primitive and Reformed Churches, that it gave an alarm to some Great Men.

A High Tory declaration of this firmness was clearly intended to reassure the *Examiners'* readers that Harley's administration was not contemplating any compromise of their ideology.

Manley also takes the opportunity to repeat accusations that the Whigs were Republicans at heart, mentioning the "great Care" that the Whigs, in their guise as Turks, took that

> Monarchical Principles should not spread too far, and that a *Diversity of Opinions in Religion* being encourag'd, Persons might at last come to have *none*; and that by learning to dissemble with their God, they might make no scruple to become *Traytors* to their *Prince*.

Viewed from this perspective, *Examiner* number 49 is simply a reiteration of the Tory creed, in which Manley makes use of all the shorthand forms with which her readership was familiar. These include the cataloguing of Charles XII's [Anne's] royal virtues ("Goodness," "Piety," "Generosity," "Grandeur of Soul," and "Penetration of Judgement"). There is also reference to the proliferation of irreligious sects who, as Whig followers, had put the Church (and her martyr, Sacheverell) into such extreme danger. Naturally, the allegory ends with a reference to recent events, as Harley is "admitted to the *Cabinet*, and made one of the superintendents of his *Majesty's Revenues*." Charles (Anne) is reunited with the loyal Tory following so that the monarch now has "*Veteran Troops* and *ancient Counsellors* about him." There was no hint, of course, that at this very time Harley was working secretly with the Whigs, in the person of Lord Halifax. Ironically this was the very same Halifax who had been ridiculed in *Examiner* number 46 and who features throughout Manley's work, as Fuimus in *Queen Zarah*, the State Mecenas in *New Atalantis*, and Julius Sergius in *Memoirs of Europe*.[69]

However, we can look beyond this representation of *Examiner* number 49 as simply a very short version of one of the secret histories. To do this we should examine more closely a passage which appears toward the end of the text. There can be no doubt that it is intended to be read as a statement of intent from the administration to their Tory supporters. Harley, the Tory readers are assured,

> will *employ none in Places of Authority and Trust, but such only as have given good Testimonies of their Duty to his Majesty, and of their Affection to the True Interest of his Kingdom.*

Such an explicit statement can only be intended as an answer to October Club complaints about the continued presence of Whigs in official positions. Ruffled High Tory feathers are equally smoothed by the vague suggestion that even the great Marlborough would eventually have to bend to the will of the new ministry:

> The *Commanding Basha* . . . made a Visit to the *New Superintendent* of the Revenue, against whom, in the beginning of my Letter, he was so implacable, that it seemed impossible for them to unite in the common Service of their Master. This occasions some Speculations: For my own part, I always interpret all Actions for the best.

None of the *Examiners* should be taken in isolation, however, and as much as any of the others, number 49 can be seen as contributing to the "drip" campaign which progressively undermined Marlborough's authority over the next few months.

It was a topic to which Manley returned in an issue two weeks later, on 19 July 1711. This issue features the second allegory in this series of *Examiners*. Frances Harris suggests that *Examiner* number 51 was inspired by the Ministry's "suspicions about Sarah's continuing influence over her husband."[70] While there must be considerable truth in this argument, it is equally likely that Manley was also contributing to the tide of classical allegory which was proving popular with anti-Marlborough pamphleteers.[71]

The theme of the *Examiner* we will now look at is the retelling of a dream sequence set in Ancient Rome at the time of Antony and his wife Fulvia, convenient aliases for Marlborough and his wife. The ambitious pair are disturbed that the Emperor Octavius (Anne) is calling upon the services of the honest Agrippa (Harley) to help him "in the Management of Affairs." Fulvia is naturally worried that this will mean the end of all of Antony's hopes to become "sole Arbitrator" of the Empire. In order to ruin Agrippa's "Virtue" she goes to the House of the Goddess of Pride. The goddess, despite the appeals of Fulvia regrets that it is impossible to corrupt Agrippa, and the best she and her Faction can do is spread "false Reports" about him and sow the seeds of dissension within Tory ranks.

Examiner number 51 is overwhelmingly Manleyan in style. Indeed, it is not unlikely that there were some readers who would have guessed the identity of the writer behind this issue. It may well be that Mainwaring deliberately repeated the word "History" in his answer to this fable to remind *Examiner* and *Medley* readers that this was the very "historian" who had already been responsible for so many outrageous secret histories featuring the duke and duchess.[72] Mainwaring certainly makes the point that "the Antients us'd to call the *Lyes* they told *Fables* and not *History*, as my Friend has done."[73]

Mainwaring would have recognized many of Manley's trademarks in the text, not least of which is the highly convoluted description of the text as a translation of a

> scarce Manuscript out of a certain Library . . . The Author is that famous *Laisan, Giovanni Adolbrandi*, who made his particular Request, that his Works might never be printed: The Manu-

script I speak of is called *Marcus Antoninus*, wrote in the same sort of Verse with the *Rinaldo* of *Tasso*, whose Senior he was.

All three of Manley's secret histories were endowed with these complex and deliberately dubious provenances. Indeed, it is possible that she intended her readers to identify her as the originator of the text through her narrator, Dolabella. This is conceivably yet another variation on her Dela or Delia (Dola), only archly referring to herself this time as "Beautiful" (Bella).

The fable is heavily symbolic and draws on contemporary propaganda to provide easily recognizable symbols for the Marlboroughs' ambitions. For instance, the inspiration for the house of pride seems likely to have been an earlier, and very popular, Tory pamphlet, *An Account of a Dream at Harwich*, published in 1708. In this pamphlet Blenheim is referred to as a "Temple to her [Sarah's] Pride."[74] Attacks on the duchess's ambition and pride had long been a regular part of Tory propaganda with descriptions of Sarah as,

> Thou earthborn Meteor, that wouldst proudly vie
> With those bright Stars that guild their native sky;
> Who like the Arch-Rebel giddy grown with Grace,
> Presum'st to insult that Pow'r that gave Thee place.[75]

Such attacks on Sarah Churchill would have been familiar to *Examiner* readers, and *Examiner* number 51, for the most part, contains fairly commonplace Tory propaganda. The attacks on Marlborough's aspirations, Sarah's pride and their capitalizing on war booty are all there. Added to all this is their unwarranted share of royal bounty. Anne's perceived lavish expenditure on Blenheim had particularly incensed her loyal Tory subjects. With all the money spent on the favorites' grand house there appeared to be nothing left in the coffers for the rebuilding of Whitehall, which had been ravaged by fire in 1691.[76] *Examiner* number 51 highlights these complaints in a description of Blenheim as being built on the "Tears and Groans of a People harrass'd with a lingring War, to gratifie the Ambition of a *Subject*, whilst the *Sovereign's Palace* lay in Ashes."

Manley's treatment of Sarah Churchill marks an interesting development in her dealings with her old adversary. Up until now the duchess had remained an essentially human, if thoroughly wicked, figure in Manley's eyes. Unlike other pamphleteers, Manley had never before directly placed her in quite such a mythologically symbolic context. It is equally significant that she was relatively complimentary about her old enemy:

> A Lady . . . Though pass'd her Meridian, her Bloom was succeeded by so graceful an Air, that Youth could scarce make her more desirable: Her fair Hair was tuck'd under a *Tiara* of Jewels made in the Fashion of a CORONET.

The description fitted the duchess very well. Sarah Churchill's worst enemy could not deny that she was still a handsome woman, even at the age of fifty-one, while over ten years later she was still described by Lady Mary Wortley Montagu as having "the finest fair hair imaginable."[77] Alongside this almost attractive figure, march Sarah Churchill's most lampooned personal characteristics. Her envy (of the new favorite Abigail Masham) is there alongside her famous temper, personified as Wrath. Tailoring her insults even more closely, Manley makes Wrath's "flaming Brand" and attendant activities occasion the famous "Toss" once caricatured by Mainwaring himself. Sarah was still recognizably that "haughty female, who (as Books declare) / Did always toss wide Nostrils in the Air."[78]

However, we should not be too sympathetic with the demon-infested duchess. She is clearly also dehumanized by pride's invitation to sit by her on her throne. Pride's praise of Sarah Churchill is lavish: "Conquress in right of her Husband. Daughter, Favorite, her Representative, her other Self." In this way, side by side with a "human" Sarah who, having lost her influential position, can be treated almost as a pathetic figure, Manley manages to present a satanic Sarah Churchill who is still intrinsically dangerous.

The final issue of the first volume of *Examiners*, number 52, is the last one we can confidently ascribe to Manley. In it she signed off as the editor. As a final issue, it was designed to give guidance to the High Flyers over the following summer months until, as she had stated in her previous issue, "the Meeting of the Parliament." The most important topic of the paper is at the end, slotted in after a conventional defence of her writing, and the ironic claim that her identity as the writer was still unknown.

After these items comes a reminder that the most pressing item on the national political agenda is still the peace negotiations. It follows extensive and lavish praise of Henry St. John, giving weight to the hypothesis that Manley's major task was to maintain a good relationship between Harley and the younger man's followers, the High Tories. In this final paper she is careful to balance her praise of Harley with a corresponding panegyric to the leader of the October Club, a figure significantly absent in her previous *Examiners*. She compares St. John to the "younger *Cato*" with "All that Love for His Country . . . Contempt of Danger, and Greatness of Soul." This praise, in itself, would be to little political purpose if Manley did not channel it towards Harley's main aim, Tory party unity. Therefore, having assured the High Flying reader that the ministry is well aware of St. John's virtues, the real message is relayed, and the first volume of *Examiners* ends with a portentous warning: "*Civil War is worse than any Tyranny*: From whence I take leave to hope we shall not easily repeat the Danger; and since all Changes are not good, let us Change no more."

We have looked at Manley's short run as sole editor of the *Examiner* and it is clear that there are several topics which recur throughout. Religion, public credit, the recent enslavement and the subsequent freedom of the queen from Junto tyranny are treated over and over again in differing ways. Perhaps the most important theme was the one she finished on, that of party unity. The success, or otherwise, of Manley's brief campaign is doubtful. The Tory party continued to split between the followers of Harley and St. John. However, in some respects this overview of Manley's half dozen *Examiners* suggests why Harley and his new ministry chose her as the new editor. For, as we have said before, her talent lay in her ability to communicate with these volatile High Tories as one of their own, something which Swift could not, or would not, do.

She, of all the professional Tory writers, had the greatest intuitive feel for what would appeal to the High Tories. Swift's appeal to them is a negative one beside Manley's effusively upbeat prose. When Swift addresses the October Men he concentrates on apologizing for what has not been done, reminding these unhappy

Tories of their "complaints."[79] Manley, in *Examiner* number 47, puts a considerably more positive gloss on the ministry's achievements:

> Could anything be more grateful to true British Spirits, who had done their utmost towards retrieving our Disorders, than to be applauded for disappointing the enemies of the Nation, *in all respects*? Not only by their raising greater Sums, than were ever granted to any Prince in one Sessions, but for restoring *Publick Credit*; a Blessing so invaluable, and so much despair'd of by our Enemies, that they concluded it impossible for the Ministry and Parliament to extricate us out those amazing Difficulties, whereunto we had been plung'd.

Manley is direct, emotive, and unequivocal, even overenthusiastic in her praise of the ministry, and indeed it could even be argued that it was Manley's deliberate strategy to sound completely different from Swift's *Examiners*, employing a radically altered structure to those of her illustrious "brother." Swift's magisterial papers take the form of essays in which a single topic is expounded with great lucidity and power. Manley tackled the task of speaking to the potentially dissident Tories in an equally effective, but deliberately less elevated, manner displaying not, as Swift did, a "contempt for party," but merely a contempt for the Whigs.[80] As such, and presumably in order to maximize her opportunities for reiterating the ministry's policies, Manley's *Examiners* do not confine themselves to one topic per number but repeat those topics continually throughout each separate *Examiner*. For instance, number 47 moves easily from a panegyric upon the queen, to a discussion of public credit, to a plea for toleration of varying styles of Anglican worship. Number 48 in the guise of answering an overflowing postbag in breathless haste, covers Dissenters and *nouveau riche* Jews, the poor quality of the queen's Whig medical care, the *Medley*, and the unpardonable treatment of the former ministry to the queen. Equally, the allegories, while concentrating on the major theme of Anne's freedom from the thrall of the Junto, are also made to carry several different messages within the overall narrative.

This multitopic approach makes Manley's *Examiners* appear to be more superficial than Swift's, and perhaps less polished.

But, these *Examiners* numbers 46 to 52 were intended, she says, to reach out to readers who are at a "distance from the Metropolis" (that is the country gentlemen and the out-of-town M.P.s).[81] With this target readership, her "portfolio" approach to their construction gives them a distinctly practical advantage over Swift's denser texts. They are not essays which need concerted concentration to be read at one sitting. They are periodicals for country gentlemen, busy with issues of estate and family. They presumably had the same appeal as John Dyer's newsletters, making them read best "over a Barrel of Brown Beer."[82] With their contents divided into "articles" they could be read in sections at convenient periods throughout the week, when each point could be taken and discussed separately.

Manley's *Examiners* are not different from Swift's merely in their construction. They also take a more direct approach toward the reader, exhibiting a conscious and ingenious policy of "reader involvement." Whereas Swift addresses his readers, Manley converses with them, inviting their response, through her easy acknowledgment of their letters. C. John Sommerville demonstrates that correspondents' letters included in the early periodicals were "part of an editorial technique" designed to create a "club" atmosphere for readers.[83] Manley's *Examiners*, unlike Swift's, actively encourage this feeling of "reader participation."

This point is easily illustrated. When pressed on the important subject of convocation, Swift graciously consents to "bestow a paper" upon the topic.[84] This, of course, involves not "answering" readers as individuals, but "delivering" an answer to them, as though they were an audience, or a congregation. Mr *Examiner* also loftily wishes that his correspondents *"give themselves the trouble to . . . consider whether what they send be proper for such a Paper to take notice of"* and regards their advice as a nuisance.[85] Manley, in an entirely more openhearted way, is the perfect hostess of *Rivella* with a "Table well furnish'd and well serv'd; [with] sparkling Wit and easy Gaiety, when at Meat with Persons of Conversation and Humour."[86] She welcomes the readers into her club as her friends. Her only worry in number 48 is that, "If I take notice of some and not of others, I proportionately disoblige."

If, as has been proposed, Manley's mission was to keep the October Club Tories in touch with Harley's ministry, this inclusiveness was a feature even more central to her project than to other periodical editors. The real October Club, which met at Westminster taverns to drink and decide political strategy, could, through the pages of the *Examiner*, maintain their "club" during the summer recess. They could meet "spiritually" via Manley's welcoming prose. In number 50 she charmingly informs them that their active interest in her paper, so far from being unwelcome, actually boosted sales. This commercial information was not, of course, simply to reassure them of the printer's prosperity. It meant that the more they corresponded, the more of their friends they could be sure of reaching. Even the printer is made to extol "that Paper wherein I had lately oblig'd so many of my Correspondents."

The strategy also had political advantages. It kept open the vital channel of communication between Harley and the backbenchers and their country supporters. It also provided them with the illusion that they retained their parliamentary voice, distant as they were from the heart of things. In a subtle way, the multiplicity of voices within the *Examiner*, she explained in number 50, also provided them with a greater chance of influencing the ministry, since "The concurrent Interest of many Authors must be much more prevailing than that of one." Essentially, Manley's *Examiners*, as other writers jibed, may have contained nothing new. But they presented the essential elements of Tory policy in a way that promoted the fiction that it had come from the readers themselves.

In this way Manley's *Examiners* are easily digestible. But equally they never lose sight that they are for Tory consumption, and are written by a committed Tory. An example of this is the invitation in number 48 for Manley to join the Whigs, because "we never refuse to accept an Enemy with open Arms." By teasing her readership with this satirical invitation to join the other side, she could assure them of her (and Harley's) unwavering Tory support. If they would only have patience they would see that she (and the new Ministry) would not betray their cause to the Whigs, however attractive the devilishly clever opposition tried to make such a defection sound.

6

"Several little pamphlets and papers": Manley's Pamphleteering

After her successful stint at the *Examiner* Manley was ready to take her place on the Tory writing team. And she was obviously pleased with what she had already produced because in 1714 she reminded Harley that she had "endeavour'd to make my self . . . useful . . . by writing several little phamplets [sic] and papers, of which, if I am rightly inform'd, some have not been disaproved by your Lordship, and the World."[1] The identification of (some of) these little pamphlets and papers is easy, despite their customary anonymity. From her own letters and Swift's *Journal to Stella*, we know that in 1711 she wrote at least three: *A True Narrative of what pass'd at the Examination of the Marquis de Guiscard*; *A Learned Comment upon Dr. Hare's Excellent Sermon Preach'd before the Duke of Marlborough;* and *The Duke of Marlborough's Vindication in Answer to a Pamphlet lately Publish'd*. Manley also probably wrote *The Honour and Prerogative of the Queen's Majesty Vindicated* (1713), for which there is a contemporary ascription to her by Abel Boyer.[2]

The first of Manley's pamphlets, *A True Narrative*, appeared on 19 April 1711. In a letter to Harley in October 1711, she begged "your lordship to know that I wrote Mons. De Guiscard's narrative."[3] Jonathan Swift wrote to his friend, Stella, that he had passed the task of writing the pamphlet over to Manley because he had not wanted to do it himself. Once again we need to query Swift's honesty. It is feasible that the pamphlet may have started out as Swift's but contemporary evidence indicates that even this is questionable. As I will show, he had already grossly misreported the assassination attempt on Harley, the incident at the center of the pamphlet. Because of this, rather than being employed as a subcontractor, it was likely to have been Manley who was to give the story a ministerial spin.[4] In this case, Swift's claim to Stella that "what you read in the narrative, I ordered to be written" does not ring true.[5]

A True Narrative was an account of the sensational assassination attempt on Robert Harley, the chancellor of the exchequer and leader of the Tory ministry in 1711. The would-be assassin was a Frenchman, the Marquis de Guiscard, a disgruntled pensioner of the British government. He had been given command of a regiment that had been destroyed at the battle of Almanza, and he had then been awarded an official pension of £500 per year, latterly reduced under Harley's chancellorship to an irregularly paid £400. Unfortunately, this sum was inadequate to support his extravagant lifestyle which, it was rumored, he enjoyed in the company of Secretary of State, Henry St. John.[6] As H. T. Dickinson explains, Guiscard, this "notorious rake" now chronically short of money, had then tried to "supplement his income by beginning a treasonable correspondence with France."[7] The offending letters were seized and he was arrested on 8 March 1711 in St. James's Park. He was taken immediately to St. John's office, where he was interviewed by the members of the privy council.

During the interview, Guiscard stabbed Harley with a penknife he had concealed in his sleeve. The blade, though impeded by Harley's richly embroidered court waistcoat, entered Harley's chest, but snapped off against the breastbone, so that Guiscard's second blow resulted in nothing more than severe bruising. With Harley temporarily stunned, Guiscard then rushed on to St. John. In the ensuing mêlée several councillors drew their swords and wounded Guiscard, who was finally brought struggling to the ground by the messengers. At the end of this extraordinary interruption to the normal course of affairs, Harley was found to have suffered a wound and extensive bruising. He was taken back to his own house in a sedan chair, and he did not return to the House of Commons until late April, some seven weeks after the attack, when he was given a rapturous welcome by his fellow members.[8]

The first newspaper reports were unequivocal about Guiscard's intended victim, making it clear that it was Harley. *The Post Man, The Daily Courant, The Post Boy, The London Gazette, The Supplement, The British Mercury, The Evening Post, Dawks's Newsletter, The Flying Post* all carried items within a day or so of the incident. The terms in which they described what had happened were all remarkably similar. Indeed, in many instances they tallied almost word-for-word with the *London Gazette*'s report of 8 March:

> This day *Monsieur Guiscard*, a French Papist, being apprehended for High Treason, and under Examination before a Committee of the Privy-Council at the Cock-pit Stabbed the Right Honourable Mr *Harley*, Chancellor of the Exchequer with a Penknife, which he had found by accident in the room where in he was confin'd before his Examination.[9]

The immediate result was a huge wave of sympathy for the brave Chancellor of the Exchequer. The most high-flying Tory could not but be impressed by Harley's calmness and presence of mind during the actual incident. Even his rival, St. John, despite their personal conflict over leadership of the Tory party, remarked on his "firmness and magnanimity" and the way neither his "countenance, nor his voice" altered.[10]

This consensus did not last. It was not long before the question of Guiscard's intended victim became a controversial issue. On 15 March 1711, Swift's *Examiner* number 33 gave a significantly different account of the matter:

> The Murderer confessed in *Newgate*, that his chief Design was against Mr. *Secretary St. John*, [and] not being able to come at the *Secretary*, as he intended, it was some satisfaction to Murder the Person whom he thought Mr. *St. John* loved best.[11]

By thus changing Guiscard's target from Harley to St. John, Swift committed a serious error of judgment. It is contemporary reaction to this error that has a direct bearing on Manley's role in writing *A True Narrative*. Harley and St. John were at that time struggling for leadership of the Tory party in the House of Commons. In fact, Harley was rescued from potential backbench mutiny by the assassination attempt. All party strife within the Tory party was forgotten in the immediate days after the incident, and Swift's version threatened to divert, or at least dilute, this goodwill. As Swift ruefully admitted later the report was unfortunate, since "if it were true, the consequence must be, that Mr. St. John had all the merit, while Mr Harley remained with nothing but the danger and the pain."[12] The rival Whig periodical, the *Medley*, was delighted with the confusion caused by Swift's difference in emphasis. The editor mischievously accused the *Examiner* of claiming that "Truly there was no design at all against Mr *H*[arle]*y*."[13]

The problem with Swift's account was that, as he later admitted, he had naïvely published what St. John had told him. It was hardly surprising, given the strained relations between himself and Harley, that when St. John read his own version of events in the original prepublication *Examiner* account he "made no alteration" to it.[14] It did, after all, give him the starring role as the hero. It was, however, only to be expected that Harley's family would resent this new slant on events, remarking on it in their letters to each other as their kinsman slowly recovered. Harley's son Edward commented to his aunt Abigail on 17 March 1711 that "The *Examiner* has mistaken in some circumstances. The best account I can pick up I will send you next post."[15] Swift's reaction to *The Medley* was to include an acknowledgment in the very next *Examiner* that some readers may have considered that he had made a *"Blunder."* He admitted that he had reported that

> *Guiscard's* Design was against Mr. *Secretary St. John*; and yet my Reasonings upon it, are, as if it were personal against Mr. *Harley*. But I say no such Thing, and my Reasonings are just; I relate only what *Guiscard* said in *Newgate*.[16]

Swift's halfhearted retraction seems not to have pacified the Harley clan. Edward wrote on 27 March, "that is a very senseless paragraph yt was in the Examiner Thursday was sevennight [sic]. The Queen was the only person he designed the blow for, besid [sic] the person he struck."[17] Lady Dupplin, Harley's daughter, wrote to her aunt Abigail, "The Examiner has made small amends for his intollerable blunder which is unpardonable having not an air of probability, people are mighty angry with the author & one more [St. John?] about it."[18] Robert's brother, Edward, remembered his indignation years later, in his unpublished memoirs.

> First the Examiner immediately came out and says that Guiscard's primary design was against Mr Secretary St. John which he afterwards corrected in another *Examiner* with saying that in so great a Hurry he might easily be excused so minute a mistake. Insert the Words out of both *Examiners*.
> Note the order of sitting [in the Secretary's office] which makes the Story improbable.
> Abel Boyer is another who in a sort not only vindicates Guiscard and dresses up the Story with other Circumstances, such as these Viz. that M. Guiscard should desire Mr. St. John to withdraw with him, that upon Mr. St. John's refusing Guiscard struck Mr. Harley with these words cest a tuy donc and declared that since he could not kill Mr. St. John He would Kill the Man he loved best, Mr. Harley. There is no need of making any remarks upon this groundless fiction.[19]

Clearly, in this instance, Edward Harley placed Swift's report on a scurrilous par with Boyer's.[20] The crux of the issue was that Swift had willingly published St. John's story, and the Harley family knew "with what industry Secretary St John took care to have it published that Guiscard's design was against himself."[21] Given the Secretary's relationship with Swift and the *Examiner*, it was clearly this journal, rather than Boyer's, to which Edward Harley referred when he wrote that St. John "had it put in the publick papers that the stab was designed for him."[22]

The Harley family's comments make it obvious that they did not have much confidence in Swift, Mr. *Examiner*, to produce an acceptable official version. It is here that the uncertainty lies, because Swift implied to Stella that it was his own decision to hand the job of writing the pamphlet over. He told her: "I had not time to do it myself, so I sent my hints to the author of the *Atalantis* [Manley], and she has cooked it into a sixpenny pamphlet, in her own style, only the first page is left as I was beginning it."[23] In the next sentence, he "was afraid of disobliging Mr Harley or Mr St. John in one critical point about it, and so would not do it myself."[24] The language Swift uses is both revealing and confusing.

Firstly, he claims he had "not time." A sentence later he has changed his mind, to say that he was frightened to do it. But the decision may not have been his at all, since we know that the ministry did not always trust him. *The Conduct of the Allies*, for instance, was endlessly checked before the ministry would allow it to go to press.[25] The ministry was aware that the unsupervised Swift could produce contentious pieces such as *The Windsor Prophecy* and the first edition of the *Public Spirit of the Whigs*.[26] Moreover, from the Harleys' viewpoint, Swift had already "blundered" once with *Examiner* number 33. In the light of the Harleys' displeasure it is interesting to note that in later years, when Swift recalled that he had "furnished [Manley] with some materials" for *A True Narrative*, he no longer claimed that it was his decision to pass on the task of writing it.[27] While this may be an instance of Swift's forgetfulness, it may be also be an indication of the truth of the matter, and in this case we must seek some explanation of why in these circumstances Manley was considered more reliable.

We have already seen that Harley was acquainted with Manley's talents in April 1711 when he or his colleagues were looking for a reliable pamphleteer. In May of 1710 she had sent him a copy of *Memoirs of Europe*.[28] He may even have received some correspondence from her before that date, since she wrote him a letter, probably on 16 April 1710, requesting an appointment.[29] They were undoubtedly in some kind of personal contact by July 1711. In a letter to Harley of that month, she mentions that she had "once had the honour of a Note from your Lordship, to command my Attendance."[30] According to the same letter, she was already well acquainted with several of his political colleagues. The weight of evidence indicates that Manley was already receiving her instructions from Harley, or at least the ministry, rather than via Swift. *A True Narrative* was written only four months before Manley mentions her missed appointment, and after she had already contributed one issue of the *Examiner*. She was already established in the stable of Tory writers.

But something even more pertinent in this instance may have made her an attractive proposition to the Harley circle. There was something more than her proven ability to write highly popular prose. The Harley camp had no doubt noted that her attitude to St. John was always expedient, a very useful quality in this instance. Unlike Swift, she was perfectly willing to adapt her writing to what was politically desirable.[31] Her personal loyalty was also probably more to their liking. We certainly know that later, when the Tory party split and Harley and St. John became open rivals for leadership, her allegiance remained with Harley. In 1714, in her last extant message to Harley, she specifically noted that she had not sent her letter "by the person I employ'd before . . . for if I am not mistaken, he is a creature of [St. John's]."[32] This partiality for Harley made her an eminently suitable candidate for the sensitive task of limiting the damage caused by Swift's *Examiner*. In addition she understood the function that *A True Narrative* had to perform on Harley's behalf.

For Manley's text is not simply a refutation of Swift's *Examiner*, although that is one of the tasks it undertakes. Swift's suggestion that the pamphlet was left as he had begun it should not persuade us that Manley simply wrote up Swift's ideas "in her own style."[33] Indeed, despite the fact that Swift claims the first page of the pamphlet as his, it actually says very little. Was it taken away from him when he had only just started it? Or did he simply want to claim some anodyne part of it to save face? We cannot know for sure, but it is certain that it is not until halfway through the second page that the propagandist purpose of the pamphlet becomes clear. And by the third page it is certainly Manley's, and she is laying great emphasis on providing a factual account of the incident. She even goes to the extent of claiming that other accounts have been "supplied with false [circumstances]" and may have been "either very imperfect, or misrepresented on purpose, by the Prejudice of Party in the Relators."[34] And while Manley's version "endeavour[s] to avoid both these Errors in the Fact I am going to relate" it also makes use of "some good Opportunities, to be informed from the first Hands, of several Passages not generally known."[35] This claim to firsthand information seems to have been true. She furnishes far more particulars than any preceding pamphleteer, and much of what she says tallies with the account by Robert Harley's brother.[36]

Since hers was the first published account that matched Edward Harley's in such detail, it seems likely that she had some official source. She is, for instance, the first writer to include information on Guiscard's demand for "bread and butter" and the presence, or otherwise, of a bread knife. Both she and Edward Harley agree that Guiscard tried to get his hands on such an implement, although they give slightly different reasons for his failure to do so.[37] Edward Harley also intriguingly refers to his own relation as a "Narrative," suggesting a subconscious reference to Manley's text.[38] In any case, the similarity between the two accounts would tend to support the view that the Harleys had supplied her with information, and that her version was designed to combat Swift's *Examiner* number 33. The *Examiner* was the most detailed account published before Manley's. It was the only one that placed St. John as the target. Therefore Manley's ambition to "endeavour to avoid [imperfect or misrepresented] Errors in the Fact I am going to relate" clearly refers to the *Examiner*.[39] The only other full version of the assassination attempt was Boyer's second reporting of the incident, which also upset Harley.[40] However, it appeared after Manley's and refers to "a little pamphlet published this day." Indeed, the first sentence of Boyer's *Political State of Great Britain* for April 1711, quotes the full title of Manley's text, and proceeds to denigrate it.[41] The "misrepresentation" to which the *Narrative* refers can therefore only be in *Examiner* No. 33. Swift's recommendation to Stella to read Manley's pamphlet because the circumstances in the *Narrative* were "all true" is a tacit acknowledgment that he had initially been misguided in his account.[42]

The *Narrative* itself focuses to a large extent on the divisive nature of party politics, with a loud call for national unity in the final section. Such a plea is completely in accord with Robert Harley's attempt to run his new ministry on cross-party principles. These principles were directly challenged by St. John's followers, the October Men. In stark contrast they were demanding a complete expulsion of Whigs from any positions in the ministry. Harley was loath to give them this, and Manley's relatively mild *True Narrative* can be compared with more virulently anti-Whig pieces that were circulating at around the same time. A good example of this kind was the acrostic on Wharton published in a Tory newspaper:

> Whig's the first letter of his odious Name;
> Hypocrisy's the second of the same
> Anarchy's his Darling; and his Aim
> Rebellion, Discord, Mutiny and Faction.[43]

If Manley was to represent Harley's moderate position, it was important that her version should be more temperate. She therefore directs her opprobrium at the demonized Guiscard in particular, and French Papists in general. There is no hint of Whig involvement, except to blame them for foolishly introducing Guiscard into the country in the first place. She was clearly under instructions to hold fire on the Whigs, a strategy easily explained by Harley's own difficult political position. The month before the attempted assassination, he had been forced to vote with the Whigs, and in early March 1711, he was still attempting to work with the center of both parties. He may even have been considering calling a new Parliament and forming a coalition ministry.[44] Manley's gentle treatment of the Whigs is therefore deliberate. Viewed from a political perspective, and quite apart from any equivocation over the intended victim, Swift's aspersions on the Whigs were ill-timed. Swift's claim that "Had such an Accident happened under [the Whigs] they would have immediately charged it upon the whole Body of those they are pleased to call *the Faction* [i.e., the Tories]" was misjudged.[45] It was not something which a minister seeking cooperation with an opposition wished to read.

Swift's linking of the Guiscard incident back to the prosecution of Harley's treasonous clerk, William Greg, was also ill-advised. Subsequent remarks by Abel Roper in The *Post Boy* were equally inappropriate, and it is significant that Swift was also strongly connected with the newspaper.[46] The *Post Boy* maliciously suggested that

> It is said that Seven Great and Excellent Men are to meet [to] find witnesses to prove that notwithstanding Mr *H*[arle]*y* discovered his Treason, as he did likewise that of Mr *Greg*, yet that he was an Accomplice of the Man, who would have Murder'd him.[47]

Even more explicitly, the same journal declared two weeks later that,

> On Tuesday Night last, several Gentlemen drinking together and talking of *Guiscard*'s Stabbing the Right Honourable Mr *Harley*, one of them, a Whigg, said, he did not like his doing of it where he did; but it had been a Glorious Action, if he had stab'd him to the Heart.[48]

Manley's text carefully avoided levelling such unhelpful accusations at the Whigs, although she could not resist maliciously noting that all the Whigs but one left the chamber of the Lords, rather than hear the panegyric Parliamentary address on Harley's stabbing.[49]

The *True Narrative* itself begins with an extensive, and highly colored, biography of the dastardly Marquis de Guiscard (formerly Abbé de Borly), which should be compared with Swift's rather more restrained efforts. Swift's Guiscard is merely "extremely prodigal and vicious."[50] Manley's history of his depravity is pure tabloid journalism. It begins sensationally with a catalogue of his sins while in holy orders. He seduces a nun, and keeps a profitable brothel in his own abbey. He abducts his brother's mistress, and subsequently poisons her. He betrays his own countrymen by raising an insurrection and then leaving them to suffer the consequences. As a soldier serving the Allies, his behavior is "Expensive, Luxurious, Vicious."[51] He lavishes his pay upon gaming and women, keeping two regular mistresses as well as enjoying a string of casual liaisons. Contemporaries recognized the lurid tone of the pamphlet, although they did not necessarily approve. Abel Boyer, for instance, considered the *Narrative* "garnish'd with Rhetorical Tinsel, unbecoming the Dignity of History."[52] There was, however, a purpose to Manley's overheated prose. As Melinda Rabb suggests, the pamphlet demonizes Guiscard to draw attention away from the uncertainty of the malevolent Frenchman's original target. The text is carefully shaped to reach a crescendo when the thoroughly evil Guiscard finally stabs the Chancellor.[53] The problem caused by Swift's idiosyncratic version was also easily solved. Manley suggests that although Harley took the brunt of the attack, the real object of the assassin's knife was the Queen. This suggestion had already been made by Edward Harley immediately after the attack, making it even more likely that Manley was in direct contact with the family during the writing of this pamphlet.[54] This third, more illustrious, target conveniently eliminates any competition for martyrdom between the two politicians. According to Manley, Guiscard had repeatedly attempted to obtain a private audience with her Majesty but:

> Failing of his Attempt there, stab'd Mr. HARLEY, as by his own Confession, he wou'd have done Mr. *St. John*, because they were the two important Lives that gave Dread and Anguish to that Monarch [Louis XIV] who has so long and often been the Terror of others.[55]

Harley, in this account, is not only a hero, but, by implication, the queen's savior.

By page 34 of the pamphlet, after Harley's triumphant journey home, Guiscard is dead and buried. Manley's prime objective of refuting the *Examiner*'s version of events has apparently been achieved. Yet the pamphlet continues for a further thirteen pages. This final section demonstrates Manley's usefulness to the ministry. It also illustrates how her facility in accommodating political expediency could, in certain circumstances, make her more modest talents preferable to Swift's greater genius. The text that Manley finally produced did more than successfully report on Guiscard's assassination attempt, thereby diverting attention away from St. John and back to Harley. It also explicitly widened Harley's political appeal to include the Dissenters, as well as traditional Anglicans. In Tory demonology, Dissenters were traditionally Whigs and would have been very unlikely to support St. John's High-Flying principles. But Harley's more moderate approach could be made to appear more attractive. Although they might be naturally wary of a Tory ministry, they could, perhaps, be wooed into supporting the Chancellor's hoped-for coalition administration.

For this reason, in the *True Narrative* both ends of the Protestant spectrum receive attention. Even the word "Moderation" takes on a new and much more sympathetic meaning than Tories had traditionally given it when Manley was writing *Queen Zarah*. In contrast to her earlier text, where readers are warned to be wary of his "prick ears" in the *True Narrative*, there is only praise for Harley's middle way. It is he who has "arriv'd by long Practice, to that difficult Attainment of possessing his Soul in all Conditions, in all Accidents, whether of Life or Death, with Moderation."[56] Manley's use of the term was clearly deliberate, since her change in emphasis was not to be seen elsewhere among the Tories. There were, of course, still party members who were not yet so fond of moderation, as can be seen in the words of a popular song of 1710:

> The brave Sons of the English Church
> Come foremost like the Wind,
> And Moderation, out of hope,
> Comes limping on behind.[57]

As if in answer to these criticisms, Manley's *True Narrative* emphasizes Harley's loyalty to Anglicanism. In the light of his well-known Dissenting background, this was something that could not be repeated too often, and it explains Manley's insistence on Harley's respect for Established modes of worship.

> Does not the flourishing Church of *England* owe him all things for her Deliverance from *Presbytery* and *Atheism*? . . . Were he not a sincere Worshipper at our increasing Altars, would he not Reduce rather than Multiply?[58]

Overall, the text is remarkable for its religious toleration, and in this it is notably different to *Memoirs of Europe*, written just over a year previously.[59] By contrast with Manley's High Church secret histories, *A True Narrative* offers an appeal for latitudinarian support. This is the only explanation for Manley's apparent *volte-face*. How else can we explain the plea that "Tho' we disagree in Religion, yet for common Good, we should, me thinks, be glad to *Unite* in Politicks: Our Ceremonies may differ, but our Essentials are the same"? The emphasis on religious inclusivity can only be understood as part of a strategy of facilitating Harley's longed-for factionless ministry.[60]

As we have seen, it was the growing personal conflict between Harley and St. John that initially made Swift inappropriate as the author of this pamphlet. It is also the subtle way in which Manley denigrates St. John through her manipulation of *A True*

Narrative that demonstrates why St. John's adversaries chose her. Having established Harley as the queen's representative for Guiscard's knife, we have seen how Manley built the text into a platform for Harley's moderate Toryism. She then, behind an apparently harmonious facade, continued to place the two men in direct opposition to each other, using St. John's faults to accentuate Harley's qualities. Her emphasis on Harley's calm assurance, even in the greatest danger, gives credibility to his policy of negotiation, rather than confrontation. St. John, by contrast, associated with the hotheaded October men, is shown to act without thought of the consequences. Within the text is the subtle replication of the positions they had taken up in the political arena. They occupy the same irreconcilable roles, with St. John, the leader of the volatile October Club, portrayed as a man who acts without thinking. His first response, after Harley has fallen, is to strike out, without reflection or consideration.[61] It was St. John's sword, Manley claims, that first wounded the assassin.[62] Since Manley's account differs from Edward Harley's in this detail we can conclude that she wanted to make St. John seem even hastier and rasher than he actually was.[63] St. John did, apparently, wound Guiscard. Manley, however, particularly pointed out that the young politician was ready to go further, until stopped by Poulett's call for restraint. Poulett was Harley's long-standing supporter, coming out against St. John when the party split.[64] Manley, by placing Poulett as a restraining influence on St. John, capitalizes on the idea of Guiscard as the extreme example of the man who acts without thinking, implicitly linking the would-be murderer with the hotheaded St. John. Guiscard was a man who, as Manley commented earlier, "was busy to Design, though full of Inconsistencies, and preposterous in his Management: His Schemes impracticable to any less rash and inconsiderate."[65]

While St. John's friends, such as Swift, may not have wished to make this particular comparison, many would have known that while Manley was writing the pamphlet, the young Secretary had a "rash and inconsiderate" scheme of his own: an expedition to Quebec, which Harley had strongly advised against. The Whigs had already abandoned it as impracticable, but St. John insisted, and, taking advantage of Harley's indisposition, it went ahead.⁶⁶ So foolhardy did Harley consider this venture, that he gave as his "dying wish," conveyed via the restraining Poulett, that the expedition be cancelled.⁶⁷

The downgrading of St. John continues even after Manley has finished with the description of the attack. She continues to emphasize Harley's central role as the victim, while St. John becomes marginalized. He is mentioned only twice more in the pamphlet. Once he is reported as being the "tenderest" friend, who hoped that Harley had only been slightly hurt.⁶⁸ If we are aware of the background to this text, and the quarrel between the two men, it is hard not to suspect conscious irony on Manley's part. Harley was certainly no longer St. John's "tenderest friend"! Thereafter, St. John's only words in the pamphlet are to pardon Guiscard. Is there some irony intended in the pardon? After all, it would have extremely convenient for St. John if Harley had actually been permanently removed from the leadership struggle.

If we turn to Manley's lavish praise of Harley, the hero, this is clearly carefully worded to present Harley as an oasis of calm in the turbulent political waters of early 1711. He was a man to whom, in direct contrast to the unthinking Secretary of State, "the Passions are in such Obedience, they never contend for Sway."⁶⁹ So calm was Harley that

> seeing them busie about taking *Guiscard*, by whom he imagin'd himself kill'd, [he] did not call or cry for Help, but getting up as well as he could of himself, apply'd his Handkerchief to the Wound to stop the Blood . . . 'till they had time to come to him, not complaining nor accusing, nor incouraging them to revenge him upon *Guiscard*.⁷⁰

As though to reinforce this feeling of calm the pamphlet finishes with a plea for "Calming our Heats and Animosities, by taking off the Veil of *Prejudice* and *Party*, which [has] so long blinded us," and the text has been subtly transformed from a defense against St. John's "industrious" self-aggrandizing propaganda into a platform for Harley's moderate Toryism.⁷¹

In *A True Narrative*, Manley had demonstrated her reliability, and had handled the tricky Guiscard situation with considerable skill. It was sufficiently impressive to lead her, as we saw in the previous chapter, to the editorship of the *Examiner* between 14

June and 26 July 1711. After her stint on the *Examiner*, Manley planned to leave London for a while. She wrote to Harley that her "infirmities and misfortunes are forcing me away into a cheaper part of the kingdom."[72] If she did manage to take a break from writing, it did not last long. She was back at work by September, answering propaganda occasioned by Marlborough's triumphant crossing of the lines of Bouchain.

This flurry of pamphlets is inextricably linked to the single most important issue that concerned the political world in 1711, the ending of the War of the Spanish Succession.[73] The Scriblerian poet/diplomat Matthew Prior spent the summer of 1711 in Paris with a mission to "hasten the pace of the negotiations."[74] The Tories were well aware of the problems involved in dealing with Louis XIV without the knowledge of the Dutch and the Empire, while also maintaining the fiction of a united front with these allies. The continued employment of the Duke of Marlborough as captain-general in the light of his opposition to peace and the ministry was also not helpful to the negotiations. Marlborough maintained a close association with the Elector of Hanover, the heir to the British throne, whose opposition to the preliminary peace proposals was unequivocal.[75] Marlborough's continued position of power and influence was considered detrimental to Tory peace efforts.

It was only to be expected that Whig anti-peace campaigners made the most of the duke's popularity. There were panegyrics to Marlborough such as,

> Victorious Hero! in Compassion give
> The panting Muses Time to breath, and live.
> Let them to Quarters of Refreshment go . . .
> Then following still the Progress of thy Sword,
> Which new arising Themes for Rapture will afford,
> They'll tell of Victorys struggling in the Womb
> Of pregnant Time, and Triumphs yet to come.[76]

In such a welter of adulatory literature in honour of the captain-general, there could be no easing of the anti-Marlborough propaganda campaign. Part of the task of the Tory government was to undermine this persistent loyalty. As one Whig pamphlet claimed, they "loose[d] their *Fault-Finders* upon him," then scandalised his family "by way of *Novel* and *Memoirs*," finally blasting "his Honours by way of *Secret Histories, to examine* his Rewards in order to deface his Merits, with many other Devices of ingenious Malice."[77] In the light of this, the timing of one of the general's most impressive successes, the crossing of the French lines at Bouchain in early September 1711, was, at the very least, inconvenient. The Whigs saw this victory as clearing the way to Paris and a means of crushing the French. For the Tories, it could not have happened at a worse time. While Marlborough was outwitting the enemy, the French and English diplomats were in talks in London, hammering out preliminary details of a treaty to end the long-running war. The preliminary articles took two forms, "public" and "private": those which the British government were prepared to show to their Allies, as opposed to those which gave distinct advantages to Britain, which were to be kept secret.[78] It is not surprising that the Whigs made the most of the victory at Bouchain. Odes to Marlborough were immediately composed and printed, trumpeting, in the words of one, the "Great Glorious Man . . . *Bouchain* shall Immortalise thy Name."[79] The Tories actively counterattacked, denigrating the victory and smearing Marlborough with the tried and tested accusations of avarice and disloyalty. With her secret histories, Manley had an impressive record in the field of invective against Marlborough, and it is hardly surprising that she was chosen to shoulder at least some of the burden. She appears to have been proud of her two efforts in this area, sending them to Harley for his approval and as part of a request for payment.[80]

The initial impetus for Manley to enter the arena after Bouchain was a pamphlet probably written, or at least revised, by her former adversary, Arthur Mainwaring, the editor of the *Medley*, although in her letter to Harley she ascribes it to Francis Hare. Mainwaring's pamphlet was entitled *Bouchain: in a Dialogue Between the Late Medley and Examiner*.[81] Manley responded with *The Duke of Marlborough's Vindication*.[82]

Mainwaring's *Bouchain* specifically attacked Swift and Manley in their roles as successive editors of the *Examiner*. It takes the form of a dialogue between the editors of *The Medley* and *The*

Examiner. The purpose of the dialogue, as Manley maintained in her answering pamphlet, was to "introduce all the fine things that are thought fit to be said of this Campaign."[83] The main body of the Whig text is taken up with a detailed description of the military exercise itself, and a glorification of Marlborough's brilliance as a general. The pamphlet also acts as a defense for the duke against accusations that he is "protract[ing] the war for the sake of his own Vanity, Ambition and Interest." It even includes a complaint that if a "scandalous Peace" is made, the Duke will have no "Footstep remain except the Building at *Woodstock*."[84] Marlborough's entirely altruistic attitude in continuing to fight the war is set against Tory accusations of his greed and self-interest. No one, says Mr. *Medley*, desires "an End of the War more earnestly and passionately than he does; that when he has been so great an Instrument in giving Rest to *Europe*, he may at last have the same himself."[85]

What Manley probably found most offensive, however, was the persona of Mr. *Examiner*.[86] He is a particularly credulous and ill-informed foil to the sensible and reasoned arguments of Mr. *Medley*. The most insulting blow, however, was probably his feeble capitulation to his superior opponent at the end of the pamphlet: "Well! what you have said has given me a great deal of Satisfaction; but I can't answer how far my Friends [the Tories] will be of the same Opinion."[87]

Perhaps it was her vigorous defense of their joint persona in the *Examiner* that prompted Swift to describe Manley's answer to this pamphlet, the *Vindication*, as "the best" of a small selection of pamphlets which he sent to Stella in Ireland.[88] And this was despite the fact that he could lay no claim to any part of it. Notwithstanding any personal considerations, Swift was right from a political perspective. The pamphlet was extremely important. The Tories, shortly to publish part of their previously clandestine peace negotiations, could not afford to have Marlborough portrayed in any light other than as a self-interested, expensive, and highly partisan warmonger. For this reason, in her *Vindication*, Manley scorns the accusations of "hard usage" which Mr. *Medley* claims Tory pamphleteers have given Marlborough, suggesting that they have overreacted to Tory accusations.[89] There is, Manley's readers will deduce from this overreaction, truth in the Tory propaganda about Marlborough. This provides Manley with the opportunity to repeat previous attacks on Marlborough. She specifically includes those from the *Examiner*, which *Bouchain: A Dialogue* unwisely reiterates.

As a way of reinforcing this point, Manley's pamphlet incorporates Mr. *Medley*'s complaints as a recurring theme. Questions such as "had he not the power to advance or retreat?" or "did any of his enemies [try to] lay [Guiscard's] villainy upon the duke?," punctuate the narrative.[90] This refrain of rhetorical questioning concerning Marlborough's true value to the nation separates the great general from any discussion of issues that pave the way for the publication of the peace preliminaries. Manley repeats Tory concerns over the cost of the war. She introduces a comparison between the old Whig ministry and the new Tory one. She urges that a dangerously powerful Empire will be the result of the Whig "No Peace without Spain" policy. It was particularly important to stress that these points were crucial to peace, given the Whigs' excitement at Marlborough's prowess at Bouchain and the idea that the next stop for the allied armies would be Paris.

Although there is a brief attempt to scale down Bouchain's importance as a military target, the victory itself is largely ignored, probably because it was, in truth, a remarkable display of military strategy and therefore difficult to denigrate. In a situation where Marlborough had to be discredited at all costs, political profit lay in belittling his overall achievements rather than in decrying one individual triumph. For this reason Manley continually disparages Marlborough's achievements as a leader, first suggesting that Marlborough has a "genius" for war or "nothing."[91] By implication, he continues the war for his own personal benefit, because it is all he can do. However, she argues, his military genius is actually unnecessary, since it was entirely the soldiers themselves who should be rewarded for the victories:

> The Hatred they had for the Enemy and their Sufferings during the late Peace gave them a double edge to War, and made them gain such glorious Victories which all must own were got by the bravery of the *English*. Their Personal Valour proved of use, when neither Genius in the General nor extraordinary Conduct was requir'd; tho' none of these will dispute his excelling in ei-

ther: It has chanc'd that our greatest Victories have been obtain'd more by the Courage of the Soldiers than the *Finesse* of the Commander; yet he has reap'd all the Advantage.[92]

Clearly, his riches have been earned under false pretenses. The reader is brought back to Marlborough's unwarranted cost later on, when the real value of Bouchain is assessed: "Consider how many Millions this one Year's War hath cost us . . . Let us consider how long we shall be able to pay such a Price for so small a Conquest!"[93]

The narrative moves from a rhetorical devaluation of Marlborough's worth to a tangible correlation on the cost of the war to the home front. The reader, now well aware of Marlborough's expenses, is invited to look at the "Number of Bankrupts . . . the decay of Trade [and the] Penury of Country-Gentlemen with small Estates and numerous Families that pay in such large Proportions to the War."[94] For these "Country-Gentlemen," the core of Tory support, this suggests an uncomfortable comparison between their comparative poverty and Marlborough's notorious personal wealth.

> Are they about . . . to confiscate all his large possessions except *Woodstock*? those vast Sums in the Banks of *Venice, Genoa* and *Amsterdam*? His stately Moveables, valuable Paintings, costly Jewels, and in a word, those immense riches of which himself and his Lady, as good an Accomptant as She is, do not yet know the Extent of?[95]

The overall strategy of this pamphlet has been to turn Mr. *Medley*'s arguments, defending Marlborough, into reminders of previous Tory propaganda. Manley does this through a close examination of Mainwaring's pamphlet. There is no doubt that Manley's paper was effective. Not surprisingly it provoked a reply from an anonymous author who roundly attacked the *Vindication's* originator for the language employed; the offending writer is accused of being "no Descendant of the old *English* Race, nor even of the manly *Dane* or *Saxons* . . . but . . . sprung from some of the Lees of those Vagabonds who came over with *William* the *Norman*"[96] Perhaps more impressively, the Duke of Marlborough himself took exception to it describing it as "villinous" [sic], and hoping that Harley would have "some feeling" of what the duke suffered from "this barbarous libel."⁹⁷ Disingenuously (Manley had already informed him that she had written the pamphlet) Harley claimed that he "neither kn[e]w nor desire[d] to know any of the authors."⁹⁸

This technique of twisting one pamphlet's words to prove the reverse is even more refined in Manley's next assault on the Duke of Marlborough and the Bouchain campaign, which appeared on 3 October 1711.⁹⁹ This was *A Learned Comment upon Dr. Hare's Excellent Sermon . . . by an Enemy to PEACE*, Manley's answer to Francis Hare's sermon *The Charge of God to Joshua*.¹⁰⁰ Somewhat unfairly, Herbert Davis implies that this work was, to all extents and purposes, by Swift. He suggests that "Swift may well have sent to the printer a copy of the original sermon with his own comments in the margin; and this material would then have been used by Mrs Manley, whose hand may be detected easily enough in many parts of the paper."¹⁰¹ This appears to be an unsubstantiated speculation. Swift described it as written by her, with "only hints sent to the printer" by himself.¹⁰² There is little or no reason to doubt this. Perhaps Manley had taken Swift's advice, but it seems unjustified to claim that he had any greater part in it than "hints."

To return to the pamphlets in question Manley's adversary, Francis Hare, was no ordinary Whig hack. He was the Duke of Marlborough's chaplain, and was therefore a personal, as well as a political, supporter of the general. Earlier in 1711 Hare had published a series of pamphlets entitled *The Management of the War in Four Letters to a Tory Member*, in which he had blatantly accused the Tories of being under "Suspicion of Favouring Popery and *France*."¹⁰³ This explains why *A Learned Comment* begins with a specific, personal attack on the integrity of Hare, casting doubt on his literary ability, his humility, and even his suitability as a man of the cloth.¹⁰⁴ Moreover, whether by chance or calculation, Hare's sermon was published at a particularly sensitive moment for the ministry. The day it appeared, 27 September 1711, was the very same day that the preliminary articles between France and England were signed. Hare's proximity to the powerful general made it imperative that this prolix cleric was completely discredited by the ministry.

The ferocity with which Manley's pamphlet proceeded to demolish the sermon is also explained by its timing. By the time Manley published her *Learned Comment*, peace plans were advancing rapidly; the ministry were actively engaged in preparing to present copies of the carefully edited "public" preliminary articles to the Allied diplomats. They did this only ten days later, on 13 October.[105]

The main body of pamphlet is a minute examination of Hare's text. The sermon, as published, uses the Israelites' initial lack of faith in God in helping them possess the Promised Land, to warn against a hasty peace. Hare's argument is that the British and the Allies have wholehearted divine support, demonstrated by their success so far. To give up at this juncture, he reasons, would, inevitably, "provoke [God] to bring on us all those *Evils*, which we have been so many Years labouring to avert."[106]

Manley's method in dealing with Hare's *Sermon* is reductive, and devastatingly effective. By taking each of his points at its most literal level, she is able to refute them, and then reinterpret them, twisting the language he uses to reflect badly upon Marlborough, and the former ministry. For instance, Hare claims that we must "wait the leisure" of God, and not give in to "our Impatience and misgiving Fears."[107] Manley archly asks: "At this rate when must we expect a Peace? May we not justly inquire whether it be God's or the D. of *M*[arlborough]'s Leisure, he would have us wait?"[108] Further on, Hare compares the taking of Bouchain to the crossing of the Jordan, and the Israelites' view of a land that was *"exceeding good."*[109] Manley points out that, in the present case, the war was being conducted, and the land taken, with the "loss of infinite Blood and Treasure," for the benefit of somebody else, not the British. If this had been the case with the Israelites, she suggests, they "might have had good reason to murmur."[110]

Manley's pamphlet seems less complex in its message than her *Vindication*. It follows Hare's text very closely and does not venture too far into the more general political arena. Because of this, on the last two pages of the pamphlet, the concluding arguments, while still tightly focused on the suffering the war has produced, have become rather more strident than in the earlier *True Narrative*. By October, some six months after the assassination attempt, Harley had all but abandoned hopes of a coalition, and both "Bouchain" pamphlets are distinctly more partisan. The conclusion of the *Learned Comment*, as a result, offers an unusually sinister prediction of the inevitable economic consequences of a long-running (Whig) war. Added to the "Dearness of Necessaries" is the "Expence of Blood and Lives of our Countrymen."[111] In this way, the comparison between the inappropriate "Plenty, nay Profuseness in the Great Officers, and Riches in the General," and the poverty of the civilian leads into a more chilling scenario.

The civilian, Manley points out, may not only lose his money in this war, but his life, and this will jeopardize the purity of the race. British women will be forced to resort to foreigners as husbands, or even the "poor Palatines," Protestant refugees from religious persecution whom the Whigs wished to naturalize. High Church Tories were horrified at this and had predicted that "by frequent intermarriages, [the Palatine refugees would] go a great way to blot out and extinguish the English race."[112] Manley lends a xenophobic voice to this:

> Of the Natives there will be scarce a Remnant preserved. Our Women, if they intend to multiply, must be reduc'd, like the *Amazons*, to go out of the Land; or take them Husbands at home of those wretched Strangers, whom our Piety and Charity relieved. [113]

The Tory suspicion of foreigners that Defoe had satirized a few years earlier with his *True-Born Englishman*, was clearly still alive and well. There are, as always, political implications embedded in this suggestion. In Manley's text, the dilution of national bloodlines through perpetual warfare becomes an unsavory reminder of how the Whig Lords defeated the Tory Commons in their attempt to repeal the Naturalisation Act in the spring of 1711.[114] By this means, Manley succeeds in "domesticating" the battlefield, demonstrating the unpalatable effects of unceasing carnage on each and every British homestead.

Carole Fabricant suggests that in this passage Manley "feminizes Tory ideology, demonstrating its adaptability to the specific interests of women."[115] This is a valid reading, but it can also be twinned with a more subversive message. In a society ruled by the ideology of heredity and hereditary rights, the specter of British land being inherited by other nationalities than the British smacks, inevitably, of Jacobite rhetoric. It can hardly have been coincidental that Manley suggests that "the *British* Name may be endanger'd once more to be lost in the *German*." For it was not only the Palatines who were German; so were the electors of Hanover and we can see this as a veiled allusion to the approaching Hanoverian succession. The phrase "once more" is difficult to decipher, referring either to the long-past Norman invasion, or the more recent "invasion" of William of Orange and his Dutch (High German?) favorites. It is also possible that, through this ambivalent reference, Manley is again attempting to make her text attractive to all shades of opinion within the Tory party, including the Jacobites.

The pamphlets on Bouchain are the last two authenticated pamphlets for Manley for 1711. There are no known pamphlets for 1712, although she may have been involved in the production of the *John Bull* series of pamphlets, an issue to be dealt with in the next chapter. The year 1713, however, saw another Manley pamphlet, *The Honour and Prerogative of the Queen's Majesty Vindicated*, in answer to an issue of the *Guardian* by her old adversary, Richard Steele.[116]

Both Steele and Manley's texts concerned themselves with the contentious issue of the demolition of Dunkirk by the British in accordance with the peace preliminaries which led to the Treaty of Utrecht in March of 1713.[117] Since the Interregnum, the port had been successively British and French. It had served as a starting point for an abortive Jacobite invasion in 1708, and it harbored corsairs who bedevilled British shipping. The possession of Dunkirk was considered "the most palpable measure of England's power and presence on the continent." It also offered an overriding justification for what many ministerial supporters considered an unsatisfactory peace.[118] Tories celebrated its acquisition: "Fam'd *Dunkirk*, that noble Invincible Pile / Now *Britain*'s Great Fortress, Barrier of Isle."[119] Nonetheless, possession was not enough; the port's destruction was considered essential to the safekeeping of British trade and national security. The importance attached to the disabling of Dunkirk explains the Whig annoyance expressed at the Tories' inexplicable tardiness in enforcing this article in the treaty.[120] This annoyance was exacerbated on 29 July 1713 by the publication of a plea from the deputy to the magistrates at Dunkirk, begging the queen (in French and English) to spare the harbor.[121] This was an outrageous request given that the destruction of the port was one of the articles of the Treaty of Utrecht.

Paul Hyland argues that the failure to implement this article aroused suspicions in the Whigs that the Tories were engaged in "secret and sinister dialogue" with the French.[122] The deputy's *Memorial* provided Richard Steele with an opportunity to raise the issue in the public mind. Using the persona of an "English Tory," he published a fierce attack on the ministry in his *Guardian* of 7 August 1713, cataloguing the reasons why "the British Nation expect the immediate Demolition of [Dunkirk]."[123]

It was an unfortunate phrase to use. In the guise of an "Old Whig," Manley riposted almost immediately, claiming that he has ruined the happy equilibrium between rural Whigs and Tories. The crux of *Honour and Prerogative* lies in Manley's interpretation of Steele's assertion that "The British Nation expect the immediate Demolition of [Dunkirk]." By the Treaty of Utrecht it lay in the British sovereign's power to order the French king to destroy Dunkirk. Therefore, Manley argues, Steele's phraseology demands a certain course of action of the queen. Steele, as the queen's subject, has no right to demand anything of her. "Expecting" the queen to take a certain course of action, in the "Old Whig's" eyes, is tantamount to an invasion of "Her Majesty's Prerogative" and an "insufferable Insult." Steele, through his disloyal "expect[ation]," was guilty of a "Threatning Unexampled Libel."[124]

Manley was only the first of the Tories to round on Steele for his "Libel." Her piece was immediately followed by two issues of the *Examiner*.[125] Daniel Defoe also weighed in with *Reasons Concerning the Immediate Demolishing of Dunkirk: being a Serious Enquiry into the State and Condition of that Affair*.[126] Steele, in his turn, defended himself against the Tory pamphleteers.[127] Swift entered into the controversy a few weeks later, with another pamphlet attacking Steele.[128]

Leading this onslaught, Manley's pamphlet is largely a rehearsal of the invective she had been aiming at Steele ever since her portrayal of him as M. L'Ingrate in *New Atalantis*.[129] Unlike Defoe, she makes no attempt to refute Steele's paper with reasoned argument. No doubt her antagonism was largely fueled by Steele's derogatory comments in the *Guardian* on their past relationship, just two months previously. He had reported rumors that they had at one time been lovers, and talked of her as an "exasperated mistress."[130] This may be why, in her own pamphlet, she blatantly ignores "the Question it self, Whether *Dunkirk* shall be demolished or no?"[131] and homes in on Steele's deceit, ingratitude, plagiarism, and hypocrisy.

Throughout the *Honour and Prerogative*, Manley's language moves steadily away from Steele's actual words, as she repeatedly reinterprets the simple sentence, "The British Nation expect the immediate Demolition of [Dunkirk]." The text begins by rewording the demand to the queen: "*Look you*, Madam, *Your Majesty had best take care that* Dunkirk *be Demolish'd, or else, &c.*"[132] The threatening nature of such a demand would naturally raise the hackles of any loyal Tory. Manley's subsequent reworking of Steele's message was even more insulting: "Madam! WE EXPECT, and we would have you take Notice that we expect it, that *Dunkirk* be Demolish'd, and that immediately."[133] Manley illustrates the full enormity of Steele's demands by comparing it to the kind of language used by an "Imperious Planter" talking to a "Negro Slave": "Look you, Sirrah, I expect this Sugar to be ground, and look to it that it be done forthwith. 'Tis enough to tell you that I EXPECT it, or else *&c*. and then he holds up his Stick at him, Take what follows."[134] The images of enslavement were a familiar theme for Manley's contemporary readers. Manley had already pictured Queen Anne as reduced to virtual servitude or enslavement by the Whigs on numerous occasions. In *Memoirs of Europe*, the physical domination of Anne by her servant, the duchess of Marlborough, was enforced through boxing the queen's ears.[135] Sarah's sway over her mistress was also achieved by psychological enslavement, so that Anne is described as "going out and coming in, rising and sitting down, signing and letting alone, as her [the Marlboroughs, Godolphin], and others of that *Junto* advised."[136]

However, the enslavement of Anne in earlier allegories had been either domestic, in the *romans à clef*, or disguised as hospitality as in the Turks' treatment of Charles XII in the *Examiners*. The interpretation that Manley now puts on Steele's words is altogether more disturbing. The plantation owner's jurisdiction over the slave is not domestic or psychological. It is legal, institutional, and physical. The reader is meant to infer that the Whigs consider that they have the same right to dictate to the queen as if she were their slave, making them Republicans by the back door. The Tories, alternatively, have a notably different attitude. In *Examiner* number 47, after all, Manley had exclaimed "God be prais'd, ... the Qu[een] is *free.*"[137] Manley therefore takes care to remind her readers that Steele "had always call'd [himself] a Whig," and as a result was simply following the Whiggish pattern of "Insult[ing] the Queen, and Affront[ing] their Sovereign in the grossest manner in the World."[138]

The force of Manley's pamphlet does not lie in its sophisticated argument. It is more significant for the speed with which she produced it, and for its direct and emotive attack on Steele's integrity, both as a politician and as a human being. Manley's pamphlet even utilizes mild Augustan scatological imagery (unheard of anywhere else in her writings):

> We sentenc'd your Paper [the *Guardian*] to be thrown into the House of Office . . . and if Mr. *Steele* himself had been here, though perhaps we might have been prevailed with not to put him in with it, yet we should not have failed to have told him he deserv'd it.[139]

The pamphlet formed part of a concerted campaign against Steele. That this is the case is made explicit at the end of the next *Examiner*, 21 August, 1713. Having expounded again on the iniquities of anyone "expecting" the queen to demolish Dunkirk, the paper ends just before an advertisement for a "Second Edition" of the *Honour and Prerogative*, with a suggestion to the reader to look out for a further pamphlet on the topic "preparing by another Hand."[140] Clearly the Tory pamphleteers were consolidating their attacks on Steele, but comparing Manley's efforts on the topic of Dunkirk with her colleagues' texts demonstrates how personal her attacks on the essayist were. Defoe's *Reasons concerning the Immediate Demolishing of Dunkirk* takes a more original line, arguing that since Dunkirk is now in British hands, it is the French, not the British, who might be expected to demand its demolition. Swift's *The Importance of the Guardian Considered*, while focusing to some extent on Steele's ingratitude and on his failings as a writer, is wittier than Manley's and does not descend into personal abuse.

With the *Honour and Prerogative* we have exhausted the pamphlets that can be securely attributed to Manley. Unfortunately, they are few in number. However, her antipathy to Steele is one of several factors that may persuade us that there may be more texts to add to her canon. In a later chapter we will examine the likelihood of these additional attributions.

7

"Pride of our Sex, and Glory of the Stage": Manley's Plays

As we have seen throughout this book, Manley's political writing was usually focused and direct. Her aims were clear. She was a Tory party writer and her job was to stay rigidly "on-message." It is not always possible to distinguish her personal beliefs from political directives, particularly after 1710 when she joined the ministerial team. She was the consummate professional. Apart from her very last set of novellas, *The Power of Love,* her prose writing can easily be interpreted as polemic tailored in one way or another to the immediate political situation.

Where did her own real loyalties lay? It is not always easy to tell, except that she appears to have believed in Harley's "middle way." So much can be said for the "official" propaganda. When we come to examine her plays the picture is not quite so clear. I will argue in this chapter that the plays were her arenas for debate. They were the authorial space she needed to work out her own complex attitude to one of the most pressing political concerns of the day: to support or to repudiate the Catholic Stuart dynasty. Therefore, while her plays are not identifiable as "party political broadcasts" as so much of the rest of her work is, they are interesting because she follows no externally prescribed line in them and they are therefore intriguingly open to interpretation.

It is certainly difficult to tease out her precise political meaning in the plays. However, from a careful reading of these texts it becomes apparent that politics was never very far from the surface. This is not surprising when we look at the plays written after she began her scandal writing, but it is true even from her very first attempts at writing for the theater.

However, we must always bear in mind that her upbringing and early life made her political awareness second nature. As we have seen, from the very beginning of her career Manley was surrounded, either through marriage or through choice, by men who would choose to make their name in politics. How could she avoid the fascination of political cut and thrust? Unfortunately, acknowledging a political slant within the plays, particularly the early ones, does not necessarily make clear the muddy waters or make their political message less elusive. Indeed, while reading them through an awareness of her lifelong immersion in politics answers some questions, it also poses others. The problem is one that is exacerbated by the clarity of our hindsight. In interpreting these early texts as tackling contemporary issues in certain ways, we are persuaded by the heavy political content of her later texts. While we must recognize in Manley's early playwriting the nascent political propagandist and polemicist, we should be wary of reading her later loyalties back into the earlier texts. While the explicit political references within her dramatic work are not difficult to find, they do not, as we shall see, always tie in so neatly with the Hanoverian loyalties she affirmed so soundly fifteen years later.

Nonetheless, it is fascinating to speculate whether the freedom of expression apparently offered by the theater in 1696 inspired her abiding interest in political argument while simultaneously providing a rewarding outlet for her talent. In this chapter, looking at this problem as objectively as possible, I will argue that there are aspects of her plays, and authorial choices taken within them, that persuade me that politics, even in the late 1690s held a fascination for her which only grew stronger. Equally, in her later plays, the indications of coherent political readings are too strong to be missed.

Manley was not a prolific playwright: four extant works and two further plays (which do not appear to have survived) are mentioned in her will.[1] None of them were written during her active periods of propaganda or journalism, although *Almyna* appeared in the years between *Zarah* and *New Atalantis*. How then should we assess their political significance? As always, a useful start is to look at the historical context within which they were written.

In the case of the first two plays the cultural ambience is equally important. They both appeared in 1696. This was the year that saw the lapse of the laws on seditious publishing, but it was before the phenomenon of the popular press had yet to reach its full extent. There was also a growing demand for comment and the drama had long been recognized as an important platform for polemic.[2] Stage plays, attractively packaged and readily comprehensible by the least perceptive of the audience were, by their very nature, seditious in both a spiritual and secular sense. For instance, while much of the Non-juring Divine Jeremy Collier's objection to the stage was its undermining of "*Morality* and *Religion*," he was equally concerned that the stage dressed "up the *Lords* in Nick Names, and expos[ed] them in *Characters* of Contempt," which could clearly lead to all manner of Republican activity.[3] Given the sensitive atmosphere, the profession recognized in this political objection a potential threat to artistic independence. They were quick to retaliate. In an answer to Collier, the playwright and critic John Dennis refuted the seditious hazards of the theater, and instead argued that far from being dangerous to the state, the stage offered a safe outlet for the naturally rebellious English:

> The Drama, and particularly Tragedy, is among other reasons useful to Government because it is proper to restrain a people from rebellion and disobedience, and to keep them in good correspondence among themselves: For this reason the Drama may be said to be instrumental in a peculiar manner to the Welfare of the *English* Government, because there is no people on the face of the Earth so prone to Rebellion as the *English*.[4]

The debate continued for years as the political atmosphere became more charged and progressive ministries became more sensitive. A few years later, when propaganda skirmishes had become the full-scale battle of Anne's reign, playwrights still recognized the theater's worth as a platform for political debate and were prepared to defend it. Some even claimed that it was opposition to the stage that was politically suspect. Thomas Baker went straight to the heart of this controversy in his dedication to *An Act at Oxford* (his banned play of 1704):

> Whatever Reformation the Stage wanted, 'tis plain that FACTION is now it's [sic] bitterest Adversary. To prove this, Your Lordship may observe, the Quarrel is chiefly managed by Enemies to the Establish'd Church, headed by the Author of the SHORT VIEW, who . . . borrows the old Phanatical Arguments to sharpen his Invectives. Thus Equipt, . . . they resolve, Hand in Hand, to venture their Lives and Fortunes in the Good Old Cause of Reformation and Ruin.[5]

A politically astute writer such as Manley would have been delighted by the theater's established role in political argument, but, as I suggested earlier, in her case the search for clues to authorial intent and partisan bias is particularly intriguing. For, unlike her prose writing, which is constructed on deliberate and overt partisan principles, it is often possible to sense internal division in the writing. We are never convinced in the plays that behind her strong Hanoverian Tory principles there did not remain the nagging conflict between loyalty to the Stuarts and their Catholicism. Reading her plays with this dilemma in mind unifies them and shows them as a series of debates around a central theme. It is a series that endlessly discusses the choice between a legitimate (Stuart) succession and a credible one (Hanover). In fact, if we were to read her plays in isolation, it is almost possible to say that under the Hanoverian Tory surface there was a crypto-Jacobite tentatively proposing and subsequently rejecting Stuart Catholic rule. Not surprisingly, the arguments that Manley continually rehearses in her plays sometimes verge on the seditious, and the authorities were ever vigilant for the theater's potential for subversion. Manley's stage writing therefore had to be subtle.

At the beginning of her career, however, the Lord Chamberlain's office may not have seen much to worry about. Manley's first produced play, *The Lost Lover*, bears the trademarks of a light romantic comedy.[6] The plot is slight, involving a superannuated and conceited Lady Young Love who is due to marry Wilmore, the lover of her daughter Marina. Marina in turn has been promised to Sir Rustick Good-Heart, Wilmore's father. Marina's fortune, which depends on the goodwill of her mother appears to be the only thing holding Wilmore back from declaring his love for his future daughter-in-law. The whole episode has been engineered by the spiteful Belira, who has been loved and abandoned by Wilmore. A stock subplot concerning Wilmore's best friend Wildman and the virtuous wife of a jealous and foolish citizen is hardly relevant and the reference to a silly young poetess named Orinda is probably little more than a dig at Catherine Trotter. The play ends happily with Lady Young Love pursued and won by the impecunious Sir Amorous Courtall, Wilmore and Wildman's preferred alternative to Sir Rustick. This happy event releases Marina and Wilmore to marry with her mother's blessing. Sir Rustick is left to ride off back to his country estate in ineffectual high dudgeon.

Despite its flimsy structure, the play has some interesting perspectives. The sexual politics seem to bear out Margaret Ezell's assertions that patriarchy, in the absence of a male head of the household, could be passed on to the female head.[7] In *The Lost Lover* it is Lady Young Love who is the most active protagonist. It is her decision to favor Sir Amorous which brings the plot to a happy ending. Sir Rustick's advice on the marriage of Wilmore to Marina is not sought; it is on Lady Young Love's favor that all decisions on Marina's fortune hangs.

Manley's early depiction of such a powerful (if unflatteringly portrayed) female is ironic, and presents us with a prototype of the vain, middle-aged women who appear throughout her scandal fictions. Women, she says, should have better things to do with themselves. The frustrations of an aspiring professional female are apparent. Depicting Lady Young Love as obsessed with fashion, appearance, and little else is an expression of the author's frustration at the paucity of outlets for female energy.[8] Her impatience is illustrated in the preface. The irony expressed in her admission of the weakness of the play appears to defer to antifeminist opinion that "Writing for the Stage is no way proper for a woman, to whom all Advantages but meer Nature, are refused." While this sounds like a condemnation of women playwrights (particularly since she ironically cites her verses written for Trotter's *Agnes de Castro*) it should probably be taken as a sardonic comment on the lack of formal education that women like Manley were likely to receive, with their resultant literary disadvantages. Having said that, since she later claimed that she was sent off to school to perfect her knowledge of languages, we must doubt Manley's own lack of faith in her abilities.[9] As always it is best not to take Manley's most ingenuous statements at face value.

None of this discussion, however, sheds any light on the political ramifications of *The Lost Lover*. While the play does not appear to be overtly topical, we cannot forget that it was produced in the year that saw a Jacobite assassination attempt on William III. She claimed that the play had been written in only seven days two years earlier, implying that there could be nothing controversial in it.[10] However, as we have seen, Manley's assertions about her life and work are often suspect. She may have written the play according to her own professed time scale. However, she must also have been aware of the Jacobite attempt on the king with its resultant upsurge of "loyalty to the crown."[11] Could she have resisted some kind of commentary on such a major event, however obscure and hidden?

Simply knowing Manley's taste for political innuendo makes the hunt for clues relevant to current affairs a useful exercise. They are certainly there, although explicitly political references are few and far between in *The Lost Lover*. However, there are two moments worthy of our attention. The first is a reference to Sir Rustick's lack of relish for his role as M.P. He states, "I never came to *London* but in times of Parliament, which thank heaven were not very frequent in our late Reigns." (p. 7) This is undoubtedly an expression of the Tory attitude to the Triennial Act (1694), which closely matched William III's dislike of overfrequent general elections. Sir Rustick's objection is apparently that parliamentary activity restricted his hunting. But of course it also meant that parliamentarians had to attend regularly because the "very short period of intermission between [elections] kept the country at large at or near the boiling point politically for years on end."[12] There is more to it than that. Manley's political astuteness should not be underestimated, and while the complaint identifies this unpleasant old man as a Williamite Tory, it also suggests that Manley, through her Rustick, is expressing Defoe's later regret that "the certainty of a new election in three years is an unhappy occasion of keeping alive the divisions and party strife among the people which would otherwise have died of course."[13] However, rather than give up standing for parliament (and the potential rewards) Sir Rustick's willingness to inconvenience himself despite his political principles, immediately marks him for the contemporary audience as a man who would willingly ignore those principles to suit his personal circumstances.[14]

While the spectators might have found this satirical swipe at members of parliament amusing, and not particularly outrageous, there are more profound questions being asked in this text. For the play takes as its central theme the provocative topic of the extent to which an individual is bound by his or her own sworn vow. In the wake of the assassination attempt the country was "swept by a wave of oath-taking" and the play's questioning of making pledges and their binding nature in a rapidly changing world betokens a troubled Tory conscience.[15] Wilmore (the son of the Williamite Tory) claims that his earlier declarations to Belira had only intimated that he "could," rather than "would," love her forever, implying that his circumstances had now altered. In a political sense this directly echoes the way that many Tories, even at the highest echelons, were willing to waive their allegiance to James, their *de justo* sovereign, and swear loyalty to William because the Dutchman was the *de facto* king.[16] As J. Douglas Canfield has pointed out, a few years earlier the centrality of oath breaking and loyalty to one's word had been a frequently rehearsed concern for playwrights. Although Canfield deals primarily with tragedies written up to and until the Glorious Revolution, his words can be taken as significant for our reading of this play (and, indeed, all of them): "There is no honor among troth-breakers, and broken words simply beget more broken words; therefore friends and lovers must remain constant and subjects loyal, no matter what."[17]

The scheming Belira, who sees herself as betrayed by Wilmore, reinforces this political undertone when she says to him: "Poor Caviller, those who can jest with Oaths, can play with Words" (p. 27) This accusation resonates interestingly with Mark Goldie's comment that it "mattered crucially not that men would conform but by what principles they did so."[18] Prefacing the accusation with a word so dangerously close to "Cavalier," Belira casts the audience's mind back to the comments on Royalists' propensity to break their vows as evidenced by Prynne in his pamphlet in the Engagement Controversy of 1650: "*He is a fool that will not take it, and he is a knave that will not break it."*[19] While the controversy itself was long gone by the time Manley was writing her play, the topic of expediency in taking oaths was one which recurred throughout the second half of the seventeenth century. After all, as John Wallace notes, Sanderson's *A Resolution of Conscience* was originally published in 1649 but was actually reprinted in 1674 and again in 1678 (at the time of the Popish Plot). It reappeared in 1685 (the accession of James II) and deals with the taking of oaths and the ways in which one may put "the lowest construction" on them to enable them to be sworn.[20] In the company she habitually kept even if Manley did not know this pamphlet, she had undoubtedly heard the arguments rehearsed. In this way, her insight into the (political) male's propensity to twist their vows to suit their temporary convenience informs her hero's attitude. Through Belira, therefore, Manley has a double hit. Tricky men will promise women what they want to hear. On a deeper level, the private deviousness betokens a public lack of principles. Indoors and out of doors they are willing to make promises and oaths to their own best advantage, and then forswear them when it becomes inconvenient. Through Wilmore, her hero, she illustrates the kind of sophistic argument that had allowed Tories to break their oath of allegiance to the divinely appointed James II because he had been so plainly unsuitable. They could switch their support to William in 1689, because there was no such thing for them as unwavering loyalty. For James's favorites such as the second earl of Sunderland and John Churchill, and even for a paragon of High Toryism, Nottingham, principles only applied when they were in their own best interests. As a result of this, oaths, allegiances and vows were constantly being reinterpreted in ways to suit themselves. By this means Manley articulates the tensions experienced by Tories torn between their previous pledges of loyalty to James the hereditary heir, and their pragmatic acceptance of William.

Discussions such as this were of fundamental importance in days when refusing to take an oath of allegiance could mean a loss of livelihood. Therefore, while Manley's first lightweight attempt at playwriting is not overburdened with discussions of such weighty matters, her next effort is fairly loaded with questions which needed to be answered. *Royal Mischief* followed almost immediately, and was more successful. Perhaps its greater critical approval was based on the way the play offers an illustration of one of the central dilemmas of the Glorious Revolution in a fascinating way.

The plot has rather more depth than *The Lost Lover*'s, and is more sensational, revolving around incest, adulterous lust, ambition, murder, and revolt. The beautiful and irresistible Homais is married to the elderly, impotent Prince of Libardian who has gone with his nephew to make war on the Abcans, a neighboring country. At the beginning of the play Homais had already been wooed by the Vizier, Osman. Osman is married to Libardian's sister. To Homais's later resentment, Osman gave up his efforts in the face of her naïve reluctance to have sex with him. His brother, Ismael, stepped into the breach and the prize of her maidenhead went to him. Ismael nurses ambitions for more than his brother's near-mistress. He also aims at his brother's official position as Vizier. Libardian wisely has doubts about Homais's fidelity, and confines her to the castle of Phasia during his absence. While languishing there she falls in love with the glowing reputation, and thereafter, the portrait of Libardian's nephew, Levan Dadian. Dadian is also away on the campaign and has recently been betrothed, for political rather than romantic reasons, to Bassima, the daugher of the king of the defeated Abcans. Osman, who originally captured Bassima and fulfilled the position of proxy during the marriage ceremony, has however actually fallen in love with Bassima, and she with him. She, however, is too virtuous (rather than naïve) to give in to his blandishments. Levan is not greatly attracted to his new bride, and predictably, when he arrives home from the war and sees Homais's seductive beauty he is immediately smitten. Homais plots with Ismael, her former lover, to take advantage of Osman's and Bassima's mutual attachment to dispose of her. She tells Levan that they are having an adulterous affair. Libardian, now aware of Homais's incestuous passion for Levan, condemns her to death. In the meantime in his camp outside the walls of the castle, Levan has condemned Bassima and Osman to death for their supposed adultery. Levan storms the castle to free Homais. The attempt ultimately fails and instead Homais is put to death by Libardian. Levan honorably falls on his sword, finally aware of the evil he has committed in the name of love for the devastating but unscrupulous Homais.

The plot is complex, but its interest lies not only in Manley's deft mapping of its twists and turns. Equally intriguing is her obfuscation of her sources, and then in her adaptation of the original story. She claims in the preface that *"There was a Princess more wicked than Homais. Sir John Chardin's Travels into Persia, whence I took the story, can inform the Reader."*[21] However, as we saw in *Queen Zarah*, it is sometimes best to do one's own investigations in regard to Manley's sources and we find in this case she has again been a heavy borrower. In the case of *Royal Mischief*, it is clear that she did not take the original plot from Sir John Chardin, although he does include the story of the love affair between Levan Dadian and his uncle's wife.[22] Her reasons for being so coy about her sources are clear. Writing as she was after Langbaine's *Momus Triumphans*, the authoritative exposé of plagiarism on the English stage, it is not surprising that Manley felt compelled to keep quiet about her liberal borrowings.[23]

In my preliminary research I had correctly assumed that Manley had taken the name Homais from one of the volumes of novels bound together by Bentley; I was delighted when I found *Homais Queen of Tunis* conveniently sited next to *Hattigé*, her source for *Queen Zarah*.[24] I have recently looked at more of Bentley's anthologies, and I now find that while I have the correct source, I identified the wrong novel. So, while Manley cites Chardin as her source, she was in fact taking much of her plot (and some of her text) from *The Rival Princesses*, a novel published by Bentley in 1689 and found in one of the twelve volumes of the publisher's "Modern Novels."[25] There can be no doubt of this, since many of the names, and most of the plot, are identical to Manley's version, including the translation of Bassima from Chardin's sluttish "none of the most faithful" to a model of virtue. It is equally clear that the delightfully wicked Homais owes more of her creation to *The Rival Princesses* rather than Chardin. Manley's inspiration for the errant princess is apparent in the novel's description of her:

> A Princess more wicked, and more ambitious than any ever was: She is guilty of all the Passions a Lover's Breast can be capable

of; for such are the regards of her passionate, tender, and languishing Eyes, that she never looks but to command Love, and inspire Hope."[26]

This fits easily with Manley's declaration of Homais' fatal attraction: "Those Eyes did never vainly shoot a Dart . . . / You never look but to command our Love, / And give your Lover hope" (p. 2).[27] There are, of course, some divergences from the original plot, and once again, as in her adaptation of *Hattigé*, the differences give the clues to the political questions that Manley wishes to pose, although unlike in *Zarah*, she seems unwilling to offer any easy answers. The most crucial of these is the depiction of the Prince of Libardian as old and impotent. In Manley's version Ismael describes him:

> . . . 'Tis none
> To take, what cannot fit anothers use;
> What boots the empty name, without possession,
> The love of Nature has Divorc'd him from her,
> Her Beauty lies neglected by his side. (p. 18)

In contrast to this, the novel describes the Prince as

> in the declension of his Age, but his conversation was sweet and amorous; his soul was amorous, and he still retain'd that part of his Youth; he had a passionate inclination for the Service of the fair Sex, and knew admirably well to make his Court.[28]

A few pages later, having been jealously guarded in the confines of the Castle of Phasia, Homais confirms this description and her husband's virility by giving birth to his child.

The simple act of reducing Libardian to a state of impotence brings Manley's Tory conscience into focus. It is once again the dichotomy facing loyal subjects of the Stuarts, a problem which she displaced onto her "truly loyal" father in *Rivella*. Sir Roger, she says, was so affected by Glorious Revolution, and his compatriots' wholesale desertion of James, that in despair at the "Misfortunes of his Royal Master" he died "soon after."[29] Manley, far from dying like her father, tackles the political conundrum felt by Tories by depicting the rightful king/husband as impotent. The explanation of this is that subjects, or wives, could be argued not to owe duty toward an impotent, or "insufficient," king or husband. James and Libardian therefore have something in common. They are neither of them viable patriarchs. The validity of this suggestion is detailed in a pamphlet that had appeared a few years before Manley's play:

> If [a husband] be insufficient [i.e. impotent] the law allows relief to such a distressed wife . . . In short, though a wife cannot put away her husband because she chose him; yet the . . . irregularities of the husband may be such as to give just cause for divorcement.[30]

Using the common comparison of the union of a prince and his people as a marriage, James's irregularities, that is his Catholicism and his tyrannical behavior, gave the English people "just cause for divorcement." On a more personal level, while Manley could not demonstrate James's impotence (he had had two legitimate heirs in Mary II and Anne) she could focus on the "mystery" surrounding the Catholic heir, James's son. By introducing the issue of impotence Manley brings into focus the rumors that the young prince was brought into the delivery chamber in a warming pan rather than from the queen's womb. While James's virility was not in question, in practice he was now unable to produce an acceptable heir. The Catholic son whom he refused to disinherit in favor of one of his Protestant daughters was out of the question. The linking of impotence with a ruler is therefore a central issue in this play. In fact, Manley may well have been influenced in her decision to make Libardian "powerless" by reports of James after 1695 as a "confused, frightened and rather pathetic old man . . . with little or no sign of the drive and determination that had been so evident before his downfall."[31] It was a compelling comparison. Libardian's flaw, his impotence, can be interpreted as James's latter-day weakness, and therefore the problem is essentially the same.

The logical extrapolation of this is the provision of a suitable, virile, or powerful, viable king. Therefore the next point of discussion in *Royal Mischief* is Lavan Dadian's right to invade the Prince of Libardian's castle, his territory, to rescue Homais. Using the relationship between husband and wife as analogous to the relationship between a king and his people Dadian's attempt to "conquer" the castle mirrors the debate over the acceptability of William's "conquest" of the English. Using the argument of "sufficiency" it is right for Dadian to free Homais from her impotent husband.

It can be compared to the way many Tories sheltered behind confused notions of James's abdication and William's right to the throne by conquest.[32] It is into the mouth of one of Homais's murderous followers that she puts the words: " . . . h'as plaid his part too long; / 'Twere time he left the Stage to other Actors" (p. 26).

This would be a typical Whig/Williamite Tory reaction. On the other side of the line, it is the (nearly) reformed Osman who gives the "loyal" view of the proceedings:

> The shameless *Homais* has undone us all;
> The Soldiers are revolted on her side,
> The Prince her Lord departed from the Castle,
> And ours Victorious now is entring here. (p. 41)

Manley's naturally Royalist sympathies are clear, but it is equally obvious that she sees her solution as untenable. She represents the unwholesome Homais and her temporarily misled Levan as short-lived victors in their struggle against the wronged Libardian. There is never much question that they will be allowed to prevail permanently. But the problems inherent in the status quo are made equally clear by the thoroughly evil Homais's accusation against the righteous, if impotent, Libardian: "My Lord [Libardian] conspired the fall of both [Homais and Levan] / Now in a Civil War he fain would steep you" (p. 40). From a Williamite perspective this is an unanswerable problem: supporting James would plunge the country back into the civil war that was still within living memory. The alternative, by contrast, is equally unacceptable, because in Manley's version of the story it is the "invaders" who are morally beyond the pale. She echoes her friend Granville's comment in another contemporary play: "Take heed . . . , Respect the King, / Who strikes at Kings, repeat the Giants Crime / And strike at *Jove*."[33]

But in one sense, Homais is right. The crux of the problem is that, as an impotent man, Libardian would effectively bring a succession crisis upon the country by defeating his own nearest relative, Dadian. There is no acceptable answer to this, and it is perhaps one of the reasons that the "caviller/Cavalier" Willmore of the earlier play found it so necessary to go back on his word: blind adherence to a set of principles is creditable, but it is also sometimes unworkable.

Throughout her writings, it is evident that High Tory principles, balanced by concerns over a Protestant succession, were the center of Manley's ideology. Her manipulation of the plot of *Royal Mistress* is therefore clearly a deliberate strategy, as evidenced by the other two versions in which inheritance is not a problem. In *The Rival Princesses*, Homais has a legitimate child by her husband; in Chardin's version Homais has three children by Levan and one purported to be by Libardian.

Having said this, Manley's determination to punish the "invaders" is perhaps an indication of Manley's hesitation in backing William wholeheartedly. She points out in her preface that she creates a painful retribution for Homais, while Chardin leaves her in "high credit."[34] The diversion from the original text is even more marked in *The Rival Princesses*. In the novel, Homais has a spectacularly successful career. The unfortunate protector, Homais's husband, retires to "the Utmost Limits of his Territories,"[35] mourns the loss of his faithless wife, and then rearming himself, takes up arms against her lover, his conquering relative, only to die in battle. Homais herself, whom Manley puts to such a spectacular and vituperative death, goes from strength to strength:

> The end of all things of this Nature, I know well, ought to be a Punishment of Vice, and Reward of Virtue; but Truth being the Thing that in all my Undertakings chiefly animates my Pen, I knew not well how to dispense my self from relating it as in reality it was. The wicked *Homais* was not long unmarried, and being the source of all the Injustice committed by *Levan*, she likewise revenged them upon him; he died by Poison, which she administered, to make room for the Coronation of her Son, *Alexander*, and her own Regency; ungratefully repaying all the Kindness and Fondness of that poor Prince. (p. 161)

In Manley's next play, which is rather more straightforward than her two earlier efforts, we find her reworking the dual problems of succession and keeping true to an oath yet again. There were, of course, differences in the contemporary context within which they appeared. While the problem of succession had not been formally resolved when *Royal Mischief* was being written, by 1707, the date of her next play, it had ostensibly been settled. The Electors of Hanover were waiting in the wings to take over from the issue-less Queen Anne. Manley, as a loyal Protestant Tory, could be expected to be satisfied with this arrangement. It is odd, therefore, that she once again features a monarch who cannot provide a direct heir. For this situation, I would argue, is the linchpin of the plot of Manley's *Almyna: or the Arabian Vow*. In this case, however, it is not his impotence, but the sultan's unpleasant habit of having his wives executed immediately after their wedding night that makes the birth of a direct heir impossible.

Manley's play is loosely based on the *Arabian Nights Entertainments,* which was enjoying an enthusiastic reception in the early eighteenth century.[36] Manley, of course, adapts the story to make her heroine far more assertive than Scheherezade, introducing a number of elements that have no place in the popular text. Perhaps the most intriguing of these is passive obedience (which I will discuss later). She also provides an heir for the sultan who, of course, plays no part in the original sequence of fantastic tales. Of course, I would not suggest we waste too much sympathy on the Sultan Almanzor's unexpressed dilemma over his succession. After all, he overcomes the problem by naming one of his brothers as his heir. At the bottom of the sultan's marital difficulties lies his wife's adultery. His anger is exacerbated when he discovers that another of his brothers has also been shamefully cuckolded. Given his family's unfortunate experiences with women, the sultan conveniently interprets his Koran as declaring females to be without a soul. He therefore takes a vow, with ingenious casuistry, that since it is not a crime to kill something without a soul, and as he never wishes to be cuckolded by a wife again, he will simply dispose of them in the morning after the marriage night. In the meantime Abdulla, the sultan's brother and heir, has fallen wildly in love with the beautiful, highly educated Almyna, despite having previously been her sister Zoradiah's clandestine fiancé. He successfully gains the approval of her father, the sultan's vizier, for Almyna's hand. Zoradiah is naturally deeply upset, but Almyna explains that she does not love Abdulla and instead intends to put herself forward as a prospective bride for the sultan (with whom she has fallen in love) in order that she can convince him that his murderous practice is wrong. She declares herself willing to become a martyr if she can persuade the sultan to make her his last victim. The Vizier, her father, already upset by his role in executing a number of young brides, is even more alarmed when he discovers this, but cannot persuade her to change her mind. The sultan, swayed by Almyna's beauty and courage, agrees that she will be his last victim. He decides to put her to a final test and watches while she is due to be executed. He is so impressed by her dignified willingness to be sacrificed for the good of others, he declares that she has a soul and immediately calls off the execution. In the meantime Abdullah has raised an army to storm the castle and free Almyna. Tragically he is killed in the fray, and Zoradiah is accidentally impaled upon his sword, also dying. The sultan and his new wife, while mourning the deaths of their siblings, live on.

Aside from the succession, a question that I have deliberately imposed upon Manley's text, there are two main themes. The first is the assertively feminist line that Manley takes with Almyna, the well-educated, determined woman who is prepared to give her life, suffragette-fashion, to demonstrate that women do, indeed, have a soul. Her protestations against the sultan's distortion of the Koran to suit his own purpose and her lists of brave women can easily be taken to underline Manley's belief that in her own society, women's worth, if not their souls, is being denied. Using the sultan as her instrument of oppression, and having him refer to himself as "like a father" (p. 46) to his people emphasises the role that patriarchal institutions such as the family play in this oppression. Brave Almyna's insistence on ramming home the point to the sultan with the question, "Cou'd the Roman Ladies . . . / Without a Soul have gain'd such endless Fames' reinforces this interpretation of the text (p. 46). Some critics maintain that Manley saw herself as Almyna, as the near-anagram of her name suggests.[37] In defence of this, it is certainly true that years later, in *Rivella*, there are echoes of her heroine. When Almyna declares. "What not thy *Vizier* none of all thy Council / Or can, or dare relate, a Woman shall!" (p. 46) it is a foretaste of Manley's declaration about herself: "She was proud of having more Courage than had any of our [male] Sex, and of throwing the first Stone" against the Whigs.[38]

The feminism is, of course, the most obvious strand to the play. In tandem with it, and perhaps with more pertinence to her political ideology, she returns to a subtle discussion of the problematic nature of oath-taking. Her decision to subtitle the play the *Arabian Vow* rules out any doubt that this is a central concern.[39] Nor can we overestimate the importance of this topic to her contemporaries. Why else would she include in the preface the statement that the "Ceremony in the first Act" will be omitted from any future productions of the play? Her insistence that she is obeying the command of her patroness is equally telling. She wished to make it absolutely clear at a time when the Junto were at the height of their power that she was not willing to risk being branded a subversive. Presumably the Countess of Sandwich "that incomparable LADY, to whom this *Play* is inscrib'd, who is Mistriss of a Genius not to be deriv'd from a less glorious Original, than the immortal Earl of *Rochester*" felt equally strongly and no doubt insisted that Manley publish her disapproval of the sententious scene.[40]

The ceremony in question sees the uxoricide sultan proclaim his brother his heir. The assembled company are required in an echo of the Act of Uniformity to swear, "By all contain'd, within this holy *Alcoran*."[41] However, it was perhaps not so much this oath that sent a shiver down the spine of Manley's dedicatee but the way Abdulla's Oath seems to conflate the coronation oaths of James II and William and Mary on their ascension to the throne. Abdalla is required to

> In Quality of King, and Lord of Realms;
> T'administer to all your People Justice,
> Maintain, and keep 'em in those Privileges:
> Your Predecessor Kings, in General,
> Or in particular, have granted 'em. (p. 7)

The words "Predecessor Kings" are significant. While James, like Abdalla, is asked to follow in the footsteps of his *"lawfull, and Religious predecessors,"* William and Mary were required to *"solemnly promise and swear to govern the people of this kingdom of England . . . according to the statutes in parliament agreed on, and the laws and customs of the same."*[42] William and Mary deliberately drew back from repeating the mistakes of their "predecessors."

Reminding readers in 1706/1707 of the nuances of the coronation oath and the debates that still raged over the rights and wrongs of monarchy by divine right or "mutual understanding" was perhaps not wise.[43] The question as always is whether Manley was promoting the Jacobite cause in doing this. I doubt that she would risk being so open, if she were toying with support for the king "over the water." But she was veering dangerously close to rehearsing the doubts raised by breaking the direct line of succession. And of course there was always the fear that this would lead to insurrection and violence on Anne's death, when the distantly related Hanoverians took over.

It was not only the monarch's oath-taking which may have caused consternation to nervous members of the audience. Oaths included in the scene evoked even stronger memories. The "Lords, . . . Governors, . . . Grandees, and Councellors" are required to

> swear and promise by your Prophet . . .
> To acknowledge, and to hold for all your Lives,
> *Abdella Abenacer*, King, and Lord,
> Of all these Realms, as Lawful Successor,
> To his great Brother, *Caliph Almanzor*. (p. 6)

Manley's wording also brought back memories of the oath of allegiance taken in 1689 in support of William and Mary. A number of M.P.s and peers had refused to take it despite an attempt to streamline it "to avoid unpleasant references to the past."[44]

It was not simply the injudicious choice of words that may have upset the countess. As well as reminding the audience of oath-taking practices twenty years earlier, the play also forces the audience to think very carefully about the fallibility of monarchs as individuals, and subsequently the very basis of their authority.

The sultan is referred to as "Commander of the faithful Musselmen" (p. 2); he is described as once having been "as a God reverenc'd, and almost pray'd to" who "Art now become their dread." It is not difficult to translate this into a definition of a monarch who believed that he had been divinely appointed. It is as much a comment of the fear that faithful Protestants felt about James II's Catholic son, the Pretender, who despite being direct in line for the throne, was never a real alternative to a Protestant succession. Manley has encapsulated the essence of the dilemma in which good Tory subjects found themselves, wishing they could support the "rightful" heir to the throne but finding it impossible. As Evelyn Cruickshank points out, for most Tories, although "the prospect of the Hanoverian succession was distasteful to them and at best a necessary evil, the party was not mainly Jacobite."[45] The Duke of Hamilton, the Scottish Jacobite put it succinctly: "There would be no difficulty at all if only King James [III] were a Protestant."[46]

Therefore in this play the figure of the sultan represents a conflation of several ideological concepts that were never far off from the contemporary political agenda. The first, and most obvious, must be passive obedience, the adherence to which gives the Sultan's subjects considerable trouble. While he is acknowledged as a ruler in whom "fair Mercy, and strickt Justice, flourish" (p. 1) he is also "Despotick is his Pow'r" (p. 2). His Vizier is caught between the necessity to obey his sovereign, and the fact that by overseeing the killing of the discarded wives, he is being asked to commit, "Under the sacred Name and Veil of Marriage / ... Murther, horrid Murther!" (p. 1) The vizier's dilemma is one of passive obedience: does he disobey the Sultan's law or God's law? They are obviously not the same. Manley presents her audience with a neat case study through which to debate Anglican principles as laid down in *The Whole Duty to Man*:

> When [the king] enjoins anything contrary to what God hath commanded, we are not to give him this active obedience; ... we must refuse to act.... But even this is a season for Passive Obedience; we must patiently suffer what the Ruler inflicts on us for such a refusal, and not ... rise up against him. *For who can stretch forth his hand against the Lord's Anointed and be guiltless.*"[47]

Manley, however, does not leave the matter here, for equally, using Almyna as her mouthpiece, she asks whether the king does not also have a duty to retreat on decisions which are clearly against the interests of the people. It is entirely conceivable that Manley was prompted in her deliberations by a public debate on a sovereign's rights through the newspapers written by the Whig John Tutchin and the High Tory Charles Leslie in August of 1706. The significance of these exchanges to Manley's play is explained in one of Tutchin's papers:

> The *Hereditary Right* to Government is a Notion advanc'd by Men of *Arbitrary Principles*, on purpose to destroy the *Native Rights* of Mankind, the Capitulations of Empires and Kingdoms, and the Stipulations betiwxt [sic] King and People; for if such a Right takes Place, the King comes to the Crown under no Terms of Government, and his Will is his Law . . . *So I will have it because I so command it. My royal Will and Pleasure is the Reason of my Action.*[48]

It is worthwhile noting that in this same issue of the *Observator* Tutchin included a section on the Coronation Oath and its significance as a "signing of the Covenant betwixt him and his People." The ideological tension underpinning the play is the vexed question of keeping one's vows, and the nature of the sovereign's vows and responsibilities to his own people. The sultan is therefore made to question the wisdom of a strict adherence to his own word, and on his breaking of his own oath admits, "We gain in losing of so false a Cause." (p. 64)

Whether Manley has a specific "cause" in mind is left tantalizingly uncertain, although the countess of Sandwich's disapproval of the "Ceremony in the first Act" suggests that there was some nervousness surrounding a detected central theme. The most obvious link is to the "false" cause of Jacobitism. There are elements that would have been timely. There is also the fact that the plot revolves around a marriage in which the weaker female partner is doomed to die. This might also indicate, albeit rather simplistically, that Manley wished to make some comment about England's forthcoming union with Scotland. Manley shows no particular animosity in her writings to the union.[49] Although she was a Tory (and Tories were suspicious of the proposed move) she seems to have been less concerned than other women of her party. For instance, nowhere does she agree with Elinor James's view that "this Union may be fatal both to *England* and *Scotland*, and therefore . . . for the love of your selves and Posterity, don't yield to it."[50]

Elinor James's terminology implies that High Tories associated the union with the death of nationhood. In contrast to this, Manley's emphasis on an amicable settlement to the potentially deadly nuptials, as demonstrated in *Almyna*, rather suggests that she agreed with James I's view of the "marriage" between England and Scotland: "What God hath conjoined let no man separate. I am the husband and the whole isle is my lawful wife; . . . I therefore think that I, a Christian King, under the Gospel, should be a polygamist and husband to two wives."[51]

But she may have felt duty bound to make some comment on an issue of such magnitude. And it was undeniable that the union was a fundamentally Whig project, even though Manley seems to have accepted it so easily. In defence of her acquiescence, we should always bear in mind that she was first and foremost a Protestant. We can speculate, given that it is a recurrent theme throughout her dramatic writing, that deep down she harbored a hope that James II's son would see sense and abandon his incomprehensible adherence to Catholicism. Until he did, however, the Pretender opposed the union, and Jacobite invasions and potential civil war were always on the horizon. Indeed, in 1706/1707, there was fear that the country might yet descend back into the chaos of the rebellion. Although written some years later, the Pretender made his objections to the union explicit in his *Declaration*. Richard Steele illustrates the perceived danger of dis-union:

> We thank and adore the Wisdom of Providence, which, by an Union of *England* and *Scotland* makes the Protection and Care of the whole Island, at this Instant of Difficulty, less subject to Delays and Distractions. We observe with Joy, the Enemy calls it an *Unhappy Union*. . . . We detest the Endeavours to dis-unite us. . . . It is an Union of Protestants and Fellow-Subjects, fighting for their Civil and Religious Liberties: An Union that we trust will be ever hateful and terrible to the Friend of Slavery and Popery.[52]

Many Englishmen felt therefore that union with Scotland would act as a defense against a return to civil war and, as such, despite High Tory reservations, it was probably a good thing.

The union is perhaps a side issue, but it is related to a central theme of the text, that of the vow. The Pretender could be said to have sworn allegiance to Catholicism. However, if he wanted his kingdom back, the argument for him to rescind the vow (to a false church) which common sense and experience demonstrated as dangerous and divisive was a strong one. We can see why Almyna begs the sultan to end "his cruel Vow" and

> Save thy precious Soul, so near to ruin,
> . . . .
> Restore thee to thy self, and to thy Glory. (p. 7)

These words surely echoed the thoughts of Hanoverian Tories whose dearest wish, however unlikely, would be to see a Protestant Stuart established as heir to the throne.

Of course, by the time Manley's last play was produced in 1717, the dilemma, if it had not actually gone away, was less acute. Queen Anne had been dead for four years and the Hanoverians were successfully ruling after a trouble-free succession. The 1715 Jacobite uprising had effectively put paid to any real prospect of a Stuart restoration and had only really succeeded in providing the ministerial Whigs with an opportunity to "exploit anti-Roman Catholic and anti-French prejudices."[53] Manley's last play, seen against this background, was an extraordinary achievement because, as we shall see, it succeeded in being interpretable as offering a message of support to either side of the political divide.

That *Lucius, First Christian King of Britain* would appeal to all may account for its unexpected theatrical host. Richard Steele, as we have seen, is reputed to have paid Manley six hundred guineas for the rights to its production and Steele was certainly no Jacobite. He may indeed have taken the play because he was "working hard to restore some of the relationships" with his former Tory friends, and Mrs. Manley obviously figured prominently among them.[54] Even so, Steele's desire for reconciliation with Manley would not have overridden his Whig sympathies, and his political wisdom, if the play had been even perceptibly Jacobite. Indeed, Steele's antipathy to the Pretender was expressed succinctly in a pamphlet that deplored James's "efforts to dis-unite us."[55] However, the inclusion in the play of a changeling prince (the true king of Britain) who has been ousted by the wicked usurper will indicate how easily the authorities could have read Jacobite sympathies into Manley's work, if they had a wish to.

The story is woven round a young prince of Britain who is on a military campaign to France. He falls in love with Rosalind, the Christian wife of the defeated king of Aquitaine. The wicked King Vortimer, ostensibly Lucius's father, has conquered the true British king and married his widow. He has claimed the British throne and is a usurper. He also falls in love with Rosalind, twice attempts to rape her and remove her from his son. In the meantime Lucius has converted and has gone through a Christian marriage ceremony with Rosalind. At the end he kills Vortimer and is revealed as the true (Christian) king of Britain. He had been passed off as Vortimer's son, but he was in fact the posthumous child of the murdered British sovereign, and is therefore the rightful heir.

The plot is excessively complex, and to a large extent predictable. The real interest lies in the explicit depiction of a usurping king, the restoration of the true hereditary heir to the British throne, and of course the heir to the throne's conversion to Christianity. All this leads once again to the Tory vision of a Protestant Stuart back on the throne. The emphasis is on Lucius being the legitimate king who has been denied his birthright by an interloper.

Such a scenario could, of course, also be conveniently appropriated by all shades of opinion. For Jacobites, Lucius, waiting to return from France to claim his inheritance, might represent James III, descended from the blood royal and ousted by the Hanoverian usurper. Equally, for the Whigs, Lucius was a good symbol of a true Christian king, with an impeccable birthright. Everyone was familiar with warming pan stories, which made the Pretender only a "Suspected Son of *James* the Second." In the eyes of Hanoverian supporters, George I was doing an excellent job keeping out "an uncertain *Popish Pretender*." Moreover, he was "of the Hereditary Blood Royal, and the nearest in Blood to the Crown of any Protestant . . . and has . . . as good a Title, as *Queen Anne* her self."[56]

The play's credentials as a vehicle for the Hanoverian succession is made explicit in the lines which Richard Steele appended to the play at its revival in 1720.

> In wanton Ease—ye Britons, learn to know,
> Nor slight, in present Welfare, distant Woe!
> Rescu'd from foreign Bonds, the happy Age
> Sees no Abuse of Power, but on the Stage:
> The Briton here, beholds the Tyrant bleed,
> The Just thro' all the Mazes of their Fate succeed.[57]

Such stirring lines present a clear warning to Hanoverian subjects that they should be grateful for their deliverance. Steele's comments echo others of around the same time: one pamphleteer asked readers to:

> Consider the Matter seriously, and tell me your Thoughts calmly . . . what will become of you if the *reputed Son*, whom ye have *Deny'd, Oppos'd, Protested* against, and *Abjur'd*, shou'd once get you into his Power, wou'd he not revenge the Affronts, abuses, and Indignities ye have put upon him, in detaining him so long from that which he vainly and arrogantly calls **His Right**?[58]

Equally, the usurper Vortimer's aim to make an inviolable league (p. 15) with the king of Gallia must have reminded the audience of Louis XIV's support of the Pretender. Again, this was a constant worry to the Whigs as contemporary pamphleteers warned:

> [Louis XIV] could have no other View in supporting the Pretender, but to use him and his Title as a Handle to kindle a Civil War in *Great Britain* so that he might with ease subdue both the contending Parties. . . . The Protestant *Jacobites* (if there were any such) wou'd then be dipp'd too far to think of a Retreat.[59]

Others went even further:

> If you can trust a *Papist* with your Lives and Liberties, and the Lives and Liberties of your Posterity; if you think a Bigotted *French* Vassal would better become, or has more Right to the

Throne than King *George*, and can make you more happy, go on and venture; call the Wretch, make him your King, and see your mistake in your Ruin.⁶⁰

Manley's success in presenting her play as acceptable to spectators of many political persuasions lies in her provision of a situation that encourages multiple interpretations. And while it would be unwise to make any kind of unequivocal judgment on where her own sympathies lay, Lucius's conversion to Christianity is probably the key feature. By joining the true faith, he is able to marry the Queen of Albany, a name that harks back to good Queen Anne's alias in *Queen Zarah*. It suggests that she and her Tory friends may still have been hoping, however unlikely it may have been, that James III will convert to Protestantism. There is evidence that this was still on the agenda for optimistic Tories. At least one contemporary mocked the Tories' faint hope that James would see sense. A Whiggish pamphleteer laughingly refers to the trip Charles Leslie, the High Tory Jacobite, was reported to have made some years earlier to

> convert a certain young Gentleman [the Pretender], and bring him over from Popery to Protestantism . . . to give Colour to the Chevalier's pretended Conversion and strengthen the Jacobite with the High Flying Interest; Which however was all Grimace.⁶¹

In the face of such taunts, it is not surprising that Manley places great emphasis on Lucius's true conversion, not the sham one of which the Chevalier, James III, might be accused.

There are, however, further clues in the text as to how Manley envisaged the play being interpreted by others in her audience. The strongest hint comes from Manley's predilection for plagiarizing. This time, however, there is no wholesale lifting of sections of an earlier work. Instead, she appears, uncharacteristically, to have taken inspiration for small portions of the text from Shakespeare's *Richard III*. The significance of these borrowings is not so much in the words themselves as the fact that Colley Cibber's version of the play had at first been refused a license. The reason given was that:

> But all the reason could get for its being refus'd, was, that *Henry the Sixth* being a Character Unfortunate and Pitied, wou'd put

the Audience in Mind of the late *King James*: Now I confess, I never thought of him in the Writing it, which possibly might proceed from there not being any likeness between 'em. [62]

The echoes of *Richard III* in *Lucius* are particularly significant. There are echoes of the scene before Bosworth in Lucius's words, "Despair and Die" (p. 51) when he believes he has killed his true father. And although it might be argued that this an unconscious borrowing, it is difficult to believe that Manley was not aware of the similarities between King Richard's "I think there be six Richmonds in the field; Five have I slain to day, instead of him" (V.iv.11–12) and the six Otharios "alike him arm'd; 'twas one of them" (p. 30). The references are tied up, if in a fairly confused manner, with the ever-present discussion of Jacobitism in the text. Murray Pittock has pointed out that the Stuarts "had linked themselves [to Henry VII]."[63] By referring the audience back to Shakespeare's play, they are reminded of Lucius as the rightful heir, their Tudor hero, restoring England to the legitimate bloodline. Jacobites would certainly have cheered at the lines, "How in these foreign Wars, and distant Climes / Forc'd us for him to carry hated Arms" (p. 3) as they recalled George I's endless, and expensive, involvement in his German disputes. How many of them would have had a wry smile at the Vortimer's original title, the Lord Verulam, clearly a reference to the Marlboroughs' links with St. Albans (Verulamium)?

There are elements that require further consideration. The near-rape of Rosalind by the disguised usurper may simply have served to excite the "Heroes in the Pit" as Steele suggested in his prologue, but rape is not something about which a woman writes lightly. Interpretation merely depended on whom you wished to place in the role of the aggressor. An unconsummated rape for the Hanoverian supporter represents the Jacobites' unsuccessful attempt to invade "Albany," or England, an invasion that was defeated by the rightful heir. For Stuart supporters of the legal monarch, it only required to place George I under Vortimer's cloak to see Lucius, or James III, come to the rescue.

Where does all this leave us? Throughout all the plays, particularly the tragedies, the balance of the argument seems to point, yet again, to Manley's love of the Stuarts, but her reluctance to accept a Catholic monarch. It seems to have been a debate that she allowed to rage in her plays, but which could find no place in her pamphleteering, where an adherence to strict Hanoverian principles was unavoidable.

8

"Ascribed to other Pens": Possible Additions to the Canon

All research into early-eighteenth-century political propaganda comes up, sooner or later, with the problem of ascription and authorship. The period was one in which writers habitually left their work unsigned, usually to avoid prosecution. Manley does not present the same problems as the most prolific of writers such as Defoe, but nevertheless there are still problems in constructing a canon for her. So far, we have looked at the material that can be ascribed to Manley with the confidence gained from external evidence. But inevitably we have to step out of the zone of absolute certainty and venture into the murky areas of probability and conjecture.

Manley undoubtedly wrote more than she owned up to. The comment by Barber's biographer that "Several Political Pieces of that Day, which common Fame ascribed to other Pens, came wholly from her own" offers strong evidence that she was more prolific than we can judge today.[1] Surprisingly, given her willingness to sign her very first plays, she seems to have adopted anonymity right from the start of her career. There is a claim made by William Langbain/Charles Gildon in 1699 that "This Lady has Publish'd several other Books, which have not her Name to 'em and which, for that Reason, I shall forbear to mention their Titles."[2]

Clearly then, Manley's "shadow" output is worth investigating, and this chapter will explore the possibility of making further ascriptions to Manley's name. The most significant suggestion is that she is extremely likely to have pubished at least one piece that has hitherto lain unclaimed: a poem entitled *An Heroick Essay Upon The Unequal'd Victory Obtain'd By Major-General Webb* (1709).³

In addition to this solus effort, she probably had a hand in other works. Writers collaborated freely during this period and there is strong evidence for Manley's participation in other texts not normally associated with her. However, I will not concern myself solely with additions to the canon: there are a couple of pamphlets widely accepted to be by Manley where the evidence for accepting her authorship is extremely questionable.

However, as suggested above, I intend to add something to her collected works before I remove any dubious items: the poem *An Heroick Essay*. This work is the only surviving panegyric to Major-General Webb, who was hailed as a Tory hero in late 1708 and early 1709.⁴ Neither Horne, Marlborough's bibliographer, nor Foxon's catalogue of eighteenth-century poetry ascribe it to any writer at all.⁵

On 27 September 1708 Webb scored a notable victory, defending essential supplies on their way to support Marlborough's siege of Lisle. His victory had been spectacular, his six thousand men had been vastly outnumbered by twenty-six thousand French troops, but the narrowness of the ground allowed him to conceal part of his force which, when called up, surprised the French infantry.⁶ Unfortunately, the dispatches subsequently sent to Marlborough did not give the credit for the engagement to Webb. The source of the misinformation seems to have been a report that gave the glory to Cadogan, who was a staunch Whig, and who did not arrive until after the main action was over.⁷ The report, originally published in Holland, was picked up by *The London Gazette* (under the editorship of Steele) and does not mention Webb at all, giving the victory at the "Wood of Winnendale" to Cadogan.⁸ The incident fueled Tory outrage, with the Commons turning a vote of thanks to their party comrade General Webb "into a demonstration against Marlborough's avarice."⁹ Thereafter, Steele was obliged to print Webb's own version of the engagement in *The London Gazette* three weeks later.¹⁰

The name Steele, of course, always raises alarm bells where Manley is concerned. But it is not only a vituperative attack on the editor of the *Gazette* that provides compelling indicators of

Manley's authorship. The poem even opens with her name: "*Delia*, who once of Courts and Empires sung."[11] Delia is practically a textual identification. It is the name that Manley chose as an alias for herself in volume 2 of *New Atalantis*, published in October 1709, only a few months after the poem. In addition to this, we know from her letters that she was familiarly known as "Dela." When they were still on speaking terms Richard Steele called her "Delia," another diminutive of Delarivier. We can only conclude that the repetition of the name "Delia," which she used in *New Atalantis*, at the beginning of the first two stanzas suggests a certain level of eagerness to implant that name in the reader's consciousness.

Even the mournful "Delia's" claim to have sung of "Courts and Empires" matches Manley's literary output exactly. Between 1705 and 1709, a large part of Manley's writing dealt with courts such as that of *Queen Zarah*, and empires as in her most recent play *Almyna*.[12] With her forthcoming secret history, she also clearly intended "courts and empires" to be an area with which her readers would associate her.

The poem continues to match Manley's own situation, with the claim that "Delia" had been

> . . . subdu'd to Rural Song,
> Where Silver *Medway* glides the Shades along;
> Near her lone Cott, too low for Storms to move,
> (For Storms fly o'er and break on those above)
> Exil'd, Forlorn, full of her Fate she lay;
> And oft regretted a more prosp'rous Day.[13]

This is reminiscent of Manley's generally regretful self-portraits. In *New Atalantis* she describes herself as Delia, "forlorn! distress'd! beggard!"[14] Delia's claim to have been in a rural location is also significant. There is no hard evidence that Manley was anywhere near the river Medway during the period prior to the publication of the poem, but in *Rivella*, her fictionalized autobiography, she claims to have written *New Atalantis* "for her own Amusement and Diversion in the Country." While we should bear in mind that Manley's chronology is often a little suspect, this assertion does correspond with the likely date of composition of this poem.[15]

Internal evidence must always be used with caution, but there are elements that argue persuasively for Manley as the poet responsible for this text. There are few, if any, other writers of this period who would have wished to include references to "the Queen of Love" so early, and so incongruously, in a poem making such a strong political point. They are also, inevitably, a reminder of Manley's own references to her expertise in writing about amatory topics, notably her comment in *Rivella* that none "of the Moderns in that Point come up to your famous Author of the *Atalantis*. She has carried the Passion farther than could be readily conceiv'd."[16] From this we may conclude that Manley, if she was the author, used the poem as some kind of self-advertisement. She had freely mixed sex and politics in her first novel; she was about to do the same again in her next one. She also understood how shows of male valor attracted women. In *Memoirs of Europe* she would equate impotence with loss of political sway. In *An Heroick Essay* the reverse is the case, as she acknowledges that there may be a rough edge to sexual attraction: "A Warrior lovely, as the God who charms, / With strenuous Force, our Beauty to his Arms."

Such explicit sexual overtones are unusual in a poem about warfare, and the central section of the poem is conventional. It would be difficult to identify it as from any particular pen, other than one writing in the Tory cause. It contains conventional complaints that the "Senate's Thanks" to Webb were "dealt with a sparing Hand."[17] Equally predictable are the claims that Webb did not simply rely on fortune for military success, as the Tories claimed Marlborough did, but he was "As *Eugene* Brave."[18]

There was nothing unusual in this central section, therefore, and certainly nothing that betrays Manley's most common stylistic features. After this, however, there are clues that the poem was written by a woman, or at least was intended to be read as such. The tone is again typically Manleyan. What is particularly interesting when we consider Manley's later career, is that it gives us a strong indication that Manley's ambition was to become a party writer. For it takes the form of a complaint that there are no opportunities for women to write political propaganda. Delia points out that while in the second stanza the Queen of Love has urged her to "new-strike the Lyre," in the world of eighteenth-century publishing,

> A Woman's Song (bright Goddess) they refuse:
> Cou'd even *Orinda, Sappho*, live again
> *Sappho, Orinda* they wou'd now disdain."[19]

It was a serious complaint; it may even help to explain why Manley wrote scandal fiction rather than straight political propaganda until she had made her name, and why she deliberately put it aside once she had. Whether this was the case or not, she clearly wished to be associated with her illustrious predecessors. She would describe herself in the same way in the self-promotional puff in *New Atalantis:*

> Delia, *had in* Apolo's *Court been bred*:
> *Nor* Astra, *nor* Orinda *knew so well,*
> *Scarce* Grecian Sapho, Delia *to excel*.[20]

Manley no doubt felt she had a right to complain about neglect. Male Whig writers did seem to be profiting from their political affiliations, while women were prevented from earning their living from such activities. She points out that John Dennis could now leave "turmoiling for the Stage" and this is a reference to the hundred pounds the Whig critic received from Marlborough for his poem in praise of Blenheim.[21] With a sour note Delia continues that :

> All *Apollo's* Sons, Apollo's *Glorys* see,
> Only the hapless Daughters mourn like me.
> A Soul depress'd cannot with lofty Ardor glow.[22]

Women (or at least Tory women) cannot hope to be rewarded for their efforts. Although the goddess attempts to make a virtue out of Delia's "stedfast Soul" whom "neither Fear, nor Hope of Favour warms," it is clearly a topic that has embittered the poetess.[23] By way of emphasizing Delia's impoverished state, she notes that the Whigs, the party who are gaining most of out of the war, pay their scribblers well: "Who can the most Reward, they mostly praise." The complaining tone of *An Heroick Essay* is a recognizably Manleyan stylistic characteristic, particularly of the year 1709. In fact, she remained aggrieved. She repeated her accusations of Tory stinginess several years later in *Rivella*: "She had chose to declare her self of a Party most Supine, and forgetful of such who served them."²⁴ How unlike the Whigs!

Manley's authorship of the poem becomes even more likely when we turn to the direct attack on Richard Steele. Manley's dislike of Steele, so noticeable throughout her political writings, is evident in this poem. The poet's virulence and obvious animosity adds a savage edge to the jibes directed at him. While Steele was not beloved by any of the Tory press, the vituperative references to him in this poem go beyond simple political hostility. They are reminiscent of the comments that occur throughout her work. It is personal rancor that appears to motivate the attack: "Ingrateful S[teel]le who forgets his *Former State* / And *Former Friends* in his new Change of Fate."²⁵ Steele's ingratitude is the *leitmotif* in all her descriptions of him. It is a point that is made explicitly in *New Atalantis*: "It is not only to her [Delia], but to all that have ever serv'd him he has shew'd himself so ingrateful."²⁶ For the poet, it is equally clearly not Steele the *Gazetteer* whom Delia, herself a "former friend," finds so offensive, but Steele the "ingrate."

There are further echoes of Manley's other later texts in her references to Joseph Addison. It is he whom Delia suggests ought to have written Webb's panegyric: "For Notes so sweet young *Addison* was raised."²⁷ The goddess's tart reminder to Delia is that "Already to great *Marlbro* he has sung," ironically suggesting that Addison, like other poets, chose the subject for his art from mercenary motives.²⁸ The goddess is probably thinking of Addison's poem *The Campaign* of December 1704, which praised Marlborough's exploits at Blenheim, and which probably helped him into the post of undersecretary of state some seven months later.²⁹ Despite Addison's regrettable choice of subject, the poet's generosity toward him foreshadows *Memoirs of Europe,* where Manley also praised the "Inchantment" in Addison's poetry while urging him not to "prostitute [his] inborn Genius."³⁰

In fairness, in ascribing this poem to Manley there are two problems that must be addressed. The first is that the publisher, Abigail Baldwin, a Whig, never appears to have handled any of Manley's other texts. This can be explained by the fluid nature of early-eighteenth-century publishing, which would not rule out a temporary arrangement, even by a politically inappropriate publisher. Morphew was after all guilty of publishing Steele's *Tatler* and Manley had not yet become a member of Morphew's stable of writers. On the other hand, maybe Baldwin insisted upon the uncharacteristically gentle treatment of Marlborough, merely suggesting that he has been "fortunate" in his victories. However, these objections seem fairly minor; they are overwhelmed by what seems to me to be a considerable amount of compelling evidence for Manley's authorship of *An Heroick Essay*.

Now we come to some more tricky attributions. A number of other texts have been attributed to Manley as sole author. One is *The Ecclesiastical and Political History of Whig-Land of Late Years*, cited by Cahoun Winton as a possible product of Manley's pen.[31] Winton's argument is persuasive, particularly when we look at the pamphlet itself (which is published by John Morphew). The text, which features an attack on Steele, contains all the hallmarks of Manley's campaign against her former friend. It includes references to a wife who is a *"West Indian* Beauty" (Steele's first wife was a West Indian heiress). The hero spends his fortune in "Pursuit of the *Philosophers Stone"* (a reference to Steele's alchemical endeavors, which Manley satirized in some detail in *New Atalantis*).[32] The pamphlet also derides Steele's supposed habit of having "his Name . . . set to the Works of others,"[33] an accusation that Manley also made in *Memoirs of Europe*. There she called him a *"Bird dress'd up in borrow'd Feathers."*[34] In addition there is a description of Steele's early background, which Winton suggests was only known to friends (including Manley) who had been acquainted with him in the 1690s.[35] Even more seductively Manleyan is an episode in which Steele deflowers, impregnates, and then abandons the daughter of a country priest.[36] As Winton says, all these factors seem to indicate Mrs. Manley as author, or at least a coauthor. On purely stylistic grounds, however, it is likely that if Manley was involved in this pamphlet, her participation ended with the descriptions of Steele. The rest of the pamphlet is unlike anything else we know to have been written by her.

Winton's notion of Manley acting as one of a team of writers is more convincing. Her ready access to the printing press gave her an unparalleled opportunity to collaborate with her contemporaries, or even to edit their work. There are two instances in which this may well have happened. The first is Swift's *A New Journey to Paris*. This pamphlet, published on 11 September 1711, was a fictitious account of Matthew Prior's mission to France to initiate peace negotiations. The provenance of the pamphlet would appear to be perfectly straightforward, if it were not for Swift's complaint to Stella that the last two pages of his work had been mauled by another hand. In a previous *Journal* entry he had told Stella that he had "writ all but the last page, that I dictated, and the printer writ."[37] Later on he claimed that the printer, Barber, had "got somebody to add" the offending pages to his original text, and that they "are so romantic, they spoil all the rest."[38] The final section, when it appeared, contained a description of a "comely Person, about Fifty, all in Rags, but with a Mien that shewed him to be of a good House." The gentleman begged charity from the departing Prior, who observed "something in his Behaviour like a Man of Quality and generously threw him a *Pistole*."[39] The point of the interpolation was clearly to illustrate the impoverished state of the French nobility as a result of the war. The insistence on inherent nobility, which showed itself in the "mien" of the beggar, is typically Manleyan but it is Swift's use of the word "romantic" that is crucial. Of all Swift's known acquaintances at this point, Manley is the only writer whose work could be described as "romantic."[40] While I find this argument persuasive in itself, in addition to this, the style of the final section of the pamphlet is reminiscent of Manley, particularly in the piling up of lavish phrases. For instance,

> I entertained him as well as I could, chiefly with the Praises of our Great Monarch, the Magnificence of his Court, the Number of his Attendants, the Awe and Veneration paid him by his Generals and Ministers, and the Immense Riches of his Kingdom[41]

This may be compared with a similar passage from *Memoirs of Europe*:

> Vertue . . . is oftentimes given 'em barely by Merit of their fleeting Possessions! Larger Banks of Gold! The Brilliancy of their Diamonds! And the Distinction of fading temporary Titles.[42]

Even the inclusion of Manley's favorite method of punctuation, the exclamation mark, in the penultimate paragraph of the pamphlet, seems to indicate her presence.[43] Moreover, the date of writing coincides with Manley's most active period of pamphleteering, when she was obviously working very closely with the printer, John Barber.[44] Unfortunately, we may never know if Manley did, indeed, tamper with her friend's work.

However, even if it was Manley who was the editor, Swift forgave her transgression and, as we have seen, even praised her work. The only other writer to whom Swift paid such a compliment was Dr. Arbuthnot, his co-Scriblerian.[45] By coincidence, Manley's name is also linked to Arbuthnot's most famous work, the *John Bull* series of pamphlets, which provides a further opportunity to explore the extent of Manley's involvement with her contemporaries. The *John Bull* pamphlets were one of the most memorable productions of 1712. At this time the English, their Allies, and the French were still wrangling over the termination of the War of the Spanish Succession. At home in Britain, Tory and Whig pamphleteers were battling over the pros and cons of the projected peace. The *John Bull* series was one of the most effective missiles in the paper war, turning the whole issue into a political lampoon allegorizing the war as a long drawn out lawsuit. The litigants were John Bull (the English) and Nic. Frog (the Dutch) against Lewis Baboon (the French king, Louis XIV). Major political figures appeared in suitably satiric guise, such as Humphrey Hocus (the duke of Marlborough) and Sir Roger Bold (Robert Harley, earl of Oxford).

Swift's frequent references to the series in his *Journal to Stella* indicates that the pamphlets were a topic of some interest at the dinners which Manley's friends, St. John and Granville, attended. Another member of the Tory Society of Brothers was Dr. Arbuthnot, the Royal Physician. It is now generally accepted that he was largely, if not entirely, responsible for the *John Bull* pamphlets, an ascription that is not without problems.[46] Charles Kirby-Miller, for instance, suggested that "there can be little doubt that Swift and others had a hand in them."[47] Earlier in the twentieth century Herman Teerink and Lester M. Beattie both suggested that Stella believed that Manley had been the author of the whole series but that Swift was quick to disillusion her.[48]

There is, however, strong evidence that Manley, if not the sole author, at least had a part to play in writing the pamphlets.[49]

The first two pamphlets in the series were published anonymously in early 1712. They proclaimed themselves to be "Printed from a Manuscript found in the Cabinet of the famous Sir Humphrey Polesworth." Polesworth was a deliberately invented amalgam of various contemporary figures, most obviously Sir Humphrey Mackworth, the Tory pamphleteer and fraudulent entrepreneur, perhaps Humfrey Wanley, the Earl of Oxford's librarian, and Sir Robert Polesworth, a Whig politician.[50] When the third part, *John Bull in His Senses*, was published on 16 April 1712, Sir Humphrey's manuscript acquired a notional publisher: the "Author of the *New Atalantis*."[51] It also acquired a short publisher's preface. Despite this bold ascription, the pamphlets have rarely, if ever, been seriously associated with Manley, which is curious, since hers is the only identifiable name which appears anywhere on the five numbers.

The "Author of the *New Atalantis*" also appeared on the front pages of the final two pamphlets. Although the fourth pamphlet has no preface, the fifth, *Lewis Baboon turned Honest*, contained a relatively long and entertaining one, ostensibly written by the imaginary Polesworth, but still said to be published by the author of the *New Atalantis*.[52] The only explicit clue in the text that the prefaces are by anyone other than Arbuthnot is a comment in the third pamphlet, *An Appendix to John Bull Still in His Senses*, that the Publisher will "bespeak the Assistance of his Friends and Acquaintances," indicating that Arbuthnot's friends, who probably included Manley, may now become involved in the production of the little satires.[53]

Several factors have to be considered in determining Manley's role in the *John Bull* prefaces. We cannot ignore the fact that Swift states unequivocally in his *Journal* that "a Scotch gentleman, a friend of mine," meaning Arbuthnot, wrote the texts.[54] Furthermore, Spence repeats Pope's remark that "Dr Arbuthnot was the sole writer of John Bull."[55] However, we must take account of the physical attributes of the pieces in question. The prefaces are "tacked on" to the *John Bull* dialogues. They could easily have been written separately from them, and it is undeniable that Manley's name is attached to three of them. Significantly, *John Bull's* Whig contemporaries appear to corroborate her involvement. The *Observator*, in a list of Tory writers, juxtaposes "the Author of the *New Atlantis*" with "John Bull brought to his Senses."⁵⁶ The *Observator* repeated the association in its next issue, stridently announcing that

> *John Bull* may low like a Calf and publish Sir Humphrey Polecat's Manuscripts till the nation be poison'd with the stench of 'em as well as by the Practices of such Persons as the Author of *The New Atalantis*.⁵⁷

The *Protestant Post Boy* was equally convinced:

> One who Midwife's *John Bull into his Senses*, ought not to be out of her own. This puts me in Mind of a Pamphlet which goes by that Name . . . said to be publish'd by that vertuous Gentlewoman.⁵⁸

Bower and Erickson suggest that the *Protestant Post Boy* "dismissed the ironic suggestion that the pamphlets were "Publish'd . . . by the Author of the NEW ATALANTIS,"⁵⁹ but it is not clear why it should be treated as an ironic suggestion. In 1712 Manley was a significant member of the Tory propaganda team.⁶⁰ There is absolutely no reason why a Whig journal should simply ironically dismiss "The Person who stiles herself Author of the *Atalantis*." The Marlboroughs themselves acknowledged the part she had played in disgracing the duke.⁶¹

On careful reading it is more likely that although the *Protestant Post Boy* believes the principal author to be Swift, it is equally convinced that Manley had some hand in it. The lengths to which *The Protestant Post Boy* goes in his attack on Manley make it clear that the editor felt her contribution was worth the effort. Indeed, the metaphor of "midwife" is apt, since Paula McDowell suggests that Manley saw herself as a literary "gossip," or the woman who attended at the generation, not of babies, but of political stories.⁶² One way of "midwifing" the last three *John Bulls* into the world was to provide them with a preface, a piece of textual paraphernalia often written by someone other than the author. There is therefore nothing unlikely in Manley offering prefaces for a popular publication such as *John Bull* and their being accepted. Sometimes the preface even appeared without the author's permission. Manley herself had experience of this. There was a preface in the form of a letter from "The Publisher to the Reader" fronting *Court Intrigues*, the unauthorized edition of *Letters Writen by Mrs Manley*.[63] We can be sure that Mrs. Manley did not write the preface herself, because she objected to the book's publication. It is even conceivable, therefore, given her proximity to the press, that she had the *John Bull* prefaces inserted on her own initiative. Arbuthnot was easygoing in his attitude to authorship, and was unlikely to object. If the *Protestant Post Boy's* attack is simply a generalized one on Manley, it is suspiciously well-timed. If it was a simple dismissal of Manley's involvement with this text, it could have been done it with considerable more brevity.

We can turn to other contemporary publications for further clues to her involvement in *John Bull*. One week after the appearance of the fourth pamphlet, the only one where the publisher's name appears but which carries no publisher's preface, a short portion of dialogue appeared in the *Examiner*. The dialogue, involving members of the Frog family (the Dutch), is purported to have been submitted by Sir Humphrey to the author of the *Examiner*. Sir Humphrey claims,

> The Person I have hitherto obliged with a free Access to my Cabinet and Manuscripts, and dignified by the Name of Publisher, to those several approved Pieces . . . hath, but whether thro' Negligence or Wilfulness I cannot positively say, omitted a very material Dialogue, designed for part of an Appendix lately Publish'd to the Third Part . . . The Dialogue is not of a sufficient length to be published by it self; and the fourth Part being not yet ready to be Transcribed for the Press; if you are not otherwise engaged I beg you would please to make room for it in your next Examiner.[64]

The "negligent" publisher was of course "the Author of New Atalantis." The fourth part of *John Bull* had been published only a few days before.[65] If, as the *Examiner* claims, this stray piece of text had been omitted by mistake, Manley, living over the printing shop, was in an ideal position to take on the persona of Sir Humphrey to correct the error. Equally, as we saw in a previous chapter, there is a strong likelihood that Manley had some involvement in the editing of the *Examiner* during the years after 1711, which would allow her free reign to insert anything she liked.[66] Unfortunately, there is little evidence to identify which of these later *Examiners* Manley wrote, but it is not impossible that Manley used the issue in question to correct an omission from the *John Bull* series.[67]

As always it is important to be wary of the evidence offered by internal textual clues. However, there are several in the preface to the fifth *John Bull* pamphlet that deserve some consideration. Once again, it is Manley's antipathy to Steele that is perhaps the most pertinent in ascribing the preface to her. The timing would have been right. On 10 July 1712 Richard Steele's *Spectator*, directed a long passage at

> a peevish old Gentlewoman [who] had for many years together outdone the whole Sisterhood of Gossips in Invention, quick Utterance and unprovoked Malice; . . . There is another Thing to be noted of her, which is, That as it is usual with old People, she has a livelier Memory of Things which passed when she was very young, than of late Years.[68]

Manley, who had gained fame initially through the retailing of gossip, was extremely sensitive to any hint of an insult from Steele, and conceivably regarded this as a direct attack on herself. The date of publication of the preface to the fifth *John Bull* pamphlet, 31 July 1712, would have meant that Steele's comments were fresh in her mind when she wrote it. Does it seem far-fetched to believe that she would take *The Spectator*'s comments as a personal affront? Perhaps we should remember that she had launched her attack on Steele in the preface of *Memoirs of Europe* on the far flimsier pretext that he had referred to her as one who published "detestable pieces."[69]

Spurred on by this real or imagined insult, Manley would not have missed the opportunity to ridicule Steele, and assuming that she wrote the preface, she did this in ways that she knew would be obvious to him. Most noticeably, there is Sir Humphrey's reference to "Cook-Maids, or mournful ditties of departing lovers" that has resonances of his impregnation of a *"Bright*

Cook-Maid" in the *Memoirs of Europe*.[70] This, in turn, was a direct quotation from one of Steele's own plays, *The Lying Lover*.[71] Even more pertinently, there is the phrase "Vulcan sweating at his Forge," which echoes metaphors that had originally appeared in *The Lady's Pacquet of Letters* in 1707, and their disputed republication in 1711.[72] In one of his letters contained in this collection, Steele wrote to Manley, "I see *Venus* . . . as busie in the Coals, as ever *Vulcan* was."[73] The phraseology of the preface therefore points to the period of Steele's alchemic experiments, of which Manley delighted in reminding him. There is even an early poem of Steele's which makes use of this same juxtaposition of Vulcan, Venus, and the ever present cook-maid with lines such as "She makes me love, not hate, my Food," "When Venus leaves her Vulcan's Call" and

> . . . she can impart
> That Beauty, to make all things Fine;
> Brightens the Floor with wondrous Art,
> And at her Touch, the Dishes shine.[74]

If we do not accept Manley as the author of this preface, we might regard these subtle references as Arbuthnot joking at Manley's expense, given that her antipathy to Steele was so public. The very detail in the jokes, however, means that he would have had to be very familiar not only with the intimate details of her stormy relationship with Steele, but also with her work. While this is not impossible, it is unlikely. I have examined the catalog of Arbuthnot's library, sold some time after his death (and therefore admittedly not necessarily complete). While this indicates that he had many volumes written by her friends, contemporaries, and colleagues, such as Pope, Bolingbroke, Addison, Gay, Prior, Swift, and Garth, there is no evidence that he owned any books by Manley.[75] Arbuthnot probably knew Manley, and undoubtedly knew of her, but on this basis it is unlikely that he knew her work intimately enough to make such detailed borrowings.

If we consider the echoes of Manley's style within this preface, we still come to no firm conclusion. Bower and Erickson suggest that the piece is an example of Arbuthnot "paying a cryptic compliment" to Manley, indicating a "debt to her." It is hard to see why he should pay any more of a compliment to her than to much closer friends such as Swift or Prior.[76] Yet there are ironic echoes of *Memoirs of Europe* in the preface to pamphlet five. Contemporary readers might call to mind Manley's customary description of Sunderland and Wharton as "Furious *Cethegus*!" and "precipitate *Cataline*!" In the preface these are transformed into the rhetorical question. *"Are* Cethegus *and* Cataline *turn'd so tame, that there will be no opportunity to cry about the Streets*, A Dangerous Plot?"[77]

This might mean that Manley, as the publisher and author of the *New Atalantis,* is gently ridiculing herself. Since we have no proof of Arbuthnot's reading of *Memoirs of Europe,* it is more likely that it was Manley choosing herself as a target for her own satire. In favor of this hypothesis is the unmistakable suspicion that the preface comes close to a deliberate parody of Manley's own writing. If we refer to the extravagant style of parts of *New Atalantis* and the deflationary techniques she uses in that text, it would not be out of character. It was typical of Manley to satirize herself and her own literary excesses.

For example, in *New Atalantis,* after describing in the most pathetic terms the horror of her own seduction and betrayal by her bigamous cousin, and her subsequent loss of position and reputation, she was able to dismiss this tragic story as an example of the "Fopperies of the Fair."[78] Therefore, the liberal use of rhetorical questions and the extravagant appeal to Grub Street, "thou fruitful Nursery of tow'ring Genius!" would be in keeping with a Manleyan act of self-mockery. Even more explicit is the reference to "Complaints of Ravish'd Virgins," which feature so strongly in her own fictions and in the Romances that inspired them. Indeed, the whole preface is a pantomime version of a writing style which she had outgrown, and which she had abandoned, at least for her political commentary. Regarded in this light, the preface to the fifth *John Bull* pamphlet may be understood as a celebration of the transition she had successfully made from scandalmonger to professional pamphleteer.

As always, the discussion of style as an indicator of authorship is contentious. If we are to use it in this way, we must do it with some conviction, and there must be strong parallels with other writings. And indeed, there are. There are several parts of the preface that parallel known Manleyan texts. There is for instance, Sir Humphrey's hiding away of the manuscript to be published when appropriate. This is reminiscent of Manley's *Examiner* number 51, which also refers to "a very scarce Manuscript" come across by chance in a library, which Manley has undertaken to translate because it "will not be unacceptable to the Town."[79] More explicitly, the reference to the "Historiographers of some Eastern Monarchs" brings to mind "Paulus Diaconus, *Secretary and Historiographer to* Desiderius *King of the* Lombards" featured in the preface of the popular *Memoirs of Europe*, which was still on sale.[80] Meanwhile, Sir Humphrey's direct references to his *Memoirs* and "ancient and modern *Historians*" recalls the long list of learned sources quoted by Manley in her earlier text: "Theophanes, Ammianus Marcellinus, Zozimus, Aurelius Victor, Eutropius, Cassidiorus, *and* Zonaras."[81] Indeed, did Manley include herself as the most modern of "historians"?

There are other circumstances surrounding the use of Manley's epithet which also need examination. The first consideration is the reason for alluding to her name, if she had no involvement with the text. One reason is that the original *John Bull* writers placed Mrs Manley's name on the pamphlets thinking it would help to sell more copies. As a marketing ploy, this makes very little sense. In fact, unauthorized use of the *New Atalantis* title, despite its popularity, was not as common as might be supposed.[82] More to the point, her name did not appear until the third pamphlet. If the intention in placing her name on prefaces were purely to capitalize on her popularity, it would have been far more effective to include it on the first pamphlet. Yet, without its help the first and second pamphlets were both issued and reprinted eight times within a short period.[83] Moreover, since printed reaction is one of the best ways of judging the efficacy of a piece of political propaganda, we can gauge the impact of the first two by noting that they provoked considerable Tory support and Whig invective.[84] Both clearly made an impact, so there was no need to add Manley's name when it had already established its popularity. We must conclude that the sudden inclusion of her name would not have been from a marketing and a propaganda standpoint. The most likely explanation, therefore, is that her name is there simply because she had become involved in the project by contributing the prefaces to the *John Bull* pamphlets.

The lateness of the inclusion of Manley's name may therefore be taken as evidence of her taking part in their composition. It must also be borne in mind that the inclusion of her name can hardly have been without her knowledge or her permission. In chapter 2 when discussing the *Secret History of Queen Zarah*, we noted how jealously she guarded her name, making it unlikely that she would have sanctioned the use of this valuable commodity without having had some personal involvement.

Further evidence suggests that the *John Bull* series was a joke between friends. It became sufficiently well established in the coterie for Lord Edward Harley to still be referring back to Sir Humphrey's "style" in 1720.[85] It is interesting therefore that a comment in the preface to pamphlet five may offer a textual clue to Manley's participation in this group. Bull says to Humphrey Polesworth, "Sir Humphrey, I know you are a plain Dealer," a phrase which was fresh in the spring of 1712 when Wagstaffe's weekly *Plain Dealer* referred to its inspiration as Captain Manly, from the play of the same name.[86] The two names "Manly" and "Plain Dealer" had actually been paired for some time, through Ned Ward's earlier pamphlet, entitled *The Manly Plain Dealer*. Wagstaffe was also a member of the Tory writing coterie, and he was said to be responsible for the 1712 key to the pamphlets. He is also supposed to have collaborated with Arbuthnot on the *Story of St Alban's Ghost*.[87] All this suggests that the reference to Sir Humphrey as a "plain Dealer" in the preface, and therefore a "Manly," was a deliberate clue. Manley's close association with the Tory wits makes this style of intertextual reference perfectly feasible, just as it does her participation in this most famous of their literary escapades.

From this likely ascription we move to some which are rather more dubious. There are, particularly, two further pamphlets which have entered the Manley canon.[88] They were originally ascribed to Manley by John Nichols along with several others whose provenance has since been proved wrong:

> Mrs Manley was also employed by Dr. Swift in . . . "A True Relation of the several Facts and Circumstances of the intended Riots and Tumults on Q. *Elizabeth*'s Birth-day." . . . Besides these three Tracts . . . she wrote "A Letter to the Examiner, concerning Dr. *Hare*'s Tract called 'The Barrier-Treaty Vindicated;' " "An Answer to Baron *Bothmar*'s Memorial"; and "A modest Enquiry into the Reasons of the Joy expressed by a certain Sett of People, upon the spreading a Report of her Majesty's Death;" from hints suggested Dr. *Swift*. The last-mentioned pamphlet in particular bears striking marks of the Dean's influence."[89]

I have found no further external evidence to support these claims, and certainly nothing as strong as that surrounding the prefaces to *John Bull*. Even the kind of circumstantial evidence which points to Manley's hand in *A New Journey to Paris* is missing. The nearest thing to proof of her responsibility for *The True Relation of the Tumult* appears to rest on a comment by Swift in the *Journal to Stella*. He informed his correspondent that he had "put an understrapper upon writing" the pamphlet, and it has been assumed that he is referring to Manley.[90] Interestingly enough, neither Swift's late-nineteenth-century editor, Thomas Roscoe nor an early twentieth-century editor of *The Journal to Stella*, Frederick Ryland, subscribes to this suggestion.[91] The ascription rests solely on the identification of Manley as "the understrapper" of the *Journal to Stella*. Elsewhere, in the *Journal*, Swift refers to Manley either by her name or as the author of the *Atalantis*. He never speaks of her as an "understrapper." To put her name to this text, without further evidence, is therefore unwise.

Manley's authorship of *A Modest Enquiry into the Reasons of the Joy Expressed by a Certain Sett of People upon the Spreading of a Report of her Majesty's Death* in 1714 is equally insecure. In support of Nichols's claim, Herbert Davis gives a reference to Swift's *Correspondence*, but on examination, the letter specified seems to have no bearing at all on Manley's authorship, or even on the queen. I have found no further evidence to ascribe this pamphlet to her.[92]

A more substantial publication, *The Female Tatler*, sits on the very outer fringes of political comment, if it can be called political, and has also from time to time been ascribed to Manley.⁹³ The evidence seems to rest on the fact that on the day Manley was arrested for *The New Atalantis*, the *Female Tatler* changed hands. I would suggest that this is simply not strong enough evidence, whereas Walter Graham's case for Thomas Baker is far stronger. *The Female Tatler*'s nonpartisan stance and its early indifference to Richard Steele suggest someone of a far different character to Manley as its author. Even the style of the early *Female Tatlers* is very different to Manley's; it is much too concerned with small cliques of women and not with larger issues. Moreover, Manley never targeted London citizens (and particularly not in 1709) because they had too little political significance. Until far stronger evidence is available, I would be very wary of including it in the Manley canon.

Charles Rivington also suggests that she wrote *The Representation of the Loyal Subjects of Albinia* (1712) but offers no supporting evidence.⁹⁴ Other ascriptions are even more mystifying, such as the Cambridge University Library catalogue, which describes *The Conduct of His Grace the Duke of Ormonde* (1715) as by Manley. The Huntington Library catalogue also lists Manley as the author of *A Short Memorial and Character of that Most Noble and Illustrious Princess Mary, Dutchess of Ormonde* which appeared in 1735, eleven years after her death.⁹⁵

Such eagerness to attribute publications to Manley testifies to her importance as a writer during the first age of party, even if the eagerness occasionally appears to be unjustified. However, despite the small legacy of known writings left to us, we do know that during her own lifetime she was a well-respected writer. In the next chapter we will discover how Manley's good name was slowly eroded and how over the centuries following her death her name became a byword for lewdness and scandalmongering.

9

"A Thousand Years Hence": Manley's Posthumous Reputation

Manley lived her last years as a celebrity in London and Oxfordshire. She was certainly not held in contempt. In fact, even just before her death her name could strike fear into the heart of opposition politicians. Even the rumor that she might be sharpening her pen against the new Hanoverian ministry was enough to send the Secretary of State's henchmen around. She had also achieved moderate wealth, fame, and respect from some of her leading contemporaries.

This was the situation when she died in July 1724 and, after the difficulties of her earlier career, we can only hope she enjoyed her last years. But however satisfied she may have been with public opinion in her later life, in the centuries since her death Swift's Prince of Posthumy has not been so generous. In fact, her reputation suffered a serious decline to the point where she was included in early-twentieth-century popular history texts with sensational titles like *Five Queer Women* and *Rogues and Scandals*.[1]

The first conclusion we could jump to is that her name became debased simply because she was a famous woman. After all, she was a significant member of the small but voluble band of early modern women writers who were regarded as little better than prostitutes simply because they had the temerity to write for a living:

> *Ephelia*, poor *Ephelia*, Ragged Jilt,
> And *Sapho*, Famous for her Gout and Guilt,
> Either of these, tho' both Debauch'd and Vile,
> Has answer'd me in a more Decent Style;
> Yet *Hackney Writers*; when their Verse did fail

> To get 'em Brandy, Bread and Cheese, and Ale,
> Their wants by prostitution were supply'd,
> Shew but a *Tester* you might up and ride:
> For *Punk* and *Poesie* agree so pat
> You cannot well be *this*, and not be *that*.[2]

Although dating from 1691, this poem was republished in 1709. It is not beyond the bounds of possibility that on its reappearance Manley was intended as one of its targets. Perhaps she was, but there is considerable contemporary evidence that offers an alternative view of Manley. Rather, indications are that instead of being universally regarded as an immoral hussy she commanded respect from her own colleagues. This is not to say that her unconventional lifestyle did not make her an easy target, but in the context of her political writing such denigration, as we shall see, was extremely rare. Indeed, in comparison to what was said of some of her male colleagues, the snide comments on her morality were remarkably restrained In fact, it is likely that her personal life was simply a politically convenient tool with which Whig writers could occasionally berate her, and I think it is in this light that most contemporary adverse comments should be viewed.

It was a shame that this could not last. But, as tastes changed and her politics went out of fashion and lost their currency she became much more interesting for the salacious rather than the topical aspects of her writing. It is not surprising therefore that her position as a (serial) mistress became the rod her detractors used to beat her. Would her reputation have suffered so much if she had been a conventional wife? We cannot know.

But we should leave speculations about her private life aside. Instead, as a precursor to identifying the roots of her decline it is contemporary opinion of her work which needs to be examined. Firstly, there are clear distinctions between the early misogynistic mockery she sometimes received as playwright and the more specific attacks she received as a pamphleteer. While early in her career she was lampooned for being one of the crowd of female writers for the stage, later on her gender was simply something which made attacks on her politics and her political writing easier.

Despite the antagonism that early modern women playwrights provoked, at the beginning of her career, she also inspired some lavish praise. Whether this was due to the quality of her writing or her impeccable breeding is hard to say. It may well be that it was her father's Royalism that brought her favor at this early stage. Was this the motivation for the glowing report of her dramatic works that appeared in *Lives and Characters of the English Dramatick Poets* in 1699? The book was dedicated, significantly, to Charles Caesar, the High Tory M.P. discussed in chapter 3:

> This lady has very happily distinguished herself from the rest of her sex and gives us living proof of what we might reasonably expect from womankind if they had the benefit of those artificial improvements of learning the men have, when by mere force of nature they so much excel. . . . Her father [was] a Gentleman of a double Merit, both in the Gown, and the Sword . . . the Republick of Learning ow'd much to his Wit and Judgment, in those Books which he was pleas'd to publish. . . . And well might our *Delarivier* prove a Muse, being begot by such a Father.[3]

Sad to say, not all critics were such fans of her father, and as a playwright Manley inevitably suffered as much as any other woman of her day. We can judge the level of the scorn with which Manley, along with other female colleagues, was sometimes viewed from a piece published in 1704, a year before the publication of her first known political text:

> The *Literati* having, some few Months since, admitted *Orinda*, Mrs *Behn*, Mrs *Manley*, and several other Poetesses, into *Parnassus*, contrary to their Ancient customs; It was observ'd that the *Virtuosi* were more assiduous at the Excises than formerly; and being Inspir'd by the Beauty of these Ladies, then by the *Muses*, made such Excellent Performances in Poetry, that even *Apollo* wonder'd at 'em: But it was not long, 'ere his *Majesty* smelt a Rat; wherefore he gave orders no more Ladies should be admitted, and that these should be Banish'd out of *Parnassus*. For he had found, that women's best Poetry consisted in their Needle and Distaff; and foresaw, that the Learned Exercises, which the *Virtuosi* and these Ladies perform'd together, would end like the Playing of Dogs, in getting upon one another's Backs.[4]

Even there, it is possible to see a political angle. All three of the poetesses were noted Royalists or Tories, although Manley was the only one still alive in 1704. It is, however, likely that Manley, even though she had long neglected stage writing, was included because she was an easy target. There was no avoiding male disapproval of women playwrights. She herself recognized the antipathy toward female authorship. She even used it to explain the failure of her unsuccessful *Lost Lover*: "I am satisfied the bare Name of being a Woman's Play damn'd it beyond its own want of Merit."[5] If she were honest, however, she might admit that she was being ingenuous: the success of her other plays suggest that the failure of the *Lost Lover* owed more to its poor quality than the sex of its author.

When the hazards inherent in the activities of a late-seventeenth-century female playwright are compared with reactions to an early-eighteenth-century woman pamphleteer, there is a marked difference. Obviously, her participation in the world of propaganda attracted derision from her political opponents, but it was not so much her gender as the (male) literary company she kept that attracted opprobrium. Accounts of her, as we shall see, were often swayed not by simple misogyny, but carefully crafted political tit-for-tat. There were private references to her lapsed virtue. One cleric, for instance was shocked at her unconventional lifestyle (although his disapproval did not stop him eagerly seeking the key to the book): "The author of *The New Atalantis* is Mrs. Manley that has been a playwright of an ordinary rank and hardly ever talked of. She has been what the wicked world call a Town-lady."[6] Comments like this rarely seem to have found their way into print. They certainly did not hamper sales.

The fact that a private correspondent felt able to refer to Manley's irregular past makes it all the more surprising that her enemies did not make more of it, particularly if we compare comments on Manley with *ad hominem* assaults on other writers. L. S. Horsley's very useful account of the topic illustrates this point extremely well. He demonstrates that late Stuart journalists often constructed scandalous public personae for their journalistic opponents in order to lessen their credibility. His research provides a standard by which to judge the attempts to ruin the reputation of Manley the pamphleteer:

When details of journalists' private lives were incorporated into these generalized attacks, their enemies were removing the encounter from the level of political dispute and defaming the man behind the journal . . . Although the *invented* details of a private history were often as stereotyped as a political epithet, they were usually joined to known or at least plausible incidents in the life of their victim and served not merely to group him with a politically dangerous faction but to lower him, morally and intellectually, in the estimation of any who read the attack.[7]

Horsley gives examples of this: Tutchin was accused of holding "Fornication but a Pastime, and Adultery a sport" while Defoe was said to be engaged in the "engendering and Procreation Trade" with his landlady.[8]

These two examples demonstrate the way in which accusations of immorality were used to discredit male journalists. Combining Manley's real life story with the scandalous nature of her most famous works should have made her an easy target. After all, Manley's openness about her marriage, desertion, and her lovers, could have provided a perfect platform for the kind of lewd accusations leveled against male contemporaries. Moreover, she occupied a position at the heart of the pamphlet wars of the Oxford ministry. Despite this, contemporary comments about Manley's personal life were markedly circumspect.

When commenting on her participation in the *Examiner*, for instance, we have already noted that Abel Boyer described her as a "poor Whore in Petticoats and tawdry Ribbons."[9] Clearly Boyer's phrase is a slur on Manley's moral integrity, but it is hardly excessive compared to the comments quoted above on Tutchin. We find another example of this caution when the *John Bull* pamphlet acquired the author of *New Atalantis* as its "publisher."[10] The popularity and high-profile nature of *John Bull* ensured that Whig journalists went on the defensive very quickly. Given that Manley was at this time openly living with the major Tory printer, her opponents were remarkably careful in using her position as his mistress against her, though they made veiled hints as to her status. The *Observator*, as we have seen, suggested that "the nation be poison'd with the stench of . . . the Practices of such Persons as the Author of *The New Atalantis*." Why was he being so disappointingly coy as to what those practices were?[11]

The comments from the Whig *Protestant Post-Boy* were a little more satisfying. The periodical prefaces its attack on Manley with a salacious story of lewd nuns, one of whom holds assignations with a cavalier. Her equally lewd Mother Superior is caught *in flagrante* with a young friar. The story ends in a fine example of hypocrisy with the nun and the Lady Abbess returning to bed with their respective lovers. But *The Protestant Post Boy*, despite the easy entry into an explicit attack on Manley's loose morals, is still surprisingly cautious in his approach:

> The Person who stiles herself Author of the *Atalantis*, may, if she thinks fitting, take the Application to herself, and consider that the Lady *Abbess* and she are much of the same Complection. Since they both equally rail at, and condemn what their selves are guilty of, and it's as proper for the one to vent Invectives against Incontinence, as for the other to read Lectures against Human Frailties. What a pity 'tis, methinks, she does not look into herself a little, and from that Inspection rest assur'd, that one who Midwife's *John Bull into his Senses*, ought not to be out of her own. This puts me in Mind of a Pamphlet . . . said to be publish'd by that vertuous Gentlewoman.[12]

The term "vertuous" is clearly intended ironically in this instance, despite the *Protestant Post Boy*'s coyness about Manley's actual misdemeanors. The lack of interest in capitalizing on them indicates that the prime motivation for all these attacks on Manley are political. They are not written by journalists who care in any way about her moral standing or her position as a "fallen" woman. The journalists' sole purpose is to discredit her position as spokesperson for the Tory ministry. It is simply convenient that she is a woman.

Even those who had a personal axe to grind seem to have exercised self-control. There were few people who knew Manley better than the editor of the *Tatler* or who had more reason to attack her. As the target for her most vicious personal vendetta, Richard Steele could have been forgiven for being more combative in his dealings with Manley. Even Steele, although he is hardly kind, steers clear of her lifestyle and generally confines himself to commenting on her pretentiousness. In *Tatler* number 6, for instance, he makes a pointed remark echoing the *Session of the Poets*:

> I am just come from visiting *Sappho*, a Fine Lady, who writes Verses, sings, dances, and can say and do whatever she please, without the Imputation of any thing that can injure her Character; for she is so well known to have no Passion but Self-love; or Folly but Affectation; that now upon any Occasion, they only cry *'Tis her Way*, and, *That's so like her*.[13]

But was this Manley? Donald Bond discusses Nichols's suggestion that Sappho may represent Manley or Eliza Haywood or Elizabeth Thomas.[14] Since Haywood was only sixteen years old at this time and Elizabeth Thomas was not particularly well-known, Manley is the most likely target. Steele certainly knew her well. His description of her inflated sense of her own importance recalls the portrait of her in *The Female Wits*. There she is "a poetess that admires her own works, and a great lover of flattery" who pretends to a knowledge of Aristotle (in translation) and is endlessly quoting other authors.[15] Steele's motivation may have been a preemptive strike. In 1709 Manley and Steele shared a publisher, John Morphew. Had he seen her attack on him in *New Atalantis* as Monsieur Le Ingrate, a "Man, whose Principles are corrupted by Hypocrisie and Covetousness"?[16] It may even have been a reaction to Manley as the probable author of *An Heroick Essay*.

Manley's (alleged) unattractive pretentiousness was something which Steele returned to in *Tatler* number 40, when Sappho "began to show her Reading" by expounding on the relative merits of Suckling and Milton.[17] With her description of him in *New Atalantis* now in print, and selling like hotcakes, Steele had every right to be resentful. His description of her as Epicene in *Tatler* number 63 is famous:

> Writer of Memoirs from the Mediterranean, who, by the Help of some artificial Poisons convey'd by Smells, has within these few weeks brought many Persons of both Sexes to an untimely Fate.[18]

It was only to be expected, given the vitriolic way in which Manley endlessly attacked Steele over the next few years, that his gentlemanly reserve eventually snapped. Finally, in 1713 in the *Guardian* he complained that he had been "credibly" reported to have "formerly lain with the Examiner" and that,

> As to the exasperated mistress, the Examiner demands in her behalf, a "reparation for offended innocence." This is pleasant language, when spoken of this person . . . I declare it was a false report, which was spread concerning me and a lady, sometimes reputed the author of the Examiner; and I can now make her no reparation, but in begging her pardon, that I never lay with her.[19]

Even though Steele denied the charge, he talks ironically of her "offended innocence." There is no doubt that Steele's animosity to Manley was in part justified retaliation tempered by party invective. In terms of its reflection on Manley's sexual morality, it is equivocal. Perhaps Steele was wary that Manley still had some very powerful friends.

Unfortunately for Manley, in the next year, her powerful friends were gone. It is essential to remember that anything written about Manley after 1714 was after the fall of the Oxford ministry. It was written in the context of Whig ascendancy and Tory party defeat. The political atmosphere was very different from those euphoric days of only four years earlier when Harley had assumed control.

Significantly for Manley's posthumous reputation, the Whigs remained in power for much of the rest of the eighteenth century. As I have suggested, following their return to office Manley's position was reversed, and she instantly became an easy prime target. Insults were inevitable from all the people who had envied her fame and position. John Oldmixon, the coeditor of The Medley, produced his own version of *New Atalantis*, calling it *The Court of Atalantis*. He generously gave Manley a starring role, introducing her twice into the text. If we agree with Horsley's suggestion that "the *invented* details . . . were usually joined to known or at least plausible incidents in the life of their victim" we can identify the strategy behind Oldmixon's fashioning of a fictional narrative incorporating known details of Manley's life.

Oldmixon's story of Delia and an unscrupulous lover called Clodius is reminiscent of the episodes in *New Atalantis*. It centers on a false marriage, which of course features in Manley's own history. In fact, Oldmixon's story is little more than a simple refashioning of Manley's life story. But it is deliberately cruel: "*DELIA* was Young, but not very Handsome. She was Fat, and had Red Hair.... *Delia's* Father was a *Mechanick*, and her Breeding answerable to her Birth."[20] The physical description of the heroine is remarkably close to what we know of her (although she describes her own hair as "Ash-colour").[21] The insistence that Delia is lowborn is clearly intended as an ironic comment on Manley's endless insistence on her own good birth, as evidenced in both *New Atalantis* and *Rivella*.[22] As Oldmixon's text progresses, his comments on Manley change from unflattering to downright malicious, and unequivocally politically motivated.

> A She Poet made her Fulsome Addresses to the Generous *Otho*, who not knowing how to distinguish Flattery from Praise, was wonderfully delighted with her Fustian Compliments, and employ'd his Domestick to pay her his Acknowledgements not only in her own kind, but also in Money. The Man not considering his own Character, and hers, takes that Infamous Office upon him, and gives the Lewdest Wretch in the Island a Certificate of her Virtue and Honour, which she exposes on all Occasions; and amidst her Lewdness and Infamy is the greatest Fury of a Zealot that it ever produc'd. Thus was the unhappy *Otho* surrounded by Persons of both Sexes, who took as little Care of his Reputation as of their own.[23]

Otho is most likely intended to be the High Tory duke of Beaufort, the dedicatee of *New Atalantis*, with his "Domestick" representing Thomas Yalden, the Grand Druid to whom Manley, as Delia, makes her plea in her own text.[24] Following Horsley's discussion of *ad hominem* satire, it is most likely that in this instance Oldmixon has no particular interest in Manley's actual history, or even her colorful sex life. He gives no explicit details of her "Lewdness" or "Infamy." The epithets are simply the best method of discrediting her and her political allies, particularly the High Tory Jacobite, Beaufort.

It is notable, however, that for several years Manley's good reputation was still too strong to be entirely destroyed. Even when her old enemy Sunderland was leading a Whig ministry, her friends did not quite desert her. *The Poetical Register* of 1719, a similar book to *The Lives and Characters of the English Poets*, affords an illuminating comparison to Oldmixon's description. By now, we might imagine that Manley would have suffered considerable loss of dignity. But in the *Register* this is not the case. The book is dedicated to Manley's old friend, George Granville, now Lord Lansdowne. Maybe it was his inclusion as dedicatee for this volume that raised Manley's prestige, and made the author bold enough to praise her as a High Tory icon. His presence certainly explains the panegyric to Manley as "the *Atalantic* Lady, being deservedly esteem'd for her Affability, Wit and Loyalty . . . In all the Writings of Mrs. *Manley* there appears a happy Sprightliness, and an easy Turn."[25]

Whig sensibilities also seem to have been ignored a few years later, when the *Historical Register* reported Manley's death. It declared her to have been "A person of polite genius and uncommon capacity which made her writings naturally delicate and easy and her conversation agreeably entertaining."[26] Nor was Manley's literary talent denied, when she appeared briefly as a gratifyingly superior writer to Behn in the dedicatory verses to a collected edition of Eliza Haywood's works in 1725. There, while Haywood is naturally judged to be superior to all others, we are still urged to read "Pathetick *Behn* or *Manley*'s greater Name."[27]

Despite this compliment, it is true to say that the literary climate slowly changed as the eighteenth century progressed. As Jocelyn Medoff argues, "creating or reinforcing the image of the respectable woman author meant not only emphasising the irreproachable nature of her behaviour and her work, but representing her as a woman who never actively sought fame."[28] Manley, with her well-publicized irregular private life and her active publishing record, did not fit this bill. It would therefore be no surprise if, by the midpoint of the eighteenth century, Manley, the antithesis of the "respectable woman female author," had seen her reputation sink without trace.

And yet, in 1741 the death of her lover, John Barber, gave rise to possibly the two most flattering compliments she ever enjoyed. The descriptions form part of two biographies of Barber, which both appeared in 1741. One of them, the ironically named *Impartial History of Mr. John Barber*, was published by Curll. His text includes the following laudatory portrait:

> Mrs *Manley* was a Gentlewoman both by Birth and Education. All who had the Happiness of her Conversation, were soon convinced how free she was from the general vain Frailties of her

Sex; what a Nobleness and Generosity of Temper she was possessed of; how distant her Views from the least Appearance of Self-Interest, or mean Design; how often have I heard her compassionately regretting the Miseries of Mankind, but never her Own, unless they prevented her Benevolence to the Afflicted!

Never was she Vindictive against the most inveterate Enemy. The innate Softness of her Soul rendered her Deportment equally obliging to all Beholders; never did she Resent but with the strictest Justice; and, with equal Humanity, forgave the Offender.[29]

This encomium is, in fact, almost word for word a direct quotation from the preface to the 1725 edition of *Letters Written by Mrs. Manley*, so while Curll was as usual plagiarizing, it is significant that he felt no need to temper the praise.[30]

The author of *The Life and Character of Mr. John Barber* was equally unafraid to pour praise upon the woman who had supported Walpole's enemies so unequivocally. It contains a different but equally positive account of Manley:

> A Lady of distinguished Merit; whose Works will be prized, whilst Eloquence, Wit and good Sense are in Esteem among Mankind . . . It seems almost needless to mention the Lady's Name; not one of the Fair Sex being at that Time so much in Vogue for these, as Mrs. MANLEY, to whom we are indebted for the *Atalantis*; *Lucius*, first Christian King of *Britain*, and a Miscellany, not yet collected, of valuable Pieces in Verse and Prose.[31]

Several pages later, the author returns to Manley, first stressing the propriety of her professional presence in Barber's house,[32] and then praising her business acumen in selling the author's benefit rights for *Lucius* for an appropriate sum:

> She knew it was a good [play, and] was resolved that if there was any Defect upon that Score [its performance], they [should] bear all the Damage, who ought to bear all the Blame.
>
> But 'twas found she judged right upon this Occasion; and, to be just to her Memory, we might add, that she was seldom or never known to do otherwise upon any Occasion.[33]

The sum total of the evidence so far is that praise for Manley easily outweighed the insults from her earliest days as a writer.

Even by the middle of the eighteenth century it seems, there was a substantial body of opinion that clung to the predominantly favorable impression that she had left on her death. We cannot escape politics even here. It is likely that the flattering descriptions of her in 1741 had something to do with her association with John Barber, who had been an active campaigner against Walpole.[34] Barber died in the year in which the "literary forces aligned against Walpole had a cohesiveness and semblance of organization in some contrast to the occasional nature" of their earlier efforts.[35]

It was also the year that the Tories had entertained hopes of regaining some of their power in the General Election. The literary men had obviously taken their lead from the opposition politicians who, despite a Whig victory in the Election, forced Walpole to resign in February 1742. It was probably no coincidence, therefore, that 1741 also saw the last eighteenth-century edition of that defiantly Tory text, *New Atalantis*.[36]

Despite this brief revival, Manley's reputation sank precipitously from the 1750s onward. Upon examination of the evidence it becomes apparent that, along with the changing status of women writers in general, the seeds of Manley's decline lie with her enemies and their followers, particularly Catharine Cockburn (née Trotter) and Richard Steele.

Manley, as we discussed in chapter 4, was particularly vindictive toward Catherine Cockburn, despite the fact that Cockburn seems to have lived an exemplary life.[37] They had once enjoyed a close friendship, although in her youth Cockburn had been warned against spending too much time with Manley.[38] Probably as a result of their cooling friendship, but also because Cockburn was associated with the Marlboroughs, Manley took pains to traduce her, even accusing her of being a early mistress of the duke.[39] She also claimed that Cockburn had once been the mistress of her own lover John Tilly.[40] There is no external evidence for these assertions, but in one of her most unpleasant assaults on anyone's character, Manley described Cockburn as "the diversion of as many of the Town as found her to their Taste, and would purchase: Yet she still assum'd an Air of *Virtue pretended*."[41] Given the disagreeable nature of these comments, it was inevitable that Cockburn's biographer, Thomas Birch, should take exception to this defamation of his subject's character. He lashed out at Manley:

> [Cockburn's good character] could not secure her from the malignity of a writer of her own sex . . . But such a pen as Mrs *Manley's* can injure no reputation but her own; and the occasion of her resentment does honour to Mrs *Cockburn*, as the only provocation to it was the withdrawing of herself from the slight acquaintance, which she once had with Mrs *Manley*, on account of the licentiousness both of her writings and her conduct.[42]

There are more than likely certain undertones of factional feeling in this description of the Whig Cockburn's association with the Tory Manley. It is significant for Manley's posterity, however, that the connection between Manley's writing and her personal life is made so unequivocally. The attack recalls the atmosphere of 1696 when the *Female Wits* had been produced.[43] But in those early days, Manley had a number of political heavyweights to come to her rescue. When, fifty years later, her personal and professional personae became confused, she could no longer defend herself. She had been dead for many years, as had most of the Tories who would have come to her defense. From this period on, and without any reaction from the Tory press, for whom she was now largely irrelevant, Manley's standing was assailed regularly, even if at times mitigating circumstances for her moral failings were allowed. For instance, in 1753 Theophilius Cibber showed some sympathy. Having detailed the whole sorry story of Manley's seduction by her cousin, he regretted, "What pity is it, that an unfortunate, as well as a false step, should damn a woman's fame."[44] However, he also allowed that Manley was a

> lady born with high powers from nature, which were afterwards cultivated by enjoying the brightest conversation, the early part of her life was unfortunate, she fell a sacrifice to a seducer, who laid the foundation for those errors she afterwards committed, and of those sufferings she underwent.

Alas, despite her talent her virtue was "nodding, and she was ready to fall into the arms of any gallant, like mellow fruit, without much trouble in the gathering."[45] Despite, or possibly because of, Cibber's mitigations, Manley's reputation did not survive long intact. In 1754 John Duncombe published his *Feminiad* extolling the virtues of female writers, while deploring a selected few, including Manley:

> The modest Muse a veil with pity throws
> O'er Vice's friends and Virtue's female foes;
> Abash'd she views the bold unblushing mien
> Of modern* Manley; Centlivre, and Behn;
> And grieves to see One nobly born disgrace
> Her modest sex, and her illustrious race.
> * The first of these wrote the scandalous memoirs call'd Atalantis.[46]

It is interesting that Duncombe felt the need to remind readers of Manley's pedigree and the "scandalous" *Atalantis*. While the plays of Centlivre and Behn were still being produced, the footnote makes it obvious that Manley's *Atalantis* had already been forgotten, despite its reissue in the previous decade. In addition, one cannot help feeling that she has been particularly singled out as having somehow betrayed her gentle origins, while Behn and Centlivre, with their less distinguished pedigree, had little family dignity to maintain.

Taking John Duncombe and Thomas Birch together it is evident that by midcentury, there had been a marked shift in the public perception of Manley's *oeuvre*. The ephemeral nature of her political journalism caused it to be largely forgotten, and likewise the remote political context of her *romans à clef* rendered them obscure. There was therefore a concomitant loss of interest in the actual contents of her writing. She may well have subsided into harmless obscurity if it had not been for John Nichols, the publisher and antiquarian who reprinted Richard Steele's periodicals and collected and published his correspondence. Just as in the case of Birch and Cockburn, Manley's reputation suffered further as a result of an editorial determination to defend a biographical subject against detractors. Nichols, unlike Birch, whose dismissal of Manley is relatively discreet, was determined that Manley's name would be as adversely affected as Steele's would be elevated. We can see this in a comparison of Nichols's two descriptions of Manley. The first one is taken from his 1779 supplement to Swift's works, before he turned his attention to Steele:

> Mrs *De La Riviere Manley*, daughter of Sir *Roger Manley*, a zealous Royalist . . . was early in life cheated into marriage with a near relation, of her own name, who had at the same time a former wife living. Deserted by her husband, she was patronized by the duchess of *Cleveland*; . . . but the duchess, being of a fickle temper, grew tired of Mrs Manley in six months, and discharged her on pretence that she intrigued with her son. Retiring into solitude, she wrote her first Tragedy; . . . she received unbounded incense from the witty and the gay. . . . In her retired hours she wrote "The Atalantis," for which, she having made free in it with several distinguished characters, her printer was apprehended . . . Mrs. Manley, unwilling an innocent person should suffer, presented herself before the court of the queen's bench as the author.. . . . On the change of the ministry, she lived in reputation and gaiety. . . . "Lucius" a well-received tragedy, was written by her . . . It was dedicated to Sir *Richard Steele*, whom she had abused in her "Atalantis," but who was then on such friendly terms with her, that he wrote the prologue to this play, as Mr *Prior* did the epilogue. While she was employed in defence of the ministry, she connected herself with Mr Barber the *printer*, and in his house she died, *July* 11, 1742 [sic].[47]

This mild description of Manley bears little resemblance to Nichols's vituperative comments a decade later. By this time Nichols had taken on the editorship of Richard Steele's letters, and in order to demonstrate that Steele was not the monster Manley had portrayed him to be, it was important to show that Manley, his most vociferous detractor, was someone who was criminally deceitful. As a result of this necessity, Nichols's description of Manley expanded dramatically:

> Upon the whole Mrs Manley's conduct in this affair [a fraud case] shews her to have been a base and wicked woman, capable of suborning perjury and forgery for gain. . . . In the latter part of Queen Anne's reign she was in high favour with the Tories, as a party-writer, and was noticed by Dr Swift, whom she assisted in *Examiner*. Whether he knew her real character is perhaps uncertain. . . . She must have been fortunate if her baseness was not known; if it was, Dr. Swift's friends at least are not much credited by their connexions with her.[48]

There is now no mention of Manley's writing apart from her role as an "assistant" to Swift. Her work as a pamphleteer has simply disappeared behind her persona of a "base and wicked woman, capable of suborning perjury and forgery for gain."[49] Nichols's image of Manley subsequently prevailed, and the result was that her nineteenth-century image was that of a scarlet woman, as wicked as the scoundrels and whores she describes in her scandal fiction. More importantly for Manley's later reputation, it could only help fuel later ages' description of her as "a woman of no character."[50] It is clear why one Victorian contributor to *Notes and Queries* described her as a "demi-rep."[51] Nineteenth-century comments about Manley, even when they are not actively hostile, often seem far more interested in her colorful love life than her writing. For instance Dr. Doran, commentating on the English stage wrote:

> Mrs Manley, the poor daughter of an old royalist had some reason to depict human nature as bad, in man and woman. The young orphan trusted herself to the guardianship of a seductive kinsman, who married her when he had a wife living . . . Mrs. Manley survived until 1724. When not under the "protection" of a friend, or in decent mourning for the lovers who died mad for her, she was engaged in composing the "Memoirs of the New Atalantis"—a satire against the Whig ministry.[52]

Once again it is Manley's life story that has taken precedence over her writing, even though Doran found it in himself to display such a laudable tolerance of Manley's predicament as a young abandoned female. Even if he had not, we could have acknowledged that he was merely writing out of the accepted mores of his period; a sexually promiscuous woman was, after all, hardly someone to be elevated as a worthy role model for other females. We can perhaps appreciate the reasons behind these judgmental attitudes so that right up until the more recent recovery and re-assessment of early-modern women writers, scholars have labelled Manley as reprehensible both in her writings and her life.

We should, however, blame Nichols for some of the most damning twentieth-century accounts of Manley, particularly from partisan supporters of her enemies. There is, for instance, this extraordinarily colorful piece from a more recent book on Steele. In contrast to the poet's "feeling heart, [and] his sentimental wit and harmless peccadilloes"[53] we are presented with the following portrait of Manley:

> She herself—ever since the penny-poor summer of 1701—had been an unremitting Steele-Watcher. She resented his minor triumphs, professional and marital. Forced by financial need to move from one man's bed to another, she would do violence to a one-time intimate who now flaunted his connubiality. Her personal prejudices, however, were seldom divorced from the political. As a consistent Tory she sneered at Steele's consistent Whiggism, particularly since his party loyalties, unlike hers, paid off in conviviality and employment. He was, she knew, a Kit-Kat; as Gazetteer he earned £300 a year less a tax of £45, surely enough "to [be] well dress'd in agreeable Company." He had respectability while she—even to the sympathetic Swift—remained a woman of that "sort" . . . Anger and hurt—always controlled—animated Mrs Manley's portrait of Steele. Through the piling up of details, each verifiable and each given a slight pejorative twist, she planned to damn him beyond the reach of human hope or, at least, to render him useless to the Whigs . . . What she succeeded in doing in May 1709 was to set a pattern for anti-Steele diatribe, a *vituperio hominis*, that reached a scatological climax in 1713–14.[54]

This somewhat overwrought picture of Manley is by no means unique. Willard Connelly describes her in a similar way:

> Wits thought she might become a successor to Aphra Behn, at which encouragement de la Riviere set up a salon; but instead of more plays coming from her quill more men crowded into her house, "which in the end," as one daring commentator puts it, "proved fatal to her virtue." Passing from one lover to another, Mary [sic] noted down for possible future utility any stray political items or bits of scandal confided to her, and was not deaf, it seems, to gossip which touched her own character.[55]

Ironically, further damage to Manley's literary reputation has undoubtedly been sustained through her close association with Swift. Her place in the propaganda canon has been hidden behind the shadow of his genius. Some Swift critics have even found it hard to believe that he was not responsible for significant portions of her work. The rationale behind this is Swift's acknowledged position as Harley's propaganda *chef d'équipe*, so that as we have already seen, some of her pamphlets are often partially ascribed to Swift (even when they are, at most, merely mentioned in the *Journal to Stella*) and included in collections of Swift's work.[56] A modern example of the justification behind this is given by Harold Williams:

> [Manley's pamphlet] was entitled *A Learned Comment upon Dr Hare's Excellent Sermon & c.*: and Swift had some part in it. In the *Journal [to Stella]* on November 3, 1711, he says that it was written by Mrs Manley—"only hints sent to the printer from Presto [Swift] to give to her." There is no reason to doubt Swift's account; the paper is therefore included . . . as a work prompted and partly written by him.[57]

Williams continues highly speculatively about the percentage of the pamphlet which *might* have been written by Swift.

From these brief examples we can see how Manley's efforts have until recently been consistently downgraded. While no critic would deny that she produced a significant amount of work for the Harley ministry, there is a reluctance to concede that she was anything more than an "understrapper," albeit a talented one, to Swift. She has therefore too often been relegated to the role of Swift's assistant, rather than acknowledged as an independent writer.[58] Even Gwendolyn Needham, who is often credited with first acknowledging Manley's importance as a political writer, is unwilling to go further than suggesting that Manley should "not be placed in exactly the same category as [other] 'understrappers.'" She too fights shy of challenging the Swiftian lobby, referring to the "harmony between her and her chief, Jonathan Swift." Rather than allowing that Manley's style and scope would inevitably mature with experience and that her writing would become more confident as senior politicians increased their trust in her abilities, Needham suggests that

> Mrs Manley undoubtedly learned much from working with Swift. Her writings reveal a growing command of exposition and argument; her style, particularly deplorable in the hasty volumes of the *New Atalantis*, improves in restraint and coherence.[59]

One unfortunate outcome of critics' reluctance to detach Manley from Swift is that the Dean's supporters have commonly been less than generous to Manley's qualities as a writer. David Woolley, for instance, has upheld Thackeray's estimate of Manley's work as "tawdry and declamatory."[60] Irvin Ehrenpreis describes her as "the hack who also served as mistress to the printer John Barber";[61] Michael Foot regards her as the "notorious author of *New Atalantis*";[62] while J. A. Downie refers to the category of "scribblers of the kidney of Delariviere Manley."[63]

It is not only literary critics and Swift scholars who have had a hand in lowering Mrs. Manley's standing as a writer. She has also suffered at the hands of historians who, given her historical insignificance, have featured her surprisingly often in accounts of the period. Generally, of course, they have taken exception to her rough treatment of her own contemporaries. Trevelyan described her a "professional libeller," dismissing *New Atalantis* as "a book of the lowest order."[64] Winston Churchill, in defense of his illustrious ancestor, the Duke of Marlborough, went further than simply labelling her "a woman of disreputable character"; he regretted that she "cannot be swept back into the cesspool from which she should never have crawled."[65]

Given the evidence of the respect that she commanded during her own day, we must argue that it is not only time to revise these opinions, but also to interrogate the conclusions which some modern scholars have drawn from them. Indeed, we must now question the validity of Carole Fabricant's suggestion that

> Critical reactions to Delariviere Manley, both in her own lifetime and in later generations, point to deep-seated commingling: of male with female . . . , of aristocracy with lower class, of neo-classical standards with those of the marketplace . . . Manley was, and continues to be, transformed into the contemptible Other that serves by contrast to shore up a culturally sanctioned Augustan identity and define the "true" Augustan moral and literary values.[66]

The evidence presented in this study also leads us to query Katharine Rogers's view that Manley suffered from a lack of prestige common to other female writers because "unfortunately, contemporaries were less impressed by their professionalism than by the immodesty of their works and the unchastity of their lives."[67] In Manley's case, as we have seen, many of her contemporaries were profoundly impressed by her professionalism, and hardly interested in her sex life. We should also therefore query Rabb's comment that she was "perceived as a 'Great Warning' by many of her contemporaries."[68] On the contrary, it could be argued that she was held up as an example to other women, since, as we have seen, her contemporaries considered her free "from the general vain Frailties of her Sex."[69]

Admittedly it could not have been helpful that Manley described herself as "the only Person of her Sex that knows how to *Live*." One could have suggested that she modify her sensational self-description: "in relation to Love, since she has so peculiar a Genius for, and has made such noble Discoveries in that Passion that it would have a *Fault in her, not to have been Faulty*."[70]

But, understandably, a colorful, gossiping woman-about-town, seduced by her bigamous cousin and then imprisoned for seditious libel, makes excellent copy. What modern tabloid could have resisted her unconventional lifestyle and her willingness to share so much of it with her readers? Unfortunately, for more scholarly writers it has meant, as Rabb has commented, that "Curiosity about Manley's life has far exceeded criticism of her work, as if her bigamous marriage, pregnancy, abandonment, and later affairs could 'explain' her work sufficiently."[71]

However, as I have argued, critics' voyeuristic interest in her personal affairs should not cloud the issue of Manley's work and standing during her own lifetime. Even among those scholars who regard the fascination with her morality as irrelevant, the perception of her is as a woman whom Swift "commissioned [to] write at least three political pamphlets," turning "over to her the editorship of the *Examiner*."[72]

The problem has been to disentangle Manley and her work from the diverse interests of those who have focused on her over the last three centuries. To separate the rumor from the writing, I have endeavored to look at her work in the political context within which it was written. I have tried, through an examination of the work and contemporary reactions to it, to peel off the layers of misconception which have accrued over the years. Manley complained feelingly "Why is it in your [men's] power, after accumulated Crimes, to regain Opinion when ours, tho' oftentimes guilty, but in appearance, are irretrievably lost?"[73]

She is usually taken to mean women in general, but perhaps she also meant female propagandists in particular.[74]

Appendix I

For a discussion of reasons for thinking that the following poem may be by Delarivier Manley, see above, pp. 231–38.

AN HEROICK ESSAY UPON THE UNEQUAL'D VICTORY
OBTAIN'D BY MAJOR-GENERAL WEBB
OVER THE COUNT DE LA MOTTE AT WYNENDALE

London: Printed and Sold by A. Baldwin in Warwick-Lane 1709.[1]

Delia, who once of Courts and Empires sung,
The Lofty Muse subdu'd to Rural Song,
Where Silver *Medway* glides the Shades along;
Near her lone Cott, too low for Storms to move,
5 (For Storms fly o'er and break on those above)
Exil'd, Forlorn, full of her Fate she lay;
And oft regretted a more prosp'rous Day:
When sudden Glory darts around the Place,
The breaking Clouds descending fill the Space;
10 On which the Queen of Love, conspicuous shone,
The Graces wait about the dazling Throne:
Her Length of flowing Hair adorn'd the Ground,
Ambrosial Odours ting'd the Air around:
Diffusive Sweetness fills the *Zephyr's* Breez
15 The catching Sweetness moves the leafy Trees.
Her features soft, as are young Lovers Hearts;
Her *Brillant* Eyes dispersing *Brillant* Darts.
The genuine Fire of *Love* her Looks inform'd,
Thus on her *Mars* she glows, so warming and so warm'd.

20 *DELIA* with pleasing Awe beheld the Sight,
Succeeding Transport swell'd the new Delight;
For thus to her the Goddess—"Nymph, arise;
Such Rustick Objects you must now despise;
Call'd to a Nobler Scene, new-strike the Lyre,

25　WEBB's[2] Theme can ev'n Inanimates inspire:
　　A Warrior lovely, as the God who charms,
　　With strenuous Force, our Beauty to his Arms:

　　As *Eugene*[3] Brave, as *Marlbro'*[4] Fortunate;
　　Whose sole Right Arm new-doom'd the Book of Fate:
30　It seem'd resolv'd the *Gallick King*[5] should stand,
　　Nor Frontier *Lisle* be wrested from his Hand;
　　The Leaguer Princes urge the Siege in vain,
　　And with united Fire the Battery sustain:
　　Never so dreadful show'd the Wrath of *Jove*,
35　Nor could the War of Heaven more mortal prove.
　　Boufflers,[6] *La Motte*,[7] their King's last Stake maintain
　　With them the Flower of all the Troops remain;
　　What were preserv'd from *Blenheim's*[8] fatal Day,
　　What *Hochstet* and th'impetuous *Rhine* not swept away:
40　Whose Current stopt, and Colour lost, in *Gallick* Blood,
　　Show'd stagnate Crimson, not the native Flood:
　　These brave Remains sustain the falling Weight,
　　And *Lewis* sinks not, whilst they prop his Fate.
　　Boufflers, like *Hector*, guards this other *Troy*,
45　Pays Fire with Fire, Terror with Dread, annoy.
　　In vain the thundring Cannon ply their Force;
　　In vain the Warrior urges on without remorse:
　　Invulnerable *Lisle* the Day commands,
　　And proudly sees their Glorys at a stand.

50　So long, so bravely, they th'Assault sustain,
　　So often fill the Trenches with the Slain:
　　So much beyond the Time that Art had set,
　　The Leaguers in their turn dread a Defeat:
　　Their Magazines of Death exhausted low,
55　And less'ning Fire proclaims the feeble Blow.
　　Supplys they want, or *Lisle* can never yield,
　　But *Vendosme*[9] and *La Motte* possess the Field
　　So from the Bird of *Jove* the Bolt if torn,
　　Jove can but vainly threaten, not perform.
60　MARLBRO's Good Fortune here stood at a gaze,
　　Dreadfully anxious how to tread the maze,
　　Fear'd this the Crisis of his Happy Days.
　　Th'Event the Factious *Britans* wait to see;
　　For Lisle untaken, *Oudenard's*[10] no Victory.

65 Ev'n *Eugene's* Laurels ravish'd at *Turin*,
Sicken and fade at this new Change of Scene:
La Motte with Numbers guards th'important Way
Through which they could only Supplys convey:
When Daring WEBB presumes to set 'em free;
70 Th'Attempt is more than any other Victory:
  Numbers affright not when he should prevail,
Nor Four to One can ponderate the Scale;
Nor all the Terrors of unequal War,
Advantages of Ground, and Cannon murd'ring from afar:
75 Full in the face of Day he charg'd the Foe;
No Odds, no Place, no Circumstance would know,
That might a moment his Resolves suspend;
United in a Point, and Victory the End:
Triumphant o'er the wondrous Field he rides,
80 Where Conquest and Amazement both preside.

  Scarce *Alexander* with more Troops the World engross'd,
Than here *La Motte* to WEBB's Six Thousand lost.
Marlbro', to whom great Actions are innate,
Thought this a stroke beyond the Arm of Fate:
85 He who had dar'd whatever Man could dare,
Found this stupendious Blow too big for War;
Nor till he saw the fated Slain, would yield
Such Honours could be gather'd from a mortal Field.
A Deed which as it has the Goal of Glory won,
90 Must ever blaze, Joint-Partner with the Sun.

  O Noble WEBB, whoe'er they Birth does claim,
Thy Mind's a Spark of the Etherial Flame;
Struck by Great *Jove* himself on such blest Nights,
When all the Godhead in one Ray unites,
95 To press the Fair, and taste supreme Delights.
As my *Adonis* lovely, as my Warrior brave;
To thee the partial Goddess Nature gave
Concurrent Charms, to make the World thy Slave.
In the first Age, when Empire went by Choice,
100 Such Worth had gain'd an Universal Choice.
O *ANNA*, draw the Hero near thy Throne,
Adorn him with the Glorys next the Crown;
Well will he wear 'em, well has thou begun.
Did not the *Prussian* King as grateful prove?

105 The *Prussian* King has much express'd his Love:
　　He in the Glory of their Order shines,
　　The Garter with the *Azure-Cross may join:
　　St *George's* Honours for the Valiant were
　　At first design'd the Recompence of War;
110 For such a Hero who can go too far?

　　　Old *Rome* for lesser Deeds wou'd Triumphs raise,
　　Ovations are too feeble for his Praise;
　　Or the cold Senate's Thanks, dealt with a sparing Hand,
　　When Joy and Shoutings fill the happy Land.
115 *Lisle* taken, the *Burgundian* looking on,
　　The *French* retire, the Field becomes their own.
　　Gaunt, Bruges, are regain'd without a Siege,
　　The fainting Troops repair their vast Fatigue:
　　The Greens reflourish on their General's Brow,
120 To *WEBB* they owe, that they are Victors now.
　　All this they gain'd—but such a Game retriev'd,
　　As can be but by wises Heads believ'd?
　　How little had they been if not reliev'd?
　　How different the Success of the Campaign?
125 Now *Lewis* grov'ling, then had proudly reign'd.
　　Rise *Delia*, take thy Lyre, and sing the Man,
　　This more than Great, who has all Men out-done."
　　To whom the Nymph;—
　　"Unequal to the mighty Task my Muse,
130 A Woman's Song (bright Goddess) they refuse:
　　Cou'd even *Orinda, Sappho,* live again,
　　Sappho, Orinda they wou'd now disdain.
　　For Notes so sweet young *Ad[dis]on*[11] was rais'd,
　　He was rewarded too as well as prais'd.
135 Ingrateful *St[ee]le*[12] forgets his former State,
　　And Former Friends, in his new Change of Fate;
　　Nay, Critick *D[ennis]*[13] in his declining Age
　　Indulg'd, may leave turmoiling for the Stage:
　　All *Apollo's* Sons, Apollo's *Glorys* see,
140 Only the hapless Daughters mourn like me.
　　A Soul depress'd cannot with lofty Ardor glow;
　　What narrow Prospect can great Buildings show?
　　Should I in Numbers dare to sing his Praise,
　　'Twould but profane the Triumphs you would raise:

*The Order of Generosity given by the King of Prussia to Major-General WEBB.

145 To *Ad[dis]on* the glorious Task enjoin,
   His Song has every Requisite Divine."
   When thus the Goddess:—
   "Already to great *Marlbro'* he has sung,
   Nay every Muse for him the Lyre has strung.
150 To Power like his new Trophys still are rais'd;
   Who can the most Reward, they mostly praise.
   But Thou, whom neither Fear, nor Hope of Favour warms,
   Whose stedfast Soul true Greatness only charms;
   Tell all the Beauteous Virgins of the Throng,
155 How worthy He of their immortal Song;

   With what enchanting Goodness, manly Grace,
   Sweetness and Courage mingles in his Face!
   How much of Human and Lofty too,
   How every Beauty there can claim a Due!
160 Then tell the Warrior Croud my Hero's Deed,
   Which no new Hero ever can exceed:
   Possessor of the highest Stand of Fame,
   The past out-done, what future shall dare claim,
   Or rank his own with *WEBB's* Immortal Name.

   FINIS.

Appendix II

Delarivier Manley's letters have never been published. They provide important information on her relationship with many of the senior Tory politicians of Oxford's ministry.

Letter No. 1[1]
Delarivier Manley to Sir John Hopkins
Pierpont Morgan Library, New York
MA 4695
[2 Nov. 1709]

Addressed to Mr Secretary Hopkins
Humbly pres[ented?]

Sir,

    The misfortune of my present Circumstances is I hope an (allowd) excuse for presuming to write to a person like you whom I have not the Honor to know. I have begged Mr Steels interest that I may be brought to a speedy Examination; there is nothing I more earnestly desire; next to the power of Atonment for the offence I have unwarily given.

    If Submission and penitence carry but a Shaddow of that Weight below as we know they do above, I may not despair of finding Grace: At least there shall be nothing unattempted on my party to deserve it.

    Consider Sir a fault arising neither from malice nor design but heat of Fancy alone the enthusiastick Dreams of some lonely country hours, yet will I not pretend (with reserve only to my intentions) to be wholly innocent since I am thought fitt to be condemn'd by you. I humbly beg a speedy hearing and your pardon for

Sr

Yr most obedient
& most humble
Servnt.

Wensday

Dela Manley.

Appendix II

Letter No. 2[2]
Delarivier Manley to Robert Harley[3]
BL, Add. MSS, 70290, Folio 1
Sunday 16 [April/July 1710?]

Sir

I had less despondence in attempting part of your character to the world, even when it was an unforgiving Sin to speak of you with Respect, than now to speak to your Self.

And, yet, Sir, my presumtion is upheld by many Great and Good, who think I deserve some Regard for exposeing the enemies of our Constitution for having, with hazzard to my Self, first Circulated their vices and open'd the ey's of the Crow'd, who were dazzled by the Shine of Power into awe and Reverence of their Persons.

I woud intreat, Sir, in favour of a young Gentleman, the Bearer, That which Time woud certainly do for him but by yr. goodness, hoping to anticipate so slow a hand, I beg the Queens recomendation (which I am told is matter of Form) to the Admiralty Board, that upon a Vacancy he may be made a Lieutenant. He has serv'd as Voluntière & pass'd Sir Richard Haddocks[4] Examination, and is every way Qualifyd for her Majestys Service.

If a Leysure (if a favourable) Moment can be found, if such a one be reserved for me I beg you will appoint it, Sir, that I may inform you of the person [——?] whom I recomend. Nay it will be hardship to debarr me from paying my duty where I have so sincerely devoted my wishes, Since 'Twas to your merit, Sir, more than your Grandeur, thus I first engaged my self with invincible respect) to be

    Sir,
    Your most Obedient
    Most humble servant
      Dela Manley

Enclosed, to Mr Markham[5] at the Bell & Dragon in Pater-Nostre Row

Letter No. 3
Delarivier Manley to Robert Harley
BL, Add. MSS, 70026 (unfoliated)
12 May 1710

Sir,

My Respect only prevents from waiting upon you in person (to beg your acceptance of this Book.)⁶ least I be thought to have the honor of your acquaintance which I can only covet never hope.

Yr. Interest [?] sir, yr. great Capacity, your Zeal for the church has made me an unwarrantable introuder. I willingly devote my ease and interest where my principles are ingaged and if I have the fortune to do some small service my Design is answered. I have attempted some faint Representations some imperfect pieces of painting of the heads of That party who have mislead Thousands. If any thing sir moves your Curiosity I will explain what you desire, if you send but a note (without a name) directed to me and under cover, to Mr Markham at the Bell and Dragon in Pater Nostre Row; I give the address to none besides therefore cant faile to know from whose Part yr. commands shall come.

Yet, perhaps I am all this time offending where I aim, and hope to please, the uncertainty of that gives me to ask yr. pardon for my presumtion, & to conclude with the profound respect of Sr.

Your most obedient servnt.
Dela Manley

Appendix II

Letter No. 4
Delarivier Manley to Earl of Oxford
BL, Add. MSS, 70028 (unfoliated)
19 July 1711

My Lord,

I had the Fortune two years agoe to publish some pieces for which I sufferd imprisonments injured my Health and prejudiced my little Fortune: Tho the performances were very indifferent yet they were reckoned to do some service having been the publick attempt made against those designs & that ministry which have been since so happily changed. My Friends have told me that I had some little pretence to be considered for what I had done as well as suffered, and my Lord Peterborow[7] as well as Mr Granvile[8] have promised to recomend me to your Lordship's Protection: I hope I may venture to add that I had once the honour of a Note from your Lordship, to command my Attendance, which I endeavoured in vain.

My Infirmities and misfortunes are forcing me away into a cheaper part of the Kingdom. If your Lordship think I have been any way serviceable, however accidentally, yr. justice will inspire you to give me your protection; if not I hope your generosity will incite you to reward my good endeavours, whether by some small pension (which in probability I shall not live long to enjoy) or some other effect your bounty, which I humbly leave to your Lordships Choice, & remain with the greatest Respect, and veneration.

My Lord
Your Lordships
most Obedient
and
most devoted humble servnt.
Dela Manley

From Mr Barbers[9] House
on Lambeth hill in Old Fish Street

Letter No. 5
Delarivier Manley to Earl of Oxford
BL, Add. MSS, 70028 (unfoliated)
October 2nd [1711]

My Lord,

I presume once more to put your Lordship in mind of my misfortunes, in hopes Mr St John[10] has spoke for me [as] he had the goodness to promise. My infirmities keep me in Town an expense I can ill bear, but if I go to a cheaper place, I lose the benefit of my physicians, who only keep me alive by Art.

In those intervals I get from sickness, I have endeavoured to make self a little serviceable; had I either instructions or incouragement I might succeed better. I beg your Lordship to know that I wrote Monsr. de Guiscard's Narrative,[11] and that Examiner of Antony and Fulvia,[12] where by Agrippa's character your Lordship's was designed I also answerd Dr Hares pamphlet of Bouchain[13] and have here sent you the inclosed upon his Sermon which will be published tomorrow.

I am told by many that your Lordship will have the goodness to consider my misfortunes, but had never so much hopes of since the gracious Secretary promised to interceed for me. If your lordship designs me any favour, I may receive your commands in a note /without a name/* directed to me, and inclosed to Mr Markham, Apothecary in Pater Nostre Row. I am with extream submission,

    My Lord
    Your Lordships
    most devoted
    humble servnt.
    Dela Manley

*This phrase is inserted above the line of writing.

Appendix II

Letter No. 6
Delarivier Manley to Earl of Oxford
BL, Add. MSS, 70032 (unfoliated)
3 June 1714

My Lord,

In Obedience to yr Lordships Commands, when I had the Honour of waiting on you three weeks agoe, I presume to send this letter by Mr. Barber the printer, att whose house I lodge.

I had likewise the honour of a note writt in your Lordships own hand some months after my sufferings and imprisonment, by order of the late ministry (for several things I had writ which they suspected to have reflected on them and their principles, and were then thought to have done the first publick service to the present cause,) but being at that time in the Country to recover my Health, which was very much disordered by my Fears and the Hardships I receiv'd, I cou'd not possible attend your Lordship.

I have since endeavour'd to make my self as useful as my ill state of Health would give leave, by writing several little phamplets [sic] and papers, of which, if I am rightly inform'd, some have not been disaproved by your Lordship, and the World.

Upon these accounts, and the promises Mr Barber was orderd to bring me from a number of Great men who were calld The Society for Rewarding of merit,[14] I had hopes yt. my poor endeavours to do service might have given me some mark of your Lordships favour; particularly I was assured that my Lord Masham[15] and Sr. William Windham,[16] two of the Society were commissiond by the rest to desire in their names, that your Lordship would send me an hundred pound, with assureances att the same time of their farther Favour. I have been likewise informed, that your Lordship agreed to their request, and that my Lord Harley ingaged to put you in mind of it.

I shall not trouble your Lordship with a tedious acct. of what I have suffered under those persecutions, or by the consequences of them ever since, both upon my Health and Circumstances; The Bearer[17] and several others could tell yr Lordship, that the little I had left of my own, or received from the generosity of some very few Friends hath been exhausted by remedies and physicians; and therefore, if I have no merit from my self, by endeavouring to serve the Cause, I att least have some by suffering by it.

I shall pretend to use no arguments moving your Compassion, yr. Generosity or your Justice, your own Head and heart are able to furnish you with infinitely better. I have heard that those who know your Lordship best affirm you to excell in Liberality and Good Nature. These are the Qualities in your Lordship which I now appeal to, and I should be easy under my appeal, if, among the croud of more importunate, more befriended and, perhaps more deserving pettitioners, I were not in danger to be forgot. In which case I have nothing left, but to wait with resignation, till it shall please God to put a period to the unfortunate life of, my Lord,

        Yr Lordships
        Most obedient and humble servant
        Dela Manley

Letter No. 7
Delarivier Manley to Earl of Oxford
BL, Add. MSS, 70032 (unfoliated)
14 June 1714

My Lord,

Having been out of Town for some time I was wholly unacquainted with yr. Lordships goodness to me; till yesterday Mr Barber took an opportunity to ride over, & put into my hands a Bill of fifty pounds from your Lordship with Commands of Secrecy which I shall punctually obey.

This supply is so noble, so seasonable, directed to make me easy under the pressure of my misfortunes; that I wish for nothing more than some opportunity, by which I may shew my gratitude & the Respect and Value I have for yr. Lordships favor,

>
> I am
> My Lord
> Yr Lordships most devoted and most obliged humble servnt.
> Dela Manley

Letter No. 8
Delarivier Manley to Earl of Oxford
BL, Add. MSS, 70033 (unfoliated)
30 August 1714

My Lord,

I take Leave, most humbly, to ask your Lordship's Opinion, whether a true account of the Changes made just Before the Death of the Queen, would not be very acceptable to the Publick?

As your Lordship has nothing to fear on this part, your Actions always aiming at the Good & Glory of the Nation and the Service of your Prince; so out of common justice, they ought to be fairly represented, to sett those men right, who only condemn for want of information, & to make others ashamed, who have only mens persons in admiration, with out regarding the interest of their Country.

Dampier[18] in the Second Vol. of his travails, has a relation of the Queen of Achins Court & Country, which would furnish a very commodious Scene.

I do not send this letter by the person I employ'd before,[19] I would have him know nothing of my design, for if I am not mistaken, he is a Creature of the Se——ys [Secretary's].[20]

I should have presumed to have waited upon you my self, but want of Mourning keeps me in the country:[21] The Bill your Lordship was so good to send me, went immediately to quiet uneasy Creditors; and now I have nothing but a starving scene before me, new interests to make without any old Merit, Ld Mal—— [Marlborough] and all his accomplices justly enraged against me; nothing saved out of the general wreck, for what indeed could I save? Your Lordships Bounty being all I ever receiv'd from the publick for what some esteem good Service to the Cause; many persons prejudiced, but none in particular thinking themselves oblig'd.

If you Lordship thinks fit to honor me with your Commands, you may please to inclose to me, & direct for Mrs Markendale,[22] att Mr Partridges house near Whetstone upon Finchley Common by the penny post.

I am with all submission
My Lord
Your Lordships
Most Obedient humble servant
D Manley

Appendix II

Letter No. 9
Institute of Historical Research, Prior Papers, Vol. 7, f. 127.
Delarivier Manley to Matthew Prior[23]
19 March 1719/20

Sir,

I have deferred till your Comeing to Town to return my most humble thanks for the honour of your letter; and for Lord Harley and Lady Harrietts Bounty.[24]

I have received several marks of your favour, and had not been this late in my thanks, if I durst have intruded myself before, but as I often begd my acknowledgements might be made to those persons that recommended my Interest, so I hope there has been so much justice done me, that I do not stand in your Esteem either as one insensible of benefit or ungrateful.

Through Ld Chamberlains wize management a play I had designed for the Town is deferrd till the next season. To make some amends, they have promisd me to revive Lucius for my Benefit; gracious Mrs Oldfield[25] has agreed to speak that admirable Epilogue you honoured me with which must ever Claim my most particular acknowledgements. But the Lady being something diffident in her performance, as much reason however as she can have got for the Contrary, enquired how she might be instructed by you, & said that rather than lose that Advantage, she would wait on you her self: next Tuesday the play is to be rehearsed, I should be glad to know your Sentiments, & be able to carry her your Commands.

       I am with Respect and Acknowledgement
       Sr
       Your most obedient
       and most obliged,
       humble servant
            Dela Manley

Notes

1. INTRODUCTION

1. Delarivier Manley, *The Adventures of Rivella; or the History of the Author of the Atalantis* (London: E. Curll, 1714), p. 117.
2. *Rivella*, p. 116.
3. *Rivella*, p. 111.
4. Delarivier Manley, *Letters Written by Mrs. Manley* (London: R. B., 1696), preface (unpaginated).
5. "Melpomene: *The Tragicle Muse. On the Death of* John Dryden, *Esq*", "Thalia: *The Comicle Muse, On the Death of* John Dryden, *Esq. A Pastoral*." See *The Nine Muses,* ed. Richard Bassett (London: [n.p.] 1700), pp. 1–2, 11–14.
6. *Nine Muses*, p. 1.
7. [Delarivier Manley], *The Secret History of Queen Zarah and the Zarazians; Being a Looking Glass for —in the Kingdom of Albigion* 2 vols. ("Albigion" [London?]: n.p., 1705).
8. Delarivier Manley, *Almyna: Or, the Arabian Vow* (London: William Turner and Egbert Sanger, 1707).
9. *Almyna*, preface, sig. A.
10. Delarivier Manley, *The Lady's Pacquet of Letters* (London: B. Bragg, 1707).
11. [Delarivier Manley], *Secret Memoirs and Manners of Persons of Quality, of Both Sexes; From the New Atalantis, an Island in the Mediterranean*, 2 vols. (London: John Morphew, 1709). As I will show later, there is a poem which is likely to have been by her published earlier the same year.
12. Delarivier Manley, *Memoirs of Europe, Towards the Close of the Eighth Century; Written by Eginardus, Secretary and Favourite to Charlemagne; and done into English by the Translator of the New Atalantis,* 2 vols. (London: John Morphew, 1710).
13. For a full discussion of this topic see J. A. Downie, *Robert Harley and the Press: Propaganda and Public Opinion in the Age of Swift and Defoe* (Cambridge: Cambridge University Press, 1979), pp. 2–3.
14. See [Charles Gildon?], *Mrs. Manley's History of her Own Life and Times . . . With a Preface Concerning the Present Publication* (London: E. Curll, J. Pemberton, 1725), sig. A2.
15. Delarivier Manley, *Lucius The First Christian King of Britain* (London: n.p., 1717).
16. Delarivier Manley, *The Power of Love* (London: John Barber, 1720).
17. See J. Paul Hunter, *Before Novels: The Cultural Contexts of Eighteenth Century English Fiction* (New York: W. W. Norton, 1990), *passim*; Michael Mc-

Keon, *The Origins of the English Novel* (Baltimore: Johns Hopkins University Press, 1987), pp. 232–33; John J. Richetti, *Popular Fiction before Richardson: Narrative Patterns, 1700–1739* (Oxford: Clarendon Press, 1969), pp. 123–55 and *passim*, and *The English Novel in History, 1700–1780* (London: Routledge, 1999), p. 31; Richetti and Paula Backscheider, eds., *Popular Fiction by Women, 1660–1730* (Oxford: Clarendon Press, 1996), p. 46; Robert Adams Day, *Told in Letters: Epistolary Fiction before Richardson* (Ann Arbor: University of Michigan Press 1966), pp. 43–45 and *passim*.

18. Lennard Davis, *Factual Fictions: The Origins of the English Novel* (New York: Columbia University Press, 1983), pp. 110–21.

19. Richetti and Backscheider include *The Secret History of Queen Zarah* in their *Popular Fiction by Women*, pp. 43–81.

20. Ros Ballaster, *Seductive Forms: Women's Amatory Fiction from 1684 to 1740* (Oxford: Oxford University Press, 1992), pp. 125–29.

21. Janet Todd, *The Sign of Angelica: Women, Writing, and Fiction, 1660–1800* (London: Virago, 1989), p. 93.

22. Caroline Gonda, *Reading Daughters' Fictions, 1709–1834* (Cambridge: Cambridge University Press, 1996), pp. 45–51.

23. Bradford K. Mudge, *The Whore's Story: Women, Pornography, and the British Novel, 1684–1830* (Oxford: Oxford University Press, 2000), pp. 136–47.

24. See Jerry C. Beasley, "Politics and Moral Idealism: The Achievement of Some Early Women Novelists," in *Fetter'd or Free?: British Women Novelists, 1670–1815* ed. Mary Anne Schofield and Cecilia Macheski, (Athens: Ohio University Press, 1986), pp. 222–24.

25. For this reason, I do not touch upon Manley's last work, *The Power of Love* (1720). While this set of short novels is clearly an important contribution to the development of prose fiction, I do not believe that Manley was especially concerned in this text with affairs of state, and therefore it would not sit particularly easily with my other discussions in this book. The same can be said of Manley's later poems, including those written as panegyrics to the family of the Whiggish earl of Bristol.

26. Rachel Weil, *Political Passions: Gender, the Family and Political Argument in England, 1680–1714* (Manchester: Manchester University Press, 1999), p. 176.

27. Kathryn R. King, *Jane Barker, Exile: A Literary Career* (Oxford: Clarendon Press, 2000), p. 130.

28. Catharine Gallagher, *Nobody's Story: The Vanishing Acts of Women Writers in the Marketplace* (Berkeley and Los Angeles: University of California Press, 1994), pp. 89–114; Paula McDowell, *Women of Grub Street: Press, Politics, and Gender in the London Literary Marketplace, 1678–1730* (Oxford: Clarendon Press, 1998), pp. 225–84.

29. Melinda Alliker Rabb, "Swift and the Spider-Woman: Manley and Tory Satire," in *Locating Swift: Essays on the 250th Anniversary of the Death of Jonathan Swift, 1667–1745*, ed. Aileen Douglas, Patrick Kelly, and Ian Campbell Ross (Dublin: Four Courts Press, 1998), pp. 60–81; Carole Fabricant, "The Shared Worlds of Manley and Swift," in *Pope, Swift, and Women Writers*, ed. Donald C. Mell (London: Associated University Presses, 1996), pp. 154–78.

30. Paul Baker Patterson, "Robert Harley and the Organization of Political Propaganda" (Ph.D. diss., University of Virginia, 1974); Frances Marjorie Harris, "A Study of the Paper War Relating to the Career of the first Duke of Marlborough, 1710–1712" (doctoral thesis, University of London, 1975). Downie is cited in note 13 above.

31. Heinz-Joachim Muellenbrook, *The Culture of Contention* (Munich: Fink, 1997), pp. 86–88 and *passim*.

32. For fuller discussions of Manley's early life see Dolores Duff, "Materials Towards a Biography of Mary Delariviere Manley" (Ph.D. diss, Indiana University, 1965), and Fidelis Morgan, *A Woman of No Character: An Autobiography of Mrs. Manley* (London: Faber and Faber, 1986).

33. *Rivella*, p. 14.

34. Morgan, *Woman of No Character*, p. 37.

35. *Rivella*, p. 14.

36. *Rivella*, p. 116.

37. *The Manuscripts of the Marquess of Downshire; Papers of Sir William Trumbull*, vol. 1 (London: H. M. Stationery Office, 1924), p. 883.

38. William Cobbett, *Cobbett's Parliamentary History of England*, vol. 5, (London: R. Bagshaw; Longmans, 1806–12), p. 939; *Parliamentary Register*, vol. 1 (London: Longmans, 1807), p. 351; Duff, "Materials," p. 68.

39. A résumé of John and Delarivier Manley's marriage is given in Morgan, *Woman of No Character*, p. 47.

40. Duff, "Materials," p. 71.

41. *Rivella*, pp. 31–33.

42. *Rivella*, p. 40.

43. *Letters Writen by Mrs. Manley*, p. 2.

44. *Letters Writen by Mrs. Manley*, p. 49.

45. *Letters Writen by Mrs. Manley*, pp. 49–50.

46. See Rosemary Foxton, "Delariviere Manley and 'Astrea's Vacant Throne,'" *Notes and Queries*, (1986): pp. 41–42.

47. *Letters Writen by Mrs. Manley*, p. 3.

48. Geoffrey Holmes, *British Politics in the Age of Anne* (London: MacMillan, 1967), p. 264.

49. Elizabeth Handasyde, *Granville the Polite: The Life of George Granville, Lord Landsdowne, 1666–1735* (Oxford: Oxford University Press, 1933), p. 72.

50. Morgan, *Woman of No Character*, p. 70.

51. Catharine Cockburn, *The Works of Mrs. Catharine Cockburn*, ed. T. Birch, 2 vols. (London: J. and P. Knapton), I, p. 8; the poem is reproduced in vol. 2, p. 465.

52. See *A New Miscellany of Original Poems, Translations and Imitations, By the most Eminent Hands* (London: T. Jauncy, 1720), p. 228; and *An Impartial History of the Life of Mr John Barber* (London: E. Curll, 1741), p. 47.

53. Bevil Higgons, epilogue to *Heroick Love*, by George Granville, in *Four Plays of the Right Honourable the Lord Landsdowne* (London: W. Feales, 1732), unpaginated.

54. Higgons, prologue to *The Jew of Venice*, by Granville, in *Four Plays*.

55. Giles Jacob, *Lives and Characters of the English Dramatick Poets* (London: E. Curll, 1719), p. 170.

56. *Rivella*, p. 42.
57. *Rivella*, p. 45.
58. Charles Gildon, *A Comparison Between Two Stages* (London: n.p., 1702), p. 15.
59. *New Atalantis*, I, pp. 177–78.
60. [Mr. W. M.], *The Female Wits or the Triumvirate of Poets: A Rehearsal* (London, 1704), cast list (unpaginated).
61. George Granville, *British Enchanters: or no Magick like Love* (London: Jacob Tonson, 1706).
62. *Power of Love* (London: John Barber, 1720), p. xiv.
63. Handasyde, *Granville the Polite*, p. 41; Henry St. John, prologue to *Heroick Love*, by Granville, in *Four Plays*.
64. *Rivella*, p. 42.
65. *Female Wits*, preface.
66. Melinda Alliker Rabb, "Angry Beauties: (Wo)Manley Satire, and the Stage," in *Cutting Edges: Postmodern Critical Essays on Eighteenth-Century Satire*, ed. James E. Gill (Knoxville: University of Tennessee Press, 1996), p. 130.
67. For accounts of Manley's relationship with Steele, see Duff, "Materials," pp. 111–43, and Paul Bunyan Anderson, "Mistress Delariviere Manley's Biography," *Modern Philology* 33 (1936): 271.
68. The letters were identified as Steele's to Manley by Anderson. Rae Blanchard reprints them as undated correspondence in *Correspondence of Richard Steele* (Oxford: Oxford University Press, 1941), pp. 425–39.
69. Steele, *Correspondence*, p. 427.
70. Duff, "Materials," p. 137.
71. Steele to Col. Edmund Revett, 2 September 1701, in Steele, *Correspondence*, p. 11.
72. "Anacreotique to Delia," in Steele, *The Occasional Verse of Richard Steele*, ed. Rae Blanchard (Oxford: Oxford University Press, 1952), p. 63. For dating, see Duff, "Materials," p. 139.
73. Steele, *Occasional Verse*, p. 63.
74. Steele, *Occasional Verse*, p. 98–99.
75. *Rivella*, p. 52.
76. The lawsuit is explained in Katherine Zelinsky's edition of *The Adventures of Rivella* (Peterborough, Ont.: Broadview Press, 1999), pp. 28–31.
77. *Rivella*, pp. 64–65.
78. *Rivella*, p. 64.
79. Duff, "Materials," p. 85; Morgan, *Woman of No Character*, p. 103.
80. *Rivella*, p. 101.
81. *New Atalantis*, I, pp. 188–92.
82. Steele to Manley, 6 September 1709 (draft), in Steele, *Correspondence*, p. 29.
83. *Rivella*, pp. 104–5.
84. Steele to Manley, 2 September 1709 (draft), in Steele, *Correspondence*, p. 29.
85. *Lucius*, dedication, sig. A2.
86. Morgan, *Women of No Character*, pp. 141–43.

87. For an account of this case, see *The Epistolary Correspondence of Sir Richard Steele*, ed. John Nichols, vol 2. (London: Nichols, 1787), p. 456.

88. For a detailed account of Barber's life see Charles A. Rivington, *Tyrant: The Story of John Barber, 1675–1741* (York: William Sessions, 1989).

89. *Life and Character of John Barber; Late Lord-Mayor of London* (London: T. Cooper, 1741), p. 9.

90. *Life and Character of John Barber*, p. 10.

91. *Impartial History*, p. 24.

92. *Life and Character of John Barber*, p. 13.

93. Madame d'Aulnoy, *Memoirs of the Court of England, . . . To which is added The Lady's Pacquet of Letters* [by Delarivier Manley] (London: B. Bragg, 1707). See Ruth Herman, "Enigmatic Gender in Delarivier Manley's New Atalantis" in C. Mounsey, ed. *Presenting Gender: Changing Sex in Early-Modern Culture* (Lewisburg: Bucknell University Press, 2001) pp. 202–24 for a discussion of the significance of including this story.

94. *Life and Character of John Barber*, p. 10.

95. Downie, *Robert Harley and the Press*, pp. 2–3.

96. This letter is unfortunately only dated "Sunday 16th." It was written before Harley became a peer, and after the publication of *Memoirs of Europe*. There are only two possible dates for this letter, 16 April or 16 July 1710. See British Library, Additional MSS 70290, fol.1.

97. See Swift's entry for 29 September in *Journal to Stella*, ed. Harold Williams, vol 1 (Oxford: Oxford University Press, 1948), pp. 34–35.

98. Swift to Addison, 22 August 1710, in *The Correspondence of Jonathan Swift*, ed. Harold Williams, vol 1. (Oxford: Clarendon Press, 1963), p. 170–71.

99. Swift, entry for 7 October 1710, in *Journal*, I, p. 46.

100. Swift, became sole editor of *The Examiner* with the issue of 2 November 1710.

101. Swift, entry for 3 November 1710, in *Journal*, I, p. 80.

102. Swift, entry for 4 January 1711, in *Journal*, I, p. 154.

103. Swift, entries for 1 October and 14 December 1710, in *Journal* I, p. 37, 125.

104. Swift, entry for 16 November 1710, in *Journal*, p. 97.

105. Charles Ford to Swift, 10 July 1714, in *Correspondence of Jonathan Swift*, II, p. 59.

106. Rivington, *Tyrant*, p. 128.

107. See Swift, *The Account Books of Jonathan Swift*, ed. Paul V. Thomson and Dorothy Jay Thompson (Newark: University of Delaware Press, 1984), p. 116, xxxix.

108. Swift, *Account Books*, p. 130; Irvin Ehrenpreis, *Swift: The Man, His Works, and the Age*, vol 2 (London: Methuen, 1967), p. 644.

109. Swift, *The Complete Poems*, ed. Pat Rogers (London: Penguin , 1983), p. 120.

110. See *Impartial History*, p. xxviii.

111. Swift records dining at his printer's house on thirteen occasions between January 1711 and April 1713.

112. Manley to Robert Harley, earl of Oxford, 19 July 1711, BL, Add. MSS 70028 (unfoliated).

113. Swift, entry for 3 July 1711, in *Journal*, I, p. 306.
114. See chapter 7 on *New Atalantis*.
115. Swift, entry for 21 June 1711, in *Journal*, I, p. 294.
116. See G. W. Cooke, *Memoirs of Lord Bolingbroke*, vol 1 (London: Richard Bentley, 1835), pp. 183–84.
117. Swift, entry for 13 March 1712, in *Journal*, II, p. 512.
118. Manley to Robert Harley, earl of Oxford, 14 June 1714, BL, Add. MSS 70032 (unfoliated).
119. Swift, entry for [9/20] June 1711, in *Journal*, p. 294.
120. Duchess of Marlborough to Queen Anne [1709], in *Correspondence of the Duchess of Marlborough*, vol 1 (London: Henry Colburn, 1838), I, p. 236.
121. See BL, Add. MSS 70290, fol. 1, and 70026 (unfoliated).
122. See Manley to Robert Harley, earl of Oxford, 14 June 1714, BL, Add. MSS 70032 (unfoliated).
123. Swift, entries for 7 February 1711 and 7 March 1711 in *Journal*, I, pp. 182, 208.
124. Manley to Robert Harley, earl of Oxford, 30 August 1714, BL, Add. MSS 70033 (unfoliated).
125. Manley to Prior, 19 March 1720, Prior Papers, Institute of Historical Research, vol. 7, fol. 127.
126. Rivington, *Tyrant*, pp. 24–25.
127. Swift, entry for 29 July 1711, in *Journal*, I, p. 323.
128. Swift to Ford, 16 February 1718/19, in *Correspondence of Jonathan Swift*, I, p. 313.
129. Delarivier Manley's will, dated 6 October 1723, Public Record Office, PROB II 599.
130. *Life and Character of John Barber*, p. 14.
131. James Moore to Dr. Sewell, undated, in *Mr Pope's Literary Correspondence* (London: E. Curll, 1735), p. 9.
132. *A New Miscellany of Original Poems, Translations and Imitations, By the most Eminent Hands, Viz. Mr Prior, Mr. Harcourt, Mr. Pope, Mr. Hughes, Lady M. W. M[ontague] Mrs. Manley &c.* (London: T. Jauncy, 1720), p. 192.
133. John Hervey, first earl of Bristol, to Mrs. Manley, 12 July 1720, in *The letter books of John Hervey, 1st earl of Bristol, 1651–1750*, [ed. S. H. A. Hervey], vol. 2 (Wells: Jackson, 1894), p. 125.
134. *Letter books of John Hervey*, II, p. 68 n; *The Diary of John Hervey, First Earl of Bristol with Extracts from his Book of Expenses, 1688–1742*, [ed. S. H. A. Hervey], (Wells: Jackson, 1894), p. 151; *New Miscellany*, pp. 201–7.
135. Curll to Robert Walpole, 2 March 1723; quoted in Ralph Straus, *The Unspeakable Curll* (London: Chapman and Hall, 1927), p. 94.
136. PRO, SP 44, vol. 81, p. 339.
137. John Tutchin, *Observator*, 7–10 May 1712.

2. A LIBERTY TO ABUSE THEIR BETTERS

1. *Queen Zarah and the Zarazians; Being a Looking-glass for — In the Kingdom of Albigion*, 2 vols. (Albigion [London?]: n.p., 1705), I, p. 2. (all page refer-

ences are to this first edition, and included in parentheses in the text). Doubts have been raised about Manley's authorship of this text. The issue is discussed at the end of this chapter.

2. See C. R. Kropf, "Libel and Satire in the Eighteenth Century," *Eighteenth-Century Studies* 8 (1974/1975): 153–68.

3. "Faction Display'd," in *Poems on Affairs of State*, ed. George deForest Lord, 7 vol. (New Haven: Yale University Press, 1970), VI, p. 668. This work will be abbreviated as *POAS* throughout.

4. There appears to be little or no research available on the keys and their relationships to the original texts. It is generally unclear how long it took for a relevant key to be published, or whether it was issued by the writer, the printer, or some other interested party. For further brief discussions see Patricia Köster, ed., *The Novels of Mary Delariviere Manley*, vol. 1 (Gainesville, Fl.: Scholars' Facsimiles and Reprints, 1971), p. xxiii, and Gallagher, *Nobody's Story*, pp. 125–26.

5. *Histoire Secrette de la Reine Zarah ou la Duchesse de Marlborough Demasqué* (Oxford: Alexandre le Vertueux, 1711), p. 202.

6. The index to Köster's edition of the novels will provide the key to Manley's texts in this book.

7. Davis, *Factual Fictions*, p. 114.

8. For further details on politics in this period see Geoffrey Holmes, *British Politics in the Age of Anne* (London: MacMillan, 1967); Keith Feiling, *A History of the Tory Party* (Oxford: Clarendon Press, 1924); Tim Harris, *Politics under the Later Stuarts: Party Conflict in a Divided Society, 1660–1715*, (London: Longman, 1993); and G. V. Bennett, *The Tory Crisis in Church and State, 1688–1730: The Career of Francis Atterbury, Bishop of Rochester* (Oxford: Clarendon Press, 1975).

9. See W. A. Speck, *Tory and Whig: The Struggle in the Constituencies, 1701–1715* (London: Macmillan, 1970), p. 98.

10. Feiling, *History of the Tory Party*, p. 149.

11. *A Kit-Kat C[lu]b Describ'd; O Monstrous Moderation!* ([London?]: n.p., 1705), p. 6.

12. Henry L. Snyder, "The Defeat of the Occasional Conformity Bill and the Tack," in *Bulletin of the Institute of Historical Research* 61 (1968): 172.

13. "An Address," in *A New Collection of Poems Relating to State Affairs, from Oliver Cromwell to this Present Time; by the Greatest Wits of the Age* (London: n.p., 1705), p. 564.

14. Frances Harris, *A Passion for Government: The Life of Sarah, Duchess of Marlborough* (Oxford: Clarendon Press, 1991), p. 63.

15. John Evelyn, quoted in A. L. Rowse, *The Early Churchills* (London: Penguin, 1956), p. 227.

16. Holmes, *British Politics*, p. 189.

17. Daniel Defoe, *A Review of the Affairs of France, with Observations on Transactions at Home*, 17 April 1705.

18. Churchill, quoted in Speck, *Tory and Whig*, p. 109.

19. Paul Bunyan Anderson, "Mistress Manley's Prose Fiction," *Philological Quarterly* 13 (1934): 170, and "Mistress Delariviere Manley's Biography," p. 272.

20. See, for instance, *A Health to the Tackers* (Oxford: n.p., 1705); *The Tackers Vindicated* (London: n.p., 1705); *Daniel the Prophet no Conjurer* ([London?]:

n.p., 1705); *A Letter from a Dissenter in the City, to his Country-Friend* ([London?]: n.p., 1705); *The Oxfordshire Nine* (London: n.p., 1705); *The Perkinite Jacks: Presbyterian Loyalty in two letters* ([London?]: n.p., [1705?]); *Tom Tell-Truth's Letter to a dissenter in vindication of the L[ord]s Against the Tackers* (London: n.p., [1705?]); *The Tackers vindicated; or an Answer to the Whigs New Black-List* ([London?]: n.p., 1705).

21. See Bennet, *Tory Crisis in Church and State*, p. 81.

22. *The Term Catalogues, 1668–1709 A.D*, ed. Edward Arber, vol. 3 (London: 1906), p. 61; Henry L. Snyder, "The Reports of a Press Spy for Robert Harley: New Bibliographical Date for the Reign of Queen Anne," *The Library* 22 (1967): 333.

23. See, for example, William Shippen "Moderation Display'd" (1704), *POAS*, VII, p. 27, and Joseph Browne, *The Fox set to Watch the Geese* (London: n.p., 1705).

24. *Jenny Cromwells Complaint against Sodomy* (1692/93), Portland Collection MSS University of Nottingham.

25. "The Female Nine," *POAS*, V, p. 209.

26. "Faction Display'd," *POAS*, VI, p. 670.

27. Harris, *Passion for Government*, pp. 83, 121; Holmes, *British Politics*, p. 210–12.

28. *Gilbert Burnet's History of his own time*, vol.5 (Oxford: Clarendon Press, 1823), p. 224.

29. Harris, *Passion for Government*, pp. 82, 97, 110.

30. "A New Ballad Writ by Jacob Tonson and Sung at the Kit Kat Clubb on the 8th of March 1705," *POAS*, VII, p. 57.

31. Harris, *Passion for Government*, p. 88.

32. Sunderland to the duchess of Marlborough, 8/19 September, 1705; quoted in Holmes, *British Politics*, p. 211.

33. See Todd, *Sign of Angelica*, p. 57.

34. John L. Sutton, "The Sources of Mrs. Manley's Preface to *Queen Zarah*," *Modern Philology* 82 (1984): 171; Ballaster, *Seductive Forms*, p. 83; see also McDowell, *Women of Grub Street*, pp. 262–63.

35. William B. Warner, *Licensing Entertainment: The Elevation of Novel Reading in Britain, 1684–1750* (London: University of California Press, 1998), p. 97.

36. See *Seven Wise Men* ([London?]: n.p., 1705); *St James's Park* (London: n.p., 1708); and *Assembly at Kensington* [[London?]: n.p., 1699].

37. Warner, *Licensing Entertainment*, p. 97.

38. Weil, *Political Passions*, p. 175.

39. See James Sutherland, *The Restoration Newspaper and Its Development* (Cambridge: Cambridge University Press, 1986), p. 180.

40. For a discussion of the differences between Manley and d'Aulnoy see Melvin D. Palmer, "Madam d'Aulnoy in England," *Comparative Literature* 27 (1975): 237–53.

41. Paula Backscheider, *Spectacular Politics: Theatrical Power and Mass Culture in Early Modern England* (Baltimore: Johns Hopkins University Press, 1993), pp. 111–12.

42. Sutton, for instance, has established that her preface, once regarded as a fresh and creative view of fiction as it stood in the early eighteenth century, is a direct translation from an earlier French text. Sutton, "Sources of Mrs. Manley's Preface to *Queen Zarah*," 168–69.

43. *Hattigé or The Amours of the King of Tamaran: A Novel* (Amsterdam: n.p., 1680).

44. *Hattigé*, p. 18.

45. For a discussion of this intertextual borrowing, see Ruth Herman, "Similarities between Delarivier Manley's *Secret History of Queen Zarah* and the English Translation of *Hattigé*," *Notes and Queries* 47, no. 2 (2000), pp. 193–96. Both Paulina Kewes in *Authorship and Appropriations: Writing for the Stage in England, 1660–1710* (Oxford: Oxford University Press, 1998), and Brean Hammond in *Professional Imaginative Writing in England, 1670–1740: "Hackney for Bread"* (Oxford: Clarendon Press, 1997) comment extensively on the practice of authorial borrowings.

46. Holmes, *British Politics*, p. 150.

47. Harris, *Passion for Government*, pp. 8–10.

48. "The Universal Health," *POAS*, V, p. 337, n. 33.

49. William Shippen, "Moderation Display'd," *POAS*, VII, p. 36.

50. For Churchill's relationship with Barbara Villiers, see Harris, *Passion for Government*, p. 18.

51. See Speck, *Reluctant Revolutionaries: Englishmen and the Revolution of 1688* (Oxford: Oxford University Press, 1988), p. 87 and Paul Hopkins, "Sham Plots and Real Plots in the 1690s," in *Ideology and Conspiracy: Aspects of Jacobitism, 1689–1759*, ed. Eveline Cruickshanks (Edinburgh: John Donald, 1982), pp. 89–110.

52. See Arthur Mainwaring, "Tarquin and Tullia," *POAS*, V, p. 50–51; and "The False Favourite's Downfall," in *POAS*, V, pp. 330, 331, n. 7. For a modern discussion see Harris, *Politics under the Later Stuarts*, p. 159.

53. "The Nine," *POAS*, V, p. 199.

54. "False Favourite's Downfall," p. 333.

55. "The Female Nine," *POAS*, V, p. 209.

56. [James Drake], *The Memorial of the Church of England* (London, n.p., 1705), p. 6.

57. David Green, *Queen Anne* (London: Collins, 1970), p. 144.

58. "Faction Display'd," *POAS*, VI, p. 651; William Garth, "The Dispensary," *POAS*, VI, p. 64.

59. Swift, *Examiner*, no. 31 (8 March 1711), in *Prose Works*, III, p. 103.

60. Shippen, "Moderation Display'd," p. 23; Harris, *Passion for Government*, p. 15 for a contemporary description of Sarah Churchill.

61. See *The Dream of the Solan Goose* (London: n.p., 1709); H. G. L. Mag, *The Eagle and The Robin* ([London?]: n.p., 1709); and *The Fable of the Housewife and her Cock* ([London?]: n.p.,1712).

62. [Drake], *Memorial of the Church of England*, p. 22.

63. *Mercurius Politicus*, ([London]: n.p., 1705), p. 7.

64. William Shippen, *The Devil upon Dun: or Moderation in Masquerade; A Poem*, ([London?]: n.p. [1705?]), p. 2.

65. [Drake], *Memorial of the Church of England*, p. 27; See also *Presbyterian Loyalty, in Two Letters: One directed to the Moderate Church-Men* ([London?]: n.p., 1705); and *A Word of Advice to the Citizens of London* (London: n.p., 1705).

66. *Moderation Displayed: A Poem* (London: n.p., 1704), preface (unpaginated).

67. [Drake], *Memorial of the Church of England*, p. 27.

68. Speck, *Tory and Whig*, p. 100.

69. For a view of the monstrosity of political factioneering, see *The Monster: or The World turn'd Topsy Turvy; A Satyr* (London: B. Bragg, 1705).

70. See "Faction Display'd," pp. 658, 661.

71. Swift, "The History of the Four Last Years of Queen Anne's Reign," in *Prose Works*, VII, p. 9.

72. *A Kit-Kat C[lu]b Describ'd*, p. 6.

73. Browne, *Fox set to Watch the Geese* pp. 2–4.

74. Snyder, "Reports of a Press Spy," p. 339.

76. Swift, "History of the Four Last Years of Queen Anne's Reign," p. 9.

77. Melinda Alliker Rabb, "The Manl(e)y Style: Delariviere Manley and Jonathan Swift," in *Pope, Swift, and Women Writers*, ed. Donald C. Mell (London: Associated University Presses, 1996), p. 135.

78. Feiling, *History of the Tory Party*, pp. 322, 365.

79. J. H. Plumb, *The Growth of Political Stability in England, 1675–1725* (London: Macmillan, 1967), p. 135, 139.

80. Holmes, *British Politics*, p. 385. For a contemporary account see Burnet, *Bishop Burnet's History of his own time*, V, pp. 112–16.

81. *A Health to the Tackers*.

82. *Ashby and White: or The Great Question* (London: n.p., 1705), p. 1.

83. See *An Appeal to the Freeholders of England* (London: n.p., 1705).

84. For a discussion of the feminist readings of this trope, see Gallagher, *Nobody's Story*, p. 102.

85. See Bennet, *Tory Crisis in Church and State*, pp. 78–79.

86. Speck, *Tory and Whig*, pp. 14–21.

87. Charles Leslie, *The Rehearsal*, 21 July 1705.

88. Holmes, *British Politics*, pp. 313–14. See also Speck, "The Electorate in the First Age of Party," in *Britain in the First Age of Party: Essays Presented to Geoffrey Holmes*, ed. Clyve Jones (London: Hambledon Press, 1987), p. 46, Plumb, *Growth of Political Stability*, p. 28. For a full discussion of the 1705 general election see Speck, *Tory and Whig*, pp. 98–109.

89. See Frances Harris, "The Electioneering of Sarah, Duchess of Marlborough," *Parliamentary History* 2 (1983), p. 75.

90. Speck, *Tory and Whig*, pp. 101, 103.

91. Speck, *Tory and Whig*, p. 101 for details of the queen's visit to Oxford in 1705.

92. Holmes, *British Politics*, pp. 41, 262.

93. William Dyer, newsletter of 19 May 1705, in *A Collection from Dyer's Letters*, (London: n.p., 1706), pp. 3–8.

94. Shippen, "Moderation Display'd," p. 31, n. 185.

95. Arthur Mainwaring, "The History and Fall of the Conformity Bill," *POAS*, VII, p. 1l, n. 109. For details of Harley's upbringing and education, see

Brian W. Hill, *Robert Harley: Speaker, Secretary of State, and Premier* (New Haven: Yale University Press, 1988), pp 4–9.

96. [Drake], *Memorial of the Church of England*, p. 21; *POAS*, VII, p. 144 n. 1.
97. "On The New Promotion," *POAS*, VII, p. 144.
98. Feiling, *History of the Tory Party*, p. 375.
99. Harley, quoted in Green, *Queen Anne*, p. 159.
100. *Impartial History of the Life of Mr. John Barber*, p. 46.
101. [Delarivier Manley], *The Secret History, of Queen Zarah, and the Zarazians; By way of Appendix to the New Atalantis; Containing The True Reasons of the Necessity of the Revolution that lately happen'd in the Kingdom of Albigion*, 2d ed., (London: n.p., 1711); for a recent commentary on Manley's authorship of *Queen Zarah*, see Ros Ballaster, *Seductive Forms*, p. 137, n. 40.
102. Advertisement in *The Examiner*, 12 April 1714.
103. Curll's preface to *Mrs Manley's History*, pp. iv, vii.
104. Rivington, *Tyrant*, p. 16.
105. Advertisement in The *Examiner*, 14 June 1711.
106. Joseph Browne, *State Tracts: Containing Many Necessary Observations and Reflections on the State of our Affairs at Home and Abroad; with some Secret Memoirs*, 2 vols. (London: Sawbridge *et al*, 1715).
107. Mark Noble, *A Biographical History of England*, vol. 2. (London: W. Richardson, 1806), p. 232.
108. Köster, *Novels*, I, p. x.
109. Robert J. Allen, "William Oldisworth: 'the Author of *The Examiner*,'" *Philological Quarterly* 36 (1947): 162.
110. Within the body of the collection, the *Secret Memoirs* of the title (i.e., *Queen Zarah*) is renamed *A Secret History Faithfully handed down from a Committee of Safety, to a Committee of Secrecy &c.*
111. *The Devil of a Whigg: or Zarazian Subtilty Detected* (London: n.p., 1708).

3. "SOME ARTIFICIAL POISONS"

1. The full title is *Secret Memoirs and Manners of Several Persons of Quality, of both Sexes; From the New Atalantis, an Island in the Mediterranean*. 2 vols. (London: John Morphew, 1709). All quotations are from this edition, and volume and page references are included in parentheses in the text. The first volume of *The New Atalantis* was announced in *The Tatler*, no. 19, 25 May 1709. Manley's arrest is dealt with later in the chapter.
2. Richetti, *Popular Fiction before Richardson*, p. 121.
3. *The Secret History of Arlus and Odolphus, Ministers to the Empress of Grandinsula* (London: n.p., 1710).
4. There are two conflicting identifications. See Köster, *Novels*, II, p. 862.
5. Sutton, *"Sources of Mrs. Manley's Preface to Queen Zarah,"* 172.
6. Thomas Hearne, *Remarks and Collections of Thomas Hearne*, ed. C. E. Noble *et al.*, 11 vols. (Oxford: Clarendon Press, 1884–1918), II, pp. 292, 389–90.
7. Delarivier Manley to earl of Oxford, 19 July 1711, BL, Add. MSS 70028 (unfoliated).

8. G. M. Trevelyan, *England under Queen Anne*, 3 vols. (London: Collins, 1965), I, p. 194; II, p. 62.

9. Gwendolyn B. Needham, "Mary de la Riviere Manley, Tory Defender," *Huntington Library Quarterly* (1948–49): 263.

10. Anne, quoted in Feiling, *History of the Tory Party*, p. 390.

11. Speck, *Tory and Whig*, p. 123.

12. Harris, *Passion for Government*, p. 132.

13. Ros Ballaster mistakenly states that Robert Harley was Abigail Masham's brother-in-law; See Ballaster's edition of *New Atalantis* (London: Penguin, 1992), p. v. The relationship was either through marriage or as a distant cousin, but according to the *DNB* "the actual relationship between Robert Harley . . . and Abigail Masham has never been discovered," however, the duchess of Marlborough believed that Masham "was in the relation to Mr. Harley as she was to me," i.e., a distant cousin.

14. Hill, *Robert Harley*, p. 118.

15. Feiling, *History of the Tory Party*, p. 405.

16. Feiling, *History of the Tory Party*, p. 408.

17. Swift, *Examiner*, no. 44, 31 May 1711 in *Prose Works*, III, p. 169.

18. See *A View of the Queen and Kingdom's Enemies in the case of the poor Palatines* (London: n.p., [1709?]); *A view of the Queen and Kingdom's enemies in the case of the poor Palatines: to which is added a list of the . . . members of the late Parliament that voted for the Naturalization-Bill* (London: n.p., 1709). See also Swift, *Examiner*, nos. 21/25, 21 December 1710 18 January 1711 in *Prose Works*, III, pp. 48, 71.

19. Swift, "Argument to Prove that the Abolishing of Christianity in England May . . . Be Attended with Some Inconveniences," in *Prose Works*, II, p. 28.

20. Bennett, *Tory Crisis in Church and State*, p. 101.

21. Narcissus Luttrell, *A Brief Relation of State Affairs from September 1678 to April 1714*, 6 vols. (Oxford: n.p., 1857), VI, pp. 505, 506, 508.

22. Lady Mary Wortley Montague to Mrs. Frances Hewet, 12 November [1709], in *The Complete Letters of Lady Mary Wortley Montague*, ed. Roberts Halsband, vol. 1 (Oxford: Clarendon Press, 1965) p.18.

23. *Rivella*, pp. 108, 109.

24. Public Records Office, State Papers 34, 11 (fol. 69). Unfortunately the records of the Queen's Bench proceedings for this period are no longer extant. I have also found no record of her imprisonment or her interview with Sunderland.

25. Luttrell, *A Brief Relation of State Affairs*, VI, p. 508.

26. *Rivella*, p. 113.

27. Luttrell, *A Brief Relation of State Affairs*, VI, p. 546.

28. Manley, *Memoirs of Europe*, I, preface (unpaginated).

29. Delarivier Manley to Sir John Hopkins, 2 November 1709. Pierpont Morgan Library, New York, MA4695.

30. *Rivella*, pp. 110, 113.

31. *Hearne*, II, p. 292.

32. Lady Mary Wortley Montague to Mrs Frances Hewet, 12 November [1709], in *Complete Letters of Lady Mary Wortley Montague*, p. 15.

33. Charles Spencer, 3rd Earl of Sunderland to Sarah, Duchess of Marlborough, 4 November 1709, BL, Add. MSS 61443, f.35.

34. Duchess of Marlborough to Queen Anne [1709], in *Private Correspondence of Sarah, Duchess of Marlborough*, (London: Henry Colburn, 1838), I, p. 236.

35. Manley's first known letter to Harley was probably written in 1710.

36. Mainwaring to Duchess of Marlborough, undated, 1709, in *Correspondence of Duchess of Marlborough*, I, p. 228.

37. Mainwaring to Duchess of Marlborough, undated, 1709, in *Correspondence of Duchess of Marlborough*, I, p. 230.

38. Sarah Churchill to Queen Anne, 1709 [u.d.] in *Correspondence of Duchess of Marlborough*, I, p. 235.

39. *Correspondence of Duchess of Marlborough*, I, p. 235.

40. *The Rival Dutchess: Or Court Incendiary* (London: n.p., 1708).

41. See the many poems in vols. V, VI and VII of *POAS*.

42. Mainwaring to Duchess of Marlborough, [u.d., 1709], in *Correspondence of Duchess of Marlborough*, I, p. 228.

43. See Michael S. Kimmel, "Love Letters Between a Certain Late Nobleman and the Famous Mr Wilson," *Journal of Homosexuality* 19 (1990): xiii–124; *The Conspirators; or the Case of Catiline* (London: n.p., 1721), p. 24.

44. Manley, *The Lady's Pacquet of Letters*, pp. 522–47.

45. See Ruth Herman, "Enigmatic Gender in Delarivier Manley's *New Atalantis*," in *Presenting Gender*, ed. C. Mounsey (Lewisburg: Bucknell University Press, 2001), pp. 202–24.

46. A fuller discussion of William III's court can be found in Dennis Rubini, "Sexuality and Augustan England: Sodomy, Politics, Elite Circles and Society," in Kent Gerard and Gert Hekma, eds., *The Pursuit of Sodomy: Male Homosexuality in Renaissance and Enlightenment Europe* (London: Harington Park Press Inc., 1989), p. 351.

47. Francis Bacon, *The Advancement of Learning* and *New Atlantis*, ed. Arthur Johnston (Oxford: Clarendon Press, 1974), p. 229.

48. Bacon, *New Atlantis*, p. 247.

49. Bacon, *New Atlantis* , p. 231.

50. Holmes, *British Politics*, p. 270.

51. Ballaster, *New Atalantis*, p. 270, n.17.

52. Manley, *Memoirs of Europe*, I, p. 167.

53. *Devil of a Whigg; or Zarazian Subtilty Detected* (London: n.p., 1708), p. 13.

54. For a discussion of this see Paula McDowell, *Women of Grub Street*, pp. 233–34.

55. See R. O. Bucholz, *The Augustan Court: Queen Anne and the Decline of Court Culture* (Stanford: Stanford University Press, 1993), pp. 205–6. See *A True Relation of the Several Facts and Circumstances of the Intended Riot and Tumult on Queen Elizabeth's Birthday* (London: John Morphew, 1711).

56. Frances A. Yates, *Astrea: The Imperial Theme in the Sixteenth Century* (London: Routledge & Kegan Paul, 1975), p. 47.

57. McDowell, *Women of Grub Street*, p. 237.

58. For contemporary accounts of Mackworth's dubious financial affairs see *The Case of Sir Humphrey Mackworth, and the Mine Adventurers.* (London: n.p., 1707), or [Sir Humphrey Mackworth] *A Familiar Discourse, or Dialogue concerning the Mine-Adventure.* (London: n.p., 1709). For a discussion of Mackworth's involvement in pamphleteering see Downie, *Robert Harley and the Press*, pp. 86–88.

59. For a discussion of this see Ballaster's *New Atalantis* pp. 291–92, and Köster, *Novels*, p. 909.

60. *Some Memoirs Relating to the Life of the Right Honourable John Lord Haversham from the Year 1640 to 1710* (London: n.p., 1711), p. iv.

61. Holmes, *British Politics*, p. 92.

62. *Queen Zarah*, II, p. 21.

63. *The Augustan Court*, p. 331, n. 110. Holmes, *British Politics*, p. 138.

64. For a discussion of this story see Koster, *Novels*, I, p. xix.

65. Holmes, *British Politics*, p. 91. Caesar did not name Marlborough but there was no doubt who he meant.

66. Holmes, *British Politics*, p. 265. Holmes records that, despite a personal affinity, Caesar did not always vote with Harley.

67. Feiling, *History of the Tory Party*, p. 387.

68. "The Golden Age Restor'd," *POAS*, VI, p. 503; "The Golden Age," *POAS*, VI, p. 462.

69. See Downie, *Robert Harley and the Press*, pp. 94–96.

70. Joseph Browne, *St. James's Park: A Satyr* (London: H. Hills, 1708), 7.

71. Holmes, *British Politics*, p. 264.

72. *St. James's Park*, p. 8.

73. *Memoirs of Thomas, Earl of Ailesbury, Written by himself.* Printed for the Roxburgh Club, (London: Nicholls & Son, 1890) vol.1, p. 618; *The Welsh Monster* (London: undated), p. A2.r.

74. See Feiling, *History of the Tory Party*, pp. 399–400.

75. *The Address of the Lords concerning W. Gregg* (London: n.p., 1708); *P. Lorrain, Ordinary of Newgate, his account of the Life and Death of W. Gregg* (London: n.p., 1708); *A Copy of W. Gregg's Paper delivered to the Sheriffs* (London: n.p., 1708); *A Letter to the Seven Lords appointed to examine Gregg*, (London: J. Baker, 1711).

76. Hill, *Robert Harley*, p. 121

77. Holmes, *British Politics*, p. 212.

78. See William Walsh, "Abigail's Lamentation," *POAS*, VII, pp. 303–4; Arthur Mainwaring, "A New Ballad," *POAS*, VII, pp. 309–16; Arthur Mainwaring, "Masham Display'd," *POAS*, VII, pp. 319–21. Joseph Browne, "The Humble Memorial," *POAS*, vol. VII, p. 327.

79. *Memoirs of Thomas, Earl of Ailesbury*, pp. 618–19.

80. *Rivella*, pp. 111–12.

81. See Henry Horwitcz, "The Structure of Parliamentary Politics," in *Britain after the Glorious Revolution*, ed. Geoffrey Holmes (London: Macmillan, 1978), p. 107.

82. Feiling, *History of the Tory Party*, p. 404.

83. W. A. Speck and J. A. Downie, "Plaine English to all who are honest or would be so if they knew how," *Literature and History* 3 (1976): p. 101.

84. *Zarah,* I, p. 83.
85. Rowse, *The Early Churchills,* p. 198
86. Ibid. p. 210.
87. Feiling, *History of the Tory Party,* p. 207.
88. Rowse, *The Early Churchills,* p. 195.
89. See earlier chapter. *Zarah,* vol. I, p. 65.
90. *Zarah,* I, p. 83.
91. Prince Eugene was a commander of the imperial army. "The Thanksgiving," *POAS,* VII, pp. 374–75
92. Harris, *A Passion for Government,* p. 44.
93. *Rivella,* p. 110.
94. William Nicolson, bishop of Carlisle, 8 February 1703. Quoted in *POAS,* VI, p. 419, n. 486.
95. See *The Hertford Letter Containing Several Brief Observations on a late Printed Tryal.* (London: u.p., 1699).
96. Defoe was much less bashful. Seven years earlier he had written a far more vicious attack on the younger brother: "The innocent lies unreveng'd in Death / He stopp'd the growing Scandal in her Breath: / Till Time shall lay the horrid Murther bare." "Reformation of Manners," *POAS,* VI, p. 420.
97. Hertfordshire Records Office, Panshanger MSS D/EP F37, f. 12. Lady Sarah Cowper, Journal, 11 July 1709.

4. "SOME FAINT REPRESENTATIONS"

The quotation in the title of this chapter was taken from: BL, Add. MSS, 70026, Delarivier Manley to Robert Harley, 12 May 1710.

1. Delarivier Manley, *Memoirs of Europe, Towards the Close of the Eighth Century. Written by Eginardus, Secretary and Favourite to Charlemagne; and done into English by the Translator of the New Atalantis,* 2 vols. (London: John Morphew, 1710). All quotations are from the first edition of volume 1 and the second, corrected, edition of volume 2 (1710). Volume and page references are included in parentheses in the text.
2. Advertised as "This Day is Publish'd" in *The Examiner,* 16 November 1710.
3. *The Examiner,* 3 August 1710.
4. Stationers Hall Records, vol. I, BL, M985/6, f. 21; Volume II, BL, M985/6, f. 86, 23 November 1710.
5. BL, Add. MSS, 70026 (unfoliated), Manley to Harley 12 May 1710.
6. *The Tatler,* 3 September 1709, I, pp. 439–40.
7. *The Tatler,* 10 November 1709, II, p. 77.
8. Steele to Manley, [6 September 1709] Blanchard, *Correspondence of Richard Steele,* p. 29.
9. John Nichols ed., *Epistolary Correspondence of Sir Richard Steele,* (London: J. Nichols, 1787), II, p. 274.
10. Feiling, *History of the Tory Party,* p. 419.
11. David Green, *Queen Anne,* p. 216.

12. Swift to Archbishop King, 9 September 1710, *Correspondence of Jonathan Swift*, I, p. 174.

13. Holmes, *British Politics*, p. 22.

14. For a full account of the Spanish theater of the war and Peterborough's activities see David Francis, *The First Peninsular War: 1702–1713* (London: Ernest Benn, 1975), pp. 171–96.

15. Colin Ballard, *The Great Earl of Peterborough* (London: Skeffington and Son, 1929), p. 237. Ballard gives a lively account of Peterborough's problems in Spain on pp. 230-41.

16. Ballard, *The Great Earl of Peterborough*, p. 237.

17. Cunningham, *The History of Great Britain from the Revolution in 1688 to the Accession of George I*, ed. William Thomson (London: Hollingsby, 1787), I, p. 465.

18. John Freind, *An Account of the Earl of Peterborough's Conduct in Spain, Chiefly since the raising of the Siege of Barcelona, 1706.*, 2d. ed. (London: Jonah Bowyer, 1707), p. 2.

19. Freind, *An Account of the Earl of Peterborough*, p. 4.

20. Ballard, *The Great Earl of Peterborough*, pp. 244–45.

21. Holmes, *British Politics*, p. 202.

22. See *Earl of Peterborough. Impartial remarks on the Earl of Peterborow's conduct in Spain. Written by a gentleman who was an eye-witness of his Lordship's transaction in that kingdom* (London: n.p., 1707), and *The Earl of Peterborough's Vindication anent the bad Success in Spain* (London: n.p., [1707?]).

23. George Farquhar, *Barcellona: A Poem on the Spanish Expedition* (London: n.p., 1710).

24. Duchess of Marlborough to Queen Anne, *Correspondence of Sarah, Duchess of Marlborough*, undated, I, p. 236.

25. David Francis, *The First Peninsular War 1702–1713*, pp. 243–44.

26. Feiling, *History of the Tory Party*, p. 398.

27. Cunningham, I, p. 466.

28. *Barcellona*, dedication, sig. A2. See also *A Genuine Copy of the Duke of Marlborough's Letter to the Earl of Peterborough* (London: n.p., 1706[?]).

29. Downie, *Robert Harley and the Press*, p. 119. For a full discussion of *Faults on Both Sides* see Paul Baker Patterson, "Robert Harley and the Organization of Political Propaganda," pp. 231–51. See also Henry L. Snyder, "The Authorship of *Faults on Both Sides*," *Philological Quarterly* 56 (1977): 266–72.

30. [Simon Clement], *Faults on Both Sides* (London: n.p., 1710), p. 28

31. *Faults on Both Sides*, p. 29.

32. Francis, *The First Peninsula War*, p. 315.

33. Howard D. Weinbrot, "Johnson, Jacobitism, and Swedish Charles: The Vanity of Human Wishes and Scholarly Method," *English Literary History* 64 (1997): 950.

34. Catharine Trotter, *The Revolution of Sweden* (London: James Knapton, George Strahan, 1706), prologue (unpaginated).

35. For a further discussion of Charles's standing in England, see Howard D. Weinbrot, "Who Said He Was a Jacobite?: The Political Genealogy of Johnson's Charles of Sweden," *Philological Quarterly*. 75 (1996): pp. 411–50.

36. Samuell Puffendorf, *The Compleat History of Sweden from its Origin to this Time: Faithfully translated from the Original High Dutch and carefully Continued down to this present Year* (London: Joseph Will, 1702), p. 607.
37. *New Atalantis*, I, p. 18.
38. William Doyle, *The Old European Order 1660–1800*, 2d. ed., (Oxford: Oxford University Press, 1992), p. 279.
39. Köster's key gives this as Nerva. *Novels*, p. 903.
40. Doyle, *The Old European Order*, p. 230.
41. *The Second Part of Arlus, Fortunatus, & Odolphus* (London: n.p., 1710), p. 3.
42. *Faults on Both Sides*, p. 50.
43. *Faults on Both Sides* (London: 1710), p. 51.
44. Bernard Connor, *The History of Poland in Several Letters to Persons of Quality* (London: Savage, 1698), II, p. 12.
45. Daniel Defoe, "The Dyet of Poland." The allegorical implications of the poem are explained fully in *POAS*, VII, pp. 72–132.
46. Bernard Connor, *The History of Poland*, II, p. 189
47. *Faults on Both Sides*, pp. 33–34.
48. *Faults on Both Sides*, p. 34.
49. See for instance, *The Secret History of Arlus and Odolphus*; *The Second Part of the Impartial Secret History of Arlus, Fortunatus, & Odolphus* (London: n.p., 1710); *An Abridgment of the Secret History of Crete* (London: 1711). Texts produced only a couple of years earlier, such as *The Devil of a Whigg*, or *The Glorious Life and Actions of St. Whigg* (London: n.p., 1708) are far less explicit.
50. Harris, *A Passion for Government*, p. 173.
51. Harris, *A Passion for Government*, pp. 60–61.
52. Arthur Mainwaring, "A New Ballad," *POAS*, VII, p. 311.
53. See *The Loyal Trimmer* (London: n.p., 1712).
54. Peter Wentworth to Thomas Wentworth, 29 June 1714. *Wentworth Papers 1705–1739*, ed. James J. Cartwright (London: Wyman and Sons, 1883), p. 395.
55. *Journal*, 24 August 1711, I, p. 339.
56. Geoffrey Holmes, *The Trial of Dr. Sacheverell* (London: Eyre Methuen, 1973), p. 31. This book contains a full account of Sacheverell's sermon, his trial, and the aftermath.
57. Henry Sacheverell, *The Perils of False Brethren both in Church and State set Forth in a Sermon Preach'd before the Right Honourable Lord Mayor* (London: Henry Clements, 1709), p. 22.
58. See *The Tatler*, 7 March 1710, II, pp. 310–11.
59. *The Officers Address to the Ladies* (London: n.p., 1710), p.2.
60. See *The Age of Mad Folks* (London: 1710).
61. For contemporary comment on the celebrations see *A Trip from Westminster Hall to Oxford* (London: n.p., 1710).
62. See F. F. Madan, *A Critical Bibliography of Dr. Henry Sacheverell*, ed. W. A. Speck (Lawrence: University of Kansas Libraries, 1978).
63. *The Tatler*, 4 March 1710, II, p. 306.
64. *Aminadab, or the Quaker's Vision, Explain'd and Answer'd Paragraph by Paragraph* ([London]: n.p., 1710), p. 5.

65. George Cunningham, *The History of Great Britain from the Revolution in 1688 to the Accession of George I*, ed. William Thomson, (London: Hollingsby, 1787), II, p. 277.

66. Cunningham, II, p. 277.

67. *A Compleat History of the Whole Proceedings of the Parliament of Great Britain against Dr Henry Sacheverell with his Tryal before the House of Peers* (London: J. Baker, 1710), [section 2], p. 84.

68. *Bellisarius: A Great Commander and Zariana His Lady* (London: n.p., 1710), p. 7. The poem also contains Sarah's complaint at the way pamphleteers treat her. p. 13.

69. Holmes, *British Politics*, p. 75.

70. Defoe noted that as a way of attacking Marlborough, his Duchess "shall have all the Spite/That Fools can put upon her." "The Age of Wonders," *POAS*, VII, p. 470.

71. For instance, *Oliver's Pocket Looking-Glass New Fram'd and Clean'd to give a Clear View of the Great Modern Colossus* (London: n.p., 1711); *The Fable of Midas* (London: n.p., 1711). For a fuller list see Robert D. Horn, *Marlborough: A Survey. Penegyrics, Satires and Biographical Writings 1688–1788* (Folkestone: Dawsons, 1975).

72. Harris, *A Passion for Government*, p. 150.

73. Harris, *A Passion for Government*, p. 154.

74. David Green, *Queen Anne*, pp. 213–14.

75. *The Fate of Manlius Capitolinus* (London: n.p., 1712), p. 4; *M. Manlius Capitolinus* (London: n.p., 1711); *A Roman Story* (London: n.p., 1711); See also *The Queen's and the Duke of Ormonde's Toast* (London: n.p., 1712) which suggests that Marlborough had once aimed to be styled "John the Second."

76. For a discussion of Somers's affair with Elizabeth Blount, see Robert M. Adams, "In Search of Baron Somers," in *Culture and Politics From Puritanism to the Enlightenment*, ed. Perez Zagorin (Berkeley and Los Angeles: University of California Press, 1980), pp. 183–85; also "Fathers Nown Child," *POAS*, V, p. 427; and *A Letter from the Grecian Coffee-house, In Answer to the Taunton-Dean Letter* ([London?]: n.p., 1711), p. 7.

77. Swift, *Prose Works*, III, p. 180.

78. *An Acrostick on Wharton*, in *The Post Boy*, 12 December 1710.

79. Swift, *Examiner* 17 23 November 1710, *Prose Works*, III, p. 28.

80. Holmes, *British Politics*, p. 27.

81. Holmes, *British Politics*, p. 239.

82. "On the Queen's Speech," in *POAS*, VII, p. 412.

83. *The Devil of a Whigg*, p. 3; *Arlus and Odolphus*, p. 15.

84. There were a great many pamphlets written against the Marlboroughs and/or the Junto. See, for instance, William Shippen, *Duke Humphrey's Answer* (London: n.p., 1708); *The Widow and her Cat* (London: n.p.,[1710?]); *The Junto* (London: n.p., [1710?]).

85. *Arlus and Odolphus*, p. 31. See also *On the Queen's Speech* (London: n.p., 1710) in which Anne is depicted as merely a spokesperson for the Junto.

86. *A Modest Enquiry into the Reasons of the Joy Express'd by a Certain Sett of People, upon the Spreading of a Report of Her Majesty's Death* (London: John Morphew, 1714), p. 7.

87. *The Examiner*, no. 47, 21 June 1711.
88. R. O. Bucholz, *The Augustan Court*, p. 207.
89. *Arlus and Odolphus*, p. 19.
90. Arthur Mainwaring, "A New Ballad," *POAS*, VII, p. 309.

5. MISTRESS *EXAMINER*

1. Holmes, *British Politics*, pp. 371–72; Feiling, *History of the Tory Party*, p. 419.
2. Feiling, *History of the Tory Party*, p. 422.
3. Feiling, *History of the Tory Party*, p. 419
4. Joseph Addison, *The Freeholder*, 24 February 1716. Quoted in Patterson, "Robert Harley and the Organization of Political Propaganda," p. 154.
5. Nichols, *A Supplement to Dr Swift's Work* (London: John Nichols, 1779), pp. 62–63.
6. For a concise description of the early *Examiner* see F. P. Lock, *Swift's Tory Politics* (London: Duckworth, 1983), p. 28.
7. Paul Baker Patterson, "Robert Harley and the Organization of Political Propaganda," p. 154.
8. For a full discussion of Swift's editorship, see Frank Ellis, *Swift versus Mainwaring: The Examiner and The Medley* (Oxford: Oxford University Press, 1985), pp. xxi–xlix.
9. *Journal*, 3 November 1711.
10. BL, Add. MSS, 70028 (unfoliated), Manley to Harley, 2 October [1711]. The issue to which Manley refers is the *Examiner* of 19 July 1711.
11. Ellis, *Swift versus Mainwaring*, p. lviii.
12. As Ellis comments, Mainwaring appears to be unaware that the consortium of writers had by this time (February 1711) given way to Swift. *Medley*, 19 February 1711; Ellis, *Swift versus Mainwaring*, pp. 253–54.
13. Jonathan Swift, *Prose Works*, VIII, pp. 123–24.
14. Gwendolyn Needham also suggests that Manley is the probable author of number 7, "Mary de la Riviere Manley: Tory Defender," *Huntington Library Quarterly* 12 (1948–49), 271–72.
15. J. A. Downie, "Swift and the Oxford Ministry," *Swift Studies* 1 (1986): 4.
16. BL, Add. MSS, 70026 (unfoliated).
17. *Medley*, 18 June 1711; Ellis, *Swift versus Mainwaring*, p. 486.
18. *Medley*, 18 June 1711; Ellis, *Swift versus Mainwaring*, p. 487.
19. *Medley*, 16 July 1711.
20. Sarah Churchill to Dr. David Hamilton, Blenheim, G-I-8, quoted in Green, *Queen Anne*, p. 235.
21. *The Life and Character of John Barber*, p. 16.
22. "The Medley," in *The Flying Post or Post Master*, 4 October 1712.
23. *Flying Post or Post Master*, 26–28 February 1713.
24. Abel Boyer, *Quadirennium Annae; The Political State of Great Britain*, (London: n.p., 1719), VI, pp. 253–54.
25. Doyle, *The Old European Order*, p. 277.
26. *The Daily Courant*, 4 August, 1710.

27. In *The Daily Courant* alone, Swedish news is included in the issues of 11, 15, 17 and 23 August 1711; 9, 11and 13 September 1711.
28. Joseph Addison, *The Spectator*, no. 619, 12 November 1714.
29. *The Daily Courant*, 11 September 1710.
30. *Evening Post*, 29 August 1710. The reports of Charles's release were soon discounted in later editions.
31. Holmes, *British Politics*, p. 174.
32. Bucholz, *Court Life and Culture*, p. 205.
33. John Oldmixon, *Memoirs of the Press, Historical and Political For Thirty Years Past From 1710–1740* (London: T. Cox, 1742), pp. 7–8.
34. Swift, *Journal to Stella*, 3 November 1711, II, p. 402.
35. For a discussion of the end of Swift's editorship see David Nokes, *Jonathan Swift, a Hypocrite Reversed* (Oxford: Oxford University Press, 1985), p. 132; Ellis, *Swift vs. Mainwaring* p. xxxiii; J. A. Downie, *Robert Harley and The Press*, p. 137.
36. Downie, *Robert Harley and The Press*, p. 137.
37. Swift, *Journal to Stella*, 7 June 1711, I, p. 291.
38. For example, see Paula McDowell, *Women of Grub Street*, p. 276.
39. Melinda Alliker Rabb, "Swift and the Spider-woman: Manley and Tory Satire," in *Locating Swift: Essays on the 250th Anniversary of the Death of Jonathan Swift 1667–1745*, eds. Aileen Douglas, Patrick Kelly, Ian Campbell Ross (Dublin: Four Courts Press, 1998), p. 62.
40. Hill, *Robert Harley*, p. 155.
41. Hill, *Robert Harley*, p. 157.
42. Ellis, *Swift vs. Mainwaring*, pp. xl–xli.
43. *Examiner* no. 45, 7 June 1711.
44. Hill, *Robert Harley*, p. 154.
45. Feiling, *History of the Tory Party*, p. 432.
46. Holmes, *British Politics*, p. 343.
47. W. A. Speck, "The Examiner *Re-Examined*," *Prose Studies* 16 (1993): 35.
48. Hill, *Robert Harley*, p. 146.
49. Hill, *Robert Harley*, p. 156.
50. W. A. Speck, "The Examiner *Re-Examined*," p. 42.
51. J. A. Downie, "Swift and the Oxford Ministry," p. 4.
52. *Examiner*, 14 June 1711, Ellis, *Swift vs. Mainwaring*, p. 477.
53. *Journal*, 22 June 1711, I, p. 296.
54. See *Journal*, 8–20 June, I, p. 293.
55. *Examiner*, 14 June 1711, Ellis, *Swift vs. Mainwaring*, p. 477, n. 2.
56. Manley, *Rivella*, p.10.
57. *Examiner*, 14 June 1711, Ellis, *Swift vs. Mainwaring*, p. 478, n. 23.
58. *New Atalantis*, I, p. 183.
59. Downie, *Harley and the Press*, p. 138.
60. See Addison's *Spectator*, no. 3, 3 March 1711.
61. For a discussion of the "Representation" see G. V. Bennett, *The Tory Crisis in Church and State*, pp. 136–38.
62. Swift, "The History of Four Last Years of Queen Anne's Reign," in *Prose Works*, VII, p. 66.

63. *The Medley*, 2 July 1711.
64. *The Post Man*, 2 June 1711.
65. Feiling, *The History of the Tory Party*, p. 400.
66. Manley, *Rivella*, p. 109.
67. See chapter on *Memoirs of Europe*.
68. *Dr. Sacheverell turn'd Oculist: or Sir W[illiam] R——ds [?] Lamentation for the loss of his Business* (London: n.p., 1710).
69. Feiling, *History of the Tory Party*, p. 430.
70. Harris, *A Passion for Government*, p. 183.
71. See, for instance, *M. Manlius Capitolinus* (London: n.p., 1711); *The Fable of M. Manlius Capitolinus* (London: n.p., 1712); Jonathan Swift, *The Fable of Midas* (London: n.p., 1712).
72. *The Medley*, 23 July 1711.
73. Ibid.
74. *An Account of a Dream at Harwich. In a Letter to a Member of Parliament about the Camisars* (London: n.p., 1708), p.12.
75. William Shippen, "Duke Humphrey's Answer," *POAS*, VII, p. 334.
76. Green, *Queen Anne*, p. 136.
77. Quoted in Harris, *A Passion for Government*, p. 252.
78. Arthur Mainwaring, "Tarquin and Tullia," *POAS*, V, pp. 50–51. It is ironic that this early lampooning of Sarah Churchill was written by Arthur Mainwaring, later her secretary and editor of the *Medley*.
79. See Swift, "Advice Humbly Offer'd to the Members of the October Club," in *Prose Works*, VI, p. 73.
80. Swift, *Prose Works*, III, p. xiii.
81. *Examiner*, no. 46, 14 June 1711.
82. Downie, *Robert Harley and the Press*, p. 96; "The Infernal Congress," quoted in Ellis, *Swift vs. Mainwaring*, p. xli.
83. C. John Sommerville, *The News Revolution in England* (Oxford: Oxford University Press, 1996), p. 150.
84. *Examiner*, 24 May 1711, Ellis, *Swift vs. Mainwaring*, p. 440.
85. *Examiner*, 12 April 1711, Ellis, *Swift vs. Mainwaring*, p. 362. *Rivella*, p. 119.

6. "SEVERAL LITTLE PAMPHLETS AND PAPERS"

1. BL, Add. MSS, 70032 (unfoliated). Manley to Oxford, 14 June 1714.
2. J. R. Moore subsequently attributed it to Defoe, but this ascription has been shown to be in error. See P. N. Furbank and W. R. Owens, *Defoe De-Attributions: A Critique of J. R. Moore's Checklist* (London: Hambledon Press, 1994), p. 61.
3. British Library. Add. MSS 70028 (unfoliated): Manley to Oxford, 2 October [1711].
4. A full discussion of this topic is contained in Ruth Herman, "Swift, Manley and the Commissioning of *A True Narrative*," *Swift Studies* 16 (2000): 88–101.

5. Swift, *Prose Works*, XV, p. 254.
6. Harley's brother believed they were intimates. See BL, Lansdowne MSS 885 (f. 30). For the story that St. John and Guiscard's intimacy resulted in a paternity dispute with a shared mistress, see *The Life and History of the right Honourable Henry St. John., Lord Visc. Bolingbroke* (London: M. Cooper, C. Sympson, 1754), pp. 10–11.
7. H. T. Dickinson, "The Attempt to Assassinate Harley, 1711," *History Today* 15 (1965): 790–91.
8. See, for example, *The Congratulatory Speech of William Bromley . . . to the Right Honourable Robert Harley, Esq.* (London: Samuel Keble, 1711). Panegyrics also appeared in verse; see for example, *To the Right Honourable Mr. Harley* (London: Richard Sare, 1711); Joseph Trapp, *To the Right Honourable Mr. Harley, on his first appearing in public, after the wound given him by Guiscard* (London: John Morphew, 1711).
9. *London Gazette*, 8 March 1711. See also *The British Mercury*, 9 March 1711; *The Post Boy*, 10 March 1711; *The Flying Post*, 10 March 1711; *Evening Post*, 10 March 1711.
10. St. John to Drummond, 13 March 1711, in *Letters and Correspondence, Public and Private of the Right Honourable Henry St. John, Lord Viscount Bolingbroke, During the Time he was Secretary of State to Queen Anne*, ed. Gilbert Parke (London: n.p., 1798), VI, p. 63.
11. Ellis, *Swift vs. Mainwaring*, p. 303.
12. Swift, *Prose Works*, VIII, p. 128.
13. Ellis, *Swift vs. Mainwaring*, pp. 312–13.
14. Swift, *Prose Works*, VIII, p. 128.
15. BL Add. MSS, 70144 (unfoliated); Edward Harley to Abigail Harley, 17 March 1711.
16. Ellis, *Swift vs. Mainwaring*, p. 320.
17. BL, Add. MSS, 70144 (unfoliated); Edward Harley to Abigail Harley, 27 March 1711.
18. BL, Add. MSS, 70147 (bundle 2); Lady Dupplin to Abigail Harley, 22 March 1711.
19. BL, Lansdowne MSS, 885 f.68.
20. See Sheila Biddle for a full discussion of the likely truth behind the theory that Guiscard had intended to kill St. John; *Bolingbroke and Harley* (New York: A. Knopf, 1974), pp. 206–7.
21. BL, Add. MSS, 70088 (j); Edward Harley's draft *Memoirs*.
22. BL, Add. MSS, 70142 (bundle 2) f.4; Edward Harley's draft *Memoirs*.
23. Swift, *Prose Works*, XV, p. 244.
24. Swift, *Prose Works*, XV, p. 244.
25. Swift, *Prose Works*, XVI, p. 408.
26. For a discussion of *The Windsor Prophecy* see Hermann J. Real, "The Most Fateful Piece Swift ever Wrote," *Swift Studies* 9 (1994): 76–99; for comment on *The Public Spirit of the Whigs*, see J. A. Downie, *Robert Harley and the Press*, p. 180.
27. Swift, *Prose Works*, VIII, p. 127.
28. BL, Add. MSS, 70026 (unfoliated): Delarivier Manley to Robert Harley, 12 May 1710.

29. BL, Add. MSS, 70290, f.1: Delarivier Manley to Robert Harley, 16 April [1710?].
30. BL, Add. MSS, 70028 (unfoliated): Delarivier Manley to Earl of Oxford, 19 July 1711.
31. See previous chapters on *New Atalantis* and *Memoirs of Europe*.
32. BL, Add. MSS, 70028 (unfoliated): Delarivier Manley to Oxford, 30 August 1714.
33. Swift, *Prose Works*, XV, p. 245.
34. *A True Narrative*, pp. 6–7.
35. *A True Narrative*, p. 7.
36. See various versions of Edward Harley's memoirs, BL, Lansdowne MSS, 885; BL, Add. MSS 70088; 70142.
37. *A True Narrative*, p. 16.
38. BL, Lansdowne MSS, 885, f.39.
39. *A True Narrative*, p. 7.
40. Downie, *Robert Harley and the Press*, p. 136.
41. Abel Boyer, *Political State of Great Britain*, I, p. 210.
42. Swift, *Prose Works*, XV, 245.
43. *An Acrostick on Wharton*.
44. For the details of Harley's parliamentary difficulties see Brian W. Hill, *Robert Harley*, p. 149.
45. Ellis, *Swift vs. Mainwaring*, p. 301.
46. Downie, *Robert Harley and the Press*, p. 163.
47. *The Post Boy*, 10 March 1711.
48. *The Post Boy*, 24 March 1711. See also *The Spectator's Address to the Whigs* (advertised in the *Post Boy* as published on 17 March 1711).
49. *A True Narrative*, p. 32.
50. Ellis, *Swift vs. Mainwaring*, p. 300.
51. *A True Narrative*. p. 10.
52. Boyer, *The Political State of Great Britain*, I, p. 211.
53. Melinda Alliker Rabb, "The Manl(e)y Style: Delariviere Manley and Jonathan Swift," in *Pope, Swift, and Women Writers*, ed. Donald C. Mell (Newark and London: Associated University Presses, 1996), p. 146.
54. See n. 17 above. Edward Harley to Abigail Harley, 27 March 1711.
55. *A True Narrative*, p. 31
56. *A True Narrative*, p. 23. For Manley's earlier attitude to Harley and Moderation see chapter on *Queen Zarah*. See also Brian Hill, *Robert Harley*, pp. 5-6.
57. F. G. Stevens, *Catalogue of Prints and Drawings in the British Museum: Political and Personal Satires*, vol. 2 (1873), no. 1549; see also nos. 1495, 1496, 1505 and in engravings such as nos. 1497, 1540.
58. *A True Narrative*, p. 34. On the increase in building churches, see Boyer, *The Political State of Great Britain*, I, p. 256.
59. See chapter on *Memoirs of Europe*.
60. *A True Narrative*, p. 39.
61. *A True Narrative*, p. 22.
62. For St. John's precipitate action, see also *The Changes: Or Faction Vanquished* (London: John Morphew, 1711), p. 13.
63. BL, Lansdowne MSS, 885, f.30.

64. See Feiling, *A History of the Tory Party*, p. 470.
65. *A True Narrative*, p. 7.
66. Holmes, *British Politics*, p. 75.
67. BL, Add. MSS, 70088, f.v.
68. *A True Narrative*, p. 24.
69. *A True Narrative*, pp. 23–24.
70. *A True Narrative*, p. 24.
71. *A True Narrative*, p. 42.
72. BL, Add. MSS, 70028 (unfoliated).
73. For a discussion of the peace negotiations see A. D. MacLachlan, "The Road to Peace: 1710–1713," in *Britain after the Glorious Revolution*, ed. Geoffrey Holmes (London: Macmillan, 1969), pp. 197–215; J. A. Downie, *To Settle the Succession of the State* (London: Macmillan, 1994), pp. 76–82.
74. Edward Gregg, *The Protestant Succession in International Politics, 1710–1716* (London: Garland Publishing, 1986) pp. 119–22.
75. For Marlborough's decision to oppose the peace, see Gregg, *The Protestant Succession*, pp. 132–33.
76. *The Nature of Man*, 3 vols. (London: Samuel Buckley, 1711), book 2, p. 64.
77. *The Speech of Lord Haversham's Ghost* (London: n.p., 1711), p. 4. For another vigorous defence of the Duke see *A short Narrative of the Life and Actions of His Grace John, Duke of Marlborough, from the Revolution to the Present Time* (London: n.p., 1711); *The Windsor Prophecy Found in a Marlborough Rock* (London: n.p., 1711). This is not Swift's poem of almost the same name.
78. See Gregg, *The Protestant Succession*, pp 126–28.
79. *To the Duke of Marlborough On the Taking of Bouchain* (London: S. Popping, 1711).
80. BL, Add. MSS, 70028 (unfoliated), Manley to Oxford, 2 October 1711.
81. [Francis Hare/Arthur Mainwaring], *Bouchain: In a Dialogue Between the Late Medley and Examiner* (London: A. Baldwin, 1711). Advertised as "Yesterday was Publish'd" on 20 September 1711. Oldmixon later claimed that Mainwaring "revis'd and Publish'd" this pamphlet. This seems more likely. Robert D. Horne, *Marlborough: A Survey*, p. 322.
82. Delarivier Manley, *The D. of M[arlboroug]h's Vindication: In Answer to a Pamphlet, lately Published, called Bouchain; or a Dialogue Between the Medley and the Examiner* (London: John Morphew, 1711). Published 2 October 1711.
83. *Vindication*, p. 3.
84. *Bouchain: In a Dialogue*, pp. 41, 42.
85. *Bouchain: In a Dialogue*, pp. 41–42
86. To avoid confusion in discussion of this pamphlet, *Bouchain: In a Dialogue*, I shall refer to the protagonists as Mr *Medley* and Mr *Examiner*.
87. *Bouchain:In a Dialogue*, p. 42.
88. *Journal*, 22 October 1711.
89. Specifically Swift's *Examiner* on Marcus Crassus (no. 27), *Prose Works*, III, pp. 83–85 and Manley's *Examiner* on Antony and Fulvia (no. 51). *Vindication*, p. 4.
90. *Vindication*, p. 7.
91. *Vindication*, p. 5

92. *Vindication*, pp. 5–6.
93. *Vindication*, p. 14.
94. *Vindication*, p. 14.
95. *Vindication*, p. 15.
96. [Anon] *The Duke of Marlborough's Vindication In Answer to a Pamphlet falsely so called* (London: A. Baldwin, 1712), p. 13. See also the later Tory pamphlet, *A Modest Attempt to Prove Dr H[are] not the Author of the Bouchain Dialogue* (London: n.p., 1712).
97. Quoted in Winston Churchill, *Marlborough* (London: George G. Harrap & Co, 1947); Duke of Marlborough to Duchess of Marlborough, (undated) II, p. 868; Marlborough to Oxford, 19 October 1711, II, p. 869.
98. Oxford to Marlborough, 30 October. Quoted in Winston Churchill, *Marlborough: His Life and Times*, II, p. 869; BL, Add. MSS 70028 Manley to Harley, 2 October [1711].
99. Date confirmed in Manley's letter to Oxford of 2 October [1711].
100. Francis Hare, *The Charge of God to Joshua: in a Sermon Preach'd Before his Grace the Duke of Marlborough at Avennes le Sec September 9. 1711* (London: n.p., 1711).
101. Swift, *Prose Works*, III, p. xxxiii.
102. *Journal*, 3 November, 1711.
103. Francis Hare, *The Management of the War in Four Letters to a Tory Member* (London: Egbert Sanger, 1711), p. 3.
104. *Learned Comment*, p. 3.
105. Gregg, *The Protestant Succession*, p. 128.
106. *Charge of God to Joshua*, p. 16.
107. *Charge of God to Joshua*, p. 6.
108. *Learned Comment*, p. 4
109. *Charge of God to Joshua*, p. 7.
110. *Learned Comment*, p. 5. The same sentiment is still being expressed in 1712. See *The Fable of Cods Heads* (London: n.p., 1712); *The Queen's and the Duke of Ormond's New Toast* (London: n.p., 1712).
111. *Learned Comment*, p. 15.
112. *Parliamentary History*, VI. p. 780, quoted in Holmes, *British Politics*, p. 69.
113. *Learned Comment*, p. 15.
114. *Learned Comment*, p. 15. The most obvious reference here is the fact that the Tory Commons had failed to achieve the repeal of the Naturalization Act only a few months before. See Bennett, *Tory Crisis in Church and State*, p. 134.
115. Carole Fabricant, "The Shared Worlds of Manley and Swift," p. 172.
116. Delarivier Manley, *The Honour and Prerogative of the Queen's Majesty Vindicated against the Unexampled Insolence of the Author of the Guardian; in a Letter from a Country Whig to Mr. Steele*. (London: John Morphew, 1713). Advertised as "This Day is Published" in *The Examiner*, 14 August 1713, and *Mercator*, 13 August 1713.
117. I have taken the details of the arguments over Dunkirk from Paul Hyland, "A breach of the peace: the controversy over the ninth article of the Treaty of Utrecht," *British Journal for Eighteenth Century Studies* 1, no. 22 (1999):

51–66. See also J. R. Moore, 'Defoe, Steele, and the Demolition of Dunkirk," *Huntington Library Quarterly* 13 (1950): 279–302.

118. Moore, "Defoe, Steele, and the Demolition of Dunkirk," p. 92.

119. [Anon], *French Sincerity Exemplified in the Surrender of Dunkirk to Her Britainnick Majesty Queen Anne.* ([London?]: n.p., [1713?]).

120. See for instance, John Toland's *Dunkirk or Dover; or the Queen's Honour, the Nation's Safety, The Liberties of Europe, and the Peace of the World* (London: n.p., 1713).

121. *A most humble address or memorial presented to Her Majesty the Queen of Great Britain* ([London?]: n.p., 1713).

122. Hyland, "A breach of the peace," p. 56.

123. Richard Steele, *The Guardian*, 7 August, 1713.

124. *Honour and Prerogative*, p. 19.

125. The *Examiner*, 21 and 24 August 1713.

126. Daniel Defoe, *Reasons Concerning the Immediate Demolishing of Dunkirk: being a Serious Enquiry into the State and Condition of that Affair* (London: John Morphew, 1713).

127. Richard Steele, *The Importance of Dunkirk Consider'd: in Defence of the Guardian of August the 7th in a Letter to the Bailiff of Stockbridge* (London: n.p., 1713).

128. Swift, "The Importance of the Guardian Consider'd: in Defence of the Guardian of August the 7th in a Second Letter to the Bailiff of Stockbridge," *Prose Works*, VIII, pp. 3–25.

129. See *New Atalantis*, I, p. 187.

130. Richard Steele, *Guardian*, 12 May 1713.

131. *Honour and Prerogative*, p. 21.

132. *Honour and Prerogative*, p. 10.

133. *Honour and Prerogative*, p. 10. See also Melinda Alliker Rabb, "Swift and the Spider-Woman," p. 79.

134. *Honour and Prerogative*, p. 10.

135. *Memoirs of Europe*, I, p. 216.

136. *Memoirs of Europe*, I, p. 217.

137. *Examiner*, no. 47, 21 June 1711.

138. *Honour and Prerogative*, p. 11.

139. *Honour and Prerogative*, p. 13.

140. *Examiner*, 21 August 1713.

7. "PRIDE OF OUR SEX, AND GLORY OF THE STAGE"

The quotation in this chapter title is taken from: Mary Pix, "To *Mrs Manley*, upon her Tragedy call'd *The Royal Mischief*," *The Royal Mischief* (London: R. Bentley, 1696), unpaginated.

1. In her will, Manley named a tragedy, *The Duke of Somerset*, and a comedy, *The Double Mistress*, "which may perhaps turn to some account." PRO 11, 599.

2. See Susan J. Owen, *Restoration Theatre and Crisis* (Cambridge: Cambridge University Press, 1996), for the centrality of politics to the Restoration stage prior to the Glorious Revolution.

3. Jeremy Collier, *A Short View of the Immorality, and Profaneness of the English Stage* (London: S. Keble, 1698), p. 1. As a non-Juror Collier had refused to swear an oath of allegience to William and Mary.

4. John Dennis, *The Usefulness of the Stage, to the Happiness of Mankind To Government, and To Religion* (London: Rich. Parker, 1698), p. 12.

5. Thomas Baker, *An Act at Oxford* (London: Bernard Lintott), Epistle Dedicatory a2V, unpaginated.

6. First performed by Thomas Betterton's company in Drury Lane, probably in March 1696.

7. See Margaret J. M. Ezell, *The Patriarch's Wife: Literary Evidence and the History of the Family* (Chapel Hill: University of North Carolina Press, 1987), p. 18.

8. This is perhaps why the authors of *The Female Wits* emphasized vanity in Marsilia, their Manley figure. She was not alone in expressing these concerns. See for instance Defoe's suggestions for an Academy for Women in *An Essay on Projects*.

9. See *Rivella*.

10. Delarivier Manley, *The Lost Lover: or the Jealous Husband* (London: R. Bentley, 1696), preface, unpaginated.

11. For details of this see Jane Garrett, *The Triumphs of Providence: The Assassination Plot 1696* (Cambridge: Cambridge University Press, 1980), p. 262.

12. E. L. Ellis, "William III and the Politicians," in *Britain after the Glorious Revolution*, p. 119.

13. Defoe, *The Review*, 1708, ed. A. W. Secord, V, p. 142, quoted in Ellis, "William III and the Politicians" p. 119

14. See H. T. Dickenson, *Liberty and Property: Political Ideology in Eighteenth Century Britain* (London: Weidenfeld and Nicolson, 1977), p. 28. William III was essentially in agreement on the inadvisability of overly frequent parliaments and the consequent restriction on the monarchy. Dickenson, p. 44.

15. Rachel Weil, *Political Passions* (Manchester: University of Manchester Press, 1999), p. 149.

16. See J. P. Kenyon, *Revolution Principles: The Politics of Party 1689–1720* (Cambridge: Cambridge University Press, 1990), p. 33. This willingness to support William even included that paragon of High Toryism, Nottingham,

17. J. Douglas Canfield, "Royalism's Last Dramatic Stand: English Political Tragedy, 1679–1689," *Studies in Philology* 82 (1985): 246.

18. Mark Goldie, "The Revolution of 1689: Pamphlets on the Allegiance Controversy' in *Bulletin of Research in the Humanities*, 83 (1980), p. 484.

19. Quoted in John M. Wallace, "The Engagement Controversy 1649–1652: An annotated list of pamphlets" in *Bulletin of the New York Public Library* 68, no. 6 (1964): 397, n. 34.

20. Wallace, "The Engagement Controversy," p. 394, n. 17.

21. Delarivier Manley, "To the Reader," *The Royal Mischief* (London: R. Bentley, 1696), unpaginated.

22. Sir John Chardin, *The Travels of Sir John Chardin into Persia and the East-Indies* (London: George Monke, William Ewley, 1689), pp. 133–36.

23. For a full discussion of this issue see Paulina Kewes, *Authorship and Appropriation* (Oxford: Clarendon Press, 1998), pp. 112–28. Dr Kewes also points out that (unlike Manley) authors usually acknowledged their sources fully, pp. 77–79.

24. Ruth Herman, "Similarities between Delarivier Manley's *Secret History of Queen Zarah* and the English Translation of *Hattigé*."

25. [Anon] *The Rival Princesses: or, The Colchian Court: A Novel* (London: R. Bentley, 1689).

26. *The Rival Princesses*, p. 8.

27. There are further textual similarities. Compare Manley's "Alive we cram'd him in the Fatal Canon which in a moment was discharg'd in Air / Carcass shattering in a thousand pieces' (p. 44) to the original: [Osman] cram'd alive, and shot off into the Air, so that his Carkass shatter'd into a thousand Pieces" (*The Rival Princesses*, p. 160)

28. *The Rival Princesses*, p. 52.

29. *Rivella*, p. 28.

30. White Kennet, *A dialogue between two friends, occasioned by the late revolution of affairs* (London: Richard Chiswell, 1689), pp. 17–18. The parallels between marriage and government is discussed at some length in Weil's *Political Passions* pp. 122–25.

31. Garrett, *The Triumphs of Providence*, p. 71.

32. See Dickenson, *Liberty and Property*, pp. 34–35, for a discussion of William's right to the throne "by conquest."

33. George Granville, *Heroick Love: A Tragedy* (London: F. Saunders, 1698), p. 13.

34. In contrast, Granville apologizes for the fact that he does not punish his wicked heroine, Briseis. See the preface to *Heroick Love*.

35. *Rival Princesses*, p. 160

36. By 1706 Galland's translation published by Andrew Bell had already been through several editions. Whether it was coincidence or a deliberate ploy, an edition was conveniently published early in December when *Almyna* was produced. See *The Flying Post*, 3 December 1706.

37. As Gwendolyn Needham suggests in "Mrs Manley: An Eighteenth Century Wife of Bath," p. 266.

38. *Rivella*, p. 109.

39. In the original the nearest the sultan comes to debating the issue of vows is when he declares, "It shall always be in my Power to keep the Oath I have made." *Arabian Nights Entertainments: Translated into the French from the Arabian MSS by M. Galland, of the Royal Academy: And now done into English*, 5th ed. (London: A. Bell, 1718), I, p. 114.

40. Delarivier Manley, *Almyna: or, the Arabian Vow* (London: William Turner, 1707), preface, unpaginated.

41. See Susan Staves, *Players' Sceptres: Fictions of Authority in the Restoration* (Lincoln: University of Nebraska Press, 1979), p. 194.

42. E. Neville Williams, ed., *The Eighteenth-Century Constitution 1688–1815* (Cambridge: Cambridge University Press, 1970), p. 37. For further discussion of this see Jennifer Carter, "The Revolution and The Constitution," in *Britain after the Glorious Revolution*, p. 40.

43. See Kenyon, *Revolution Principles*, p. 23. No doubt the parliamentary wrangling over the Whig-favored Regency Act of 1706 highlighted the timeliness of this debate. See Holmes, *British Politics*, pp. 132–33.

44. For further discussion of this see Staves, p. 197.

45. Evelyn Cruickshank, *Political Untouchables* (London: Duckworth, 1979), p. 3.

46. Quoted in John S. Gibson, *Playing the Scottish Card: The Franco-Jacobite Invasion of 1708* (Edinburgh: Edinburgh University Press, 1988), p. 55.

47. Quoted in H. T. Dickenson, *Liberty and Property*, p. 21.

48. John Tutchin, *The Observator*, 7 August 1706.

49. Although in *Queen Zarah*, II, 43, she does suggest that the money it is costing to engineer the union is more "than some Kingdoms are worth."

50. Elinor James, untitled (n.p.: 1706/1707)

51. JamesI/VI, *The Political Works of James I* (1918), pp. 271–73, quoted in William Ferguson, *Scotland's Relations with England* (1977), p. 236.

52. Richard Steele, *The British Subject's Answer to the Pretender's Declaration* (London: 1715?), unpaginated verso.

53. See Bruce Lenman, *The Jacobite Risings in Britain 1699–1746* (London: Eyre Methuen, 1980), p. 157.

54. Calhoun Winton, *Sir Richard Steele, M. P.* (Baltimore: Johns Hopkins University Press, 1970), p. 118

55. Richard Steele, *The British Subject's Answer to the Pretender's Declaration* (London: n.p. [1715?])

56. *Clarendon against Lesley; or the Difference between Two Restorations* (London: R. Burleigh, 1715), pp. 3–4.

57. *Richard Steele's The Theatre,* ed. John Loftis, (Oxford: Clarendon Press, 1962), p. 112.

58. Thomas Baldwin, *The Folly of Preferring a Popish Pretender to a Protestant King* (Liverpool: S. Terry, A. Eaton, D. Birchall, 1716), pp. 17–18. See also pamphlets such as E. D., *A Serious Presentation to the People of Great-Britain concerning the Pretender* (London: J. Baker, 1715), p. 2.

59. *Justice done to the Late Ministry: or the Charge of Their Designing to make the Pretender King of Great Britain* (London: J. Baker, 1715), p. 5.

60. E. D., *A Serious Presentation tot he People of Great-Britain concerning the Pre*tender (London: J. Baker, 1715), p. 12

61. *Remarks on Lesley's Two Letters from Bar le Duc* (London: J. Roberts, 1715), pp. 2–3.

62. Colley Cibber, *The Tragical History of King Richard III: As it is acted at The Theatre Royal* (London: B. Lintott, 1700), preface, unpaginated.

63. Murray Pittock, *Poetry and Jacobite Politics in Eighteenth Century Britain and Ireland* (Cambridge: Cambridge University Press, 1994), p. 36.

8. "ASCRIBED TO OTHER PENS"

1. *Life and Character of John Barber*, p. 16.
2. Gerard Langbain [and Charles Gildon], *The Lives and Characters of the English Dramatick Poets* (London: Tho. Leigh, Wm Turner, 1699), p. 91.
3. See Ruth Herman, "A New Ascription for Delarivier Manley," *Notes and Queries*, 246 cont. series, new series vol. 48, no. 4 (Dec. 2001): pp. 401–3.
4. The full text of the poem has not been reproduced since its first publication, and is included at the end of this book as Appendix I.
5. See Robert D. Horne, *Marlborough: A Survey. Penegyrics, Satires and Biographical Writings, 1688–1788* (Folkestone: Dawsons, 1975); D. F. Foxon, *English Verse, 1701–1750: A Catalogue of Separately Printed Poems with Notes on Contemporary Collected Editions*, 2 vols. (Cambridge: Cambridge University Press, 1975), H. 154.
6. For an account of this encounter, see David Chandler, *Marlborough as Military Commander* (Tunbridge Wells: Spellmount Ltd, 1989), pp. 231–33.
7. See Winston Churchill, *Marlborough, His Life and Times*, (London: Harrap, 1933–38), II, pp. 449–50.
8. [Richard Steele], *The London Gazette*, 27 September 1708.
9. Feiling, *History of the Tory Party*, p. 415.
10. [Richard Steele], *The London Gazette*, 14 October 1708. See also *The Daily Courant*, 11 October 1708.
11. *An Heroick Essay upon the Unequal'd Victory Obtain'd by Major-General Webb over the Count dela Motte at Wynendale* (London: A. Baldwin, 1709), p. 3. Advertised as "Recently publish'd" in the *Daily Courant* on 22 February 1709.
12. Delarivier Manley, *Almyna: or the Arabian Vow.*
13. *An Heroick Essay*, p. 4.
14. *New Atalantis*, II, p. 189.
15. *Rivella*, p. 113.
16. *Rivella*, p. 4.
17. *An Heroick Essay*, p. 8.
18. *An Heroick Essay*, p. 5.
19. *An Heroick Essay*, p. 9.
20. *New Atalantis*, I, p. 96.
21. *The Life of Mr John Dennis* (London: J. Roberts, 1734), p. 24.
22. *An Heroick Essay*, p. 10.
23. *An Heroick Essay*, p. 11.
24. *Rivella*, p. 110.
25. *An Heroick Essay*, p. 9.
26. *New Atalantis*, I, p. 193.
27. *An Heroick Essay*, p. 9.
28. Joseph Addison, *The Campaign, A Poem, To His Grace the Duke of Marlborough* (London: Jacob Tonson, 1705).
29. See *POAS*, VII, p. 166, n.1.
30. *Memoirs of Europe*, I, pp. 259–60.
31. Cahoun Winton, "Steele, Mrs. Manley, and John Lacy," *Philological Quarterly* 62, no. 2 (1963): 272–75.

32. *New Atalantis*, pp. 102–3.
33. *The Ecclesiastical and Political History of Whig-Land of Late Years; To Which are Prefix'd the Characters of a Late Ecclesiastical Historian . . . By John Lacy* (London: J. Morphew, 1714), pp. 12, 14, 22.
34. *Memoirs of Europe*, II, p. 312.
35. Winton, *Steele, Mrs. Manley and John Lacy*, p. 275.
36. *The Ecclesiastical and Political History of Whig-Land*, pp. 15–18.
37. *Journal*, 11 September 1711, I, p. 357.
38. *Journal*, 13 September 1711, I, p. 359.
39. Swift, "A New Journey to Paris," *Prose Works*, III, p. 217.
40. I am grateful to Professor Hermann H. Real of the Ehrenpreis Center, Muenster, for his brief discussion with me on this point.
41. Swift, *Prose Works*, III, p. 217.
42. *Memoirs of Europe*, II, p. 16.
43. Swift, *Prose Works*, III, p. 217. For a calculation of Manley's use of the exclamation mark see Köster, *Novels*, I, p. xi.
44. See earlier chapter.
45. *Arbuthnotiana: The Story of St Alb-n's Ghost (1712); A Catalogue of Dr Arbuthnot's Library (1779)*, introduction by Patricia Köster, (Los Angeles: William Andrews Clark Memorial Library, 1972), pp. vi, 3–23.
46. For discussion of authorship, *The History of John Bull*, ed. Alan W. Bower and Robert A. Erickson (Oxford: Clarendon Press, 1976), pp. xxii–xxiii. All references to the *John Bull* pamphlets are from this book.
47. *Memoirs of the Extraordinary Life, Works, and Discoveries of Martinus Scriblerus: Written in Collaboration by the Members of the Scriblerus Club, John Arbuthnot, Alexander Pope, Jonathan Swift, John Gay, Thomas Parnell*, ed. Charles Kerby-Miller, 2d ed. (Oxford: Oxford University Press, 1988), p. 7.
48. See Herman Teerink, *The History of John Bull for the first time faithfully re-issued from the original pamphlets, 1712, together with an investigation into its composition, publication and authorship.* (Arnhem: H. J. Paris, 1925), p. 62, and Lester M. Beattie, *John Arbuthnot: Mathematician and Satirist* (Cambridge, Mass: Harvard University Press, 1935), p. 44.
49. *John Bull*, p. 1.
50. For a discusion of Mackworth as the origin of Sir Humphry Polesworth, see *The History of John Bull*, pp. lxxvii–lxxix, 177.
51. *John Bull*, p. 47.
52. Published 31 July 1712.
53. *John Bull*, p. 43.
54. *Journal*, 10 May 1712, II, p. 532.
55. *Anecdotes, Observations, and Characters of Books and Men. Collected from the Conversation of Mr Pope, and other eminent Persons of His time, by the Rev. Joseph Spence. Now first published from the original papers*, with notes and a life of the author by Samuel Weller Singer (London: W. H. Carpenter, 1820), p. 145.
56. *Observator* 10 May 1712
57. *Observator* 24 May, 1712
58. *Protestant Post Boy*, 26 April 1712.
59. *John Bull*, p. xxii.

60. For a longer discussion of this attack on Manley see chapter 8.
61. Harris, "A Study of the Paper War," pp. 205, 207, 234.
62. McDowell, *Women of Grub Street*, p. 222.
63. Delarivier Manley, *Court Intrigues* (London: John Morphew, 1711), unpaginated.
64. *Examiner*, 15 May 1712.
65. See advertisement, "tomorrow will be publish'd An Appendix to John Bull Still in his Senses," *Examiner*, 8 May 1712.
66. *The Life and Character of John Barber*, p. 16.
67. *Examiner*, 15 May 1712.
68. *The Spectator*, 10 July 1712.
69. *Tatler*, 10 November 1709, II, p. 77.
70. *Memoirs of Europe*, II, p. 309.
71. Richard Steele, *The Lying Lover: or the Lady's Friendship* (London: u.p., 1704), p. 43.
72. *The Lady's Pacquet*, p. 575.
73. *The Lady's Pacquet*, p. 577.
74. Blanchard, *The Occasional Verse of Richard Steele*, pp. 19–20.
75. Köster, *Arbuthnotiana*, pp 3–23.
76. *John Bull*, p. lxxxviii
77. *Memoirs of Europe*, I, p. 200; *John Bull*, p. 94.
78. *New Atalantis*, II, p. 192.
79. *Examiner*, 19 July 1711.
80. See advertisement columns of *Examiner*, vol. 2, 1711–12.
81. *Memoirs of Europe*, I, preface.
82. The British Library catalogue reveals only one spoof title in 1710 and two instances in real publications up until 1712: " 'Tale about or W'are coming to You. A farce acted by the Wh[i]ggs. With a Prologue and Epilogue. By the Ingenious Author of the Atlantis," in *The Instructive Library or, an Entertainment for the Curious, the Improvement of the Learned, the Information of the Ignorant, The Satisfaction of all Good Men, the Confusion of the Bad* (London: n.p., 1710), p. 14; PARIS Appendix, Miscellaneous. *The Idol of Paris with what may be expected, if ever the High-flying Party should establish a Government agreeable to that . . . Doctrine of absolute passive obedience & c. Written by a young Lady, now upon her departure for the New Atalantis. 1710, Occasioned by the affair of Henry Sacheverell* (London: n.p., 1710).
83. For a list of editions see *John Bull*, pp 279–82
84. *John Bull*, p. xviii.
85. Quoted in Beattie, *John Arbuthnot*, pp. 167, 168.
86. There is considerable discussion over the authorship of *The Plain Dealer*. However, Wagstaffe is generally considered to be the author of the periodical. See *The Papers of a Critic, selected from the writings of the late Charles Wentworth Dilke*, ed. Charles Wentworth Dilke 2 vols (London: John Murray, 1875), vol.1 p. 378.
87. See *John Bull*, pp. xxxii, 168.
88. See, for instance, the bibliography to Ros Ballaster's edition of *New Atalantis*, p. xxv.

89. *A Supplement to Dr. Swift's Works*, I, p. 2.
90. *Journal*, 26 November 1711, II, p. 421.
91. *The Works of Jonathan Swift DD*, ed. Thomas Roscoe, 2 vols. (London: G. Bell, 1880), pp. 524–27; *Journal to Stella*, ed. Frederick Ryland (London: G. Bell, 1924), p. 287.
92. Swift, *Prose Works*, VIII, xvi.
93. See Paul Bunyan Anderson, "The History and Authorship of Mrs Crackenthorpe's *Female Tatler*," *Modern Philology* 38 (1931): 354–60; Walter Graham, "Thomas Baker, Mrs Manley and the *Female Tatler*," *Modern Philology* 34 (1936–7): 267–72; J. H. Smith, "Thomas Baker and the *Female Tatler*," *Modern Philology* 49, (1952): 182–88; *The Female Tatler*, ed. Fidelis Morgan (London: Everyman, 1992), pp. vii–ix.
94. Charles A. Rivington, *Tyrant*, p. 247.
95. This pamphlet is bound in with *Mr Pope's Literary Correspondence*, 3 vols. (London: E. Curll, 1735), vol. 3.

9. "A THOUSAND YEARS HENCE"

The quote in the chapter title is taken from: *Memoirs of Europe*, II, dedication, unpaginated.

1. Walter and Clare Jerrold, *Five Queer Women* (London: Brentano's, 1929), pp. 83–138; Philip Sergeant, *Rogues and Scoundrels* (London: Hutchinson & Co., 1929), pp. 171–209.
2. Robert Gould, *A Satyrical Epistle to the Female Author of a Poem call'd Sylvia's Revenge* (London: R. Bentley, 1709), p. 5. The poem was originally published in by R. Bentley in 1691.
3. Langbain, Gerard [& Charles Gildon], *The Lives and Characters of the English Dramatick Poets* (London: Tho. Leigh, William Turner, 1699), p. 90.
4. [N. N. Esq.] *Advertisements from Parnassus, Written originally in Italian by the Famous Trajano Boccalini Newly Done into English, and adapted to the Present times*, (London: Richard Smith, 1704), Advertisement XXII.
5. Delarivier Manley, *The Lost Lover*, preface, unpaginated.
6. HMC Downshire, vol. 1, pt. 2, p. 883, Rev. Ralph Bridges to Sir William Trumbull, 11 November 1709.
7. L. S. Horsley, "The Public Characters of Queen Anne Journalists," *Texas Studies in Literature and Language* 18 (1976): 203.
8. Quoted in Horsley, "The Public Characters," pp. 207, 208.
9. Abel Boyer, *The Political State of Great Britain*, VI, pp. 253–54.
10. Bower and Erickson, *John Bull* p. lxxviii.
11. *Observator*, 24 May 1712
12. *Protestant Post Boy*, 26 April 1712.
13. *The Tatler*, 23 April 1709, I, p. 54.
14. *The Tatler*, 23 April 1709, I, p. 54, n.1.
15. See *The Female Wits*, passim.
16. *The New Atalantis*, I, p. 193.

17. *Tatler*, 12 July 1709, I, p. 291.
18. *Tatler*, 3 September 1709, I, pp. 439–40.
19. *Guardian*, 23 May 1713.
20. [Oldmixon] *The Court of Atalantis* (London: J. Roberts, 1714), p. 78.
21. *Rivella*, p. 8.
22. *New Atalantis*, II, p. 181, *Rivella*, p. 14.
23. Oldmixon, *Court of Atalantis*, p. 87.
24. *New Atalantis*, II, p. 180.
25. Giles Jacob, *The Poetical Register of the Lives and Characters of the English Dramatick Poets* (London: E. Curll, 1719), p. 167.
26. *Historical Register*, IX, 1724, p. 35.
27. James Sterling, "To Mrs Haywood on Her Writings," in *Secret Histories, Novels, and Poems: Written by Mrs Eliza Haywood*, 2d ed. (London: Ran. Browne; S. Chapman, 1725), I, p. A2.
28. Jocelyn Medoff, "The Daughters of Behn," *Women, Writing, History 1640–1740*, ed. Isobel Grundy and Susan Wiseman (London: B. T. Batsford, 1992), p. 53.
29. *An Impartial History of Mr. John Barber*, pp. 44–45.
30. Manley, *A Stage Coach Journey to Exeter* (London: J. Roberts, 1725), sig. A2.
31. *Life and Character of John Barber*, p. 10
32. *Life and Character of John Barber*, p. 13.
33. *Life and Character of John Barber*, pp. 14–15.
34. Henry Horwitz, "Party in a Civic Context: London from the Exclusion Crisis to the Fall of Walpole," *Britain in the First Age of Party*, ed. Clyve Jones (London: Hambledon Press, 1987), p. 189.
35. Bertrand A. Goldgar, *Walpole and the Wits: The Relation of Politics to Literature, 1722–1742* (Lincoln and London: University of Nebraska Press, 1976), p. 188.
36. A "seventh edition" of *New Atalantis*, 4 volumes, was published by James Hedges in 1741.
37. For a recent account of Cockburn's life see A. V. Kelley, "Catharine Trotter (1679–1749): A Re-evaluation of her literary and philosophical writing, and their inter-relationship" (Ph.D. diss: University of Hertfordshire, 1998).
38. BL, Add. MSS, 4264, fol. 265.
39. *New Atalantis*, II, p. 53.
40. *Rivella*, p. 101.
41. *Rivella*, pp. 101–2; *New Atalantis*, II, p. 55.
42. Thomas Birch, *The Works of Mrs. Catharine Cockburn* (London: J. & P. Knapton, 1751), pp. xlvii–xlviii.
43. See chapter 1 for a discussion of the *Female Wits*.
44. Theophilus Cibber, *Lives of the Poets of Great Britain and Ireland, to the Time of Dean Swift* (London: R. Griffiths, 1753), IV, p. 10.
45. Cibber, *Lives of the Poets of Great Britain and Ireland*, IV, p. 18.
46. John Duncombe, *The Feminiad*, intro. by Jocelyn Harris (Los Angeles: William Andrews Clark Memorial Library, publication no. 207, 1981), pp. 14–15.
47. *A Supplement to Dr Swift's Works* (London: J. Nichols, 1779), introduction to "A True Narrative . . . of the Marquis de Guiscard," p. [2].
48. *The Epistolary Correspondence of Sir Richard Steele*, ed. John Nichols (London: John Nichols, 1787), II, p. 457n.

49. *Epistolary Correspondence of Sir Richard Steele*, p. 456–57, n.
50. Winston S. Churchill, *Marlborough, His Life and Times* (London: Harrap, 1933), I, p. 130.
51. R. Brook Aspland, *Notes and Queries* 46 (1856): 390–91.
52. Dr Doran, *Their Majesties' Servants: Annals of the English Stage* (London: 1865), p. 85.
53. Edward A. Bloom and Lillian D. Bloom, ed., *Addison and Steele, The Critical Heritage*, (London: Routledge and Kegan Paul, 1980), p. xi.
54. Edward A Bloom and Lillian D Bloom, "Steele and his Answerers: May 1709–February 1714," *The Dress of Words*, ed. Robert B White Jr. (Kansas: University of Kansas Libraries, 1978), pp. 169–70.
55. Willard Connelly, *Sir Richard Steele* (London: Jonathan Cape, 1934), p. 78.
56. For instance, Roscoe, *The Works of Jonathan Swift*, 2 vols. (London: G. Bell, 1880), I, pp. 512, 517, 520.
57. Swift, *Prose Works*, III, p. xxxiii.
58. For instance, David Nokes, *Jonathan Swift: A Hypocrite Reversed* (Oxford: Oxford University Press, 1987), pp. 131, 147.
59. Gwendolyn Needham, "Mary de la Riviere Manley: Tory Defender," pp. 272, 273, 285.
60. David Woolley, "The Canon of Swift's Pamphleteering, 1710-1714," in *Swift Studies* 3 (1988): 102.
61. Irvin Ehrenpreis, *Swift: The Man, his Works and the Age*, II, p. 471.
62. Michael Foot, *The Pen and the Sword* (London: MacGibbon and Key, 1957), p. 218.
63. J. A. Downie, *Jonathan Swift: Political Writer*, p. 185.
64. G. M. Trevelyan, *England under Queen Anne*, 3 vols. (London: Collins, 1965), I, p. 194; II, p. 62.
65. Churchill, *Marlborough His Life and Times*, I, pp. 53, 130.
66. Carole Fabricant, "The Shared Worlds of Manley and Swift," p. 154.
67. Katharine M. Rogers, *Feminism in Eighteenth-Century England* (London: Harvester Press, 1982), p. 21.
68. Jeslyn Medoff, "The Daughters of Behn," p. 42.
69. *An Impartial History of the Life of John Barber*, p. 44.
70. *Rivella*, p. 120.
71. Rabb, "The Man(ley) Style" in James Gill, ed., *Cutting Edges: Postmodern Critical Essays on Eighteenth Century Satire* (Tennessee: University of Tennessee, 1996), p. 128.
72. McDowell, *Women of Grub Street*, p. 276.
73. *New Atalantis*, II, p. 190–91.
74. The myth continues. See Ophelia Field, *The Favourite: Sarah, Duchess of Marlborough* (London: Hodder and Stoughton, 2002), pp.17-18.

APPENDIX I

1. Foxon H154. Advertised in *Daily Courant* 22 February 1709.
2. General John Richmond Webb (1667?–1724).

3. Prince Eugene (1663–1736). Prince of Savoy.
4. John Churchill (1650–1722). First Duke of Marlborough.
5. Louis XIV of France (1638–1715).
6. De Lamothe, French commander. Dates unknown.
7. Duc de Boufflers (1644–1711). Marshal of France.
8. Battle of Blenheim, 13 August 1704.
9. Philippe Vendôme (1655-1727). French General.
10. Battle of Oudenarde, 28 October 1708.
11. Joseph Addison (1672–1719). Poet, essayist.
12. Sir Richard Steele (1672–1729). Poet, essayist, MP.
13. John Dennis (1657–1734). Critic.

APPENDIX II

1. Written during Manley's imprisonment.
2. Earlier Manley scholars do not appear to have been aware of the existence of this letter.
3. Robert Harley, First Earl of Oxford (1661–1724). First Lord of the Treasury 1711–14.
4. Sir Richard Haddock (1629–1715). Controller of the Navy 1690–1715.
5. John Barber (1675–1741) left £100 to John Markham, apothecary, in his will.
6. Volume 1 of *Memoirs of Europe*.
7. Charles Mordaunt, third Earl of Peterborough (1658–1735).
8. George Granville, Baron Lansdowne (1667–1735).
9. John Barber (1675–1741). Printer.
10. Henry St. John, Viscount Bolingbroke (1678–1751).
11. *A True Narrative of What Passed at the Examination of Monsieur de Guiscard at the Cock-pit the 8th of March 1710/11* (London: John Morphew, 1711).
12. *Examiner* no. 51, 19 July 1711.
13. Francis Hare, *The Charge of God to Joshua; In a Sermon preach'd before the Duke of Marlborough at Avenes le Sec* (London: n.p., 1711), answered by Manley's *A Learned Comment on Doctor Hare's Sermon* (London: John Morphew, 1711).
14. Tory dining club instituted in 1711 by Henry St. John to offer, among other things, financial support to Tory writers.
15. Samuel Masham, first Baron Masham (1679?–1758), husband of Abigail Masham (née Hill).
16. Sir William Wyndham (1678–1740). 1713 Chancellor of the Exchequer
17. John Barber.
18. William Dampier, "buccaneer, pirate, circumnavigator, captain" (*DNB*). Wrote several account of his travels: *New Voyage round the World*, 1697; *Voyages and Descriptions* (1699), *Voyage to New Holland in the Year 1699* (two parts, 1703 and 1709).
19. John Barber.
20. Viscount Bolingbroke.
21. Queen Anne had died two weeks earlier.

22. Manley's sister.
23. Matthew Prior (1664–1721), poet and diplomat.
24. Edward Harley, (1689–1741) second Earl of Oxford, son of Robert Harley, and Lady Henrietta Harley (née Cavendish Holles).
25. Anne Oldfield (1683–1730), actress.

Bibliography

PRIMARY SOURCES

Manuscript Sources

British Library, Additional MSS.
British Library, Lansdowne MSS.
British Library, Sloane MSS.
British Library, Thynne Papers.
Hertfordshire Records Office, Panshanger MSS.
HMC Downshire MSS: *The Manuscripts of the Marquess of Downshire, Papers of Sir William Trumbull,* 2 vols. (London: H.M. Stationery Office, 1924).
Huntington Library, Bishop Percy Collection.
Institute of Historical Research, Prior Papers.
Public Records Office, PROB II 599.
Public Records Office, State Papers Domestic Anne.
University of Nottingham MSS, Portland Collection.

Works by Delarivier Manley

The Adventures of Rivella; or the History of the Author of the Atalantis. London: E. Curll, 1714.
Almyna: or the Arabian Vow. London: William Turner, Egbert Sanger, 1707.
The Duke of Marlborough's Vindication: In Answer to a Pamphlet, lately Published, called Bouchain; or a Dialogue Between the Medley and the Examiner. London: John Morphew, 1711.
The Examiner. London: John Morphew, 1711.
An Heroick Essay upon the Unequal'd Victory Obtain'd by Major-General Webb over the Count dela Motte at Wynendale. London: A. Baldwin, 1709.
The Honour and Prerogative of the Queen's Majesty Vindicated and Defended against the Unexampled Insolence of the Author of the Guardian. London: John Morphew, 1713.
The Lady's Pacquet of Letters in *Memoirs of the Court of England*. London: B. Bragg, 1707. Re-issued as *Court Intrigues as a Collection of Original Letters from the Island of New Atalantis*. London: John Morphew, 1711.
A Learned Comment on Doctor Hare's Sermon. London: John Morphew, 1711.
Letters Written by Mrs Manley. London: R. B., 1696.

The Lost Lover; or the Jealous Husband. London: n.p., 1696.
Lucius The First Christian King of Britain. London: n.p., 1717.
Memoirs of Europe Towards the Close of the Eighth Century, Written by Eginardus, Secretary and Favourite to Charlemagne, and Done into English by the Translator of the New Atalantis. London: 1710.
The Nine Muses. London: Richard Basset, 1700.
The Power of Love in Seven Novels. London: John Barber, 1720.
The Royal Mischief. London: n.p., 1696.
The Secret History of Queen Zarah and the Zarazians; being a Looking-Glass for ——— In the Kingdom of Albigion. London[?]: n.p., 1705.
Secret Memoirs and Manners of Several Persons of Quality of both Sexes, From the New Atalantis, and Island in the Mediterranean. London: John Morphew, 1709.
A True Narrative of What Passed at the Examination of Monsieur de Guiscard at the Cock-pit the 8th of March 1710/11. His Stabbing of Mr. Harley and Other Precedent and Subsequent Facts Relating to the Life of the Said Guiscard. London: John Morphew, 1711.

Other Works

A Ballad on the Junto. To the Tune of Lilly Bullero. [London?]: n.p., undated.
A Burlesque Poem in Praise of Ignorance By Edmund Hickeringill. [London?]: 1708.
A Caveat Against the Whigs. London: John Morphew, 1710.
A Compleat History of the Whole Proceedings of the Parliament of Great Britain against Dr Henry Sacheverell with his Tryal before the House of Peers. London: J. Baker, 1710.
A Complete Key to the Three Parts of Law is a Bottomless Pit and the Story of St. Albans Ghost. London: n.p., 1712.
A Copy of W. Gregg's Paper delivered to the Sheriffs. London: n.p., 1708.
A Dialogue between Jest, An East-India Stock-Jobber and Earnest An Honest Merchant. London: n.p., 1708.
A Dialogue Between Louis le Petite and Harlequin le Grand. London: n.p., [1708?].
A Dialogue or New Friendly Debate between A High and Low Church-Man, Concerning Elections. London: n.p., 1705.
A Fable of the Shepherd and his Dog. London: n.p., 1712.
A Fair Way with the Dissenters and their Patrons. Not Writ by Mr L—y, or any Other Furious Jacobite. London: R. Wilkin, 1704.
A Fox Set to Watch the Geese. London: n.p., 1705.
A Friendly Letter from Honest Tom Boggy to the Reverend Mr G—d, Canon of Windsor. London: n.p., 1710.
A Funeral Satyr in Memory of the Worthy Treatment of the Late Mr. anthony Bowyer of Camberwell By a Friend of Dr. Sacheverell's Club. London: n.p., 1709.

Bibliography 303

A Genuine Copy of the Duke of Marlborough's Letter to the Earl of Peterborough. London: n.p., [1706?].

A Health to the Tackers: A New Song. Oxford. n.p., 1705.

A History of Great Britain from the Revolution in 1688 to the Accession of George I, [Cunningham]. Ed. William Thomson, 2 vols. London: Hollingsby, 1787.

A Kit-Kat C[lu]b Describ'd; O Monstrous Moderation!. [London?]: n.p., 1705.

A Letter from a Dissenter in the City, to his Country-Friend. [London?]: n.p., 1705.

A Letter From a Foreign Minister in England to Monsieur Pettecum Containing the True Reasons of the Late Change in the Ministry. London: J. Baker, 1710.

A Letter from a Member of Parliament to his Friend in the Country. London: n.p., 1705.

A Letter in Vindication of L[ord] N[ottingham]. [London?]: n.p., 1711.

A Letter to a Member of the October Club: shewing That to yield Spain to the Duke of Anjou by a Peace, wou'd be the Ruin of Great Britain. London: A. Baldwin, 1711.

A Letter to a Minister of the Church of England Concerning the Societies for Reformation of Manners. London: Joseph Downing, 1710.

A Letter to a Newly Elected Member of Parliament Concerning His Behaviour There, about Occasional Conformity, &c. London: n.p., 1705.

A Letter to the Examiner. London: John Morphew., 1710.

A Letter to the Seven Lords appointed to examine Gregg,. London: J. Baker, 1711.

A List of Those Worthy Patriots. Oxford: n.p., 1705.

A Mess for the Devil; or An Excellent New Recipt to Make a Junto. [London?]: n.p., 1711.

A Modest Attempt to Prove Dr. H—Not the Author of the Bouchain Dialogue. London: n.p., 1712.

A Most Humble Address or Memorial Presented to Her Majesty the Queen of Great Britain by the Deputies of the Magistrates of Dunkirk to Her Majesty. [London?]: n.p., [1713?].

A New Collection of Poems Relating to State Affairs, from Oliver Cromwell to this Present Time by the Greatest Wits of the Age. London: n.p., 1705.

A New Dialogue between The Horse at Charing Cross and The Horse at Stock-Market. London: n.p., 1703.

A New Miscellany of Original Poems, Translations and Imitations By the most Eminent Hands, Viz Mr Prior, Mr Harcourt, Mr Pope, Mr Hughes, Lady M W M —, Mrs Manley &c. London: T. Jauncy, 1720.

A New Years Gift for the Renegado and Hansel to his Whisper. [London?]: n.p., 1705.

A Pair of Spectacles for Oliver's Looking Glass Maker. London: J. Baker, 1711.

A Prince and No Prince or Mother Red Cap's Strange and Wonderful Prophecy. London: J. Reed, 1714.

A Review of the Dangers of the Church. London: n.p., 1705.

A Review of the State of the British Nation. London: 1704–1711.

A Roman Story. London: n.p., 1711.

A Short Account of a Dialogue betwixt the D—l and Mr Spintext, a P—n T—r. London: n.p., 1711.

A Short Memorial, and Character of that Most Noble and Illustrious Princess, Mary Dutchess of Ormonde. London: E. Curll, 1735.

A Short Narrative of the Life and Actions of His Grace John, Duke of Marlborough, from the Revolution to this Present Time. With Some Remarks on His Conduct. London: John Baker, 1711.

A Speech by A- B-Esq; on the Ninth of March. Upon the Marquis of Guiscard's Stabbing the right Honourable Robert Harley, Esq. London: n.p., 1711.

A Speech Without Doors. London: A. Baldwin, 1710.

A Stage Coach Journey to Exeter. London: J. Roberts, 1725.

A Supplement to Dr. Swift's Works: Containing Miscellaneous in Prose and Verse, by the Dean; Dr Delany, Dr. Sheridan, Mrs Johnson and others, his Intimate Friends. Ed. John Nichols. 3 vols. London: John Nichols, 1779.

A Tale of J—n and S—h or Both Turned out of Court at Last. [London?]: n.p., 1711.

A Toast for A[nn]e and Robbin, in the French Wine. London: John Turnham, 1711.

A Trip from Westminster Hall to Oxford. London: n.p., 1710.

A True and Faithful Account of the Last Distemper and Death of Tom Whigg Esq. London: n.p., 1710.

A True Relation of the Several Facts and Circumstances of the Intended Riot and Tumult on Queen Elizabeth's Birthday. London: John Morphew, 1711.

A view of the Queen and Kingdom's enemies in the case of the poor Palatines: to which is added a list of the . . . members of the late Parliament that voted for the Naturalization-Bill. London: n.p., 1709.

A Vindication of the Present Ministry from the Clamours Rais'd Against Them upon the Occasion of the New Preliminaries. London: n.p., 1711.

A Word of Advice to the Citizens of London concerning the Choice of Members of Parliament at the Ensuing Election. London: n.p., 1705.

A Letter from the Grecian Coffee-house, In Answer to the Taunton-Dean Letter

Addison, Joseph. *The Campaign, A Poem, To His Grace the Duke of Marlborough.* London: Jacob Tonson, 1705.

Advice to a Painter. London: n.p., 1705.

Aesop at the Bell Tavern in Westminster or A Present from the October Club. London: n.p., 1711.

Aminadab, or the Quaker's Vision, Explain'd and Answer'd Paragraph by Paragraph. London and Dublin: n.p., 1710.

An Abridgment of the Secret History of Crete. London: S. Popping, 1711.

An Account of a Dream at Harwich. In a Letter to a Member of Parliament about the Camisars. London: n.p., 1708.

An Acrostick on Wharton. London: *The Post Boy*, 1710.

An Address of the Lords concerning W. Gregg. London: n.p., 1708.

An Answer to the Great Noise. [London?]: n.p., [1705?].

An Appeal to the Freeholders of England on behalf of themselves against the unwarrantable Proceedings of Sir Samuel Eckly late High Sherriff of the County of Gloucester & co. London: n.p., 1705.

An Elegy on the Author of the True-Born-English-Man with an Essay on the Late Storm. London: n.p., 1708.
An Elegy on the Much Lamented Death of Charles, Earl of Sunderland. [London?]: n.p., undated.
An Epistle from Sempronia to Cethegus To Which is Added Cethegus's Reply. London: John Holmes, 1713.
An Examination of the Management of theWar in a Letter to My Lord ***. London: J. Morphew, 1711.
An Excellent New Song Being the Intended Speech of a Famous Orator Against Peace. [London?]:[1711?].
An Excellent New Song Called An End to our Sorrows. [London?]:1711.
An Excellent New Song Called Credit Restor'd in the Year of our Lord God, 1711. [London?]: 1711.
An Historical and Political Essay, Discovering the Affinity or Resemblance of the Ancient and Modern Governments. London: n.p., 1706.
An Impartial History of the Life of Mr. John Barber. London: E. Curll, 1741.
An Old Story that Every One Knows: Or the Religion of the Whigs Enquired Into. London: n.p., 1712.
Anecdotes, Observations, and Characters of Books and Men. Collected from the Conversation of Mr Pope, and other eminent Persons of His time, by the Rev. Joseph Spence. Ed. Singer Samuel Weller. London: W. H. Carpenter, 1820.
Arabian Nights Entertainments: Translated into the French from the Arabian MSS by M. Galland, of the Royal Academy: And now done into English, 12 vols. 5th ed. London: A. Bell, 1718.
Arbuthnot, John, *The History of John Bull*. Ed. Alan W. Bower and Robert A. Erickson. Oxford: Clarendon Press, 1976.
Arbuthnotiana: The Story of St Alb-n's Ghost. 1712.; A Catalogue of Dr Arbuthnot's Librar (1779). Ed. Patricia Köster. Los Angeles: William Andrews Clark Memorial Library, 1972.
As Bob as a Robin. London: n.p., 1712.
Ashby and White: or The Great Question, Whether an Action lies at Common Law for an Elector who is deny'd his Vote for Members of Parliament?. London. n.p., 1705.
Authentick Memoirs of the Life and Conduct of her Grace, Sarah, late Duchess of Marlborough. London: R. Walker, 1744.
Baker, Thomas, *An Act at Oxford*. London: Bernard Lintott.
Baldwin, Thomas, *The Folly of Preferring a Popish Pretender to a Protestant King*. Liverpool: S. Terry, A. Eaton, D. Birchall, 1716.
Beasts in Power or Robins Song; with an Old Cat's Prophecy. London: n.p., 1709.
Bellisarius: A Great Commander and Zariana His Lady. London: n.p., 1710.
Benefits of a Theatre. London: n.p., 1705.
Bishop Burnet's History of his own time with the suppressed passages of the first volume and notes by the Earls of Dartmouth and Hardwicke and Speaker Onslow, 6 vols. Oxford: Clarendon, 1823.
Black Bird's Second Tale. London: Ed. Lewis, 1710.

Boccalini, Tragario, *Advertisements From Parnassus* 2 vols,. London: Richard Smith, 1794.

Bosse, Malcom, J., *The Secret History of Queen Zarah and the Zarazians*,. London: Garland Publishing, 1972.

Boyer, Abel. *Quadriennum Annae Postremum; or the Political State of Great Britain during the Four Last Years of the Late Queen's Reign*, 2d. ed. 8 vols. London: n.p., 1718.

British Apollo: or Curious Amusements. London: n.p., 1708–1711.

British Mercury. London: n.p., 1711–12.

Browne, Joseph *The Fox set to Watch the Geese; a State Paradox Being a Welcome from Newmarket by Way of Fable*. London: n.p., 1705.

Browne, Joseph, *Almonds for Parrots*. London: n.p., 1708.

Browne, Joseph, *Letter to Mr Secretary Harley*. London: n.p., 1706.

Browne, Joseph, *St. James's Park: A Satyr*. London: John Morphew, 1708.

Browne, Joseph, *State Tracts: Containing Many Necessary Observations and Reflections on the State of our Affairs at Home and Abroad; with some Secret Memoirs. By the Author of the Examiner*, 2 vols. London: Sawbridge, et al., 1715.

Browne, Joseph, *The British Court*. London: The Publishing Office, 1707.

Browne, Joseph, *The Gothick Hero*. London: n.p., 1708.

Browne, Joseph, *The Lawyer's Answer to the Country Parson's Good Advice*. London: n.p., 1706.

Character of a Whigg under Several Denominations. London: n.p., 1700.

Chardin, Sir John. *The Travels of Sir John Chardin into Persia and the East-Indies*. London: George Monke, William Ewley, 1689.

Cibber, Colley. *The Tragical History of King Richard III: As it is acted at The Theatre Royal*. London: B. Lintott, 1700.

Cibber, Theophilus. *Lives of the Poets of Great Britain and Ireland, to the Time of Dean Swift*. 5 vols. London: R. Griffiths, 1753.

Clarendon against Lesley; or the Difference between Two Restorations. London: R. Burleigh, 1715.

Clark, John. *Churchill's Annals; Being a Short History of the Great Duke of Marlborough with his Character*. London: n.p., 1722.

Collier, Jeremy. *A Short View of the Immorality, and Profaneness of the English Stage*. London: S. Keble, 1698.

Concordia Discors; or, An Argument to Prove that the Possession of Dunkirk, Port Mahon, Gibralter. London: n.p., 1712.

Connors, Bernard. *The History of Poland in Several Letters to Persons of Quality, Vol. 2 compos'd and Publish'd by Mr Savage*, 2 vols. London: n.p., 1698.

Cupid in Quest of Beauty: or, Venus at Stratford A Lampoon By the Author of the British Apollo. London: n.p., 1709.

Daily Courant. London: Samuel Buckley, 1702–1714.

Daniel the Prophet no Conjurer. [London?]: n.p., 1705.

Defoe, Daniel. *A Letter from Captain Tom to the Mobb*. London: J. Baker, 1710.

Defoe, Daniel. *A New Test of the Church of England Loyalty; Or Whiggish Loyalty and Church Loyalty Compar'd*. London: n.p., 1702.

Defoe, Daniel. *A Spectator's Address to the Whigs, on the Occasion of the Stabbing of Mr Harley*. London: n.p., 1711.

Defoe, Daniel. *Advice to all Parties*. London: Benj. Bragg, 1705.

Defoe, Daniel. *Atalantis Major*. Olreeky [London?]: n.p., 1711.

Defoe, Daniel. *The Consolidator; or Memoirs of Sundry Transactions from the World in the Moon*. London: Benj. Bragg, 1705.

Defoe, Daniel. *The Dyet of Poland*. [London]: n.p., 1705.

Defoe, Daniel. *The High Church Legion: or The Memorial Examin'd: Being a New Test of Moderation*. London: n.p., 1705.

Defoe, Daniel. *The Reasons concerning the Immediate Demolishing of Dunkirk: being a Serious Enquiry into the State and Condition of that Affair*. London: John Morphew, 1713.

Defoe, Daniel. *The Secret History of the October Club*. London: n.p., 1711.

Dennis, John. *The Usefulness of the Stage, to the Happiness of Mankind To Government, and To Religion*. London: Rich. Parker, 1698.

Distinction of High Church and Low Church distinctly consider'd and faithfully stated. With some reflections on the popular plea of moderation etc. London: n.p., 1705.

Diverting Post. London: H. Playford, 1704–1706.

Dr Sacheverell turn'd Oculist: or Sir W[—] R—ds' Lamentation for the loss of his Business. London: n.p., 1710.

[Drake, James] *The Memorial of the Church of England Humbly Offer'd to the Consideration of all True Lovers of our Church and Constitution*. London: n.p., 1705.

Duncombe, John. *The Feminiad*. Intro. by Jocelyn Harris. Los Angeles: William Andrews Clark Memorial Library, publication no. 207, 1981.

Dunton, John. *A Cat May Look at A Queen; or a Satire on Her Present Majesty*. London: John Morphew, 1708.

Dunton, John. *King Abigail: Or the Secret Reign of the She Favourite*. London: S. Popping, J. Harrison, 1715.

Duntor., John. *Neck or Nothing*. London: T. Warner, 1713.

Dunton's Whipping Post: A Satyr upon Everybody. London: B. Bragg, 1706.

Dyer, William. *A Collection from Dyer's Letters, Concerning the Elections of the Present Parliament with an APPENDIX, relating to some other Publick Matters. 19 May 1705*. London: n.p., 1706.

E. D., *A Serious Presentation to the People of Great-Britain concerning the Pretender*. London: J. Baker, 1715.

Eleven Opinions About Mr Harley with Observations. London: J. Baker, 1711.

Fable of the Housewife and her Cock. London: n.p., 1712.

Farquhar, George. *Barcellona: A Poem on the Spanish Expedition Publish'd for the Benefit of the Author's Widow and Children*. [London]: n.p., 1710.

Faults in the Fault-Finder: or a Specimen of Errors in the Pamphlet, Entitul'd Faults on Both Sides. London: A.Baldwin, 1710.

Faults on Both Sides: or an Essay upon the Original Cause, Progress, and Mischievous Consequences of the Factions in this Nation. London: n.p., 1710.
Female Apostacy: or The True Born Englishwoman. A Satyr. London: n.p., 1705.
Four Plays of the Right Honourable the Lord Landsdowne. London: W. Feales, 1732.
Freind, John. *An Account of the Earl of Peterborough's Conduct in Spain, Chiefly since the raising of the Siege of Barcelona, 1706,* 2d. ed. London: n.p., 1707.
French Sincerity Exemplified in the Surrender of Dunkirk to Her Britainnick Majesty Queen Anne: Interspers'd with a Medley of Whigg Loyalty and Low Ch-ch Moderation; Compil'd to expose the Moderate Faction, by an Arch Anti-Whigg. [London?]: n.p., 1712.
G. B., Ingraver. *The Whigs Medley. The Three False Brethren.* [London?]: n.p., 1711.
Gildon, Charles. *A Comparison Between the Two Stages.* London: n.p., 1702.
Gildon, Charles. *The Golden Spy.* London: J. Woodward, John Morphew, 1709.
Gould, Robert. *The Works of Mr. Robert Gould Consisting of those Poems which were formerly printed, and corrected since by the author; as also of the many more which he design'd for the press.* 2 vols. London: W. Lewis, 1709.
Granville, George. *Heroick Love: a Tragedy.* London: F. Saunders, 1698.
Hare, Francis [and Arthur Mainwaring]. *Bouchain: In a Dialogue Between the Late Medley and Examiner.* London: A. Baldwin, 1711.
Hare, Francis. *The Charge of God to Joshua; In a Sermon preach'd before the Duke of Marlborough at Avenes le Sec.* London: n.p., 1711.
Hare, Francis. *The Management of the War in Four Letters to a Tory Member.* London: Egbert Sanger, 1711.
Hattigé or the Amours of the King of Tamaran: A Novel. Amsterdam: n.p., 1680.
Hattigé ou Les Amours du Roy de Tamaran Nouvelle. Cologne: Simon l'Africain, 1676.
He's Welcome Home; or a Dialogue Between John and Sarah. London: n.p., 1711.
Hickelty Pickelty: or a Medly of Characters Adapted to the Age. London: J. Morphew, 1708.
Higden, William, *The Case of the Admission of Occasional Conformists to the Holy Communion.* London: Samuel Keble, Francis Coggan, 1705.
Histoire Secrete de la Reine Zarah et des Zaraziens, ou la Duchesse de Marlborough demasquee. Oxford: Alexandre le Vertueux, 1711.
Honour Retriv'd From Faction: in a Dialogue between Smith and Johnson. London: J. Baker, 1713.
Hudibras Redivivus: or a Burlesque Poem on the times. Part the Second. London: n.p., 1709.
Impartial Remarks on the Earl of Peterborow's Conduct in Spain. London: n.p., 1707.
Jacob, Giles. *The Poetical Register of the Lives and Characters of the English Dramatick Poets.* London: E. Curll, 1719.
John the Bailiff's Letter to Robin the Steward. London: J. Read, [1712?].

Justice done to the Late Ministry: or the Charge of Their Designing to make the Pretender King of Great Britain. London: J. Baker, 1715.
Kennet, White. *A dialogue between two friends, occasioned by the late revolution of affairs*. London: Richard Chiswell, 1689.
Kiss Me if You Dare; or a Royal Favourite Turn'd Out. London: n.p., 1710.
Langbaine, G. [and Charles Gildon]. *The Lives and Characters of the English*. London: Tho. Leigh, William Turner, 1712.
Langbaine, G. *The Lives and Characters of the English Dramatic Poets*. London: W. Turner, 1699.
Leslie, Charles, *The New Association etc. Cassandra.—But I hope not.—Telling what will come of it*. London: n.p., 1709.
Letters and Correspondence, Public and Private of the Right Honourable Henry St. John, Lord Viscount Bolingbroke, During the Time he was Secretary of State to Queen Anne. Ed. Gilbert Parke. 7 vols. London: n.p., 1798.
Letters Illustrative of the Reign of William III From 1696 to 1708 addressed to the Duke of Shrewsbury by James Vernon Es. Secretary of State, Now First Published From the Originals. Ed. P. R. James. 3 vols. London: Henry Colburn, 1841.
Lord Haversham's Speech in the House of Lords, on the first article of the Impeachment of Dr. Henry Sacheverell. Dublin: John Hyde, 1710.
Lord Hervey's Memoirs. Ed. Romney Sedgewick. London: William Kimber, 1952.
Luttrell, Narcissus. *A Brief Relation of State Affairs from September 1678 to April 1714*. 6 vols. Oxford: n.p., 1857.
M. Manlius Capitolinus. London: n.p., 1711.
Mackworth, Humphrey. *A Brief Account of the Tack in a letter to a Friend*. [London?]: n.p., 1705.
Mackworth, Humphrey. *A Letter from a Member of Parliament to his Friends in the Country*. London: n.p., 1705.
Mackworth, Humphrey. *A Treatise Concerning the Divine Authority of the Scriptures*. London: n.p., 1704.
Mackworth, Sir Humphrey. *A Discourse, or Dialogue concerning the Mine-Adventure*. [London?], n.p., 1709.
Mackworth, Sir Humphrey. *Real Vindication or the True University Answer to the Pretended University Ballad*. London: n.p., 1705.
Macky. *Memoirs of the Secret Services of J. Macky*. London: n.p., 1733.
Mag, H. G. L. *The Eagle and The Robin*. London: John Morphew, 1709.
Manley, Delarivier. *New Atalantis*. Ed. Rosalind Ballaster. London: Penguin Books, 1992.
Manley, Roger. *History of the Late Warres in Denmark*. London: n.p., 1670.
Manley, Roger. *The History of the Rebellions in England and Scotland*. London: L. Meredith, T. Newborough, 1691.
Memoirs of John, Lord Haversham, from the Year 1640 to 1710. London: n.p., 1711.
Memoirs of the Extraordinary Life, Works, and Discoveries of Martinus Scriblerus: Written in Collaboration by the Members of the Scriblerus Club, John

Arbuthnot, Alexander Pope, Jonathan Swift, John Gay, Thomas Parnell. Ed. Charles Kerby-Miller. 2d ed. Oxford: Oxford University Press, 1988.

Memoirs of the Marquis de Guiscard: or an Account of his Secret Transactions in the Southern Provinces of France, Particularly in Ronergue and the Cevenne to Rescue the Nation from Slavery. London: B. Bragg, 1705.

Mercurius Politicus. [London]: n.p., [1705]

Moderation Displayed: A Poem. London: n.p., 1704.

Moderation in Fashion: or an Answer to a Treatise, Written by Mr Francis Tallents, Entituled, A Short History of Schism &c. London: W. B. for G. Sawbridge, 1705.

Moderation Still a Virtue. London: J. Taylor, 1705.

Modern Novels in XII Volumes. London: R. Bentley, 1692.

A Modest Enquiry into the Reasons of the Joy Express'd by a Certain Sett of People, upon the Spreading of a Report of Her Majesty's Death. (London, John Morphew, 1714.

Monarchy and Church As Explain'd by Dr. Henry Sacheverell. London: J. Baker, 1710.

Mr. Pope's Literary Correspondence for Thirty Years; from 1704 to 1734, 5 vols. London: E. Curll, 1735–1737.

Mrs Manley's History of Her Own Life and Times. London: Edmund Curll, J. Pemberton, 1725.

N. N. Esq. *Advertisements from Parnassus, Written originally in Italian by the Famous Trajano Boccalini Newly Done into English, and adapted to the Present times.* London: Richard Smith, 1704.

New Song Warbled out of the Oracular Oven of The Baker Just After the D. of M—gh's Triumphal Procession thro' the City of London. [London?]: n.p., [1714?].

Novels of Mary Delariviere Manley. Ed. Patricia Köster. 2 vols. Gainesville, Fla: Scholars Facsimiles and Reprints, 1971.

Oldmixon, John. *Memoirs of the Press, Historical and Political For Thirty Years Past From 1710–1740.* London: T. Cox, 1742.

Oldmixon, John. *The Court of Atalantis.* London: J. Roberts, 1714.

Oliver's Pocket Looking Glass, New Fram'd and Clean'd to giv a clear View of the Great Modern Colossus. London: n.p., 1711.

On the Duke of B[uckingham]s House. London: n.p., 1705.

On the Queen's Speech. London: n.p., 1710.

Once more, by you Inspir'd, my Muse her Long Meglected Arts Renews. London: Richard Sare, 1711.

Orrery, Earl of Boyle. *Altermira, a Tragedy.* Revised Hon. Charles Boyle. Prologue by Henry St. John, Esq. London: John Nutt, 1702.

Out With 'Em While You Are About It: or a Great Change at Court. [London?]: n.p., 1710.

The Ox—d Dialogue between a Master of Arts and a Stranger. (London: 1705.

P. Lorrain, Ordinary of Newgate, his account of the Life and Death of W. Gregg. London: n.p., 1708.

PARIS Appendix, Miscellaneous. The Idol of Paris with what may be expected, if ever the High-flying Party should establish a Government agreeable to that . . . Doctrine of absolute passive obedience & c. Written by a young Lady, now upon her departure for the New Atalantis. 1710, Occasioned by the affair of Henry Sacheverell. London, 1710.

Perkinite Jacks; Presbyterian Loyalty in two letters one directed to the moderate Church-men. [London?]: n.p., [1705?].

Pittis, William. *Hymn to Nature.* London: R.Basset, 1705.

Pittis, William. *Seven Wise Men.* [London?]: n.p., 1705.

Pittis, William. *The Case of the Church of England's Memorial Fairly Stated.* London: n.p., 1705.

Presbyterian Loyalty, in Two Letters: One directed to the Moderate Church-Men . . . The Other a Tacking Member. London: n.p., 1705.

Prior, Matthew, *To the Right Honourable Mr Harley, Wounded by Guiscard.* London: Jacob Tonson, 1711.

Pro Aris et Focis: or A Vindication of the Proceedings of the Commons on the Writs of Habeus Corpus and Writ of Error in the Case of the Aylesbury Men. London: n.p., 1705.

Puffendorf, Samuell. *The Compleat History of SWEDEN from its Origin to this Time: Faithfully translated fromt he Original High Dutch and carefully Continued down to this present Year.* London: Joseph Will, 1702.

Queen Elizabeth's Day or the Downfall of the Devil, Pope and Pretender. London: n.p., 1711.

Reasons for Restoring the Whigs. London: n.p., 1711.

Remarks and Collections of Thomas Hearne. Ed. C. E. Doble *et al.*, 11 vols. Oxford: Clarendon Press, 1884–1918.

Remarks on Lesley's Two Letters from Bar le Duc. London: J. Roberts, 1715.

Representation of the Loyal Subjects. London: n.p., 1712.

Resistance and Non-Resistance Stated and Decided: Dialogue between a Hotspur High Flyer, a Canting-Low-Church Man and B—f Censor of Great Britain. London: J. Baker, 1710.

Richard Steele's The Theatre. Ed. John Loftis. Oxford: Clarendon Press, 1962.

R—s on Both Sides: In Which ar the Characters of Some R—'s not yet Describ'd. London: John Baker, 1711.

Rufinus or an Historical Essay on the Favourite Ministry under Theodosius the Great and his son Arcadius To Which is added a Version of Claudian's Rufinus. London: John Morphew, 1712.

Sacheverell, Henry. *The Perils of False Brethren both in Church and State set Forth in a Sermon Preach'd before the Right Honourable Lord Mayor.* London: Samuel Clements, 1709.

Sackville, Tufton. *The History of Faction alias Hypocrisy alias Moderation.* London: Benj. Bragg, 1705.

Sarah's Farewel to C—t or A Trip from St. James's to St. Albans. London: n.p., 1710.

Savage, Richard. *An Author To Be Let.* London: n.p., 1732.

Secret Histories, Novels and Poems, Written by Mrs Haywood. Ed. James Sterling. 2 vols. London: Ron. Browne; S. Chapman, 1725.

Shippen, William. *Duke Humphrey's Answer*. London: n.p., 1708.

Shippen, William. *Moderation Display'd*. London: n.p., 1704.

Shippen, William. *The Devil upon Dun: or Moderation in Masquerade. A Poem*. London: n.p., 1705.

Sir Humphrey Mackworth's Real Vindication Or The True University Answer To the Pretended University Ballad. London: B. Bragg, [1705?].

Sir Thomas Double at Court and in High Preferments. London: n.p., 1710.

Some Memoirs Relating to the Life of the Right Honourable John Lord Haversham From the Year 1640 to 1710. London: J. Baker, 1711.

Some Remarks upon a Pamphlet entitled 'A Letter to the Seven Lords of the Committee appointed to examine Gregg. By the Author of the Examiner. London: n.p., 1711.

Steele, Richard. *The Importance of Dunkirk Consider'd: in Defence of the Guardian of August the 7th in a Letter to the Bailiff of Stockbridge*. London: n.p., 1713.

Steele, Richard, *The British Subject's Answer to the Pretender's Declaration*. London: [1715?].

Steele, Richard. *The Lying Lover: or the Lady's Friendship*. London: n.p., 1704.

Stinking Fish; or a Foolish Poem attempted by John the Hermit. London: John Morphew, 1708.

Swift Jonathan. *The Complete Poems*. Ed. Pat Rogers. London: Penguin Books, 1983.

Swift, Jonathan. *Prose Works*. Eds. Herbert Davis *et al.*, 16 vols. Oxford: Blackwell, 1939–68.

Swift, Jonathan. *The Fable of Midas*. London: n.p., 1712.

The Adventures of Rivella. Delarivier Manley. Ed. Katherine Zelinsky. Ontario: Broadview Press, 1998.

The Age of Mad Folks. London: n.p., 1710.

The Age of Wonders. London: n.p., 1710.

The Apparition. [London?]: n.p., [1711?].

Theatre Royal. London: B. Lintott, 1700.

The British Court: A Poem Describing The Most Celebrated Beauties at St. James's the Parl and the Mall. London: n.p., 1707.

The Case of Sir Humphrey Mackworth, and of the Mine Adventurers. London: n.p., 1705.

The Changes: Or Faction Vanquished. London: John Morphew, 1711.

The Character of Richard St[ee]le, Esq; with Some Remarks by Toby, Abel's Kinsman. London: J. Morphew, 1713.

The Character of the Present Set of Whigs. London: n.p., 1711.

The Cheating Age Found Out. London: n.p., [1705?].

The Circus, or British Olympics; A Satyr on the Ring in Hide-Park. London: n.p., 1709.

The Complete Letters of Lady Mary Wortley Montague. Ed. Robert Halsband, 3 vols. Oxford: Clarendon Press, 1965.

The Conduct of His Grace The Duke of Ormonde in the Campaign of 1712. London: John Morphew, 1715.
The Congratulatory Speech of William Bromley [. . .] *to the Right Honourable Robert Harley, Esq*. London: Samuel Keble, 1711.
The Conspirators; or the Case of Catiline. London: n.p., 1721.
The Correspondence of Jonathan Swift D. D. Ed. F. Elrington Ball. 6 vols. (London: 1910–1914.)
The Correspondence of Jonathan Swift. Ed. H. Williams. 5 vols. Oxford: Oxford University Press, 1963–1972.
The Correspondence of Richard Steele. Ed. Rae Blanchard. Oxford: Oxford University Press, 1941.
The D— Deputies; A Satyr. London: n.p., 1705.
The D—e and D—s of M—h's Loss; Being an Estimate of their Former Yearly Income. London: n.p., 1711.
The Devil and the Peers: Or the Princely Way of Sabbath-Breaking; Being a True Account of a Famous Cricket Match between the Duke M—, another Lord and Two Boys. London: 1712.
The Devil of a Whigg; or Zarazian Subtilty Detected. London: n.p., 1708.
The Diary of John Evelyn. Ed. Austin Dobson. 3 vols. London: Routledge, 1996.
The Diary of Sir David Hamilton 1709–1714. Ed. Philip Roberts. Oxford: Clarendon Press, 1975.
The Dream of the Solan Goose. London: n.p., 1709.
The Duchess of Marlborough's Vision. London: n.p., 1711.
The Duke of Marlborough's Vindication In Answer to a Pamphlet falsely so called. London: A. Baldwin, 1712.
The Dutch Won't Let us Have Dunkirk, and High Treason Happily Discover'd or the Dutch Un—'d. London: n.p., 1712.
The Earl of Peterborough's Vindication anent the bad Success in Spain. London: n.p., 1708.
The Ecclesiastical and Political History of Whig-Land of Late Years; To Which are Prefix'd the Characters of a Late Ecclesiastical Historian . . . By John Lacy. London: J. Morphew, 1714.
The Epistolary Correspondence of Sir Richard Steele. Ed. John Nichols. 2 vols. London: J. Nichols, 1787.
The Examiner. London: J. Morphew, 1710–1714.
The Exchequer's Answer. London: n.p., 1711.
The Fable of M. Manlius Capitolinus. London: n.p., 1712.
The Fable of the Cods Heads: Or a Reply to the Dutch-Men's Answer to the Resolutions of the House of Commons. London: n.p., 1712.
The Fable of the Widow and her Cat. (London: n.p., 1712.
The Fate of Manlius Capitolinus. London: n.p., 1712.
The Female Monster; or The World Turn'd Topsy Turvy. London: n.p., 1705.
The Female Nine. London: n.p., 1690.
The Female Tatler. London: B. Bragg, R. Baldwin, 1709–1710.
The Female Tatler. Ed. Fidelis Morgan. London: Everyman, 1992.

The Flying Post or The Post Master. London: G. Ridpath, 1702–1713.
The Gates of Hell Opened: In a Dialogue Between the Observator and the Review. London: John Morphew, 1711.
The Glorious Life and Actions of St. Whigg. London: n.p., 1708.
The Golden Age Revers'd. [London?]: n.p., 1702.
The Golden Spy or a Political Journal of the British Night's Entertainment of War and Peace. London: J. Woodward, J. Morphew: 1709.
The Grand Enquiry or What's to be done with Him. London: n.p., 1712.
The Guardian. London: 1713.
The Hertford Letter Containing Several Brief Observations on a late Printed Tryal. London: n.p., 1699.
The High Church Bully; or the Praises of Mr. Higgins. [London?]: n.p., [17?].
The Historical Register. London: n.p., 1724.
The History of Prince Mirabel's Infancy, Rise and Disgrace. London: J. Baker, 1712.
The History of the Three Goddesses and the Golden Apple of Prince Paris and Prince Araro. [London?]: n.p., 1712.
The Impartial Secret History of Arlus and Odolphus, Ministers to the Empress of Grandinsula. London: n.p., 1710.
The Instructive Library or, an Entertainment for the Curious, the Improvement of the Learned, the Information of the Ignorant, The Satisfaction of all Good Men, the Confusion of the Bad,. London: n.p., 1710.
Swift, Jonathan. *The Journal to Stella.* Ed. Harold Williams. Oxford: OUP, 1948.
The Junto. London: n.p., 1710.
The Kit-Kats; A Poem. London: E. Sanger, E. Curll, 1708.
The L— T—'s Out at Last And Deliver'd up his S—f. London: n.p., 1710.
The Letter Books of John Hervey, 1st Earl of Bristol. Ed. S. H .A. 3 vols. Wells: 1894.
The Letters of Jonathan Swift to Charles Ford. Ed. D. Nichols Smith. London, 1953.
The Life and Character of Mr Alderman Barber. London: T. Cooper, 1741.
The Life and History of the Right Honourable Henry St. John., Lord Visc. Bolingbroke. London: n.p., 1754.
The Life of Mr John Dennis. London: J. Roberts, 1734.
The London Gazette. London: H. Muddiman, 1702–1712.
The Loyal Trimmer. London: n.p., 1712.
The Medley. London, n.p., 1710–1711.
The Memoirs of Thomas, Earl of Ailesbury, Written by himself. Printed for the Roxburgh Club, 2 vols. London: Nicholls & Son, 1890.
The Monster: or The World turn'd Topsy Turvy. A Satyr. London. B. Bragg. 1705.
The Nature of Man. 3 vols. London: Sam Buckley, 1711.
The New Loyal Health; French Sincerity Exemplified In the Surrender of Dunkirk to Her Brittanick Najesty Queen Anne. [London?]: n.p., [1713?].
The Night Mr Collins, one of Her Majesty's Messengers, arrived here being dispatched Express by his Grace of the Duke of Marlborough, with the following Account of the Surrender of Bouchain. London: Tooke and Barber, [1711].

The Nine K—s. London: n.p., 1705.
The Observations on the Estimate of the Debts of the Navy consider'd in a Letter to a Friend. London: n.p., 1712.
The Observator. London: John Tuchin, 1702–1712.
The Observator's Letter to his Learned Counsel. [London?]:1711.
The Officers Address to the Ladies. [London]: A. Baldwin, [1710?].
The Old and True Way of Manning the Fleet, Or How to Retrieve the Glory of the English Arms by Sea, as it is Done by Land. London: n.p., 1707.
The Oxfordshire Nine. London: n.p., 1705.
The Papers of a Critic, selected from the writings of the late Charles Wentworth Dilke. Ed. Charles Wentworth Dilke. London. John Murray, 1875.
The Perkinite Jacks; or a New Ballad on the Tackers. [London?]: n.p., [1705?].
The Petticoat Plotters; or The D—ss of M—h's Club. London: T. Wellard, 1712.
The Plain Dealer. London: n.p., 1712.
The Post Boy. London: A. Roper, 1709–1714.
The Post Man: and the Historical Account. London: R. Baldwin, 1702–1710; 1714.
The Private Correspondence of the Duchess of Marlborough 2 vols. London: Henry Colburn, 1838.
The Prophesy: Or Masham's Lamentation for Harley. London: Abel Roper, 1710.
The Protestant Post Boy. London: n.p., 1711–1712.
The Quaker's Sermon: Or, A Holding Forth Concerning Barabbas. London: A Baldwin, 1711.
The Queen's and the Duke of Ormond's New Toast. London: n.p., 1712.
The Reheasal. London: Charles Leslie, 1704–1709.
The Republican Procession. [London?]: n.p., 1714.
The Rival Dutchess: Or Court Incendiary. London: n.p., 1708.
The Rival Princesses: or, The Colchian Court: A Novel. London: R. Bentley, 1689.
The Second Part of the Impartial Secret History of Arlus, Fortunatus, & Odolphus, Ministers of State to the Empress of Grand-Insula. London: n.p., 1710.
The Secret History, of Queen Zarah, and the Zarazians; By way of Appendix to the New Atalantis. Containing The True Reasons of the Necessity of the Revolution that lately happen'd in the Kingdom of Albigion, 2d ed. London: n.p., 1711.
The Seven Extinguishers. London: n.p., 1710.
The Spectator. London: Samuel Buckley, J. Tonson, 1711–1712.
The Speech of Lord Haversham's Ghost. London: n.p., 1710.
The State of the Case Between Ashby and White. London: B. Bragg, 1705.
The Tackers vindicated; or an Answer to the Whigs New Black-List. London: n.p., 1705.
The Tatler. Ed. Donald F. Bond, 3 vols. Oxford: Clarendon Press, 1987.
The Taunton Dean Letter. London: n.p., 1701.
The Theatre. London: n.p., 1720.
The Thoughts of an Honest Tory upon the Present Proceeedings of that Party in a Letter to a Friend in Town. London: A. Baldwin, 1710.

The Toasters Compleat With the Last Additions. London: n.p., 1704.
The True Patriots Vindicated or A Justification of the Late Earl of Rochester. London: n.p., 1711.
The Welsh Monster; or the Rise and Downfual of that Late Upstart the R—t H—le Innuendo Scribble. [London?]: n.p., [1710?].
The Wentworth Papers, 1705–1739 selected from the private and family correspondence of Thomas Wentworth. Ed. J. J. Cartwright. London: Wyman and Sons, 1883.
The Whigs Appeal to the Tories, In a Letter to Sir T—H—, With a Postscript Concerning the Proceedings of P—. London: S. Popping, 1711.
The Windsor Prophecy Found in a Marlborough Rock. London: n.p., 1711.
The Wolf Stript of His Shepherd's Clothing address'd to Dr. Sacheverell. London: n.p., 1710.
The Wolf Stript of His Shepherd's Clothing In answer to Moderation and Vertue. London: n.p., 1704.
The Woman Haters Lamentation: or a New Copy on the Fatal End of Mr Grant, a Woollen-Draper. London: J. Robinson, 1707.
The Works of the Learned, 13 vols. London: H. Rhodes, T. Bennet, A. Bell, D. Midwinter, 1699–1711.
To the Duke of Marlborough On the Taking of Bouchain. London: S. Popping, 1711.
To the Right Honourable Mr Harley. London: Richard Sare, 1711.
To The Right Honourable R— H— Esq. London: Bernard Lintott, 1711.
Tofts and Margarita. London: n.p., 1705.
Toland, John, *Dunkirk or Dover; or the Queen's Honour, the Nation's Safety, The Liberties of Europe, and the Peace of the World: All at Stake till that Fort and Port be totally demolish'd by the French*. London: n.p., 1713.
Tom Tell-Truth's Letter to a dissenter in vindication of the L[ord]s Against the Tackers. London: n.p., [1705?].
Trapp, Joseph *The True, Genuine Modern Whigg-Address*. [London?]: n.p., 1710.
Trapp, Joseph, *To the Right Honourable Mr. Harley, on his first appearing in public, after the wound given him by Guiscard*. London: John Morphew, 1711.
Trapp, Joseph, *The Character and Principles of thePresent Set of Whigs*. London: John Morphew, 1711.
Trapp, Joseph, *The Mischiefs of Changes in Government*. Oxford: n.p., 1705.
Trotter, Catharine *The Revolution of Sweden*. London: James Knapton, George Strahan, 1706.
Trotter, Catharine *Unhappy Penitent*. London: William Turner and John Nutt, 1701.
Truth If You can Find it: Or A Character of the Present M—y and P—t: In a Letter to a Member of the March Club. London: n.p., 1712.
Freeman, A. Martin, ed. *Vanessa and Her Correspondence with Jonathan Swift*, London: Selwyn and Blount, 1921.
Vernon, James *Letters Illustrative of the Reign of William III from 1696 to 1708 addressed to the Duke of Shrewsbury*. Ed. G. P. R. James, 3 vols. London, n.p., 1841.

Vulgus Brittanicus; or the British Hudibras in Fifteen Cantos By the Author of the London Spy. London, Sam Briscoe, 1711.

W. M., *The Female Wits: or the Triumvirate of Poets: A Rehearsal*. London: Wm. Turner, William Davis, Bernard Lintott; Thom. Brown, 1704.

Wagstaffe, Thomas, *The Case of Moderation and Occasional Communion*. London: R. Wilkinson, 1705.

Walker, T., *The Wit of a Woman*. London: n.p., 1705.

Ward. Edward, *Hudibras Redivivius*, 2 vols. London: n.p., 1706–1709.

Ward. Edward, *The Secret History of the Calves Head Club*, 5th ed. London: B. Bragg, 1710.

Ward. Edward. *A Fair Shell, But a Rotten Kernel*. London: n.p., 1705.

Wesley, Samuel, *Marlborough; Or the Fate of Europe*. London: C. Harper, 1705.

Where's Your Impeachment Now? Or the D—Safe Delivery. [London?]: n.p., 1712.

Whig and Tory; Or Wit on Both Sides. London: n.p., 1712.

Whincop, Thomas, *A Compleat List of all the English Dramatic Poets, and of All the Plays ever printed in the English Language, to the Present Year, 1747*. London: W. Reeve, 1747.

Index

Works by Manley (DM) appear directly under title; works by others under author's name

Account of a Dream at Harwich, An (pamphlet), 146
Acrostick on Wharton, 120
Act of Uniformity, 195
Addison, Joseph: Swift and, 26; on origins of *Examiner*, 126; and Charles XII at Bender, 130; on public credit, 138; DM's references to, 211; *The Campaign*, 211
Adventures of Rivella, The (DM): publication, 14, 63; as biographical source, 17–18, 20, 142, 208, 233; on DM's affair with Tilly, 22–23; and DM's supposed Jacobitism, 85; and DM's caution in *The New Atalantis*, 92; on DM's corpulence, 137; tone and style, 150; and loyalty to Stuarts, 189; and DM's amatory writings, 209
Allen, Robert, 64–65
Almyna, or the Arabian Vow (DM; play): publication and performance, 12, 25, 180; plot, 193–94, 198; royal succession theme, 193–94, 197–98; sources, 193; women's role in, 194–95; and oath-taking, 196–97; and Jacobitism, 198
Aminabad or the Quaker's Vision, 117
Anderson, Paul Bunyan, 41
Anglicanism. *See* Church of England
Anne, Queen: in DM's writings, 12; dominated by Marlboroughs, 12–13, 50, 52–53, 58, 61, 91, 97; death, 14, 30–31, 200, 260; and pamphlet war, 16; as Albania in *The Secret History of Queen Zarah*, 36–37, 44, 50–52, 58, 60–61, 203; Sarah Churchill's early friendship with, 39; and universities, 61; as Olympia in *The New Atalantis*, 68, 84, 91–92; Whig influence on, 70, 108–9, 118, 139, 176–77; Harley's relations with, 71; defends established Church, 78; as Constantine/Augustus in *Memoirs of Europe*, 97–100, 113, 121–24; gains independence from Junto, 99; succeeds to throne, 100; dismisses Sarah Churchill, 112; deprecates Marlborough's ambitions, 119; sexual preferences, 124; allegorized in *Examiner*, 131–32, 143–45; expenditure on Blenheim, 146; and Guiscard's assassination attempt, 161–62, 164; and demolition of Dunkirk, 175–76; Hanoverian succession to, 193, 200, 202
Annesley, Arthur (fifth earl of Anglesey), 61
Arabian Nights Entertainments, 193
Arbuthnot, Dr. John: in Society of Brothers, 29; and authorship of *John Bull* pamphlets, 34, 214–15, 219; as Tory propagandist, 34; knowledge of DM, 219–20; *The Story of St Alban's Ghost* (?with Wagstaffe), 222
Arlus and Odolphus (pamphlet), 68, 111, 122
Ashburne, Sir James, 81
Ashby-versus-White controversy, 58–59
Atterbury, Francis: edits *Examiner*, 64–65, 129; contributes to *Examiner*, 128

Augustus II, King of Poland, 106–7
Aulnoy, Marie Catherine Le Jumel de Barneville, baronne d', 14, 43; *Memoirs of the Court of England*, 25

Backscheider, Paula, 44
Bacon, Sir Edmund, 68
Bacon, Francis: *New Atlantis*, 76
Baker, Thomas: *An Act at Oxford*, 181; *The Female Tatler* ascribed to, 224
Baldwin, Abigail, 211–12
Ballaster, Ros, 14, 43, 77, 79
Barber, John: relations with DM, 24–25, 27–28, 31, 214, 234–36, 243, 255, 257; publishes DM's works, 25–26, 95; arrested, 27; attends Society of Brothers dinners, 29; and DM's death, 33; publishes *Examiner*, 128–30; and DM ascriptions, 206; and Swift's *New Journey to Paris*, 213; death, 234, 236
Baron, Sir William, 68
Bath, John Granville, first Earl of, 19, 23
Beattie, Lester M., 214
Beaufort, Henry Somerset, second duke of, 29, 77, 233
Beckley, near Oxford, 32
Behn, Aphra: supposedly portrayed as Astrea in *The New Atalantis*, 78; reputation, 227, 234, 238, 241; *Love Letters between a Noble-Man and his Sister*, 43
Bender: Charles XII at, 130–31, 140
Bentley, R. (publisher), 188
Bickerstaffe, Isaac. *See* Steele, Sir Richard
Birch, Thomas, 236, 238
Blanchard, Rae, 22
Blenheim, battle of (1704), 100, 210–11
Blenheim Palace, Oxfordshire, 60, 98, 146
Blount, Elizabeth, 119
Bolingbroke, first viscount. *See* St. John, Henry
Bond, Donald, 231

Bouchain, 166–74, 256
Bower, Alan W.: and Robert A. Erickson, 216, 219
Boyer, Abel, 130, 152, 156, 161, 229; *Political State of Great Britain*, 159
Bridgewater, Elizabeth, countess of (née Churchill), 42
Bristol, John Hervey, first earl of, 32–33
British Mercury, The, 154
Bromley, William, 61
Browne, Joseph, 56, 64–65; *Gothick Hero*, 106; *St James' Park*, 82
Buckingham, George Villiers, first duke of, 124
Buckingham, John Sheffield, first duke of: as Mulgarvius in *The Secret History of Queen Zarah*, 36, 45, 54–55
Burnet, Gilbert, Bishop of Salisbury, 42

Cadogan, General William, first earl, 207
Caesar, Charles, 81, 227
Cambridge University: political sympathies, 60–61
Canfield, J. Douglas, 185
Castlemaine, countess of. *See* Cleveland, duchess of
Catherine de Medici, Queen of France, 53
Catholicism: and Jacobitism, 85; and Gunpowder Plot, 115; and Stuarts, 115, 179, 190, 199–200, 205
Centlivre, Susannah, 238
Chardin, Sir John, 188, 192
Charles II, King, 12
Charles XII, King of Sweden: as Theodorick in *Memoirs of Europe*, 97, 105–8, 111; Tory view of, 106, 141; military campaigns, 107–8, 130–31; in DM's *Examiner*, 111, 127, 130–32, 141, 143, 177; represented as parallel with Queen Anne, 132, 143; *Post Man* attacks, 141
Church of England: and Dissenters, 38–39; and threat of treachery, 50,

53; Whig attitude to, 72; Sacheverell defends, 115–16; *Examiner* on, 139; Harley's loyalty to, 163

Churchill, John (first duke of Marlborough): domination of Queen Anne, 12–13, 50, 58; as Hippolito in *The Secret History of Queen Zarah*, 36, 44, 47–49, 52, 57, 87; political machinations and opportunism, 39–40, 48; progress in War of Spanish Succession, 39; campaign expenses, 40; seduced by Sarah, 46; and Church of England, 50; Tory mistrust of, 57; enfranchises dependents in local constituency, 60; downfall, 68, 91, 100, 118; loses influence with Queen Anne, 70, 100; submits to Whig Junto, 70; Harley's relations with, 71; Ashburne attacks, 81; DM's consistent criticism of, 86, 96; military successes, 86, 91, 108, 168, 209; abandons James II, 87–91; affair with duchess of Cleveland, 87; attacked in *The New Atalantis*, 87–92, 118; Steele defends against DM, 96; as Stauracius in *Memoirs of Europe*, 98–100, 119; ambitions for power, 118–19, 146; Tory attacks on, 118; as Commander Basha in *Examiner*, 127, 132, 141–42, 144; Medina pays for army bread contracts, 140; forces Harley's resignation (1708), 141; in *Examiner* dream sequence, 145; Sarah's influence on, 145; Bouchain victory, 166–72; opposes peace negotiations with French, 166, 168; DM attacks over militarism in Bouchain action, 167–70; as James II's favourite, 186; and Major-General Webb, 207; payment to John Dennis, 210; Addison praises, 211; satirized in *John Bull* pamphlets, 214; hostility to DM, 260

Churchill, Sarah (duchess of Marlborough): domination of Queen Anne, 12–13, 50, 52–53, 91, 118, 176; on DM's correspondence with Robert Harley, 30; as Zarah in *The Secret History of Queen Zarah*, 36–38, 41, 43, 44–49, 51–59, 61–62, 87, 90, 114; early friendship with Anne, 39; sexual reputation, 41–42, 46; Tory antagonism to, 41–43, 47; children's marriages, 42–43; Godolphin's supposed relations with, 42, 53, 56–57, 89; political influence, 49–53, 58–59, 61; and Church of England, 50; as "Faction," 52; and General Election (1705), 59–60; electioneering, 61–62; letter from Sunderland on *The New Atalantis*, 74–75; as Jeanitin/Marchioness de Caria in *The New Atalantis*, 87, 89–92, 110, 114; DM prophesies downfall, 97; as Irene in *Memoirs of Europe*, 97, 99, 105, 109–11, 119, 122, 124, 131, 176; on Abigail Masham's ingratitude, 112; dismissed from court appointments, 112, 114, 118; as Lady Hautisara in *Arlus and Odolphus*, 122; on DM's editorship of *Examiner*, 129; in *Examiner* dream sequence, 145–46; influence on husband, 145; ambitiousness and pride, 146–47; appearance, 147; DM demonizes, 147; envy of Abigail Masham, 147

Churchill, Sir Winston S., 243
Cibber, Colley, 203
Cibber, Theophilus, 237–38
Clare, Robert, 41
Clement, Simon: *Faults on Both Sides*, 104–5, 108, 110
Cleveland, Barbara Villiers, duchess of (*earlier* countess of Castlemaine): DM works for, 13, 239; as Clelia in *The Secret History of Queen Zarah*, 36, 45, 47–49; Marlborough's affair with, 87; as Duchess de l'Inconstant in *The New Atalantis*, 91
Cockburn, Catherine (née Trotter): John Hughes sends verses to, 19;

introduces DM to Tilly, 23; DM attacks in *Memoirs of Europe*, 101–2; praises Charles XII of Sweden, 106–7; DM defames, 236; *Agnes de Castro* (play), 18, 183
Coke family, 80
Coke, Cary, 68, 80
Coke, Thomas, 80–81
Collier, Jeremy, 181
Conduct of His Grace the Duke of Ormonde, The : ascribed to DM, 224
Connelly, Willard, 241
Connor, Bernard: *History of Poland*, 108–9
Constantinople, 97, 107–8
Copyright Act (1710), 95
Court Intrigues (unauthorized edition of *Letters Writen by Mrs Manley*), 217
Cowper, Spencer, 93
Cowper, William (*later* first earl), 93
Cunningham, George, 117
Curll, Edmund, 33, 63, 234–35

Daily Courant, 130, 154
Dampier, William, 260
Davis, Herbert, 223
Davis, Lennard, 14, 37
Dawks's Newsletter, 154
Day, Robert Adams, 14
Defoe, Daniel: study of, 15; on High-Flying Tories, 40; on frequency of elections, 184; ascriptions problem, 206; accused of immorality, 229; *The Diet of Poland*, 109; *Reasons concerning the Immediate Demolishing of Dunkirk*, 177
"Delia": as DM pseudonym, 20, 22, 130, 208, 210–11
Dennis, John, 181, 210
Devil of a Whigg, The, 65, 77–78, 121
Dickinson, H. T., 153
Dissenters (nonconformists), 38, 50, 56, 62, 162
Doran, Dr. John, 240
Downie, J. A., 104, 128, 133, 243; *Robert Harley and the Press*, 17
Drury Lane Theatre, 20–21, 24
Dryden, John, 12

Duff, Dolores, 22
Duke of Marlborough's Vindication in Answer to a Pamphlet lately Publish'd, The (DM), 152, 167–70, 172
Duncombe, John: *Feminiad*, 238
Dunkirk: demolition of, 174–77
Dupplin, Abigail, viscountess (Harley's daughter), 155
Duumvirs (Marlborough/Godolphin), 40, 51, 54–56, 62, 71, 86, 141
Dyer, John, 150

Ecclesiastical and Political History of Whig-Land in Late Years, The : ascribed to DM, 212
Egerton, Sarah Fyge, 24–25, 69
Ehrenpreis, Irvin, 243
Elizabeth I, Queen, 78, 124
Ellis, Frank, 133, 136–38
Erickson, Robert A. *See* Bower, Alan W.
Engagement Controversy (1650), 185
Evening Post, The, 154
Examiner, The (periodical): DM's editorship, 14, 64, 125, 126, 128–33, 136, 145, 147–51, 165–66, 218, 229, 239; Swift and, 14, 26, 31, 52, 118, 120, 127, 129, 133–36, 148–50, 239; DM first contributes to, 26, 111, 128–29, 157; discontinued, 64; begins, 126; Harley subsidizes, 126, 128, 133, 136; contributors, 128; allegorical references in, 131–33, 141–45; political themes, 138–40, 143–45, 148; on Church, 139; Mainwaring attacks, 140–41, 167–68; dream sequence in, 145; as Tory journal, 151; on Guiscard's assassination attempt on Harley, 154–56, 158–59, 162; on demolition of Dunkirk, 175, 177
Examiner, The (periodical; ed. Browne), 64–65
Ezell, Margaret, 183

Fabricant, Carole, 16, 173, 243
Faction, 51–52, 54
"Faction Display'd," 35, 52
Farquhar, George: *Barcellona*, 103

Index

Farquhar, Margaret, 103–4
Female Tatler, The : ascribed to DM, 223–24
Female Wits, The (play; [by Mr. W.M.]), 20–21, 231, 237
Fielding, Henry, 68
Flying Post, The (journal), 130, 154
Ford, Charles, 27, 31
Fowler, Katherine ("Orinda"), 227
Foxon, D. F., 207
France: war with Britain, 71; peace negotiations with Britain, 166–67, 171; and demolition of Dunkirk, 178
Frederick, Prince of Wales, 77
Freind, Dr. John: contributes to *Examiner*, 128–29; *Account of the Earl of Peterborough's Conduct in Spain*, 103

Gage, Catherine, 101
Gallagher, Catherine, 16
Gape, John, 62
Garth, William: "The Dispensary," 52
Gazette : publication and printing, 31
General Elections: (1705), 40, 59–62; (1708), 70; (1710), 112
George I, King (*earlier* Elector of Hanover), 166, 201, 204
George II, King (*earlier* Prince), 77
George, Prince of Denmark, 92, 98
Gildon, Charles, 206
Glorious Revolution (1688), 39, 89, 185, 187, 189
Godolphin, Francis, 61
Godolphin, Henrietta (née Churchill), 39
Godolphin, Sidney, first earl of: as Volpone in *The Secret History of Queen Zarah*, 35, 37, 50, 51, 53–55, 56–57, 116; political orientation, 40, 53–54; relations with Sarah Churchill, 42, 53, 56–57, 89, 91; and Church of England, 50; downfall, 68, 118; attacked (as Biron and Aemilius) in *The New Atalantis*, 69, 74, 84, 87, 89–92, 118; submits to Whig Junto, 70; Harley discredits, 71; and Harley's resignation (1708), 83, 141; DM's consistent criticism of, 86–87; political decline, 86; as Aemilius in *Memoirs of Europe*, 98, 113, 121; loses office as Lord Treasurer, 99–100; antipathy to Peterborough, 103; and Junto control of Queen Anne, 109; Sacheverell attacks, 116; in DM's *Examiner*, 141

Goldie, Mark, 185
Gonda, Caroline, 14
Graham, Walter, 224
Granville family, 22–23
Granville, George (baron Lansdowne): as DM's sponsor, 18–20; political career, 19, 28; DM praises, 20, 82; membership of Society of Brothers, 29; supports Harley, 82; royalist sentiments, 191; and *John Bull* pamphlets, 214; recommends DM to Harley, 255; *The British Enchanters*, 20; *Heroick Love* (play), 19–20; *The Jew of Venice*, 19; *The She Gallants* (play), 19
Greg, William, 83, 160
Griffin, Mrs. Edward, 101
Guardian (periodical), 174–75, 177, 231
Guiscard, Marquis de (*formerly* Abbé de Borly), 153–56, 159–62, 164–65, 169, 256
Gunpowder Plot (1605), 115

Haddock, Sir Richard, 253
Halifax, Charles Montagu, first earl of: in *New Atalantis*, 94; as Julius Sergius in *Memoirs of Europe*, 120–21, 144; DM satirizes, 136, 144; as Fuimus in *Queen Zarah*, 144; Harley negotiates with, 144
Hamilton, Dr. Sir David, 129
Hamilton, James Douglas, fourth duke of, 197
Hanoverian dynasty, 77, 182, 193, 200–202
Harcourt, Sir Simon, 85
Hare, Francis: DM attacks in *Learned Comment*, 152, 171–72, 256; DM ascribes *Bouchain* to, 167; *The*

Barrier-Treaty Vindicated, 223; *The Management of the War in Four Letters to a Tory Member* (pamphlet series), 171
Hargreaves, James, 19
Harley, Edward, second baron (*later* second earl of Oxford; Robert's son), 30, 155, 222
Harley, Edward (Robert's brother), 156, 159, 161, 164
Harley, Lady Henrietta (Harriet; née Cavendish Holles), 261
Harley, Robert (first earl of Oxford): heads Tory ministry (1710), 13–14, 80, 100; DM's relations with, 26, 28, 30–31, 157–58, 165; and Society of Brothers, 29–30; Parliamentary dominance, 40; as Secretary of State (1705), 40; receives Cambridge degree, 61; attacked in *Queen Zarah*, 62, 83, 162; DM's changing attitude to, 62–63, 83–85; supports Whigs in General Election (1705), 62, 83; as Don Haro in *The New Atalantis*, 68, 83–84, 92; abandons cooperation with Whigs, 70; accepted by Tories, 71; uses Abigail Masham as intermediary with Queen Anne, 71, 74; Sarah Churchill suspects of complicity with DM, 74; supports and advances St. John, 81–83; resigns (1708), 82–83, 85, 141–42; DM sends copy of *Memoirs of Europe* to, 96; as Herminius in *Memoirs of Europe*, 98–99, 113, 124–25; appointed Chancellor of Exchequer, 100, 126; unable to form coalition with Whigs, 114; criticism of in *Memoirs of Europe*, 125; subsidizes *Examiner*, 126, 128, 133, 136; relations with St. John, 134, 148; Swift on, 135; and Tory dissidents, 135, 138, 144, 148, 151; DM defends in *Examiner*, 143; secret negotiations with Halifax, 144; and DM's Tory propaganda, 152, 157; assassination attempt on, 153–56, 159–65; St. John's rivalry with, 154, 158,

163; DM sends *Memoirs of Europe* to, 157; mistrusts Swift, 157; Anglican sympathies, 163; opposes Poulett's suggested Quebec expedition, 165; and Marlborough's reaction to DM's *Vindication* pamphlet, 171; political "middle way," 179; satirized in *John Bull* pamphlets, 214; fall from power, 232; Swift writes for, 242; letters from DM (texts), 253–60; sends money to DM, 259, 261
Harris, Frances, 17, 145
Hattigé (French novella), 45, 48, 52, 188–89
Haversham, Sir John Thompson, first baron, 79–80
Haywood, Eliza, 231, 234
Hearne, Thomas, 69, 73
Henry III, King of France, 53
Heroick Essay Upon the Unequal'd Victory Obtained by Major-General Webb, An (attrib. DM), 207–12, 231; text, 247–51
Hervey, John. *See* Bristol, first earl of
Higgons, Bevil, 19
Hill, Brian, 135
Hill, Jack, 29
Historical Register, 234
Holland. *See* Netherlands
Holmes, Geoffrey, 15, 46, 101, 135
Honour and Prerogative of the Queen's Majesty Vindicated (attrib. DM), 152, 174–78
Hopkins, Sir John, 73; letter from DM, 252
Horne, Robert D., 207
Horsley, L. S., 228–29, 232–33
Howard, Stuarta, 67
Hughes, John, 19
Hunter, J. Paul, 14
Hyland, Paul, 175

Impartial History of Mr. John Barber, 234

Jacob, Giles: *Lives and Characters of the English Dramatick Poets*, 19

Index

Jacobitism: in *Lucius*, 14, 201–4; Tories and, 132–33; and threat from foreigners, 174; and Catholic Stuart dynasty, 182; and assassination attempt on William III, 184; and divine right of monarchs, 196
James I, King, 124, 199
James II, King (*earlier* Duke of York): in DM's writings, 12; as Albanio in *The Secret History of Queen Zarah*, 36, 50; and John Churchill (Marlborough), 48–49, 87, 90–91; homosexuality, 76; in *The New Atalantis*, 85–88, 90; deposed by William of Orange, 106, 191; despotism, 108; Catholicism, 115, 190; reputation, 124; loyalty to, 186, 189; in *Royal Mischief*, 189–90; coronation oath, 195–96
James, Elinor, 199
James Francis Edward Stuart, Prince ("the old Pretender"; "James III"), 197, 199–201, 203–4
Jennings, Frances, 36
John Bull (pamphlets), 174, 214–22, 292
Jonson, Ben, 54
Junto: DM satirizes, 12–13, 69; cooperation with Tories, 40; and Tory attacks on Sarah Churchill, 42; Sarah Churchill's influence in, 49, 51; in *The Secret History of Queen Zarah*, 50, 55; tolerance of Dissenters, 56; Tory mistrust of, 57; and rebellious clergy, 59; political dominance, 69–70, 92, 109; Anne gains independence from, 99; loses power (1710), 101, 118; satirized in *Memoirs of Europe*, 111, 113–14, 121, 123; identified with Turks, 131, 143; attacked in *Examiner*, 132. *See also* Whigs

Kent, Henry Grey, duke of, 99
King, Kathryn, 16
King, William, 128
Kirby-Miller, Charles, 214
Kit Kat club, 29

Königsmark, countess of, 107
Köster, Patricia, 64, 79

Lady's Pacquet of Letters, The (DM): publication, 13, 21, 25; pirated edition, 64; and Beau Wilson affair, 75; Steele in, 219
La Fayette, Marie Madeleine de: *The Princess of Cleves*, 68
Langbain, William, 206
Langbaine, Gerard: *Momus Triumphans*, 188
Lansdowne, baron. *See* Granville, George
Lansdowne, Mary, Lady, 20
Learned Comment upon Dr Hare's Excellent Sermon Preach'd before the Duke of Marlborough, A (DM), 152, 171–73, 242
Leiden Gazette, 130
Leslie, Charles, 60, 141, 198
Letter to the Examiner (ascribed DM), 223
Letters Written by Mrs Manley (DM), 12, 18, 217, 235
Life and Character of Mr. John Barber, 235
Lincoln's Inn Theatre, 21
Lindsey (singer): as Philomela in *Memoirs of Europe*, 120
Lisle, siege of (1708), 207
Lives and Characters of the English Dramatick Poets, 227, 233
London Gazette, The, 154, 207
Lost Lover, The (DM; play): political content, 12, 184–86; produced, 19, 20; plot, 182–83; failure, 228
Louis XIV, King of France, 71, 89, 166, 202, 214
Lucius the First King of Britain (DM; play): proto-Jacobite sentiments, 14, 201–4; Steele produces and pays for, 24, 32, 200; plot and themes, 201–3; influenced by Shakespeare's *Richard III*, 203–4; dedicated to Steele, 239
Luttrell, Narcissus, 72–73

McDowell, Paula, 16, 78, 216

326 Index

McKeon, Michael, 14
Mackworth, Sir Humphry, 79, 215
Madan, F. F., 116
Mainwaring, Arthur: as duchess of Marlborough's secretary, 62, 140; on Harley and the Church of England, 62; dismisses *New Atalantis*, 74–75; attacks on *Examiner*, 128–29, 140–41, 145, 167; edits *Medley*, 128, 140, 167; caricatures "Toss" of duchess of Marlborough, 147; *Bouchain*, 167, 169–70
Malplaquet, battle of (1709), 86
Manley, Delarivier: output as writer, 11–13, 33–34; arrest and imprisonment, 13, 17, 27, 66, 72–73, 95, 142, 224, 255; and development of narrative fiction, 14–16; editorship of *Examiner*, 14, 64, 125, 126–34, 136, 145, 147–51, 165–66, 218, 229; as Tory propagandist, 14, 17–18, 95–96, 117, 125, 138, 148–49, 152, 179, 209–10; birth and background, 17, 233; career, 18–19, 24; marriage to cousin John and birth of son, 18, 22, 239; Delia pseudonym, 20, 22, 130, 208, 210–11; satirized in *The Female Wits*, 20–21; social connections, 20, 25–26; friendship with Steele, 21–23; affair with Tilly, 22–23; breach and reconciliation with Steele, 23–24; relations with Barber, 24–28, 31, 214, 234–36, 243, 255, 257; contributes to *Examiner*, 26, 111, 128–29, 157; friendship with Swift, 26–29; relations with Robert Harley, 26, 28, 30–31; Swift teases in *Corinna*, 28; finances and business interests, 30–32; ill-health in later years, 32; late writings, 32–33; poetry, 32; death, 33, 225, 234; authorship and attributions, 63–65, 206–24; humor, 78; supposed Jacobite sympathies, 85; openly admits authorship of *Memoirs of Europe*, 95; reputation, 95, 224, 225–28, 233–45; attacks Steele, 96–97, 175–77; corpulence, 136–37; secret histories, 145–46; attacks Francis Hare, 152, 171–72; on Guiscard assassination attempt on Harley, 152–53, 156–65; attacks Marlborough over Bouchain actions, 167–71; Mainwaring on, 167; feminizes Tory ideology, 173; on threat from foreigners, 173–74; on demolition of Dunkirk, 174–77; plays seen as expression of DM's beliefs, 179–82; political beliefs, 179–80, 192; and women's role, 183–84, 194–95, 209–10, 245; collaborates on Swift works, 213–14; and *John Bull* prefaces, 215–22; private life and morals, 228–30, 232, 237, 240, 244; Steele criticizes, 230–32; in Oldmixon's *Court of Atalantis*, 232–33; letters (texts), 252–61; complains of sickness and misfortune, 255–57
Manley, Isaac (John's brother), 27
Manley, John (DM's cousin and "husband"): DM's irregular marriage to, 18; political career, 19; acts in Granville-Montagu lawsuit, 22–23; supports brother Isaac, 27; satirized in *The New Atalantis*, 68, 78
Manley, Sir Roger (DM's father), 17, 189, 227, 239
Markendale, Cornelia (DM's sister), 28, 260
Markham, John, 253–54, 256
Marlborough, first duke of. *See* Churchill, John
Marlborough, duchess of. *See* Churchill, Sarah
Mary II, Queen: in DM's writings, 12; coronation oath, 195–96
Mary of Modena, Queen of James II, 85
Masham, Abigail, Lady (née Hill): as Queen Anne's favourite, 13, 70, 74; *Memoirs of Europe* dedicated to, 29, 112; DM thanks, 31; attacked in *State Tracts*, 64; as Hilaria in *The New Atalantis*, 68, 84, 91–92; attacked in *The Rival Dutchess*, 75; association with Harley and St.

John, 84–85; offers patronage to DM, 84; as Theodecta and Leonidas in *Memoirs of Europe*, 98–99, 110–11, 113, 124; brother awarded Essex Regiment, 100; Sarah Churchill rescues, 112; attacks Marlborough's ambitions, 119; and rumors of Anne's sexual preferences, 124; Sarah Churchill's envy of, 147; and assassination attempt on Harley, 155
Masham, Samuel, first baron, 29–31, 257
Medina, Sir Solomon, 140
Medley (periodical), 128–29, 137, 140–41, 154, 167–68, 170, 232
"Melpomene": as DM pseudonym, 12
Memoirs of Europe (DM): reputation, 12; publication, 13, 26, 30, 98, 104; dedicated to Abigail Masham, 29, 112; Peterborough depicted in, 29, 95, 97, 102–5, 110; DM thanks Steele in, 73; praises Sophia, Electress of Hanover, 77; DM openly admits authorship, 95; plot and themes, 97–99, 109–10; Queen Anne represented in, 97–100, 113, 121–24, 176; and Tory confidence, 100, 124; structure, 101–2, 111; Poland and Northern Wars in, 108–9; characterizations, 110–11, 119, 131; on Sacheverell case, 116–17; on new Tory ministry's program, 117–18; scandal in, 119–21; extols DM, 142; religious intolerance in, 163; impotence and political sway equated in, 209; praises Addison, 211; style, 213; DM's self-satire in, 220; and *John Bull* pamphlets, 220–21
Memorial of the Church of England, 50, 53, 55, 62
"Moderation" (political), 40, 53–55, 62, 162–63
Modest Enquiry into the Reasons of the Joy . . . of Her Majesty's Death, A (ascribed DM), 223
Mohun, Charles, 101

Monmouth, James Scott, duke of, 88–89
Montagu family, 22
Montagu, John, duke of, 120
Montagu, Mary, duchess (*earlier* countess) of (née Churchill), 42, 120
Montagu, Lady Mary Wortley, 72, 74, 147
Moore, James, 32
Morgan, Fidelis, 19
Morphew, John, 64, 73, 211–12, 231
Mudge, Bradford K.: *The Whore's Story*, 14
Müllenbrock, Heinz-Joachim, 17

narrative fiction: DM and development of, 14–16
Narva, 107
Naturalization Act (1709), 71; repealed (1711), 173
navy (British): mismanagement satirized in *The New Atalantis*, 67
Nedoff, Jocelyn, 234
Needham, Gwendolyn, 70, 242
Netherlands: and negotiations to end War of Spanish Succession, 166
New Atalantis, The (DM): reputation and popularity, 12, 66, 73–74, 96, 238, 243; political allegory in, 13, 67–70, 76, 103; Charlot character in, 14, 16, 67; incest and lasciviousness in, 14; publication, 17, 26–27, 30; Granville described in, 20; on Steele's speculative investment, 23; dedicated to duke of Beaufort, 29; writing, 29, 65, 66, 71, 208; supposed fifth volume, 33; and *Queen Zarah*, 63; structure and organization, 66–69, 101–2; and arrest of DM and associates, 72–73; homosexuality in, 75; and Bacon's *New Atlantis*, 76; Astrea figure in, 78; DM's caution in, 92–94; role of Sarah Churchill in, 114; on Tories' program, 118; on Whig immorality, 119; Halifax satirized in, 137; DM as "Delia" in, 208; DM's self-promotion in, 210;

self-mockery in, 220; on DM's background, 233; later edition (1741), 236
New Atalantis for the Year 1713, 63
Nichols, John: on origins of *Examiner*, 126; ascribes works to DM, 222–23; and DM's later reputation, 238–40; republishes Steele, 238–39
Nine Muses, The (anthology), 12
Nottingham, Daniel Finch, second earl of, 61, 80, 186

oath-taking, 185–86, 195–96, 198
Observator (periodical), 198, 216
October Club, 134, 136, 138, 144, 148, 151, 159, 164
Oldfield, Anne, 261
Oldisworth, William, 64
Oldmixon, John, 133; *The Court of Atalantis*, 232–33
"On the New Promotion" (anon.), 62
Orford, Edward Russell, earl of, 94
Orinda. *See* Fowler, Katherine
Orrery, Charles Boyle, fourth earl of, 29
Oxford, first earl of. *See* Harley, Robert
Oxford University: Tory sympathies, 60–61

Parliament: prorogued (1711), 135–36
Patterson, Paul Baker, 17
Peter I (the Great), Tsar, 107
Peterborough, Charles Mordaunt, third earl of: recommends DM to Harley, 28–29, 255; as Horatio in *Memoirs of Europe*, 29, 95, 97, 102–6, 110; in *The New Atalantis*, 74, 94, 95, 103; background and career, 102–4, 107–8; changes political sympathies, 102–5
Pittock, Murray, 204
Pix, Mary, 80
Plain Dealer (periodical), 222
Poetical Register, The, 233–34
Poland, 106, 108–9

"Polesworth, Sir Humphrey" (composite figure), 215, 217, 222
Polesworth, Sir Robert, 215
Polignac, Melchior de, Cardinal, 101, 106–7
Poltava, battle of (1709), 108
Popish Plot (1678), 186
Portland, William Bentinck, first earl of, 67, 75–76
Post Boy (periodical), 140–41, 154, 160
Post Man (periodical), 141, 154
Poulett, John, first earl, 164–65
Power of Love, The (DM; novellas), 14, 20, 32, 179
Prior, Matthew, 31, 64, 128, 166, 213; letter from DM, 261
Protestant Post Boy, The, 216–17, 230
Prynne, William, 185
Puffendorff, Samuell: *History of Sweden*, 106

Quebec, 164

Rabb, Melinda Alliker, 16, 134, 161, 244
Rehearsal (periodical), 141
Representation of the Loyal Subjects of Albinia, The : ascribed to DM, 224
Richetti, John, 14, 67
Rival Dutchess, The (anon. play), 75
Rival Princesses, The (anon. novel), 188, 192
Rivington, Charles, 224
Rochester, John Wilmot, second earl of, 195
Rogers, Katharine, 243
Roman Catholicism. *See* Catholicism
Roper, Abel, 140–41, 160
Roscoe, Thomas, 223
Royal Mischief (DM; play): political references in, 12, 187, 189–92; commendatory verses in, 19; Higgons writes verses in, 19; transfers to Lincoln's Inn Theatre, 21; success, 186–87; plot, 187–88, 192;

sources, 188–89; and royal succession, 191–93
Ryland, Frederick, 223

Sacheverell, Henry: as Plato the Patriarch in *Memoirs of Europe*, 98–99, 115, 116–17; impeached and tried, 115–17, 142–43; depicted in *Examiner*, 142–43
St. Albans, Hertfordshire, 62
St. John, Henry (first viscount Bolingbroke): writes prologue to Granville's *Heroick Love*, 20; and Barber, 24–25; encourages DM to write for *Examiner*, 26; political career, 28; forms Society of Brothers, 29–30; DM's antipathy to, 81–82; Harley advances, 81–83; support for Marlborough, 81; resigns (1708), 82; relations with Abigail Masham, 84–85; depicted in *Memoirs of Europe*, 114–15; as Secretary of State, 114; womanizing, 115; and origins of *Examiner*, 126, 129; contributes to *Examiner*, 128; relations with Harley, 134, 148; DM praises in *Examiner*, 148; Guiscard's association with, 153; and assassination attempt on Harley, 154–56, 159, 162, 164–65; rivalry with Harley, 154, 158, 163; DM's attitude to, 158; and *John Bull* pamphlets, 214; recommends DM to Harley, 256
Sanderson, Robert: *A Resolution of Conscience*, 186
Sandwich, Elizabeth, countess of (née Wilmot), 13, 195, 198
Scotland: union with England, 198–200
Secret History of Queen Zarah, The (DM): publication and reputation, 12, 24–25, 35; narrative style, 16; character identification and aliases in, 35–36; plot and themes, 36–37, 44–50, 114; as political commentary, 36–37, 43, 63; dating of, 41; French influence on, 43–45, 48, 52, 189; amatory element in, 44, 47–48, 57; authorship questioned, 63–65, 222; influence, 65; and "Moderation," 162
Sedgemoor, battle of (1685), 89
sex: and politics in DM's writings, 15
Shakespeare, William: *Richard III*, 203–4
Short Memorial . . . of . . . Princess Mary, Dutchess of Ormonde : ascribed to DM, 224
Shrewsbury, Charles Talbot, duke of: supposed liaison with Sarah Churchill, 41, 57; as Salopius in *The Secret History of Queen Zarah*, 57; in *The New Atalantis*, 74; appointed Lord Chamberlain, 99
Skipwith, Sir Thomas, 20
Society of Brothers, 29–30
Society for Rewarding of Merit, 257
Somers, John, baron: republicanism, 55; awarded honorary Cambridge degree, 61; in *New Atalantis*, 94; as Julius Sergius in *Memoirs of Europe*, 102; opposes impeachment of Sacheverell, 116–17; relations with Elizabeth Blount, 119–20; pretensions to wit, 137
Sommerville, C. John, 150
Sophia, Electress of Hanover, 77
Spanish Succession, War of, 39, 71, 117, 214; ends, 166
Speck, W. A., 135–36
Spectator, The (journal), 138, 218
Spence, Rev. Joseph, 215
Stanhope, Brigadier General James (first earl), 103
State Tracts . . . with some Secret Memoirs (attrib. Joseph Browne), 64–65
Steele, Sir Richard: correspondence with DM published, 13, 21, 25; friendship with DM, 21–23; DM's breach and reconciliation with, 23–24, 200, 208; financial speculation, 23; backs *Lucius*, 24, 32, 200, 239; relations with Swift, 26; Swift disparages, 27; payment to DM, 32; criticizes *The New Atalantis*, 66; as M. L'Ingrate in *The New Ata-*

lantis, 69, 96, 176, 211, 231; and DM's release after arrest, 73; DM attacks in *Memoirs of Europe*, 96–97, 101, 114, 212, 218–19; refers to DM as *Epicene*, 96; on Sacheverell trial, 116; DM attacks over demolition of Dunkirk, 174–78; on union with Scotland, 199; antipathy to Old Pretender, 201; adds lines to revival of *Lucius*, 202, 204; edits *London Gazette*, 207; attacked in *An Heroick Essay*, 211, 231; accused of falsely claiming authorship, 212; and publication of *Tatler*, 212; references to in *Ecclesiastical and Political History of Whig-Land*, 212; attacks DM for gossip, 218; ridiculed in *John Bull*, 218–19; alchemic interests, 219; and *The Female Tatler*, 224; criticisms of DM, 230–32; Nichol reprints works, 238; and DM's posthumous reputation, 240–41; recommends DM to Hopkins, 252; *The Lying Lover*, 219

Stella (i.e., Esther Johnson and Rebecca Dingley): letters from Swift, 27–28, 115, 133–34, 152–53, 156, 159, 168, 213–14

Stout, Sarah, 93

Stuart dynasty: DM's attitude to, 179, 182, 189; Catholicism, 199–200, 205; association with Henry VII, 204

succession (royal), 191–93, 199–204

Sunderland, Anne, countess of (née Churchill), 42

Sunderland, Charles Spencer, third earl of: issues warrant for DM's arrest over *The New Atalantis*, 13, 73–75, 142; marries Anne Churchill, 42; on Sarah Churchill's political influence, 43; antimonarchy, 55; political ambitions, 63; absence from *The New Atalantis*, 75, 94; sexuality questioned, 75; as Cethegus in *Memoirs of Europe*, 98–99, 119, 220; dismissed as Secretary of State (1710), 99, 101, 142; Peterborough's antipathy to, 103–4; in Manley's *Examiner*, 142; heads Whig ministry, 233

Sunderland, Robert Spencer, second earl of, 186

Supplement, The (periodical), 154

Sutton, John L., 43

Swift, Jonathan: editorship of *Examiner*, 14, 26, 31, 52, 64, 127–29, 133–36, 148–50, 167, 239; study of, 15; relations with DM, 26–29; as Tory propagandist, 26; excludes Robert Harley from Society of Brothers, 30; and DM's business interests, 31–32; literary achievements, 33; depicts "Miss Faction," 52; on Godolphin's relations with Sarah Churchill, 57; on Naturalization Bill, 71; on demand for peace, 100; on St. John's profligacy, 115; attacks Marlborough, 118; on Wharton, 120; and High Tories, 148; and DM's pamphlet on Guiscard, 152–53, 156–58; on Guiscard's assassination attempt, 154–56, 159–64; Mainwaring on, 167; praises DM's *Vindication* pamphlet, 168; attacks Steele over demolition of Dunkirk, 175; and authorship of *John Bull* pamphlets, 214–16; Nichols reprints, 238; and DM's posthumous reputation, 241, 244; *The Conduct of the Allies*, 157; *Corinna*, 28; *The Importance of the Guardian Considered*, 178; *Journal to Stella*, 152, 213–15, 223, 242; *A New Journey to Paris*, 213, 223; *The Public Spirit of the Whigs*, 157; *Tale of a Tub*, 129; *The True Relation of the Tumult*, 223; *The Windsor Prophecy*, 157

Tack and Tackers, 38–39, 41, 60

Tatler (magazine), 96, 212, 230–31

Teerink, Herman, 214

Temple, Sir Richard, 120

Test and Corporation Act, 38, 72

Thackeray, William Makepeace, 243

"Thalia": as DM pseudonym, 12

theater: and morality, 181–82
Theatre Royal, London, 19
Thomas, Elizabeth, 231
Tilly, John, 22–23
Todd, Janet, 14
Tooke, Benjamin, 31–32
Tories: assume government (1710), 13, 112, 114; DM's support and propaganda for, 14, 17–18, 26, 37, 95–96, 117, 138, 148–49, 152, 179; conflict with Whigs and Junto, 15, 55; ministry falls (1705), 31; divisions in, 38; and established Church, 38–39; concern over Marlboroughs' influence, 39; High-Flyers, 40, 60, 114, 147; antagonism to Churchills, 41–43, 47–48; and right to govern, 46; on "Moderation," 54–55; oppose extension of franchise, 60; attitude to Queen Anne, 61; and general election (1705), 61–62; early mistrust of Harley, 62, 83; satirized in *The New Atalantis*, 68, 78–80; and Naturalization Bill, 71–72; on Whig corruption, 76–77; celebrated in *Memoirs of Europe*, 100, 124–25; support Sacheverell, 116; and Jacobitism, 132–33, 203; anti-Harley faction in, 135–36, 138, 144, 148, 151; supported by *Examiner*, 151; peace negotiations with French, 166–67; Hare accuses of favouring Popery and France, 171; suspicion of foreigners, 173–74; and royal succession, 192, 197, 200; reservations over union with Scotland, 198–200; DM accuses of stinginess, 210–11; and *John Bull* prefaces, 221; fall from power (1714), 232
Townshend, Charles, second viscount, 33
Trevelyan, George Macaulay, 70, 243
Triennial Act (1694), 184
Trotter, Catherine. *See* Cockburn, Catherine
True Narrative of what pass'd at the Examination of the Marquis de Guiscard, A (DM), 152, 154, 157, 161–65, 172, 256
True Relation of the Tumult (attrib. DM), 223
Turkey (Ottoman Empire), 108–9, 130–31, 177
Tutchin, John, 198, 229

Utrecht, Treaty of (1713), 174–75

Wagstaffe, Thomas, 222
Wallace, John, 186
Walpole, Robert, 33, 235–36
Walsh, William: *The Golden Age Restored*, 81
Wanley, Humfrey, 215
Ward, Ned: *The Manly Plain Dealer*, 222
Warner, William, 43
Webb, Major-General John Richmond, 207, 209, 211
Weil, Rachel, 15, 44
Wentworth, Peter, 115
Wharton, Lucy, 120
Wharton, Thomas, first marquis of, 55; as Artonio in *The Secret History of Queen Zarah*, 58; receives Cambridge degree, 61; portrayed in *The New Atalantis*, 93–94; as Catiline in *Memoirs of Europe*, 114, 119–20, 220; supposed impotence, 119–20; acrostic on, 159–60
Whigs: DM satirizes, 12–13; conflict with Tories, 15; toleration of Dissenters, 38, 50, 72, 131, 162; and "Moderation," 53–54; Parliamentary malpractice, 58; in General Election (1705), 59, 60–62; abused by *Queen Zarah*, 65; satirized in *The New Atalantis*, 69–70, 72, 92; domination of Queen Anne, 70, 108–9, 118, 139, 176–77; corruption charges against, 76–77; fall from power (1710), 100–101, 112, 118, 126; and Peterborough's switch to Tories, 104–5; attitude to Charles XII of Sweden, 106–7, 141; satirized in *Memoirs of Europe*, 111–12, 114; identified with Turks,

131, 143; accuse Tories of Jacobitism, 132–33; and public credit, 138–39; republicanism, 143; attacked in *Examiner*, 149; and Guiscard assassination attempt, 160–61; and Marlborough's Bouchain success, 167–69; and Spanish peace negotiations, 169; favour union with Scotland, 199; payments to propagandists, 210–11; and *John Bull* prefaces, 221; regain power (1714), 232. *See also* Junto

Whitehall: improvements to, 146

Whole Duty to Man, The, 197

William III (of Orange), King: in DM's writings, 12; as Aurantio in *The Secret History of Queen Zarah*, 36; Marlborough's relations with, 39, 48–49, 88–90; and Whig Junto, 40; homosexuality at court of, 41, 75–76; death, 67; invasion of England, 85, 89, 174; in *The New Atalantis*, 88–90; in *Memoirs of Europe*, 98; Anne succeeds, 100; deposes James II, 106; assassination attempt on, 184–85; dislikes over-frequent elections, 184; allegiance to, 186; accession, 191; coronation oath, 195–96

Williams, Harold, 242

Wilson, Beau, 25, 75

Winton, Cahoun, 212

women: DM on role of, 183–84, 194–95, 209–10, 245; in DM's fiction, 183; as writers, 209–10

Woodstock, John, 73

Woolley, David, 243

Wyndham, Sir William, 30, 257

OHIO UNIVERSITY LIBRARY
Please return this book as soon as you have finished with it. In order to avoid a fine it must be returned by the latest date stamped below. All books are subject to recall after two weeks or immediately if needed for reserve.

CF